Enterprise and the Welfare State

Enterprise and the Welfare State

Edited by

Martin Rein
Professor of Social Policy, Massachusetts Institute of Technology, US

Eskil Wadensjö
Professor of Labour Economics, Swedish Institute for Social Research, University of Stockholm, Sweden

Edward Elgar
Cheltenham, UK • Lyme, US

Published by
Edward Elgar Publishing Limited
8 Lansdown Place
Cheltenham
Glos GL50 2HU
UK

Edward Elgar Publishing, Inc.
1 Pinnacle Hill Road
Lyme
NH 03768
US

3 2280 00613 5644
ᴦ.

A catalogue record for this book
is available from the British Library

Library of Congress Cataloguing-in-Publication Data
Enterprise and the welfare state / edited by Martin Rein, Eskil
    Wadensjö.
        Includes bibliographical references and index.
        1. Old age pensions—Cross-cultural studies. 2. Pension trusts–
    –Cross-cultural studies. 3. Retirement income—Cross-cultural
    studies. 4. Welfare economics—Cross-cultural studies. I. Rein,
    Martin, 1928- . II. Wadensjö, Eskil, 1944- .
    HD7105.3.E58   1997
    331.25'2'0973—dc21   97-24228
                                                                CIP

ISBN 1 85898 379 7 (cased)

Printed and bound in Great Britain by
Hartnolls Limited, Bodmin, Cornwall

Contents

List of figures — vii

List of tables — viii

Notes on the Authors — xii

Preface — xvi

1   The Emerging Role of Enterprise in Social Policy   1
Martin Rein and Eskil Wadensjö

2   The Austrian Pension System   33
Peter Rosner, Thomas Url and Andreas Wörgötter

3   France: A National and Contractual Second Tier   65
Emmanuel Reynaud

4   The Public-private Mix in Pension Provision in Germany: 99
The Role of Employer-based Pension Arrangements
and the Influence of Public Activities
Winfried Schmähl

5   The Retirement Provision Mix in Italy: The Dominant   149
Role of the Public System
*Rita Di Biase, Aldo Gandiglio, Maria Cozzolino
and Gaetano Proto*

6   The Role of the Japanese Company in Compensating   195
Income Loss after Retirement
Yoko Kimura

7   The Netherlands: Growing Importance of Private   220
Sector Arrangements
Martin Blomsma and Roel Jansweijer

v

Contents

8   The Welfare Mix in Pension Provisions in Sweden   266
     Eskil Wadensjö

9   The British Case   309
     Tony Lynes

10   Enterprise and the State: Interactions in the Provision 352
     of Employees' Retirement Income in the United States
     Lucy apRoberts and John Turner

Index   381

Figures

4.1	Types of pension schemes for various groups of the population in the Federal Republic of Germany	105
4.2	Options for the transition to retirement provided for under social insurance legislation	108
4.3	Scale of tariffs in the pension schemes of the public sector and the statutory pension insurance	129
6.1	Retirement pay of high school graduates at 55 to the final monthly salary	199
6.2	Structure of employees' pension funds and national pensions	201
6.3	Structure of the pension schemes	204
6.4	Distribution of coverage 1980–90	208
6.5	The balance of the pension funds	208
6.6	Company pension plans	211
6.7	Coverage of the employees' pension funds	213
6.8	Distribution of retirement pay by types	214
7.1	Average retirement age	226
7.2	Differences in growth rate between the net minimum benefits and the net average negotiated wages since 1970	236
7.3	Social protection expenditures in the first and second tier, age 55–64	247
7.4	Social protection expenditures in the first, second and third tier, age 65 and over	249

Tables

2.1   Average replacement ratios for new pensions in 1990   36

2.2   Annual increase of pensions, inflation and real growth rates   38

2.3   Average pension of men, women and total, January each year   39

2.4   Increase of average nominal pension (VDPPS), rate of inflation, and increase of average real pension, January each year   40

2.5   Number of retired per 1000 active people in 1993   42

2.6   Coverage of old age pension by contributions   44

2.7   Contributions of the federal budget to the pension system   46

2.8   Development of average retirement age   47

2.9   Percentage of new disability pensions as percentage of all new pensions   49

2.10   Monthly median firm pension and median public old age pension for employed persons in 1993   59

3.1   Sources of income of retirees, for selected former occupations (1984)   66

3.2   Benefits paid by the general scheme and compulsory supplementary schemes (1990)   73

3.3   Average old age monthly pensions (1988)   81

3.4   Average old age monthly pensions for employees with a full career (1988)   81

3.5   Net replacement rate (%) for employees with a full career (1988)   83

3.6   Net replacement rate (%) for male and female employees with a full career (1988)   83

Tables

4.1	Population in Germany age 55 and older: absolute number and socio-economic status (1992)	103
4.2	Expenditures of institutions for old age security in Germany (1992)	112
4.3	Number of beneficiaries in selected systems of old age provision	114
4.4	Shares of pensioners with occupations pension (OP) and pension amounts by last occupational status and sex	123
4.5	Cohort-specific coverage and pension amounts in private supplementary pension schemes in 1986	125
4.6	Shares of pensioners with an own supplementary pension in the public sector and pension amounts by last occupational status and sex	130
4.7	Cohort-specific coverage and pension amounts in public supplementary pension schemes in 1986	131
5.1	Italian public general pension scheme: sources of funding in 1992	155
5.2	Italian public general pension schemes in 1992	156
5.3	Accrual rates in 1995	167
5.4	Pensioners in 1991: number, type of pension, and values	171
5.5	Households' sources of income in 1991	172
5.6	Yearly earnings, pensions and severance pay in 1995	177
5.7	Average pension amounts and economic ratios based on pre-reform rules	179
5.8	Assets of the second and third pillars	183
6.1a	Public pension schemes	202
6.1b	Public pension schemes (as of end of March 1992)	203
6.2	Distribution of the ratio of fringe benefits to the total cash wage	210
6.3	Retirement pay by education and length of service	217
7.1	Total payments from the three tiers for those aged 55 and over, as a percentage of GDP, 1980–93	250

7.2	Composition of income for people aged 65 and over	251
7.3	Average gross incomes of people aged 65 and over as a percentage of average earnings for those aged 25–64	252
7.4	Social security premiums paid by employers and employees, as a percentage of the total labour costs (1978–92)	254
8.1	A comparison of the four occupational pension schemes	292
8.2	The share of people in 1994 with taxable income, who receive tax deductions for private pension payments	294
8.3	Income sources for households headed by people aged 20–64 and 65 or older in 1993	295
8.4	Average old age pensions paid out in 1994 for men and women aged 65 and over compared to average earnings for men and women aged 25–60	295
8.5	The percentage of people with a pension in 1994 and average size of the pension according to age	296
8.6	The percentage of people with different forms of pensions in 1991	297
8.7	Average pensions in 1991	297
8.8	Assets of the two systems (in billion SEK and as a percentage of GDP)	298
8.9	Total costs for payments of old age pension	305
8.10	The situation of the pension schemes in 1992	306
9.1	1986 estimates of cost of retirement pensions	319
9.2	1986 estimates of contribution rates for employees not contracted out	320
9.3	Employees in occupational pension schemes 1953–91, United Kingdom	323
9.4	Manner of calculation of pension, private sector, 1963	326
9.5	Part-time employees' pension scheme coverage, 1991	329
9.6	Insurance companies' annuity rates: average of best four, 1990–94	343

9.7   Average gross incomes of pensioner units, by source,   344
      1979, 1989 and 1993, at July 1993 prices, and percentage
      change 1979–93

9.8   State pension payable to a man on average male earnings   346
      reaching age 65 in selected years from 1996 to 2040, at
      1996 prices and as a percentage of average male earnings

10.1 Coverage rate of the work force by occupational plans   366
      in the private sector, 1975, 1987 and 1992: defined
      benefit plans and defined contribution plans (percentage
      of the private sector work force)

10.2 Total cash payments from the three pillars for those   370
      age 55 or older, 1992

10.3 Total cash payments from the three pillars for those   371
      age 55 or older, 1980

10.4 Cash payments from the three pillars for those age 55   372
      or older as a percentage of GDP, 1980 and 1992

10.5 Percentage of units aged 65 and older with money   373
      income from specified sources, 1962–92

10.6 Percentage shares of aggregate income of units aged   374
      55 and older, 1984 and 1992

10.7 Distribution of income from each source by quintile,   375
      units aged 65 and older, 1990

Notes on the Authors

Lucy apRoberts is a researcher on the economics of social welfare at IRES (Institut de Recherches Economiques et Sociales – Social and Economic Research Institute) in France. Her work focuses on links between state-run social insurance and occupational benefit plans in the United States and in France. She has recently co-edited *International Perspectives on Supplementary Pensions: Actors and Issues* (Quorum Books).

Martin Blomsma studied history at the Free University in Amsterdam. Between 1983 and 1989 he was employed at the Welfare Policy Harmonization Council (HRWB), and since 1993 is a senior researcher at the Ministry of Social Affairs and Employment in The Hague.

Maria Cozzolino is a researcher at the Italian Institute for Studies on Economic Planning (ISPE). She is the author of studies on labour costs and on the Italian social security system and has recently coordinated an international research team on fringe benefits in major OECD countries (with A. Gandiglio and G. Proto) and published 'Contribution-based vs. earnings-related retirement pension systems: some policy proposals for Italy' (with F. Padoa Schioppa Kostoris), *Ricerche Economiche* 1995.

Rita Di Biase graduated from the University of Ancona, Italy. She was, in turn, researcher there, then consultant to the Board of Foreign Trade, and is at present research director at the Institute for Studies on Economic Planning and member of the Bureau of the Working Party on Social Policy at OECD. She is the author of essays in public finance and particularly in the field of social security financing.

Aldo Gandiglio graduated from the University of Turin. He is currently a senior researcher at the Institute for Studies on Economic Planning specializing in public finance, work and training. He is also a member of Official Government Commissions and author of essays in public finance and related policies. Currently, he is involved in public sector employment analyses and in the redistributive effect of expenditures on education.

Roel Jansweijer studied sociology at the University of Amsterdam. Since 1980, he is employed as a member of staff at the Scientific Council for Government Policy (WRR) in The Hague. During the last few years hc has done extensive research on the influence of a sustainable old age pension system on the distribution of income.

Yoko Kimura is Associate Professor of public economics at National Nara Women's University, Nara, Japan. She has written many articles and co-authored books on pensions, medical care, community care, and public finance including public debt and public expenditure, and distribution of income and wealth in Japan. She is also a member of advisory boards for the government, including the Financial System Council for Ministry of Finance, and the Pension Council for Small and Medium-sized Businesses for the Ministry of Labour.

Tony Lynes has worked in the field of social security and pensions for nearly forty years. His work has included research, writing (academic, political and journalistic), policy-making and political campaigning. He is now a pensioner.

Gaetano Proto is a researcher at the Italian Institute for Studies on Economic Planning (ISPE). He is the author of studies on the redistributive effects of Italian fiscal policy and on fringe benefits in a comparative perspective. He has recently coordinated an international research team on fringe benefits in major OECD countries (with A. Gandiglio and M. Cozzolino) and published 'ITAXMOD. A microsimulation model of the Italian personal income tax and of social security contributions' (with R. Di Biase, M. Di Marco, and F. Di Nicola), *Documenti di Lavoro ISPE* 1995.

Martin Rein is Professor of Social Policy at the Massachusetts Institute of Technology in Cambridge, Massachusetts. He is a member of the external faculty of the European Centre for Social Welfare Training and Research and a frequent consultant for the Institute for Advanced Studies in Vienna. Among his recent publications are *Frame Reflection: Toward the Resolution of Intractable Policy Controversies* (with Donald Schon); *Age, Work, and Social Security* (co-edited); *Time for Retirement: Comparative Studies of the Decreasing Age of Exit from the Labor Force* (co-edited).

Emmanuel Reynaud received a Ph.D. in sociology from l'Ecole des Hautes en Sciences Sociales in Paris. He is a researcher at the Institut de Recherches Economiques et Sociales in Paris. He is the French representative of the European Commission's Observatory on Supplementary Pensions and the chairman of the European Network for Research on Supplementary Pensions. He has written a number of publications on retirement provision in France and in other industrialized countries, and is co-author of *Les systèmes de retraites à l'étranger: Etats-Unis, Allemagne, Royaume-Uni.* He has recently co-edited *International Perspectives on Supplementary Pensions: Actors and Issues* (Quorum Books).

Peter Rosner is Doz. Dr., Associate Professor at the Department of Economics, University of Vienna. His fields of research are social policy and history of economic theory.

Winfried Schmähl holds the degree of Dr. rer. pol. Since 1989 he is Professor of Economics, specializing in Social Policy, and Director of the Economics Department at the Centre for Social Policy Research, University of Bremen, Germany. He is Chairman of the Social Advisory Council of the German Federal Government since 1986. His fields of research are economic aspects of social policy and demographic aging, retirement, financing of social security, old age security, long-term care, lifetime income development, and social policy in former socialist countries. He is a member of several expert commissions of the German Federal Government and the German Parliament, on, for example, income redistribution, demographic changes, and social security.

John Turner has a Ph.D. in economics from the University of Chicago.

He is Special Social Security Advisor to the International Labor Office and adjunct lecturer at George Washington University, where he teaches the Economics of Aging. He was formerly Deputy Director of the Office of Research, Pension and Welfare Benefits Administration, US Department of Labor, and before that he worked in the research office of the Social Security Administration. He received a Fulbright Scholar award to do pension research at the Institut de Recherches Economiques et Sociales in Paris in 1994. He has written or edited eight books on pensions.

Thomas Url received his Ph.D. in economics at the University of Graz and Vienna in 1993. He currently holds a position at the Austrian Institute of Economic Research. He is also Lecturer at the University of Business Administration and Economics, Vienna, and at the Joint Vienna Institute.

Eskil Wadensjö is Professor of labour economics at the Swedish Institute for Social Research (SOFI), Stockholm University, and Dean of the faculty of social sciences, Stockholm University. His fields of research are labour economics, social policy and the history of economic thought. He is the author of several governmental reports on occupational pensions. Among his recent publications may be mentioned: *The Nordic Labour Market in the 1990s* (edited) (North-Holland), and *Arbetsmarknaden* (*The Labour Market*) (co-authored), which is a textbook in labour economics (SNS 1996).

Andreas Wörgötter is Chairman of the Department of Economics at the Institute for Advanced Studies, Vienna. He is also affiliated with the Central European University in Budapest and the Center for Economic Research and Graduate Education at Charles University in Prague. He has previously held positions at New York University and the University of Technology in Vienna.

Preface

The assumption on which the present study rests is that there is more to welfare than what the state provides. If we accept this premise, then the conclusion that follows is that the welfare state is too narrow a framework to capture the details about the economic well-being of the residents and citizens of a society. A new and broader intellectual perspective is required, namely a transition from the welfare state to the welfare society. These ideas were developed in a book that Martin Rein and Lee Rainwater titled *The Interplay Between the Public and Private Institutions of Social Protection*, published in 1989. From an American perspective, the focus only on the state led to an underestimate of the level of social protection in society. When the broader welfare society perspective is adopted, America no longer looks like an exceptional case characterized as a welfare laggard.

In the 1980s, Eskil Wadensjö, writing about the Swedish welfare state, also observed that contractual welfare provisions were neglected in favour of a more ideologically committed perspective which views the state as the central actor in the creation of a universal citizen provision of social benefits. In two books written together with Per Gunnar Edebalk, *Avgångsbidrag* (*Severance Pay Insurance Schemes*, 1980) and *Arbetsmarknadsförsäkringar* (*Occupational Insurances*, 1989), various parts of the system of occupational insurances were described. As a result of the widespread acceptance of a bias in favour of universal state provision as the guarantor of egalitarian social policy, the role of contractual social benefits in Swedish social policy was neglected. In practice, however, since the introduction of earnings-related social insurance (ATP) in 1960 white-collar workers managed to preserve contractual social benefits they had before the introduction of ATP. Blue-collar workers interested in equity claims insisted on an expansion of contractual benefits as well. Without being fully recognized, the result was the development of a mixed welfare system. In the 1990s state spending was under pressure and a major pension reform has been decided on, which provided even greater interest in the potential of contractual benefits to offset the projected decline in state benefits. Both trends combined to create a substantially mixed welfare system of contractual and public provision.

To take the concept of a welfare society rather than a welfare state seriously requires a different system of statistical accounting and a different focus of case studies. This issue of measuring trends is reflected internationally in the creation of two different data sets designed to measure the differing intellectual perspectives. OECD statistics on social policy measures state spending and include education as well as health and welfare. By contrast, the European Community tried to develop a social protection framework to include public and private provision for dealing with interrupted and inadequate income and high and unexpected social consumption costs. Education as a public good was not included in this approach. The implications of the different measures are discussed at length in the book by Rein and Rainwater.

Intuitively, the welfare society concept is reasonably clear. The state is a general provider of insurance and means-tested social security benefits for the aged and their survivors, which we conventionally identify as public benefits. In addition there are contractual benefits that act to supplement the public programme which take the form of occupational pensions and age-conditioned severance pay. Finally there are personal or individual accounts which take the form of individual savings through insurance companies and tax deferred annuities of different types. The state indirectly promotes these benefits largely via the tax system or what is know as off budget or tax expenditures.

While the intuition is clear, the devil is in the details. Without reviewing all the complexities it is enough here to state three problems. First, the state is both an employer and a general provider, which poses a problem of how to deal with a system in transition where government employment is privatized, like the railroads or the post office (Germany), or there is a decision to phase out the programme and require future generations to receive only general public benefits (the United States). Secondly, what to do if the public employment system is an alternative to the general government scheme, Beamten or Civil Service Pensions rather than a supplement to it (Germany). Third, how to handle the government mandating of contractual benefits, where the government requires that enterprise provide a pension supplement but provides only broad guidelines leaving the details to be worked out in contractual agreements (the French story). The European Community is still struggling to resolve these conceptual and measurement issues. In

1996 it issued a new revised statistical series, which took into account the revised basic definitions.

With all its limits a statistical series now exists which permits the first international comparisons of welfare society spending in most mature industrial societies. The present book draws on national statistics supplemented by these statistics. Here we owe a special debt to Laura Bardone, for help in the early phases of our study.

More specifically the ideas for the present project draw on a network of specialists that created a book on early exit from the labour market called *Time for Retirement*. This work was supported by the WZB, the Science Centre in Berlin, for whom we owe a special debt to Frieder Naschold and Wolfgang Zapf, who was then director of the Science Centre. The idea for this present study grew out of this early effort to study entry and exit from the welfare state. Martin Rein was asked by Edward Elgar Press to produce a book of readings on public pensions. He proposed an alternative approach, namely to focus on the changing welfare mix and the developments of occupational pension schemes. They thought the shift in focus not only made sense, but was exciting. Martin Rein and Eskil Wadensjö then agreed to act as the editors.

A range of countries with different institutional welfare mixes was chosen. One of the persistent issues about contractual schemes is whether they arise to offset a weak welfare state or whether they build on the strengths of the foundation established by mature welfare states. It was therefore essential to include in our study accounts of the strongest welfare states: France, Germany, the Netherlands and Sweden. What emerges when we consider the experiences of these countries is that they all show evidence of strong occupational pensions. Sometimes, as in Germany, they appear within the public sector, reflecting a struggle for equity between civil servants and other public employees. In comparison the private sector schemes are relatively weak. By contrast, Sweden's occupational programmes were fed by a desire for equity between white-collar and blue-collar workers. In the Netherlands supplementary schemes flourish in both the public and private sectors, but almost 20 per cent of workers are still excluded. The tendency for the government to raid the public schemes when it needed resources created pressure to privatize the civil service pension schemes. In France mandating occupational schemes was widely accepted, creating both mandating and weak regulation resulting in variations across industries. Given such a variety of practice, typologies of welfare state regimes as distinct and stable can be misleading. But not all strong welfare states developed contractual or supplementary pension arrangements. Hence the inclusion of Italy and Austria as examples of an opposite trend to that of most countries in continental Europe was of interest.

In contrast there is the account of weak welfare states as characterized by the experience of Japan, United Kingdom and the United States. It was essential to include the story of these countries as well. Briefly we see that like the strong welfare states, each developed contractual schemes. In Japan and the United Kingdom rules for contracting out of the state programmes were important. In the United States there was the opposite pattern of contracting in the federal, state and local civil servant into the general public social security programme, but transforming the basic structure of occupational programmes, from a defined benefit to a defined contribution plan. The details are in the chapter on the USA. Given this variety our interpretative framework is not based on regimes, but on the interaction between state and enterprise.

A group of specialists were invited to join the project from different disciplines: history, economics, political science and sociology. The first meeting was held in Paris. Emmanuel Reynaud managed to help secure funds for a meeting that was financed by l'Observatoire des Retraites. The meeting was very stimulating. It is unusual for a group of experts to feel that they learned so much from the participants. The reason seemed clear. The world was changing and this was a first occasion to learn about the major projected and realized changes that were developing in each country. The framework provided some unity to the diversity of country experience.

With the financial help of the Institute for Advanced Studies (IHS) and The European Centre in Vienna, we arranged a second meeting held at IHS in April 1995. The papers were reviewed and criticized by the participants at the meeting. This was followed by comments from the two editors.

The last stage in the production of the final manuscript was organized at the Swedish Institute for Social Research, Stockholm University. Jean Parr assisted with the editing, Ingvar Nilsson and Mats Lindahl did the technical editing and MediaMontage the desk-top originals.

Cambridge, Mass. and Stockholm

Martin Rein   *Eskil Wadensjö*

1

The Emerging Role of Enterprise in Social Policy

Martin Rein and Eskil Wadensjö

The thesis of this chapter is that the institutional arrangements for distributing social protection against the risk of income loss and income inadequacy are changing in mature industrial societies. This signals a major new development for the evolution of the intergenerational contract. Indeed, we believe that the future of the welfare state is already developing in the present realignment of the mix of institutions that are designed to protect individual well-being at the last stage of the working career. Many countries have revised their pension systems in the last few years.[1] In many countries enterprise-based social policy, for example occupational pensions, is a growing part of that mix. However, these developments are rather new and therefore it is difficult to judge the durability of the changes that are now increasingly becoming visible. Before exploring these questions, some preliminary comments are necessary.

There are many reasons for studying occupational welfare. There is more to welfare than what the state provides and the exclusion of employment-based occupational welfare from the system of accounting for total welfare spending leads to distortions in our understanding of laggard and leading welfare state countries (see Rein 1996). In the present study we are not trying to develop a general model of occupational pensions, nor are we trying to account for the historical origins of this system of protection, which in many countries pre-dated the state system and was regarded as an alternative to the state. For our present purposes we assume that we are in the middle of an evolving story.

Our intention is to show how changes in one system (the public sec-

---

[1] For a recent international survey and a proposal for change see World Bank (1994).

tor) shape or more modestly influence changes in another system (occupational pensions). Both systems are influenced by broader changes in the economic and political system. We begin with an interpretation of what is driving the state, on the assumption that the firm-state interaction is probably the overriding factor in creating a change in the welfare mix. Hence it is most important to understand why the state does what it does, since its action activates the ongoing process of action and reaction.

1. The dynamics of accommodation

Our analysis rests on the assumption that both continuity and transformation are essential to maintain the ongoing viability of the welfare society, which constitutes a mix of public, occupational and personal systems of social protection. This approach implies that the welfare society must be understood in the framework of continuous institutional accommodation to the policy environment in which it is situated. This means accommodating both to the actions of the three main pillars of social protection and to the broader context changes. Over time societies change. There has been a remarkable growth of long-term unemployment in Europe since the early 1970s, a rise in part-time employment, an increase in the number of lone parents, and a rise in unprotected full-time careers. These developments have created problems for the state social security system which depended on the assumption of full employment and a male breadwinner model of economic dependence and family structure. The change in economic conditions and the shifts of political regimes are entwined with these social changes.

A long-term perspective of accommodation is needed since an understanding of pension policy must take account of at least a 30 to 40 year time horizon from entry into the labour market as a young worker to exit from work at the last stage of the working career. But there is an impatient demand by some analysts for abrupt, discretionary reduction in benefits rather than gradually, by deindexation. But as Assar Lindbeck also points out, welfare state policies not only mitigate market risks but may also create new risks in the form of unpredictable changes in politically determined rules or rule instability. These unstable rules in turn are bound to influence people's behaviour in various markets. The avoidance of rule instability may be one of the reasons why unwinding the welfare state may be difficult (Lindbeck 1995, p. 14). But it is not only individual behaviour, but the behaviour of institutions that come into play in response to the new market risks and political disturbance

2

created by rule instability. Rather, what is implied is that the unwinding of welfare state spending in some areas may often call forth rewinding of the regulatory role of the welfare state as personal and occupational welfare systems of social protection arise in response to the vacuum created by the state's initiative. In brief, our main argument is that the welfare state changes in response to changes in the socio-economic-political system in which it is embedded. Other institutions of the welfare society accommodate to the changes initiated by the state. Of course, it is not a perfect accommodation. There are lags, fall-backs and leaps forward. There are continuous discoveries of design flaws within a country, but also a borrowing of ideas from the experience of other countries. There seems little doubt that the UK exported its social policy of contracting out of state pensions to occupational and then later personal pensions. In practice 'poorly trained agents, working on a commission basis, oversold inappropriate policies (for example, to those already in occupational schemes providing better returns)' (Silburn 1994). There was also the cautious lesson to be learned from the overselling of personal pensions as a substitute for occupational pensions as part of the same experience. But the main lesson is that countries accommodate to changes in their policy environment and occupational pensions are part and parcel of that accommodation.

The arguments that follow are presented as follows: set out a simplified state-firm interaction framework to explain why the welfare mix (state, occupational, and personal pensions) at the last stage of the working career has changed in many countries and to consider how this framework differs from current approaches to the welfare state; we elaborate the framework; we define the concept of pension policy; we summarize empirical evidence to document that a change in pension policy has occurred in many countries; we show how the recent pension reform of the state is likely to affect the development of occupational pensions; we consider what the effect a change in the welfare mix would have on the distribution of economic well-being; and finally we relate the changes in the nine countries covered in this book to the development.

2. The framework to describe the processes that are changing the welfare mix

The main elements of the framework are briefly the following: (1) There have been significant changes in the policy environment in which the state is located (political, economic and normative). (2) The state adjusts to these changes in its environment by introducing pension reforms. (3) The enterprise/occupational pension system primarily adjusts to the changes of the state pension scheme while taking account of the changes in its own product market, production regime shaped by changes in technology, and in internal labour market requirements (described by some as the lean and mean era).

Of course, it is not surprising that enterprises are not necessarily driven by the same forces that activate the state. The demography of the society is, after all, not the same as that of specific enterprises. One example is Renault, the auto company in France, which has a large share of older workers. Renault hired many foreign workers during the 1960s, all of about the same age, and they are still in the firm since these workers have low job mobility. It is not clear if the firm's problem with the age composition of the work force is due to migrant workers lacking literacy and hence capacity to adjust to new technologies, or to age discrimination, or the lower productivity of older workers.

Still another problem facing enterprise is the changing labour market conditions. At one time, granting pensions was a means to recruit and retain workers with special skills. In a tight labour market with unemployment in the double digits the labour considerations guiding the development of enterprise-financed pensions have retreated.

We want to make explicit the theoretical framework within which we examine the emerging role of enterprise in social policy and to contrast our framework with other theories about the welfare state. A firm-state interaction which focuses on a change in the welfare mix can be contrasted with two other perspectives: the theory of the welfare state crisis and the theory of welfare state regimes.

The welfare state crisis literature assumes that the state is caught in a legitimacy crisis which inhibits its capacity for flexible adaptation to its changing environment without undermining its democratic mandate. The state is paralysed and unable to accommodate to a changing environment, hence a welfare state crisis. See Offe (1984).

Theorizing about the welfare state regimes has its origins in Richard Titmuss's inaugural lecture at the London School of Economics in the mid 1950s. He first argued in his essay on the 'Social Division of Welfare' that there are three forms in which welfare can be distributed: fiscal, occupational and social welfare – the tax system, the enterprise fringe benefit system and the state redistribution system of direct benefits. He later generalized a modified version of the social division of welfare found within a country into a description of types of welfare societies. He suggested that there were three main types: an industrial achievement model which used occupational social benefits as an incentive to promote productive and efficient labour; an institutional redistributive model which used direct state benefits and the fiscal system to redistribute resources to create a more egalitarian society; and finally a residual system which relied upon means testing and modest benefits to concentrate resources among the poor. This effort was elaborated many years later into a theory that countries had relatively stable welfare regimes. See Esping-Andersen (1990).

If our thesis about emergence is correct, then regimes can be expected to change over time. There are several other problems with the theory of regimes. There is hardly any agreement among experts as to which countries should be assigned to which regime types. Transfer and service regimes appear to be quite different. Moreover, political regimes appear to have changed dramatically while there is substantial continuity in pension policy. Germany is the prototypic case of political regime shifts and stable policy. The literature blurred the ideological and normative issues surrounding regimes with an analytical account of the elements that constitute a regime. A welfare regime is constituted by its parts; the number of civil servants, the role of occupational and personal pensions, and the form and generosity of public provisions, its reliance on means testing etc. However, the constellation of these elements has been assigned a political label. A welfare regime is thus confused with the naming of a political regime as 'liberal, social democratic or conservative corporatist'. It is one thing, of course, to identify a pattern of welfare elements at one point in time, which constitutes a portrait of the welfare landscape with a characterization of regimes as processes, where the different elements change over time. Our focus on 'emergence' through the interaction of the firm and the state addresses the issue of the processes which lead to a change in the relationship of the welfare elements to each other.

We will elaborate below the way in which the state is the prime actor, creating a system of public provision and a regulatory and incentive structure for the development of occupational and personal pensions. The firm tries to use the existing infrastructure of public provisions for its own purposes, as it did when creating the phenomenon of early retirement. See Kohli et al. (1991). The state, in turn, responds to the action of the enterprise by trying to slow down or reverse the drain of its resources. The enterprise responds to the state and the process continues creating, over time, not stable regimes but dramatic changes in the social division of welfare now conceptualized as state, occupational and personal pensions.

3. The framework elaborated: the state confronts a new perceived policy environment

This new environment is characterized by the 'perception' that pensions will not be affordable in the future, that the existing system of pensions is also not intergenerationally and gender fair; and finally there has been a change in philosophy growing out of the belief that too much attention has been given to developing state social benefits as a system of market protection against market failures and thereby neglecting the equally important phenomenon of state failure. The story is surprisingly similar in all the countries we are studying.

What then is driving the state? There are at least three intellectually interesting challenges to the generational contract between the actively employed who currently pay for the retirement income of those who are retired in a system of financing that is based on paying for benefits as society goes along (pay-as-you-go). We believe that the future of the welfare state can best be understood by examining the present response to these challenges. In this sense the future is in the present. These challenges are: (1) that the generational contract in its present form is no longer practical given demographic changes and the erosion of full employment, (2) that it is not fair, given the better information derived from a future-oriented generational accounting scheme, and (3) that it is not viable given the shift in priorities from redistribution to monetary stability, monetary integration, and market making by encouraging the deregulation of labour markets.

The first argument is designed to show that the generational contract will become too expensive. Sometimes the causal agent is demographic change, i.e. the growth of the aging population relative to the working population where benefits to the aging are paid directly through the wages of the actively employed. This 'too expensive' or 'can't afford' argument is based on the commonly accepted projections of rapid growth in the size of the older cohorts, usually referred to as the aging of society.

The increased price of social security benefits due to demographic factors can be simply illustrated: 'When the ratio of retirees to workers is

6

1 to 4, it costs the average worker $0.25 to raise average benefits by $1. If the ratio falls to 1 to 3, it then costs the average worker $0.33 to raise benefits' (Turner and Watanabe 1995). The World Bank estimates that if the Swedish system does not change, payroll taxes are projected to exceed 25 per cent in the year 2000 and 40 per cent twenty years later. Austria and Germany spend almost 40 per cent of the consolidated public budget on old age pensions.

Population aging is only one factor behind increasing costs; the other is the effective lowering of the age of entry into the pension system due to the massive increase in early retirement in the last two decades.

The rapid growth in early retirement has effectively lowered the age of entry into the pension system and transformed the labour force participation rates at the last stage of the working life. We would stress the role of early retirement more than the demographic argument. Consider the situation in Austria, which has one of the lowest labour force participation rates of older men in the Western economies. The rate is below 15 per cent for men aged 60–64. Not surprisingly the cost of adaptability is affordability. Austria has the highest ratio of public pension spending to GDP, 16.1 per cent in 1986 (World Bank 1994, pp. 41 and 361).

Most studies take account of expenditures and the dependency ratio. The essay by Van den Noord and Herd (1994) provides a sophisticated estimate of pension liabilities in seven countries. This is perhaps the best summary of the 'too expensive' argument. But even though costs and the ratio of the retired to the working population have increased due to the aging of the population when productivity per worker is taken into account, GDP per worker has declined in virtually all countries. Cutler et al. (1990) have developed an interesting model which shows that the demographic impact of the baby boom generation was to generate more than the per capita capital requirements the current working age population needs to sustain itself and to become more productive. Hence the 'too expensive' argument is overstated. See also the critique of Abel-Smith (1993). This counterevidence suggests that the best conclusion is that the 'too expensive' argument is a subtle mixture of political and economic reasoning. Therefore the policy environment is better interpreted as 'perceived' rather than as necessarily 'real'.

The second argument is about fairness. Unfairness exists not only between generations, but also within generations, for example, between men and women and blue-collar and white-collar workers. How the gender and class issue arises differs across countries. Consider some differences between Sweden and Germany. In Germany the class difference is focused on how workers in the public sector improve their economic position relative to the civil servants. The Swedish discussion is mainly about equity between blue-collar and white-collar workers and between men and women, not between those employed in the private and the public sector. The main difference between the German and the Swedish labour market is the high labour force participation among Swedish women (almost the same as among men). This difference contributes to an explanation of the differences in the development of the pension systems.

In Germany Julia Allmendinger (1994) has eloquently argued that women do best financially in retirement if they marry well. Their economic position in the state system is most likely to depend on derived benefits from their status as survivor. Some 40 per cent of all beneficiaries receive survivor benefits which have lower value than earned benefits. But the size of women's earnings in the labour market is hardly enough to earn them entitlement to private occupational pensions – only 7 per cent of women in the private sector have a private pension compared to 40 per cent of male pensioners who worked in the private sector. In brief the marriage market, rather than the labour market or the welfare state, would be more likely to assure women an adequate income in retirement. On the face of it such a system is outrageously unfair to women.

We want to focus next on how the unfairness argument is expressed across generations. The most recent expression of this position is found with the introduction in the US of a new system of generational accounting. The basic argument is that a new system of budgeting is needed because the tax and transfer budget is 'present-oriented' and the costs to our children and to citizens not yet born are excluded from the account (see Auerbach, Gokhale and Kotlikoff 1994). A generational accounting scheme is based on the assumption that the present tax and transfer system when projected to the future displays a high degree of generational imbalance. Today's 65-year-olds have a net gain of $65 000, whereas today's 30-year-olds have a net loss of $200 000, and citizens not yet born have a deficit at birth of $167 000. The generational contract of today produces perverse distributional effects when future generations are taken into account. Using a different assumption the authors still find that 'future generations will have to pay 65 per cent more than current new-borns' assuming a discount rate of 3 per cent and economic growth of 1.25 per cent. 'Thus, the evidence for significant generational imbalances in the US fiscal policy is quite robust' (Auerbach, Gokhale and Kotlikoff 1994, p. 82).

These various arguments about fairness play as important a role in the political pressure to change the pension system as do the economic arguments about demography and early retirement.

The third challenge, concerning changing philosophy, is both more subtle and fundamental, and is based on an interpretation of why a national welfare state at the European level has not emerged and why Europe will never become a federal state capable of creating a social Europe committed to the social democratic ideals of generational solidarity and redistribution.[2]

What appears to be emerging in the European Union is a shift in priorities away from a commitment to full employment. The social security system is based on and is only sustainable with the premise of full employment as the foundation on which the social contract is to be forged. A strong state is emerging as an agent of the free market. The commitment to monetary integration and monetary stability makes it possible to promote European economic integration while preserving national autonomy. The implicit norm is not to overrule a country, but to postpone a decision till unanimity is reached. This rules out federal state aid and subsidies to protect people against the market. The focus is on the deregulation of the labour market and encouraging labour mobility, posing, of course, the problem of how to regulate the low end of the labour market.

In practice this has meant, at least so far, a deeper concern for low inflation, low public debt, and low, and decreasing, rates of growth of governmental spending as the overriding basis for the standardization of norm setting by national autonomous countries. As a result a double-digit unemployment rate is tolerable, while a 3 per cent growth of inflation or the budget deficit is unacceptable. The new vision of the Liberals threatens the community of solidarity of the Social Democratic vision. A viable European integration can only be built on the economic image of market making, open labour markets and monetary stability and integration. The only way to preserve European integration and national autonomy is to build on the Liberal vision of open markets. A federal welfare state trying to save old and declining industries by subsidization

---

[2] The analysis is based on recent research by Dobbin and Boychuk (1996).

is not viable. The development of industries of the future is replacing the rescue of declining industries. The market will, over time, equalize regions and expand citizens' free choice. No new utopia nor new vision lies on the horizon. This new Liberal vision on which European internationalization is being forged poses a threat to the generational contract of solidarity.

The state responds to its perceived or real new environment by introducing pension reforms. The response across countries while differing in detail is surprisingly similar. We highlight those reforms that are likely to have the greatest impact in the occupational personal pension systems.

4. What is a pension policy?

Part of the confusion arises from the difficulty in defining the terrain: what is retirement and what are the public and private institutions providing social protection at retirement? Consider each issue in turn. What is retirement? There are at least three different definitions. First is entry into the public old age pension programme based on age (and in some cases other qualifications, such as years of contribution, or years of residence). In this definition retirement is defined as a definite chronological stage of the life course. Secondly, retirement is defined as a definite exit from the labour market without any intention to re-enter. Thirdly, retirement is defined as exiting from the 'lifetime job', a job in which a person has worked for a major part of his working career.

For most of this century there has been a development towards a division of the life cycle into three distinct phases: childhood and education, adulthood and work, old age and retirement.[3] The age of entering and leaving the labour market have tended to become more and more uniform for greater and greater segments of the labour force. Fewer people, for example, have continued to work after the age for receiving an old age pension. The three definitions of retirement tended to coincide – a person left a long-term full-time employment at the age for receiving an old age pension and also left the labour market at the same time. This trend towards conformity and simultaneity has been broken. During the last decades new patterns have emerged.

---

[3] See Kohli (1985).

10

The first part of that development is a discrepancy between the age of leaving the labour market and the age of receiving an old age pension. Many people leave the labour market several years before they receive an old age pension. In most cases they do so through different pathways where they receive compensation through other social insurance programmes.[4] The most important pathways are disability, sickness, and unemployment insurance. The unemployment insurance received by an older worker can be the functional equivalent to a pension, since many countries no longer require that older workers be registered as unemployed and be actively seeking employment. This development means a gradual withdrawal from the labour force of the *population* of older workers.

The other development is that in some countries people leave their long-term full-time jobs before the age of retirement but continue to work. Japan, the US and Sweden are three examples, but with different forms for changing employment. In Japan after the *teinen* age (the age of retirement from the 'life-long' job), workers are redeployed to other jobs in daughter companies of the enterprise, to other related companies, or to new lower-paid positions in the same enterprise as they have been employed in, or start a small firm utilizing the severance pay paid upon reaching the teinen age.[5] In the US there are bridging jobs of workers who get a pension and continue to work elsewhere.[6] In Japan the company takes the initiative, in the US it is left to the individual. What they share in common is combining work and retirement after leaving their last job. In Sweden, partial pensions make it possible to combine work and pensions in the same job.[7] This means that many people in Sweden aged 60 to 65 continue to work but with reduced working hours. The developments in Japan, the US and Sweden are three different models where *individuals* are gradually withdrawing from the labour market.

Separating the public and private domains is equally challenging. The main difficulty is that the state has several roles.[8] We identify several

---

[4] See Kohli et al. (1991) for the development in several industrial countries.

[5] See Oka (1992), Takayama (1992) and Kimura et al. (1994) for the Japanese system.

[6] See Burkhauser and Quinn (1989), Sheppard (1991) and Gustman, Mitchell and Steinmeier (1994) for the US system.

[7] See Wadensjö (1996) for an overview of the Swedish system.

[8] For a discussion of the different roles of states regarding pensions see Rein (1988).

11

roles, all of which influence the evolution of the mix of public and private institutions providing social protection. The state, for example, is both provider of social security, and employer. Sometimes the civil servants have their own alternative scheme (Germany and the US). But the state is also active in stimulating occupational welfare by a complicated system of tax exemptions and tax deferments and the state is an active regulator of life insurance, pension funds and company pensions. The state is also the guarantor of pensions in case of insolvency.

Given these different definitions of retirement and the multiple roles of the government, how shall we name and frame the social protection at old age? There are two strong competing metaphors that offer some conceptual unity to our subject: the image of 'pillars' and that of a 'welfare mix'. The former is more eloquent, but the latter more adequate to our task. Pillars suggest solid, autonomous, free standing independent foundations on which the social protection edifice is built. The mix metaphor suggests a mixture of elements that change in the course of their interaction. The fusion, linkage, and interrelations of the elements makes the task of demarcation most elusive.

The three main institutional elements in the mix are, as we have suggested above, state, occupational/enterprise and personal. Each element is difficult to separate since the state is both an employer and a provider of social security, and the personal life insurance field not only serves the individual, but is, especially for small firms, the main provider for the enterprise's occupational welfare. We will, however, concentrate on changes in the social security pension system and their effects on the occupational/enterprise pension system.

5. Pension reforms

The following main pension reforms are found in most countries:

1) The most obvious way of advancing the economic situation of the pension system is to raise the pension age. Several countries, including Germany, Japan, Sweden, and the US have decided to raise the pension age.

2) The reference period for calculating pension rights has been lengthened. There are three systems for calculating these rights: the last year, the best years, all years. Several countries (Italy, Sweden etc.) are shifting from last and best year systems to an all years system. The US

12

already has the all years system. This will lower pension benefits for all individuals whose income rises with age and experience – i.e., better educated and higher paid workers.

3) There is some pressure to modify the pay-as-you-go financing into a quasi-funded scheme. In the US the size of the social security trust fund will increase from 4 per cent of GDP in 1990 to 24 per cent in 2018, and then decline thereafter (Van den Noord and Herd 1994, p. 159). Many systems are in fact combinations of pay-as-you-go and quasi-funded. These systems are difficult to sustain in practice, because of the tendency for governments to use the surplus to lower the debt or reduce government spending. The Dutch supplementary civil service pension and the US experience illustrate the problems. Briefly, in the Netherlands the state took contributional holidays from their financial obligation to contribute to the funded scheme, and constrained the investment portfolios of these funds. The result is the decision to privatize the public pension scheme to give it more autonomy. In the US, Senator Moynihan proposed legislation (which failed to pass) to reduce contributions to the Trust Fund, because the money was going to finance the debt rather than build a reserve in anticipation of future demographic changes.

4) Legislation has been passed to decrease access to public programmes which are 'pension-like' because they serve the same function as old age pensions by permitting exit from work at the last stage of the working career. The main pathways vary by country but include severance pay, disability, sickness, and unemployment benefits. Since 1991, in Sweden, disability pensions for labour market reasons are not granted; in the Netherlands disability benefits have been lowered and access made more difficult.

5) Tax incentives to encourage the development of occupational and personal pensions have been expanded. Britain has created legislation to provide strong economic incentives to promote the development of personal pensions. The 1994 White Paper further establishes the intention to extend these incentives to other age groups. At present the programme is most attractive to those under 40 years of age. But British social security policy has a history of 'doing and undoing' with different political regime shifts. The durability of the change in direction toward a minimal welfare state remains politically unsettled, given the past history. In the US there is tension between the desire to reduce tax losses, by for example setting a ceiling on benefits and contributions, and increasing tax losses by permitting

employees, for the first time, to make tax deductible contributions to enterprise-created pension schemes (401k programmes). This tension is also found in most other countries. At the same time that countries provide incentive for expansions, they increase the regulations to place safeguards ensuring that company-sponsored programmes will not be plundered and that the entitlement of future pensioners is protected. The stronger the regulation the less attractive the schemes are for employers and the more attractive to employees.

6.   Main types of changes in the welfare mix

It seems useful to describe the enterprise response in two different ways: first, to consider in more qualitative terms the response of enterprise to the pensions reform by suggesting different types of firm-state interaction; second, to document the empirical evidence for a growing share of supplementary occupational pensions. This is now possible because of the availability of a new statistical Eurostat series documenting trends in supplementary pensions from 1980 to 1993.

How do employers, employers' associations, unions and households respond to these changes in the state's pension policy caused by the various challenges which that policy faces (too expensive, fairness, and changing philosophy)?

A comparison of countries shows diverse developments. In some countries the state and the occupational/personal pension systems show a *parallel development*. They decline at the same time or, as was common in earlier periods, they expand at the same time. In other countries a decline in the public pension scheme is counteracted by an expansion of occupational and personal pensions. In earlier periods the reverse pattern was common – an expansion of the public pension system simultaneously with a decline in the occupational and personal systems.

One explanation for a *double decline* is that lower earnings lead to less demand for most goods and services including various forms of pensions. Another explanation is that public and occupational pensions are complements. For example, together they may form a pathway for early exit from the labour market. If the conditions for eligibility and benefit levels at early retirement deteriorate in the public scheme, this may lead people to stay longer in the labour market and therefore the demand for occupational early retirement pensions which complement the state programme may decrease. Another example is given by what happened

14

when the replacement rate in the state partial pension scheme in Sweden decreased from 65 to 50 per cent. A corresponding cut of the replacement rate was made in the occupational partial pension scheme for white-collar workers, a scheme which compensates for earnings over a certain ceiling.

The most obvious explanation for a decline in the public pension schemes and an increase in the occupational/private pension schemes at the same time is that compensation from the schemes are substitutes for each other. They are all means to guarantee income replacement after retirement and if, as has recently often been the case, the government makes cutbacks in the public scheme, the demand for other forms of pension schemes increases. In earlier periods the opposite development was common – an expansion of public pensions replacing occupational and private pensions. A decline in the public system and an increase in the occupational and private system at the same time mainly appears in two forms: *cross over* (individuals leave the public scheme for occupational or private pensions) and *offsets* (declines in the public scheme are counteracted by offsetting increases in occupational schemes).

We will give some examples below of the three patterns mentioned: cross over, offsets and parallel development. This is a first step in investigating the striking international differences that exist. Sometimes more than one pattern can be found in a single country. This naturally makes the task of generalizing much more difficult, but also, of course, more interesting. After considering these trends we turn to the question of what difference the welfare mix makes for the level of poverty and inequality.

Cross over means that an individual can leave the public system and cross over into an occupational or personal system of savings as an alternative to the earnings-related component of the public pension system. An active process of sectorial cross over, or opting out or contracting out from state to occupational and personal pensions, is being vigorously promoted by the government of the UK. While the British system of opting out is supplemented by a flat-rate public pension which over time will become less important, it is nevertheless unique in encouraging the replacement of a part of the social security system with an occupational or personal pension.

In the British context the cost of contracting out is quite considerable. The British government paid 10.5 billion pounds to people who opted for personal pensions in the form of rebates on social security contributions. Companies selling personal pensions take 4–13 per cent in com-

15

missions and charges for sales agents and management fees (Turner and Watanabe 1995, p. 49). About a third of a million who contracted out will receive lower benefits on retirement than if they remained in the public scheme. The incentive to oversell the product was very strong. Life insurance companies were fined one million pounds for advising people to buy unsuitable products (*The Economist*, 11–17 December, 1993, p. 75). For a critique and a proposal of an alternative system see also *Social Justice* (1994).

In addition to the rebate on contributions, an incentive payment of 2 per cent of covered earnings is made to those newly contracting out. The government determination to promote personal over occupational pensions is clear from the fact that the 2 per cent incentive payment is also available to workers who have already contracted out to an occupational pension if they have been in the plan for less than two years. About two-thirds of those contracted out are in employer-sponsored schemes and one-third are in personal pension plans. It is one of the ironies of British pension policy that the government has been forced to raise the base social security tax by 1 per cent to cover the cost of the subsidy to encourage cross overs.

Britain is not the only country where cross over is possible. The Japanese government encourages contracting out but does not subsidize it. In Britain about half of private sector workers and virtually all public setor workers are contracted out. In Japan about 25–30 per cent of all workers are contracted out.

It should be clear from the UK experience that a highly subsidized cross over can hardly be seen as a solution to the 'too expensive' arguments. But it is important in response to arguments that the pension system gives too little incentive for working and saving and that pension reforms should promote increased labour supply and savings. Such schemes encourage the separation of redistribution from saving and raise in a fresh way the question of which type of system is preferable as the saving-annuity complement to the public redistributive system. By making the personal pillar so visible in its pension policy the whole issue of the relevant welfare mix surfaces.

A special form of cross over, in this case mainly between different occupational pension schemes, is that which follows from nationalization or privatization. Such a change regularly means a change of occupational pension scheme which often leads to tensions. Whereas cross over is important in the UK, offsets seem to play a much larger role in the Netherlands and Sweden.

In the Netherlands contractual arrangements with enterprises were introduced, not to expand social protection but to offset the decline that had been created in the public sector.[9] Labour force participation among workers aged 55 and older started to fall already in the 1960s. This development could be explained with reference to the Dutch social insurance system. Already from 1967 labour market reasons could be taken into account when granting a disability pension. This rule explains why the Netherlands is the country that has the highest rate of people with disability pensions. The unemployment insurance system has also contributed to the high exit rate by unlimited compensation periods for older workers and high replacement rates.

Already in the late 1970s there was a change in the opinion regarding the desirability of early exit. The replacement rate was lowered and the maximal compensation period of the unemployment insurance system lengthened. The next attempt, made in 1987, was an abolishment of the rule that labour market reasons should be taken into account when granting a disability pension. Benefit cuts, a periodic review of disability status and a new principle of tying benefits to age are other parts of the attempts to decrease disability pensioning and early exit.

The attempts to change the development, however, have mainly failed due to the offsetting influence of occupational insurance schemes. The first reaction from the employers was to establish, together with the unions, social plans (SOP) using elements from social insurance, occupational insurance and the employers' own contributions to stimulate early exit. The next step was to create a new form of occupational insurances for early retirement pensions on the industry level. When these schemes, VUT, started to appear in 1977, 63 or 64 was the age from which compensation could be paid out. Now 60 or 61 is the common age limit, and in some cases a limit as low as 55 has been established.

In the 1990s there has been considerable pressure on the state for benefit cutbacks in Sweden. Disability for labour market reasons was eliminated in 1991. Partial pensions survived two attempts to eliminate or radically reduce them, but were finally reduced in 1994 as a part of a new pension reform. The new Swedish pension system which the *Riksdag* decided to adopt in June 1994 points to a decline in benefits when a

---

[9] See de Vroom and Blomsma (1991), Trommel and de Vroom (1994) and OECD (1993) for the development in the Netherlands.

system of lifetime earnings as the basis for calculating benefits is introduced. The government made a commitment to reduce new entries into the disability system by 25 per cent. At major restructuring and as an alternative to the terminated disability pensions for labour market reasons, the employers have started to buy 'garantipensioner' (guarantee pensions) for older employees (the age limit is often set to 55). Lately the unions and employers have discussed the introduction of early retirement pensions of the same type as the Dutch VUPs. A first step in that direction is a new collectively bargained insurance scheme (TUFS) agreed upon by LO (the blue-collar workers' confederation) and SAF (the association of employers in the private sector) in June 1993 (discontinued in 1996). Compensation (93.75 per cent of the unemployment compensation) is paid to people aged 62 to 65 who have exhausted their unemployment benefits and who have become unemployed as a consequence of a layoff and at that time received support from the severance pay insurance scheme (another occupational pension scheme). The compensation is paid out monthly until the person receives a full old age pension at the age of 65.

Co-mingling public and private arrangements is not so much an issue of principle, but of pragmatism. When a clear secular trend is in evidence and one pathway for enactment is blocked, some substitute pathway to realize the same objective emerges through creative problem solving. This is what happened in the Netherlands when enterprise was interested in maintaining the trend toward early retirement and the state set up obstacles, making it more difficult to make use of the unemployment and disability system to achieve early labour market exit. 'Instrument substitution', another social mechanism, was invented and the trend continued.

The third pattern is a parallel development in the benefits provided by the state and the coverage and benefit levels of the occupational pension system. The US offers a good example. We consider this development in a historical perspective to highlight its changing importance in recent years.

During the 1970s, counter to the conventional wisdom which held that a generous public provision of social insurance made employment embedded social protection unnecessary, came fresh evidence that 'by establishing a "floor" of state provision, state pensions actually encourage additional private pension saving' (Hannah 1992). This suggests a pattern of *complementarity* rather than substitution. The expansion of social security benefits had the effect of reducing the cost of private pensions in schemes which guaranteed a defined benefit level based on the cumulation of the public and private schemes. One conclusion was that 'private coverage appears to grow in response to the establishment and expansion of public coverage'. See Dobbin and Boychuk (1996).

In the US this is exactly what happened in the period of *double expansion.* Congressional concern about the low level of benefits led to five separate increases in benefits and the creation of an automatic cost-of-living increase in 1974. It was at this time, in the last half of the 1970s, that there was a huge increase in private pension coverage (data cited in Dobbin and Boychuk).

The political and economic setting in the 1980s and 1990s changed as a period of slow economic growth, high unemployment, and declining real wages emerged. In this new environment we are witnessing a period of *double decline* in occupational pensions coverage and public social security benefits. Consider each of these trends in turn.

The percentage of full-time private sector workers covered by a pension scheme declined from 50 per cent in 1979 to 43 per cent in 1988. Results differ somewhat, depending on whether one uses a legal definition, workers' perception, or employer financed pensions (Turner and Watanabe 1995, p. 124). The decline according to the latter definition appears to be related to a decrease in union membership, in real earnings and in the relative size of the manufacturing sector. A similar decline in coverage is also occurring in other countries such as the UK and Germany. In the UK public policy is actively seeking a shift from occupational to personal pensions in an attempt to create a minimum welfare state. In Germany occupational pension coverage has also recently decreased but without a similar political intention. According to the survey of IFO in 1993 the number of employees in the industrial sector with a company pension decreased from 70 per cent in 1990 to 66 per cent in 1993. Thus the downward trend of occupational pensions which began at the end of the 1980s is continuing into the 1990s. It is not that companies are not honouring existing pension obligations, but that they are not extending them to new employees. The economic recession and many other factors play a role here. See Ahrend (1995, p. 27).

But in the US it is not only the decline in occupational coverage that has occurred but also a decline in state pension as a share of the household income of older Americans. This development can be traced to legislation passed by Congress in 1983 in response to the widely held belief that the social security system was in imminent danger of collapse unless a dramatic rescue was planned. This legislation not only averted a

19

deficit, but created a massive social security surplus. The effect of this legislation was to lower benefits in a number of specific ways. The social security retirement age will be gradually raised to age 67. Those who retire before the normal age will get lower benefits. At present those retiring at age 62 get 20 per cent lower benefits for their lifetime compared to what they would have received had they retired at age 65. The rate of decrease will increase slowly to 30 per cent and apply to those who retire below age 67. Another equally important factor in lowering lifetime benefits relative to lifetime contributions is that the contribution rates were raised and the maximum taxable income was also heightened. One of the visible results of these legislative changes is that the percentage of retirement income provided by public social security declined from 39 per cent in 1980 to 36 per cent in 1990.

One of the factors leading to the double decline is the action of government in trying to reduce tax incentives in an effort to curb the growing budget deficit. More losses in federal resources are attributable to pensions than to any other programme. Pension tax forgiveness is 25 per cent larger than deductions for mortgage interests.

In the US both the employer's contribution and the interest earned from the capital of the pension funds are tax exempted. For employees the interest is tax deferred, i.e. one pays taxes on these benefits upon receiving them, usually later in the working career, when tax obligations decline with a decrease in income after retirement. One way to illustrate this is to consider the example of salary reduction plans where the worker's contributions to such a plan are deductible before tax earning. This makes them very attractive to the worker. They are also a relatively inexpensive way for firms to provide coverage for their workers. Even if the worker is the main or only contributor, the 401k plan must be set up by the employer – making the line separating firm and personal pensions difficult to draw.[10] We think it makes sense to consider these pensions as occupational pensions.

Between 1983 and 1990, participants in these defined contribution

---

[10] The 401k programme refers to the section of the Internal Revenue Code which made it possible for an individual to make a tax exempt contribution to a pension plan set up by the enterprise. Earlier, individual contributions to pension plans were taxed, only the employer's contribution was tax exempt. Although the law was passed in the late 1970s, the regulations were not written until the early 1980s. In 1992 about one-quarter of wage and salary workers made contributions to the plans. But these plans have not matured, so that contributions exceed actual benefits by more than tenfold.

plans grew by 15.1 million, while participation in defined benefit plans declined. However, the government has decided to make these plans less attractive to workers by decreasing the maximum amount that the worker can contribute tax free from $30 000 to $8000. What is clear is that a double decline has occurred, what is not clear is whether this is a temporary or long-term phenomenon.

7.   The enterprise response to the state's pension reform

Before reviewing the available trends we briefly comment on a number of conceptual issues which make it difficult to interpret the data. First, *the public-private divide.* Occupational does not mean private. The state has a double role: as provider of basic and earnings-related public pensions, and as employer distributing occupational pensions as an alternative to the public, state-sponsored, social security system. We consider the civil service pension system as an alternative system. By our definition an occupational system is a supplement to the basic and earnings-related social security system. This is consistent with the Eurostat distinction between the basic first pillar and the second pillar as a supplementary system.

We accept this distinction, but think that a further distinction is necessary for the benefits available to civil servants. We propose the concept of *supplementary advantage* to suggest that the civil servants get a disproportionate share of total expenditure relative to their share of recipients. The figures available for Germany, France and Italy illustrate the point. In 1989 in Germany, civil servants comprised 6 per cent of all beneficiaries and 18 per cent of total expenditure; in France the shares were 8 per cent and 22 per cent respectively, in Italy 6 per cent and 14 per cent respectively. Public pension expenditure as a percentage of GDP was 6.9 per cent in Germany, 9 per cent in France and 10.6 per cent in Italy. We allow an additional 2 per cent beneficiaries in each country, on the argument that civil servants have longer tenure and higher wages and therefore their share of expenditures relative to the pension population should be larger. This would mean that the civil servant has a share amounting to 1.1 per cent of GDP in Germany, 1.8 per cent in France and 1.3 per cent in Italy (Van den Noord and Herd 1994, Table 1 and Tables A3, A4 and A5).

While the example is only illustrative it does seem to suggest that the supplementary advantage of the civil service pension is between 1 and 2 per cent of GDP in these countries. The concept of supplementary advantage is one way to deal with the dual role of state as employer and provider.

A second conceptual difficulty exists in the Eurostat distinction between mandatory and voluntary supplementary pension in the second pillar. While the Netherlands and France have mandated supplementary systems, the crucial distinction is how the benefit levels and pension rules are set. In both countries the benefit structure is not set by the state but by contractual agreements between employers and unions. Moreover the benefits vary across industries and in the Netherlands close to 20 per cent of the working population is not covered by these contracts, since the system is only quasi-mandatory if an industry-wide contract is agreed upon. Moreover, Eurostat believes that the voluntary agreements are seriously underreported in most countries. For these reasons we have used the term 'occupational pensions' to make it clear that we have included all supplements to the basic scheme – both voluntary and mandatory – that are part of the labour contract, rather than embedded in the system of rules and regulations established by the legislative system.

A third conceptual difficulty concerns the distinction between occupational and personal. This classification is not used in the Eurostat classification, but is important especially in Anglo-American countries and also in Sweden. British public policy has encouraged the promotion of personal pensions, which in turn has created unanticipated side effects requiring stringent British regulations 'to compensate those who had been mis-sold personal pensions'. The trend in the US has been in the opposite direction. Personal pensions declined in the 1980s but by contrast 401k, which must be set up by the employer and is therefore an occupational rather than a personal pension, increased throughout the 1980s. These personal pensions will be important in the future, when the contribution level cited above becomes translated into actual benefits and appears as current expenditures.

To get comparable data across countries, it is important to include both old age and survivor pensions together. For example, not all countries have a special category for survivor benefits. We have not included disability benefits in our estimate, since the trends from 1980 to 1993 to be reported by Eurostat excludes them. Nevertheless these benefits are especially important in some countries. Excluding these benefits therefore underestimates the size of the supplementary occupational pensions. However, including disability without taking account of age distorts the definition of pensions that we are using, namely, as income at the last stage (over 55 years of age) of the working career.

22

After all of these caveats and struggles with definitions we can now turn to a more detailed review of the aggregate findings. We present the available data, in a simple form separating basic and occupational pensions expressed as a percentage of GDP in five-year periods from 1980, 1985, 1989, and 1993.

What does the Eurostat Social Protection evidence show? We have chosen to express the level of spending as a percentage of GDP in the currency of the country. The share of supplementary pensions is calculated by dividing supplementary by total. Using shares and ratios of absolute spending levels can yield somewhat different findings, since the annual level of GDP can change more or less rapidly than the change in the level of spending. But in practice the differences are trivial. We have therefore chosen the simplest measure.

It appears that in 1989 between 0.2 and 5 per cent of GDP was spent on supplementary or occupational pensions. To understand what these percentages signify, consider their value in relation to the basic public social security payment. In some countries a value of 5 percentage points means that almost half of total pension spending comes from occupational pensions. What is striking is the division into two groups of countries: those with relatively high levels of spending for occupational pensions and those with relatively low levels of spending. The high spending countries (4–5 per cent of GDP) include the Netherlands, the UK, and the US. The low spending countries (less than one per cent of GDP) are Austria and Italy; the medium countries (about 2 per cent of GDP) are Germany, France, and Sweden. For one of the countries included in this study, Japan, we lack comparable information. Japan should probably be classified among the high spending countries.

This grouping of countries is very interesting. Consider the low and medium spending countries first. Three of the countries – Germany, Italy and France – have what we have described above as 'supplementary advantage' (about 1–2 per cent of GDP) for their civil servants. These pensions can reasonably be considered as a supplementary pension above the basic and earnings-related state system. If we accept this logic then France can be redefined as a high spending country and Germany as a middle level country spending about 2.3 per cent of GDP.

Some countries are in transition from low to high spending. Denmark offers an example of a reversal of roles. Since the 1940s, Denmark has developed a flat-rate pension system financed from general taxation and without a well-developed system of earnings-related pensions to supplement this basic amount either in the public or in the private sector. As

23

a result, only about 4.6 per cent of GDP is allocated to old age pensions in Denmark in 1989. This is about the same level of spending as exists in the UK. There are important differences worth noting. In the UK pressure developed to supplement the basic pension with personal and occupational pensions. On the other hand, no such pressure had developed in Denmark. However, in 1992 and in 1995, this situation changed. New contractual agreements between unions and labour have encouraged the creation of occupational pensions. The state, of course, contributed to this trend by making these pensions tax deferred. Thus, there is a historic reversal of the role of occupational pensions in Denmark. This reversal has apparently not occurred in Italy, despite continued discussions about developing a funded private pension system to gradually replace the overburdened public pension scheme.

The list of high spending countries seems to challenge the dominant hypothesis that occupational pensions are a substitute for inadequate public pensions. While it could be argued that the US and the UK are countries that spend only 5.1 and 5.8 per cent of GDP on old age pensions and these low levels of public spending support the hypothesis that occupational pensions serve as a substitute for inadequate public outlays, the same argument cannot be developed for the Netherlands. That country have a relatively high level of public social security spending.

All countries, except Italy and France, witnessed increased spending for occupational pensions and in some countries the rate of increase was greater than in the basic public scheme and produced a clear change in the welfare mix. The data on trends show that the high spending countries have substantially increased their occupational pension spending since 1980 more rapidly than their basic public pension, and as a result the welfare mix has changed. In the Netherlands, the UK and the US, occupational, old age and survivors pensions, were about one-third of the total spending for public and occupational pensions combined. By 1993 they represented 43 per cent of spending in the Netherlands and half in the US. In 1988 in the UK it increased to 44 per cent.

In the countries with low spending for occupational pensions, these pensions increased only modestly and not at all in Italy. The welfare mix did not change, with the exception of Denmark which is clearly committed to expanding its supplementary pension system. By 1993 there was already evidence for a declining use of means-tested in-kind pensions to supplement the basic flat-rate pension. It will be interesting to see whether there has been any change when we get the 1993 data.

Our point in stressing these facts is that the array of non-state pension arrangements has increased quite sharply in countries like Sweden, traditionally regarded as the prototype of a highly developed public pension scheme.

8.   The redistributive impact of composition and changes of the welfare mix[11]

One of the most important policy questions is what effects different welfare mixes do have on poverty and inequality. We first examine some cross national empirical data on the link between the welfare mix and poverty and then explore this question more critically by a non-empirical review of the case of Sweden. We conclude with some notes of caution on lesson drawing.

Some preliminary remarks about the difference between a welfare state and welfare mix approach are necessary, because they will play an important role in interpreting the results. The multi-pillar view of social protection is a critique of the literature on the welfare state, which assumes that over time there is a natural evolution toward public provision. One of the main debates in the welfare state literature was how to organize public provision among three different organizing principles: *selectivity* which targets benefits on groups who are in need; *universal programmes* that provide minimum income for all groups in society and therefore are not embedded in work relationships; and *earnings-related programmes* which tie benefits and contributions to the command of market income.

The multi-pillar or welfare-mix perspective raises a different set of policy issues other than the universal selectivity question which dominates the design of public benefits. First there is the issue of the separation of the redistributive function of the state from both the savings function of personal households and the deferred earnings of occupational welfare provision. What the new model implies is a separation of public and occupational and personal protection. In fact it turns out to be very difficult to make an unambiguous demarcation. One of the many difficult issues is the dual role of the state as provider and employer. Moreover the relationship of the three pillars to each other is in flux and many mixed forms which co-mingle public and private arrangements

---

[11] See Korpi and Palme (1994) for another discussion of the effects of the organization of social insurances on equality.

are emerging. For example, the Dutch civil service pension funds will be privatized in 1995. The conceptual difficulties of demarcation of the public and private pillars make the measurement of the relative outcome of systems difficult.

A strong hypothesis regarding the impact that public protection, occupational pensions, and personal savings have on poverty and inequality at the end of the working career has been developed by Smeeding, Torrey and Rainwater (1993): 'The smaller the role of public sources of income the higher the level of income inequality.' The argument for why this outcome occurs is that 'Private sources are less stable across age and over time than public sources. These public transfer sources of income are those which are systematically adjusted for price change and which provide fail-safe sources of income among the aged.'

We think that the data supports an alternative hypothesis. The level of poverty and inequality depends on how the public and private pillars are organized and how the public and occupational pillars are demarcated. Even the most preliminary review of the data shows that Sweden, the Netherlands and in recent years even Britain have strong occupational welfare and relatively low poverty and inequality. Consider the situation in Britain in more detail. The Goode Report on Pension Law Reform (1993, pp. 152–3) reports trends in the composition of gross income of pensioners. In 1979 the state pension accounted for 61 per cent of the aged household income, occupational pension 16 per cent, saving and earnings each 12 per cent. By 1990–91 state pension declined to 50 per cent, occupational pensions grew to 22 per cent, savings to 20 per cent and earnings declined to 10 per cent. Yet during roughly the same period of time the percentage of low income persons over 60 years of age declined from 17 per cent to 6.7 per cent (Rainwater 1993, Table 7.2). Even the Gini coefficient for family heads aged 65–74 declined slightly from 0.251 to 0.235. These data are very striking – poverty and inequality declines in the face of declining state pensions and growing occupational and personal pillars. What accounts for the change in the welfare mix producing such results? One interpretation might be the slow maturation of the state earnings-related system. After many years state benefits are finally improving while contracted out pensions are required to be as good as the public and many offer even more attractive benefits. In the private sector 78 per cent of occupational pensions are contracted out. As a result of this double movement, pension benefits are increasing and poverty is being reduced.

Sweden is another country which has experienced an increase in occupational pensions. A recent estimate suggests that 13 per cent of the income of pensioners comes from occupational pensions, which is high but lower than in the UK. Yet Sweden has one of the lowest poverty and inequality rates among Western economies. What accounts for the parallel expansion of occupational pensions and low inequality? One interpretation is that inequality depends on two main factors: the level of coverage and the height of the income ceiling that is protected.

In the late 1940s the basic public pension was significantly raised, and in 1960 an earnings-related scheme (ATP) of supplements to the basic pension was introduced. Earlier only white-collar workers and public employees had earnings-related pensions through occupational pension systems. With the ATP scheme blue-collar workers and self-employed workers such as farmers are also covered. Both public reforms narrowed income differentials between the retired and the working age population and between white-collar and blue-collar workers in retirement.

A ceiling on the earnings level that was to be covered was introduced. Earnings that were 7.5 times a base amount were not protected as retirement income. However, earnings above that level were covered already at the time of the start of the ATP-system by occupational pension schemes for white-collar workers in the private sector and for public employees. The occupational pensions stabilized the distribution of income and prevented the further narrowing of the distribution of income. On the other hand, when blue-collar workers in the private sector reached an agreement on supplementary pensions in the 1970s, only earnings up to 7.5 times base amounts were covered just as in the ATP scheme. Very few blue-collar workers at that time had earnings over or close to the ceiling.

There were two options regarding the ceiling for the *Riksdag* when deciding on a reform of the pension system: to raise the maximum above 7.5 times the base, or to accept that the ATP earnings-related scheme could become a new higher basic level since an increasing share of the full time working population managed to earn above this income level. The former decision was taken in 1994 and the ceiling will be indexed in the new pension system.

The British and Swedish examples would seem to suggest that the hypothesis that 'the smaller the role of public sources the higher the level of inequality' needs to be qualified. The proposition holds under certain conditions, when coverage of occupational pension is limited to a small segment of the population and when public pensions are reasonably adequate and a strong redistributive component.

What also seems to have surfaced with the study of income packaging is the continued importance of earnings as a component of income. Our data for the US in 1990 clearly show a declining importance of male earnings, from 82 per cent of gross income for male-headed households whose head was 55–61 years of age to 60 per cent of heads aged 62 to 64, to 42 per cent for heads aged 65–69 to 19 per cent of heads aged 70 and over. But what was even more striking was that when we looked at heads without male earnings, earnings continued to play a significant role in the household income. What appears to be happening is that spouses continue to work as the economic position of the male falls in hard times.

To illustrate this point we cite American data on changes over time and over the life course. In the US in 1990 92 per cent of aged households over 65 received social security retirement benefits, 45 per cent an employer-provided pension (30 per cent a private pension and 15 per cent a pension based on government employment), 68 per cent income from savings and 22 per cent earnings from a job. Since 1962, with the exception of employment, all of these income sources increased substantially. The percentage employed has remained stable in the past decade. When we look at the income package from these different sources, the importance of the welfare mix becomes even more evident. Social security income is 36 per cent of total gross income, assets 24 per cent, and employer pensions 18 per cent. Moreover, public social security income declined from 39 to 36 per cent in the past decade, reversing the upward trend that was visible for several decades (Turner and Watanabe 1995, p. 135). The mix also changes with age. Entry into social security is possible at age 62. Comparing the welfare mix for male headed families aged 62 to 65 compared to those over 70 we see a continued growth of asset income and social security, while employer pensions are stable and earnings decline. From these data we see that there is clearly a welfare mix. Personal assets and employment are as important a component of the income package as are social security and employer-based pensions. Turner and Watanabe (1995) caution us however to remember that 'the image of retirement income as a three legged stool only applies for white couples' (p. 139).

9.   A changing welfare mix

In Chapters 2–10 the mix between social, occupational and personal pension schemes is analysed for nine industrialized countries – seven

European countries (Austria, France, Germany, Italy, the Netherlands, Sweden and the UK), Japan and the US. The emphasis is on the interaction between the national social insurance schemes and the occupational pension schemes, the first and the second pillars, and especially on the influence of the social security schemes and from the state as a regulating authority on the occupational pension schemes.

As mentioned in section 7 of this chapter, the size of the occupational pension schemes measured as a share of GDP or of the total pension schemes varies greatly between the countries included in this book. Some of the differences may be due to a lack of information. A special problem is how to deal with the pensions of public sector employees, since in some countries they get their total pension from the state as an employer and are not included in the national social insurance schemes. The correct way to handle it is to divide the pension into one part belonging to the first pillar and one to the second pillar (the supplementary advantage), but statistics are not available to make the figures fully comparable.

A comparison shows that among the countries with social insurance pension schemes with high replacement rates, there is a large variation in the extent of the occupational pension schemes: the high spending Netherlands, middle spending Sweden and low spending Austria and Italy belong to this group. However, the three countries with low replacement rates from the social security schemes, Japan, the UK and the US, all have extensive occupational pension schemes.

In most countries the government supports and subsidizes occupational pension schemes. The forms differ. In Japan and the UK the government encourages contracting out from the national pension scheme (in the UK not only to occupational but also to personal pensions); in almost all countries the tax system treats the occupational pensions favourably. In France and the Netherlands collectively bargained agreements are extended to those not primarily covered by the agreement.

In this book we have reviewed two main questions: Are countries reducing their reliance on governments' social security programmes?; and if the answer is positive how have the occupational and personal pillars responded to these changes?

The answer is that the general trend is towards an expanded role for the occupational and personal pensions compared to the national pension schemes. The occupational and personal pillars react to changes in the social security programmes. The speed of that development differs strongly between countries. However, the general trend is towards a more diversified welfare state.

The future evolution of the welfare state is being shaped by the developments we have reviewed. There appears to be some evidence of a 'shift away from employer responsibility towards individual responsibility for retirement income' (Turner and Watanabe 1995, p. 122). A more careful monitoring of the changing welfare mix may provide guides for the welfare society that will emerge in the future.

References

Abel-Smith, Brian (1993), 'Age, Work and Social Security: The Policy Context', in Anthony Atkinson and Martin Rein (eds.), *Age, Work and Social Security*, London: Macmillan.

Ahrend, Peter (1995), 'Pension Financial Security in Germany', in Zvi Brodie, Olivia Mitchell and John Turner (eds.), *Securing Employer-Provided Pensions: An International Perspective*, University of Pennsylvania Press.

Allmendinger, Julia (1994), *Lebensverlauf und Sociale Politik*, Frankfurt: Campus Verlag.

Auerbach, Alan, Gokhale, Jagadeesh and Kotlikoff, Laurence (1994), 'Generational Accounting: A Meaningful Way to Evaluate Fiscal Policy', *Journal of Economic Perspectives*, Vol. 8, Winter, 73–94.

Burkhauser, Richard and Quinn, John (1989), 'American Patterns of Work and Retirement', in Winfried Schmähl (ed.), *Redefining the Process of Retirement. An International Perspective*, Berlin: Springer-Verlag.

Cutler, David, Poterba, James, Sheiner, Louise and Summers, Lawrence (1990), 'An Aging Society: Opportunity or Challenge', *Brookings Papers on Economic Activity*, No. 1, 1–71.

Dobbin, Frank and Boychuk, Terry (1996) 'Public Policy and the Rise of Private Pension: The US Experience Since 1930', in Michael Shalev (ed.), *The Privatization of Social Policy? Occupational Welfare and the Welfare State in America, Scandinavia and Japan*, London: Macmillan.

Esping-Andersen, Gösta (1990), *The Three Worlds of Welfare Capitalism*, Cambridge: Polity.

Gustman, Alan, Mitchell, Olivia and Steinmeier, Thomas (1994), 'The Role of Pensions in the Labor Market: A Survey of the Literature', *Industrial and Labor Relations Review*, Vol. 47, No. 3, 417–438.

Hannah, Leslie (1992), 'Similarities and Differences in the Growth and Structure of Private Pensions in OECD Countries', in *Private Pension and Public Policy*, Paris, OECD Social Policy Studies, No. 9.

Kimura, Takeshi, Tagaki, Ikuro, Oka, Masato and Omori, Maki (1994), 'Japan: Shukko, Teinen and Re-employment', in Frieder Naschold and Bert de Vroom (eds.), *Regulating Employment and Welfare*, Berlin: Walter de Gruyter.

Kohli, Martin (1985), 'Die Institutionalisierung des Lebenslauf', *Kölner Zeitschrift für Soziologie und Sozialpsychologie*, Vol. 37, Nr. 1, 1–29.

Kohli, Martin, Rein, Martin, Guillemard, Ann-Marie and Herman van Gunsteren (eds.) (1991), *Time for Retirement: Comparative Studies of Early Exit from the Labor Force*, Cambridge, Cambridge University Press.

Korpi, Walter and Palme, Joakim (1994), 'The Strategy of Equality and the Paradox of Redistribution', mimeo, Swedish Institute for Social Research, Stockholm University.

Lindbeck, Assar (1995), 'Hazardous Welfare-State Dynamics', *American Economic Review*, Vol. 85, May, 9–15.

Offe, Claus (1984), *Contradictions of the Welfare State*, London: Hutchinson.

OECD (1993), *The Labour Market in the Netherlands*, OECD Documents, Paris: OECD.

Oka, Shinishi (1992), 'Older Workers: Conditions of Work and Transition to Retirement. Country Report: Japan', Working Papers Condi/T/1992/WP.2, ILO, Geneva.

Pension Law Reform (1993), The report of the pension law committee (chairman professor Roy Goode), CM2342, London: HMSO.

Rainwater, Lee (1993), 'Income Distribution in OECD Countries', mimeo, October.

Rein, Martin (1988), 'A Comparative Study of Pension Policies in the United States and Europe', in Gail Lapidus and Guy Swansen (eds.), *State and Welfare USA/USSR*, IIS, University of California, Berkeley.

Rein, Martin (1996), 'Is America Exceptional? The Role of Occupational Welfare in the United States and the European Community', in Michael Shalev (ed.), *The Privatization of Social Policy? Occupational Welfare and the Welfare State in America, Scandinavia and Japan*, London: Macmillan.

Reynaud, Emmanuel (1995), 'Financing Retirement Pensions: Pay-as-you-go and Funded Systems in the European Union', *International Social Security Review*, Vol. 48, No. 3–4, 41–57.

Sheppard, Harold (1991), 'The United States: The Privatization of Entry', in Martin Kohli, Martin Rein, Anne-Marie Guillemard and Herman van Gunsteren (eds.), *Time for Retirement: Comparative Studies of Early Exit from the Labor Force*, Cambridge, Cambridge University Press.

Silburn, Ronald (1994), 'Social Insurance: The Way Forward', *Proceedings of the First Social Security Seminar*, Nottingham University, October 1994.

Smeeding, Tim, Torrey, Barbara and Rainwater, Lee (1993), 'Going to Extremes: An International Perspective on the Economic Status of the U.S. Aged', LIS Working Paper, February.

Social Justice. Strategies for National Renewal (1994), The Report of the Commission on Social Justice, London: Vintage.

Streek, Wolfgang (1995), 'From Market-Making to State-Building? Reflections on the Political Economy of European Social Policy', in Stephan Leibfried and Paul Pierson (eds.), *Prospects for Social Europe: The European Community's Social Dimension in Comparative Perspective*, Washington, DC: The Brookings Institution.

Takayama, Noriyuki (1992), *The Greying of Japan: An Economic Perspective on Public Pensions*, Tokyo: Kinokuniya.

Trommel, Willem and de Vroom, Bert (1994), 'The Netherlands: The Loreley-Effect of Early Exit', in Frieder Naschold and Bert de Vroom (eds.), *Regulating Employment and Welfare*, Berlin: Walter de Gruyter.

Turner, John and Watanabe, Noriyusu (1995), *Private Pension Policies in Industrialized Countries*, Kalamazoo, MI: W.E. Upjohn Institute.

de Vroom, Bert and Blomsma, Martin (1991), 'The Netherlands: An Extreme Case', in Martin Kohli, Martin Rein, Anne-Marie Guillemard and Herman van Gunsteren (eds.), *Time for Retirement: Comparative Studies of Early Exit from the Labor Force*, Cambridge, Cambridge University Press.

Van den Noord, Paul and Herd, Richard (1994), 'Estimating Pension Liabilities: A Methodological Framework', *OECD Economic Studies*, No. 23, 131–66.

Wadensjö, Eskil (1996), 'Gradual Retirement in Sweden', in Lei Delsen and Geneviève Reday-Mulvey, *Gradual Retirement in the OECD-countries*, Aldershot: Dartmouth.

World Bank (1994), *Averting the Old Age Crisis*, Oxford: Oxford University Press.

2

The Austrian Pension System

Peter Rosner, Thomas Url and Andreas Wörgötter

Austria is probably the classic example of a country with a public pay-as-you-go pension system. More than 95 per cent of all pensions are paid by public pension systems. A second tier hardly exists. When the current system was started in the mid 1950s, the basic philosophy was that the public pensions should be adequate enough to maintain every person's standard of living upon retirement (except for those with high incomes). Older existing pension systems, like those for the mining industry, railway workers, and some of the banks were integrated into the general pension system. The self-employed and the farmers got their systems in the 1960s, and they were set up with the same principles as the systems for the employed.

In the first section of this chapter we give an overview of the Austrian pension system. In the second section we discuss some of its problems, namely its distributional effects and the financial problems. An understanding of the distributional effects is important as they shape the political discussion of all reforms. In the third section we discuss the retirement regulations in the public sector and in the fourth section we look at firm pensions and ask what the reasons are for firms to supply them.[1]

1. The system

The Austrian pension system covers nearly all persons active in the economy. Not only the employed but also the self-employed and the farmers are encompassed by the public system of social security. It is only professionals who are not organized within this system, their retirement

---

[1] For a better understanding of what follows, note that the Schilling was tied to the D-Mark for nearly twenty years, with 7 Schillings to the Mark.

schemes are managed by their own organizations with mandatory membership (*Kammern*).[2] Nevertheless, there is not just one single system, but rather, different systems for different social groups. There is one system for the non-agricultural self-employed, one for the farmers and a couple of systems for the employed.

Each system has different regulations and is organized in a separate institution *Pensionsversicherungsanstalt* (henceforth *PV-Anstalt*).[3] These *PV-Anstalten* are self-governing bodies (*Selbstverwaltungskörperschaften*). The federal state is only a controlling institution. For those in the civil service (which is also comprised of teachers, professors, police, armed forces, public sector health workers) who work under public law (*Dienstpragmatik*) no *PV-Anstalt* exists, because they do not formally retire (see below). All *PV-Anstalten* are under the influence of the mandatory and voluntary interest organization – i.e. the unions and the chamber of labour have political control of the *PV-Anstalten* of the employed, the *Kammer der Gewerblichen Wirtschaft* of the *PV-Anstalt* of the self-employed, and the *Kammern* for agriculture of those of farmers. The *PV-Anstalten* are therefore also lobbying institutions vis-à-vis the state on behalf of its clientele. All the *PV-Anstalten* are loosely connected at the *Hauptverband der Sozialversicherungsträger*. The federal state regulates the pensions and the contributions and covers deficits. All systems are pay-as-you-go systems; there is no fund except small ones for liquidity reserves.

In the rest of this chapter we will concentrate on the pension system for those who are employed outside the mining industry.[4] This comprises the market sector and those in the state sector under private law.[5]

Retirement age for the normal old age pension is 65 for men and 60 for women. The different retirement ages for men and women were ruled as contradicting equality. However, by an amendment to the constitution, full equalization of the retirement age was postponed to begin in the year 2018. A minimum insurance period of 15 years is required. An earlier retirement is possible (60 for men, 55 for women), if the per-

---

[2] The pension scheme of the public notaries belongs to the social security system.

[3] An amalgamation of some of the *PV-Anstalten* is currently being discussed.

[4] The annual increase of all pensions – save that of the public sector – is the same for all pensions.

[5] The pension system of state agencies which are going to be privatized or will at least be separated from the civil service, like the railway system and the postal services, will be changed. Whereas the pension system is currently similar to that of the civil service, after the reforms they will be more in line with the general pension system. However, this relates only to new entrants.

son has been insured for 35 years (37.5 years from 1997 onwards), or because of reduced ability to work or prolonged unemployment. In these cases there is only a requirement of 10 years insurance (15 years from 1997 onwards). An even earlier retirement due to disability is possible.

The pension increases with time paid into the system. For the first 30 years one gets 1.83 per cent insurance per year and for the following 15 years 1.675 per cent (until 1996 1.9 and 1.5). Periods during which earnings are below a threshold (1995 S 3400 per month) do not count for the pension (*Geringfügige Beschäftigungsverhältnisse*). This is the case for approximatly 135 000 people most of whom are women. For low wage contracts this comes to a working time not exceeding 40 hours a month, for better paid wages only about 20 hours a month. Including some extra benefits the retiree can get up to 80 per cent of his/her calculatory basis. This is based on the average income of the best 15 years. There are some provisions in the law that allow for the 80 per cent even with only 40 years of insured income, namely, if the beginning of retirement is later than 60 for men or 55 for women.

There is an upper limit for all calculations of the social security system outside the public sector (*Höchstbemessungsgrundlage*). This upper limit concerns the payments into the system and the basis for calculating the pension. This limit was S 37 800 per month in 1995.[6] While nearly all blue-collar workers (more than 99 per cent) fall below this threshold, most male employees in career jobs reach it during their working life. In the year 1993 26.3 per cent of all male employees and 4.3 per cent of female employees had an income above the *Höchstbemessungsgrundlage* (Sozialbericht, 1994, vol. II p.167). For this group the public pension falls sharply below their income during the last years of working life and the question of a second layer for retirement income is of importance. However, there is a possibility for a voluntary increase in the parts of income which are covered by insurance. The contributions are wage related, namely 22.8 per cent, out of which the employee pays 10.25 per cent and the employers pay 12.55 per cent (up to the *Höchstbemessungsgrundlage*).[7] No contributions are paid for those below the above men-

---

[6] As nearly all wages are paid 14 times a year in Austria, this amounts to S 44 100 per month calculated at an annual basis.

[7] The basis on which the payments are calculated is the gross income of the employed which includes their payment into the system, but does not include the payment of the employers. In the early 1980s there was a discussion about changing the system of contributions to a value added basis. The reason for this

Table 2.1 – Average replacement ratios for new pensions in 1990

	Gross	Net
Blue-collar workers		
Disability pension men	66.2	78.4
Disability pension women	55.7	67.6
Old age pension men	68.3	82.5
Old age pension women	55.0	67.6
White-collar workers		
Disability pension men	64.7	78.4
Disability pension women	49.7	61.4
Old age pension men	69.0	82.4
Old age pension women	53.2	65.6

Source: Wirtschafts- und sozialstatistisches Taschenbuch der AK Wien, 1992, p. 390.

tioned threshold of S 3400. All contributions reduce the basis for calculating income tax.

Pensions are paid, as are nearly all wages, 14 times a year. The retired pay 3.75 per cent of their pension into the public health system.[8] All public pensions are taxed according to the income tax law in the same way as wage incomes – i.e. only 6/7 of the annual pension after health insurance is taxed according to the normal tariff, whereas 1/7 is taxed with a flat rate of 6 per cent. The effective taxation begins at a monthly pension of S 8000. As pensioners do not pay into the pension system (10.25 per cent), nor into the unemployment system (currently 3 per cent) or into the fund for furthering housing (0.5 per cent), net pension does not fall much below the net income for those who were insured for a long time and did not have an age related wage profile until the end of their working life. For example, a blue-collar worker with 40 years of employment will have a gross pension between 70 and 80 per cent of his last income, and thus a net pension of 80 to 90 per cent of his last income.

---

proposal was that the then rising rate of unemployment was seen as a result of a rising capital intensity. (Up to 1981 Austria had nearly no unemployment. In 1982 the rate of unemployment reached the 3 per cent level for the first time.) After a few years of public excitement, the discussion abated.

[8] The *PV-Anstalten* have to pay an amount into the health system which is more than double what the pensioners pay themselves. One can therefore say that pensioners pay about 10.7 per cent for their health insurance. Thus, gross pensions are more than 7 per cent higher than they appear.

Survivors' pensions are paid to widows and widowers and to orphans. They are not means-tested and can be combined with other pensions from private insurance policies, if any. Widows (and widowers) get between 40 per cent and 60 per cent of the pension of the deceased, depending on their own income. In 1994 there were nearly 240 000 pensioners (more then 13 per cent) with more than one pension, 90 per cent of whom were women.

All pensions are linked to economic development. They are increased annually by decree of the Minister of Social Affairs. When fixing the increase, the payments into the system and the change in the relation of gross income to net income of the employed must be considered. The payments into the system are closely linked to the development of nominal wage incomes. Therefore pensions are related to the nominal income. This is not only a safeguard against inflation, but a means of ensuring that the retired also participate in the growth of the economy. The clause according to which an increasing divergence between gross and net incomes should be taken into account was introduced for not increasing pensions when the active have to pay more into the social system. Otherwise an increase of social security contributions would not dampen the increase of pensions.

There is no minimum pension in Austria. However, there is a means-tested supplement to the pension (*Ausgleichszulage*) which increased all household income of single pensioners to S 7710, and for couples to S 11 000 in 1995. In a way, this can be seen as an official poverty level. This level has been raised for many years much more than the general pensions, therefore the number of recipients of *Ausgleichszulagen* increased. In 1994 there were about 280 000 recipients of *Ausgleichszulagen* (about 17 per cent of all pensioners).

In the long term pensions followed real incomes, whereas the minimum increased much more than real income. Since 1970 pensions were increased due to the annual revaluation by 395 per cent in the market sector, by 340 per cent in the public sector, the *Ausgleichsrichtsatz* by 573 per cent, whereas prices rose by 297 per cent. Real GDP rose by 80 per cent.

The actual age of retirement is much lower than the statutory retirement age. For men it is 57.1 years, for women one year less (both without interstate pensions; source: *Wirtschafts- und sozialstatistisches Taschenbuch AK Wien*, 1995 p. 364). Note that for men the actual retirement age is below the statutory retirement age for old age pension due to long insurance (60), whereas for women it is above that mark (55). This is due to

Table 2.2 – Annual increase of pensions, inflation and real growth rates

Year	Increase of pensions due to indexation	Increase of minimum for single houshold (Ausgleichszulage)	Inflation rate	Real growth rate
1986	3.5	3.5	1.7	1.2
1987	3.8	4.2	1.4	2.0
1988	2.3	2.8	2.0	3.9
1989	2.1	2.6	2.5	3.8
1990	4.0	5.5+2.95[1]	3.3	4.6
1991	5.0	7.6	3.3	3.0
1992	4.0	8.3	4.1	1.8
1993	4.0	7.7	3.6	0.0
1994	2.5	7.15	2.9	2.8

[1] In 1990 the *Ausgleichszulagen* were raised on 1 January and 1 July.

the facts that (i) it is more difficult to get the now necessary 37.5 years by the age of 55 than by the age of 60, (ii) women do not have as continuous working lives as men do, and (iii) some programmes for still earlier retirement apply primarily to men (invalidity, regulations for mining etc.).

There is a 1.5 year difference in retirement age between blue-collar workers and white-collar workers. This difference is due to the higher percentage of blue-collar workers who end their working lives with a pension due to disability. The average retirement age of men with invalidity pension is about 53 (50 for women), whereas that for old age pension is 62 (59 for women). Whereas in 1993 about 55 per cent of all new pensions for male blue-collar workers were due to disability (30 per cent for women), only 35 per cent of new pensions of male white-collar workers were due to invalidity (20 per cent for women).

Until 1996 the pension system was connected with the unemployment insurance system in two ways. One was the possibility of early retirement due to prolonged unemployment. This possibility still exists. The other one was the *Sonderunterstützung* according to a special law, similar to the German *Vorruhestand*. This payment was an increased unemployment benefit (at most plus 25 per cent), which men could get at 59 and women at 54 and then usually led to early retirement due to long insurance. In 1992 a third of the new old age pensions of men and half of those of women due to long insurance were preceded by *Sonderunterstützung* (Tálos and Wörister 1994, p. 196). This system was abolished in 1996.

38

Table 2.3 – Average pension of men, women, and total, January each year

	Men	*Women*	*Total*
1971	1 984	1 099	1 563
1972	2 162	1 196	1 702
1973	2 346	1 299	1 845
1974	2 588	1 432	2 032
1975	2 988	1 654	2 344
1976	3 425	1 908	2 689
1977	3 870	2 173	3 044
1978	4 196	2 398	3 317
1979	4 552	2 635	3 605
1980	4 951	2 897	3 925
1981	5 363	3 170	4 252
1982	5 794	3 441	4 588
1983	6 291	3 732	4 968
1984	6 833	4 048	5 385
1985	7 307	4 317	5 746
1986	7 747	4 547	6 071
1987	8 175	4 766	6 389
1988	8 664	5 008	6 753
1989	9 054	5 182	7 037
1990	9 391	5 337	7 284
1991	9 905	5 600	7 672
1992	10 541	5 931	8 155

Source: Own calculations.

There are probably also cases of unemployment a year before retirement, as unemployment benefits are paid for one year, if the person has worked for many years. As this is usually the case and unemployment benefits are about 58 per cent of the net income of the last half year, there is an incentive to choose unemployment before leaving the employment system.

Currently only a third of male blue-collar workers enter the retirement system directly from employment (the rate for male white-collar workers is 60 per cent). The rest have received unemployment benefits, *Sonderunterstützung,* or sickness payments before retirement[9] (Stefanits and Lackner, 1995).

---

[9] Blue-collar workers get full payment for five weeks in case of sickness. If they are sick for a longer period they receive sickness payments which are much lower. In case of long-term illness, white-collar workers do much better than blue-collar workers.

Table 2.4 – Increase of average nominal pension (VDPPS), rate of inflation, and increase of average real pension, January each year

	Change of average nominal pension (%)	Inflation	Change of average real pension (%)
1972	8.85	6.45	2.40
1973	8.41	7.46	0.95
1974	10.16	9.54	0.62
1975	15.36	8.32	7.04
1976	14.72	7.31	7.41
1977	13.19	5.62	7.57
1978	8.96	3.55	5.41
1979	8.70	3.74	4.96
1980	8.85	6.31	2.55
1981	8.33	6.78	1.55
1982	7.91	5.42	2.49
1983	8.28	3.39	4.90
1984	8.39	5.58	2.81
1985	6.70	3.22	3.48
1986	5.66	1.67	3.98
1987	5.24	1.42	3.82
1988	5.70	1.94	3.76
1989	4.20	2.54	1.66
1990	3.51	3.31	0.20
1991	5.33	3.30	2.03
1992	6.30	4.07	2.23

Source: Own calculations.

As can be seen there was a real increase of pension income in most of the years. However, these tables underestimate the real increase of pension income. There has been a change in the composition of pensions throughout the years. Whereas in 1970 there were more direct pensions to men (428 028) than to women (387 977), this ratio changed dramatically up until 1992 (590 540 direct pensions for men; 628 381 for women). As women's pensions are much lower than men's, the growth of the average for both groups together underestimates the growth of the pensions for each group taken separately. The average pension for men rose by 556 per cent between 1970 and 1992, for women 539 per cent, whereas total average pension rose by only 521 per cent. Nominal national income per capita rose at the same time by 568 per cent.

2. Problems

Two problems of the Austrian pension system are continually discussed. The first one relates to distributional problems, questioning whether the system is 'fair'. The second problem concerns the question of whether the system can be maintained without major alterations.

2.1 Distributional effects

One of the complaints about the Austrian system is that all the inequalities of the earnings system are perpetuated in the pension system. Because of the *Ausgleichszulagen* this relates more to questions of justice than of poverty.[10] But as long as the system is constructed as an insurance system this is necessarily so and cannot be abandoned. However, the question of distributional justice arises as the amount of subsidies differs systematically: the higher the pension is, the higher is the subsidy in absolute terms. There is also a big difference in the amount of federal subsidies to different groups.

Redistribution in favour of the poor has never been an important issue in the pension system. The inequalities between earnings up to the *Höchstbemessungsgrundlage* are preserved as differences of pensions. This does not imply that redistributive effects of the Austrian pension systems do not exist, but they are unclear and have never been evaluated in a scientifically acceptable way.

The political discussion of redistributive effects of the pension systems has been dominated by questions of functional income distribution. This is due to the fact that there are different institutions for the self-employed, farmers, blue-collar workers, white-collar workers, railway workers, the civil service, mining etc. and of the different political institutions linked to the *PV-Anstalten*. As the deficit as a percentage of current payments is different in the different *PV-Anstalten*, due to different relations between the number of active and retired persons, the state

---

[10] There are extra benefits for the aged, as is in most other countries. All pensioners are exempt from the recently introduced fee for medical services. Some of them apply to all persons above a certain age, like reduced rates for public means of transportation, others are means tested, like a reduction in charges by the telephone system, free medicine etc. The most important extra benefit is the recently created *Pflegegeld* which is paid to those who are in need of care. It extends and supplants all previously existing public support of caretaking.

Table 2.5 – Number of retired per 1000 active people in 1993

Blue-collar workers	716
White-collar workers	374
Railway workers	694
Miners	2 922
Self-employed	688
Farmers	916
Public notaries	427
All systems	586

Source: Statistisches Handbuch der österreichischen Sozialversicherung, 1994, Tab 3.03.

has to support different *PV-Anstalten* in different amounts out of general taxes. This is often seen as a question of distributive justice between social groups.

However, it is not clear on which basis any calculation of redistributive effects can be made. The employed pay less than half of their contributions, the rest is paid by the employers (*Dienstgeberbeitrag*). But since the contribution of the employers is calculated as a percentage of wage income (together 22.8 per cent of current wages), it is doubtful whether the contribution is really paid by the firms.[11] The self-employed and farmers pay only 14.5 per cent of their income, which is roughly the same as the direct contribution of the employed. An equivalent to the *Dienstgeberbeitrag* is said to be paid by taxes which are considered to be special taxes for the farmers or the self-employed. The incidence of these taxes has never been estimated. Up to 1993 a part of the income of the *Gewerbesteuer* (otherwise a communal tax) was seen as a contribution of the self-employed to the social security system of the self-employed. This tax was a tax on the *Gewerbeertrag* which comprised both wages and profits, and therefore could hardly be seen as a tax on profits alone. However in 1994 this tax was abandoned and replaced by an increase of another communal tax, *Kommunalabgabe*, which is a tax on wages alone.[12]

---

[11] In all calculations of functional income distribution in Austria, it is customary to include the payments of the firms into the social security system on behalf of their employed as part of the wage income.

[12] Public discussions of taxes and social security contributions are usually discussed within the concepts of a purely formal incidence. Usually the unions and the chamber of labour accept everything, as long as the tax is formally paid by the employers. Questions of economic incidence are hardly looked at.

There was never a discussion about the incidence of the financing of the deficit out of general taxes. The basis for taxes cannot be much larger than the basis for public pension contributions, because the public pension system covers nearly the entire active population. The most important difference is the pensions themselves, as they are part of the tax base for the value added tax, the different consumption taxes, and (to a lesser extent) the income tax, whereas there are no contributions from pensions into the pension system.

In comparison to a fair insurance there is a lot of redistribution in this system. Income is redistributed in favour of women due to their higher life expectancy.[13] Further, income is redistributed in favour of couples due to survivors' pensions (40 per cent to 60 per cent of the pension of the partner), there is a redistribution against blue-collar workers, because, firstly, they hardly enjoy age-related income increases and, secondly, their life expectancy is lower compared with white-collar workers or the self-employed[14] (Tálos and Wörister 1994, p. 170).

A recent study (Lutz et al. 1993) estimated the coverage of old age pensions for different groups. By using income data from 1972 to 1988 and making assumptions for the development of incomes from 1958 to 1972, total payment into the system could be estimated for different groups who retired in 1989.[15] The number of years until the own contributions were 'eaten up' were calculated and by comparing this result with the average life expectancy for the different groups, the percentage of the coverage could be estimated (all excluding survivors' pensions).[16]

The number of years covered by contributions does not vary much between different groups, but due to the difference in life expectancy the amount of the average coverage varies very much. It is lower for women than for men, lower for white-collar workers than for blue-collar

---

[13] The earlier retirement possibilities for women do not result in favouring women to a great extent, for the actual retirement age of women is only a year below that of men.

[14] Because of higher risks, blue-collar workers have to pay a higher percentage of income to the health insurance than white-collar workers. It is strange that the unions of the blue-collar workers never asked for a compensating decrease of their contribution to the pension system.

[15] A real rate of interest of 2.5 per cent was assumed to calculate the fictitious value of wealth at the beginning of retirement.

[16] 'Own payments' refers in the case of employed persons to the sum of employee and employer contributions. In the case of the self-employed the fictitious contribution due to the *Gewerbesteuerbeitrag* was added.

Table 2.6 – Coverage of old age pension by contributions

	Men 60 years				Women 55 years			
	Blue-collar worker	White-collar worker	Farmer	Self-employed	Blue-collar worker	White-collar worker	Farmer	Self-employed
Years covered by own payments	7.0	6.9	6.4	6.4	7.3	7.3	7.0	7.0
Expected years of pensions	10.9	18.6	16.9	18.6	25.5	27.3	25.5	27.3
Percentage of coverage of expected pension	42	37	38	35	30	27	28	26
Amount of expected pension covered by own payment (in Mill. S)	1.734	2.798	4.039	1.932	1.688	3.365	0.773	2.073

workers, lower for self-employed people than for employees and about the same for farmers as for white-collar workers. However, because the absolute amount of the subsidy of a pension depends also on the size of the pension, the pensions of white-collar workers and those of the self-employed are much more expensive for the federal budget than the other ones. The pensions of women are cheaper for the budget than those of men.

Interestingly, the coverage ratio for men and women who retire earlier due to invalidity is much higher. Although they stop paying into the system earlier, the coverage ratio for men is about 50 per cent due to their lower life expectancy.

The coverage ratio naturally varies with the number of years people have been working. But even for those who retire after 45 years of work this ratio never reaches 80 per cent. Only for men who retire due to health reasons at the age of 55 does the coverage ratio reach nearly 90 per cent, and for those retiring at 60 due to health reasons nearly 100 per cent (Lutz et al. 1993).

2.2 Financial problems

When the system was set up for the employed in the mid 1950s, the basic idea was that the standard of living at the moment of retirement should be upheld by the pension. The pension was therefore linked to the income of the last years. Although there was already a deficit when the system was set up in the beginning, the aim of keeping up the standard of living was probably realistic at that time. Firstly, the retirement age was put at 65 for men and 60 for women and then current life expectancy was pretty low, particularly for male blue-collar workers. Secondly, the biggest part of the employed were blue-collar workers, who usually do not enjoy much of an age related earnings profile. The deficit was due to a generous minimum percentage regulation particularly favourable for women, and because of allowances for different causes of not paying into the system (political and racial captivity, war and war related events, child rearing, unemployment, higher education etc.).[17] The *Ausgleichszulagen* also were never considered to be covered by contributions.

---

[17] The minimum percentage regulation was abandoned in 1984, and the allowances for higher education were abandoned in 1987, whereas the allowances for child-rearing had been increased.

Table 2.7 – Contributions of the federal budget to the pension system (excluding *Ausgleichszulagen*)

Year	Billion Schillings	Percentage of all pensions
1983	31.8	29.8
1984	33.7	29.1
1985	34.7	27.8
1986	37.6	28.3
1987	44.4	31.3
1988	45.6	30.7
1989	46.9	29.8
1990	43.8	26.1
1991	47.9	26.6
1992	47.2	24.7
1993	47.3	23.8
1994	47.3	23.0

Source: Wirtschafts- und Sozialstatistisches Taschenbuch der Arbeiterkammer.

When the system started the federal budget was required to completely cover all deficits. This would not have been a problem, if the contributions were set to cover all expenditures on the average. In that case a deficit would arise in times of recessions and a surplus during booms. If, on the other hand, the law would clearly state once and for all which contingencies should not be covered by contributions, this would not have caused big problems for the federal budget either. However, the clause according to which the federal state simply had to cover all deficits caused problems as the size of the deficits was and still is endogenous to the political system. This clause allowed for the increase of benefits without taking care of the deficit.[18] Meanwhile this clause was changed, so that today the federal budget fully covers a deficit up to a third of all expenditures of the pension funds only.[19] If the deficit is higher, half of the remaining deficit has to be covered by increasing the contributions.

---

[18] Of course this would not be true if the political system would plan all public expenditures and all taxes. However, no political system can do this. Quite the contrary, by raising benefits one can act as a Stackelberg leader in distributional fights within the public system.

[19] This comprises not only pensions, but payments into the health system, administrative expenditures and other items as well.

Table 2.8 – Development of average retirement age

	All Pensionsversicherungs-anstalten			Blue-collar workers		White-collar workers	
	Men	*Women*	*All*	*Men*	*Women*	*Men*	*Women*
1970	61.9	60.4	61.3	59.8	59.3	63.4	59.8
1975	61.8	60.1	61.1	59.9	59.2	63.1	59.9
1980	59.2	58.3	58.7	57.5	57.8	61.0	58.2
1985	58.3	57.9	58.1	56.4	56.9	60.4	58.2
1990	58.3	57.5	58.0	57.3	57.0	59.7	57.5
1992	58.3	57.3	57.9	57.7	57.0	59.5	56.8
	Without interstate pensions						
1992				56.3	56.3	59.1	56.3
1993				56.2	56.3	58.7	56.2

The purpose of this clause is to bind the political authorities not to increase the benefits of the system without considering the financing.

Seen as a problem of the aggregate deficit of the pension system, the political system was successful in keeping the deficit stable. As a percentage of all pensions it decreased by more than 9 percentage points since the mid 1970s. However, the stability of the deficit is not due to the stability of the system but due to countervailing tendencies. Whereas the number of insured people increased almost every year, from 2.6 million in 1971 to 3.0 million in 1993, and real incomes and therefore real contributions increased as well, the number of pensions rose also. Whereas in 1971 there were only 1282 million pensions, by 1992 the number had risen to 1760 million. That there is a problem can be seen by considering that the average pension rose nearly as much as per capita national income (see above), but the number of pensions rose by more than 40 per cent. A growing part of national income is at the disposal of pensioners and has to be channelled through the public pension system.

The increase in the number of insured persons is due to the increased labour market participation of women (from 0.88 million in 1970 to 1.28 million in 1992), and to immigration (111 000 immigrants in Austria in 1970; 273 000 in 1992). The labour market participation of men declined, partly due to increasing education, but also due to the working of the pension system. Austria is amongst the countries with the lowest labour market participation of men and women over 55.

The increase in the number of pensions therefore is not only the result of the increased number of insured people in the past but the result of lowering the effective retirement age as well. This lowering in turn can partly be explained by a growing number of people who are eligible for earlier retirement due to long insurance (35 years). It is also the result of encouragement for earlier withdrawal from active labour market participation for not allowing the number of unemployed to increase too much, particularly for inhibiting the emergence of youth unemployment (Rhein-Kress 1992; Biffl 1992). There existed special programmes for earlier retirements in case workers did shift work for some time to lessen the burden of unemployment in regions which were economically dominated by heavy industry.

A third reason which contributed to the declining participation of individuals over the age of 55 in the labour market was the increased number of people ending their working life with a pension due to invalidity. This increase is not easy to interpret. On the one hand, life expectancy is still increasing, and it is therefore very unlikely that the health conditions of those over 55 had declined to such an extent. We therefore have to assume that it has become easier to get a disability pension. However, the average life expectancy of those leaving the labour market with a disability pension is far below the life expectancy of those who end labour market participation to begin drawing their old age pension. In 1993 the average age of pensioners at their death was 68.3 for men whose pension began with a disability pension (75.9 for women), whereas for men with old age pension the average age at death was 79.0 (81.0 for women) (*Sozialbericht* 1993, vol. 2, p. 113). Further, there has been no increase in life expectancy for men with invalidity pensions since 1970, whereas life expectancy for men with old age pension has risen by three years since 1970. One can therefore conclude that the increased granting of invalidity pensions, although partly due to easing labour market pressures, served a real social need. That there is some discretionary power in the system can be seen from Table 2.9.

It is very unlikely that this development can be interpreted by increasing or decreasing health conditions. Why, for example, should the health conditions of older male white-collar workers have deteriorated dramatically between 1991 and 1993, or why should the health conditions of older male blue-collar workers have improved fantastically between 1985 and 1990? Any interpretation of these data must carefully

Table 2.9 – Percentage of new disability pensions as percentage of all new pensions

	Male blue-collar workers	*Male white-collar workers*	*Female blue-collar workers*	*Female white-collar workers*
1985	63.4	28.8	37.6	19.8
1990	56.1	29.0	31.4	19.1
1991	56.6	28.2	32.3	17.9
1992	56.1	32.5	31.3	22.2
1993	55.5	35.5	29.4	20.4

Source: Sozialbericht 1993, vol. 2, p. 106.

look at the changes in the laws. A change in the law can make it worthwhile to stay half a year more at the last job, or to leave the last job a few months earlier than planned. Although the system has become extremely complicated, there are some institutions, primarily the trade unions and the Chamber of Labour, who provide very good counselling for calculating an individually optimal time for retiring.

The stress on the pension system due to decreasing labour market participation of older workers was magnified by increasing life expectancy. Whereas a 60-year-old woman could expect to live less than 19 years longer in 1970, the life expectancy of a 60-year-old woman rose to 22.5 years longer in 1992. The life expectancy for men rose from less than 15 years longer to 18.4 years.

A fact which contributed in keeping the financial problems small up to now was the demographic composition of the population. Birth rates declined between 1921 and 1937 (from 127 000 children who survived their first year to 78 000). But these are the cohorts who are already retired or will retire very soon. The stabilizing effect of the demographic composition will then be over. The birth rate increased slightly in 1938, and jumped in 1939 by more than 50 per cent. It remained on a high level throughout the war years. When these cohorts retire in the coming years, it will put a particularly high burden on the pension system.

3. The public sector

As mentioned above the pension statutes for the public sector are different from those of the rest of the economy. There is no law which is unique to the public sector but, rather, different statutes for the civil service of the federal state, of the *Bundesländer* (provinces) and the towns. There is a special law for the railways and one for the postal system. However, all systems distinguish between those who work under a private law contract and therefore retire under the same rules as those in the rest of the economy, and those under public law statutes. They comprise the core of the public sector. In the following we concentrate on the civil service of the federal state which comprises, in addition to the administrative staff of Austria, the police forces, the army, the universities, the high schools, and people who work for the judicial system.

Formally, the employees of the civil service do not retire. They discontinue working and receive a retirement wage. The formal differences from retirement are firstly, that the state can recall people to work, which actually never happens, and, secondly, that people remain under the disciplinary code for the civil service. It is possible to be expelled from the civil service even after having stopped working. This happens occasionally in criminal court cases.

A more important difference is that up to now the annual increase of the pension was bound to the annual increase of the wages in the civil service.[20] This is going to be changed now. The second difference concerns the organization of the pensions. As they are disbursed as if they were wages, there is no separate institution comparable to the *PV-Anstalten*. One consequence is that there is hardly any statistical material available concerning public sector pensions.[21]

The most important difference between public sector retirement wages and normal pensions is that the former are related to the last income. The maximum replacement rate is 80 per cent which can be reached already after only 35 years. This is seen as an unjust privilege by the general public and will probably be changed within the next years. However, it is unclear whether the civil service really enjoys privileges, because the civil service claims to have lower wage incomes while working.

---

[20] In Austria there are four unions for the public sector: one for the federal state, one for local government workers, one for the railways and one for the postal system. Up to 1992 all four of them bargained together to reach one agreement. Since 1994 when the railway system was discharged from the federal budget the railway union negotiate separately with the railways. This immediately created problems as the rather generous wage increase for the railway system was seen by the public sector as a signal of higher wage increases.

[21] This does not apply to the railway system, as they have a *PV-Anstalt* which is integrated in the *Hauptverband.*

The average pension in the public sector is much higher than in the market sector. This is partly due to different pension rules and partly due to differences in the composition of the labour force. The average qualification is much higher in the public sector than in the market sector due to the high number of jobs requiring academic qualifications.

To assess the situation of the civil service vis-à-vis the rest of the economy, one has to compare life income and the composition of people in comparable jobs. The life income of an employee in the market sector consists of his/her wage paid by the employer, the severance payment (up to one year's income) which is paid by the employer as well and the pension which, in addition to the contribution by the employee, is paid for out of general taxes through contributions from the employer and the state. In the case of the civil service the state is also the employer and pays the wage and the entire pension out of taxes. There is no severance payment in the civil service. Whether the subsidies to the pension of the civil service out of taxes are really bigger than for the market sector cannot be evaluated unless an equivalent to the employer's contribution and for the severance payment is calculated. However, the higher retirement wage of the civil service can therefore be the result of different timing of wage payments.

No systematic study of income differentials between the public sector and market economy has been done. Systematic data for incomes in the public sector which would be a precondition for any analyses do not exist. This is partly due to the fact that the wage income of the public sector not only consists of the statutory wages but of diverse supplements, some of which are group specific, whereas others are bound to specific jobs.[22] A study by Adenstedt et al. (1990) demonstrates by comparing possible curricula of blue-collar workers, white-collar workers, and civil service employees that the life income of men in the lower echelons is not much higher in the public service compared to the market sector, whereas it is much higher for women in the public service than in the market sector. This is due to the fact that the statutory equality between men and women has more effect in the public sector than it does in the market sector.[23]

---

[22] Public sector unions are not helpful in providing the data. This fact can be seen as an expression of a bad conscience concerning privileges.

[23] Private law contracts in the public sector are to be found amongst women to a greater extent than amongst men.

4. The second layer in Austria

4.1 The prevailing system

The prevailing dual system of occupational pensions in Austria consists on the one hand of mandatory severance payments and on the other hand of voluntary occupational pension plans. Severance payments are limited to persons who stay longer than three years with the same company and who either are fired, retire, or leave the company in accordance with the management. Starting with one monthly wage after three years of company membership, payments increase with the duration of the job up to a maximum value of one yearly income after 25 years. In 1993, 3.96 per cent of gross wages in Austrian industry were spent on severance payments (Wirtschaftskammer 1995). This ratio varies from year to year between 3 and 4 per cent and is probably a slight exaggeration of the amount spent in the total economy, because industrial employment is continuously being reduced, whereas other sectors of the economy increase their employment. Within the book accounting system of firms, severance payments are recorded as regular wage expenses. This is the reason why statistical data for Austria are not available.

In the following we will concentrate on voluntary occupational pension plans. Their existence is puzzling given the fact that the Austrian public pension system is based on mandatory insurance of all working persons with comparatively high income replacement ratios. Therefore, over time, consumption smoothing only plays a minor role in motivating funded occupational pensions. Consumption smoothing might be relevant only for persons with income levels above the upper ceiling for public pensions, which in 1995 was S 37 800. Slightly less than 10 per cent of all employees have earnings above that level. About 50 per cent of the male employees who are between 55 and 60 years of age – which is the usual age for entering retirement – receive incomes above the ceiling. But there is another simple rationale for occupational pensions of high income earners: a progressive tax system allows for tax evasion by deferring income into the retirement period with income levels in lower tax brackets.

Because the main bulk of employed persons have incomes in the lower income brackets, and since firms are already facing high public pension contributions of 22.8 per cent of gross wages, the motivation for firm pensions in the lower income brackets must rest on other explanations. Possible candidates are efficiency wages combined with deferred wage payments, large depreciation of human capital due to specific job characteristics, or rent sharing arguments as put forward by the insider-outsider theory.

The economic rationale behind deferred wage payments rests on a variety of models stressing efficiency wage motives. Becker (1975) suggests that economizing on hiring and training costs provides an incentive to firms for offering long-term contracts. An occupational pension plan serves as the efficiency premium and will help the firm to stabilize the turnover in its work force at low levels. A similar reasoning is developed in Shapiro and Stiglitz (1984), namely, high monitoring costs. To avoid shirking behaviour on the part of workers, an occupational pension is promised such that the detection of misbehaviour is associated with a comparatively high loss in expected income. Steep age earnings profiles may serve similar services to the firm, although pensions form a stronger commitment to actually pay out deferred wages. Both arguments emphasize the role of quitting costs for employed persons. In the case of Austria exit costs are dramatically high, since direct commitments allow for a complete slashing of pension entitlements in the case of workers quitting.

The insider-outsider approach on the other hand argues for rent sharing as an explanation for occupational pension plans. Given that a firm accrues rents from operating in a non-competitive market and that the management is confronted with a strong union, Lindbeck and Snower (1988) show that profit maximizing wages will be above the market clearing level. A related explanation relies on state ownership of firms which results in potentially low ownership interest in profit maximization. Governments often pursue industrial, regional, or labour market objectives when running enterprises. Within this setting firm pensions may serve as a means to hide sector wage differentials to owner representatives.

Differences in human capital depreciation may also explain firm pension schemes. If a job implies a great risk to health or life, a firm pension offers insurance against income losses from an accident. Particular jobs, like professional athletics or fashion modelling, imply only short periods of high income and therefore introduce a need for income smoothing.

To test for competing hypotheses, a sample of 800 Austrian firms from industry, construction, energy and water supply was analysed by Mooslechner and Url (1995). The firms provided information on the existence of an occupational pension plan, the number of entitled employed persons, the number of pensioners, the amount spent on pensions, several firm specific characteristics, and their motivation for the pension plan. This information can be combined within a logit model which allows the estimation of the probability for the existence of an occupational pension plan for a specific firm. Additionally the model reveals the main determinants for offering firm pensions.

The variables of the presented model have been selected in a specific way. Starting with a model comprising all possible explanatory variables, likelihood ratio tests have been used to arrive at a parsimonious version for the probability of firm i to offer a firm pension:

$$\Pr{(yes)}_i = \frac{1}{1 + e^{-Z_i}}$$

where the firm specific index Z_i is defined by

$Z_i = -2.56^{**} + 0.76\,base\# + 1.11\,chem^{**} - 0.40\,constmat - 0.32\,techn$
$\quad - 0.04\,cons - 1.10\,construct^{**} - 2.17\,empl1^{**} - 0.65\,empl2^{*}$
$\quad + 0.38\,empl3 + 0.46\,empl4 + 1.98\,empl5^{**} + 0.03^{**}\,old + 0.04\,highs^{*}$
$\quad + 0.07\,univ^{**} + 0.49\,demand^{**} + 0.52\,state^{**}.$

(# significant at the 10 per cent level; * significant at the 5 per cent level; ** significant at the 1 per cent level)

List of variables:

sector of activity:	base	production of basic goods and materials
	chem	chemical industry
	constmat	production of construction material
	techn	production of technical goods
	cons	production of consumer goods
	construct	construction
number of employees	empl1	up to 50 employees
	empl2	51 to 100 employees
	empl3	101 to 500 employees
	empl4	501 to 1000 employees
	empl5	more than 1000 employees

old: share of employees older than 40; *highs:* share of employees with high school degree; *univ:* share of employees with university degree; *demand:* employees' demand for occupational pensions as perceived by management (yes/no); *state:* state owns more than 50 per cent of the firm.

Variables with positive parameters increase the probability of a firm pension and those with negative values will decrease it. The model is able to forecast 87 per cent of all cases correctly, with a small bias to predict cases with no firm pension more often correctly. All variables are significant at 5 per cent or 1 per cent level, but the magnitude of parameters has to be interpreted carefully. Dichotomous variables like the sector of activity or the employment level are coded 0/1 whereas variables like the ratio of employed persons older than 40 are measured as a percentage between 0 and 100.

The signs of the estimated parameters indicate that firms operating in the base sector (base) or in the chemical industry (chem) are more likely to offer occupational pensions whereas firms in the construction industry (construct) are very unlikely to do so. A comparison of results on sector wage differentials in Austria by Hofer (1994) indicates that high wage sectors also tend to pay firm pensions. Hofer concludes that rent sharing is the prime motivation for sector wage differentials in Austria. Obviously this reasoning can be extended towards occupational pensions. Collective bargaining agreements in the Austrian banking sector (a traditional high wage sector with an oligopolistic market structure) strengthens this explanation.

The firm size measured by the number of employed persons matters also. The bigger the firms, the more likely they are to offer occupational pensions. This may be related to organizational problems of monitoring, the existence of scale economies and market power or the higher degree of unionization associated with bigger firm size.

The signs of the remaining variables indicate that firms with a large share of employed persons older than 40 or a large share of workers with high school education or university degrees tend to offer occupational pensions. The age structure may indicate a demand pull by employed persons for shifting income into the future. It may also indicate the outcome of a self-selection process by seniority rules for firing decisions. Higher educational levels foster occupational pension plans. This relation reflects the link between higher education and higher wage levels and shows the relevance of the insurance gap in the public pension system as a reason for occupational pensions.

Additionally the demand of employed persons for deferred wage payments as perceived by the management has been included in the model. Managers of firms with a pension plan share the view that their workers prefer deferred wages over cash. Whether this truly reflects workers' attitudes remains questionable.

55

An interesting aspect arises from the significance of the state ownership variable. State ownership strongly favours occupational pension plans which indicates a lack of interest in dividend payments. Industrial policy, labour market interventions or regional interests dominated pure profit maximization strategies and provide the leeway for managers and unions to share rents and increase wage payments through occupational pension plans. This incentive is emphasized by central wage bargaining in the metal working and chemical industries. Occupational pensions in these industries provide an alternative for firm-specific wage increases.

Summing up, the estimated logit model gives evidence for the importance of the insurance gap and tax reasons to engage in occupational pension plans. In addition, the firm size indicates the relevance of efficiency wages. The biggest explanatory power for occupational pension plans in Austria comes from variables associated with rent sharing: sector wage differentials are mirrored by occupational pensions and finally state ownership increases the probability of occupational pensions.

4.2   A projection for occupational pensions in Austria

The analysis of motivations for occupational pension plans provides the starting point for the first general attempt to project the number of firms, the number of entitled employed persons, the number of pensioners, the means of finance, and finally the amount spent on firm pensions in the non-agricultural market sector of Austria's economy. A projection of all these variables is necessary because pension plans are voluntary and official data on this subject are neither collected nor published up to now. Several studies are available covering special groups of firms in specific sectors of the economy but they do not attempt to generalize their results. Mooslechner and Url (1995) present results from a questionnaire which was answered by firms in Austrian industry, construction, energy and water supply and combine them with information on other sectors of the economy. An important alternative source of information is provided by a few collective bargaining agreements between unions and employer associations. The agricultural and public sectors are excluded from the projection although occupational pension plans are common among semi-official institutions in Austria. The reason for this is not only lack of sufficient data but also to facilitate comparisons with results obtained from the Statistische Bundesamt (1994) for Germany.

The projection is based on the 112 255 firms with more than three employed persons operating in January 1994. Firms are attributed to sectors of the economy according to national accounts standards. Another line of distinction goes along the firm size measured by the number of employed persons. The projection for manufacturing, construction, energy and water supply is based directly on the questionnaire and the logit model presented in the previous section. For banking and insurance collective bargaining agreements, aggregated data published by the Austrian National Bank, and a special study by Gassner-Möstl (1991) are combined to achieve reasonable estimates. Results for the remaining sectors are subject to greater uncertainty, as only information from the Austrian Association of Pension Funds, from regression results based on industry data, and comparisons with results from Germany are available.

A total of 4850 firms within the private sector offer occupational pension plans. This corresponds to roughly 5 per cent of all operating firms. Whereas only a proportion of 3–5 per cent of small firms offers occupational pensions, the ratio increases to 85 per cent for firms with more than 1000 employed persons. A comparison with Germany (see Schmähl, in this volume, Table 4.7) shows that the overall ratio of 5 per cent in Austria is significantly lower than that in Germany. The distribution over firm sizes shows that especially the behaviour of firms with less than 1000 employed persons is responsible for this pattern.

The motivational structure for occupational pensions in Austria suggests that differences among sectors should exist as well. Actually, in the banking and insurance sector with a relatively high degree of concentration and until 1994 a lack of international competition, collective bargaining agreements include occupational pension plans and thus create a relatively high proportion of firms with occupational pensions. On the other hand the dissemination of occupational pensions is small in the construction business. This is quite contrary to the experience in Germany, where collective bargaining agreements exist only within this sector. In comparison to other sectors the spread of occupational pensions among small firms in the other service sectors is surprisingly high. Tax advantages used by professionals are the prime motivation for this result.

The number of employed persons with vested claims follows the pattern already sketched out for firms. A total of 186 000 or 9 per cent of all employed persons are vested with firm pensions.

The number of pensioners actually receiving supplementary payments by firms can only be estimated for the most popular case of direct commitments and for pension funds. Beneficiaries from direct life insurance contracts receive their pension payments from the insurance company and are no longer under the control of firms after retirement. Records by the Austrian Association of Pension Funds give a total of 5907 pensioners in 1994. The projection by Mooslechner and Url indicates a further 79 000 pensioners within direct commitments.

These numbers can be compared to projections by the Austrian Central Statistical Office (Vollmann 1993 and Wolf 1991, 1995) based on the Mikrozensus, a representative sample of regular interviews with 0.7 per cent of the Austrian population. Wolf (1995) estimates a total of 99 000 persons receiving supplementary occupational pensions. Both numbers are reasonably close with the difference attributable to the inclusion of public sector pensioners and beneficiaries from life insurance contracts. The means to finance occupational pensions in Austria strongly depends on the historical development of legal restrictions. The right to establish pension funds was enacted as late as 1990, which provides the main reason for a low proportion of firms using pension funds. On the other hand direct commitments provided an attractive source of cheap inside financial resources for a considerable period of time. In 1979 the amount of tax deductible accumulation of book reserves has been reduced below the present value of pension entitlements. This resulted in a subsequent reduction in the popularity of occupational pensions. Direct insurance contracts and insurance of direct commitments became more and more popular since then. At the same time a shift towards defined contribution plans took place. The projection for 1994 gives a 62 per cent share of firms funding their pension plan by direct commitments, 17 per cent funding it by pension funds and 21 per cent using direct life insurance contracts.

The projected volume of financial transactions refers to 1993 and is disaggregated according to means of finance. Within direct commitments about S 14.7 billion are used to build up book reserves for future payments and another S 8.8 billion are paid out of the actual wage bill. This reflects the lack in appropriately funding direct commitments during the years of legal restrictions on tax deductibility (1979 to 1988). This may also be a reason why the amount might be overestimated. Firms are now required to rebuild book reserves according to present values.

Pension funds received S 880 million as premiums and about S 175 million are spent on direct insurance premiums. The total amount of S 24.5 billion spent on occupational pension plans amounts to 2.1 per

Table 2.10 – Monthly median firm pension and median public old age pension for employed persons in 1993

	Public pension		Occupational pension		As percentage of public pension	
	women	*men*	*women*	*men*	*women*	*men*
Blue-collar workers	6 470	13 173	1 300	1 500	20.1	11.4
White-collar workers	10 058	19 010	2 400	5 900	23.9	31.0

Source: Hauptverband (1994), Wolf (1995). The data refer only to firms paying supplementary pensions.

cent of wages according to the national accounts definition or to 14 per cent of public pension expenditures for employed persons in 1993.

It is interesting to compare these numbers with monthly median occupational pension according to Mikrozensus data published in Wolf (1995). Compared to public sector pensions, differences in firm pensions between women and men are smaller for blue-collar workers but larger for white-collar workers. The ratio of occupational pensions to public pensions strongly depends on gender and job positions. For women an occupational pension accounts for approximately 20 per cent of their public pension regardless of their occupational position. On the other hand men experience higher supplements within white-collar positions. This results from the ceiling for public pensions and the resulting insurance gap.

5.   Outlook

The smallness of the second tier is a consequence of the dominance of the public pension system. The structures of occupational pension plans up to now do not mirror problems of the public system, neither financial problems nor political problems, but must be seen in the framework of incentives in labour contracts and rent seeking. According to our estimates rent sharing is the prime motive for supplementary pensions for those below the public insurance limit.

However, the current system is under discussion. To continue the Austrian pension system on today's level, with its high replacement

59

ratios, the low retirement age and the still growing life expectancy, would either require a drastic increase of contributions or a rapid expansion of the active labour force. To put all the burden on an increase of contributions is politically out of the question, and would hardly be economically sensible, as it would lower incomes out of active participation in the economic system. It would therefore make it more attractive to retire still earlier.

Increasing the labour force to such an extent that it would completely eliminate the pressure on the system is also not viable, as the reproduction rate is very low in Austria. Some alleviation is to be expected from a further increase in the labour market participation of women. Immigration is kept at a low level for political reasons. However, any increase in the number of insured can only postpone the problems, unless the system is considered to grow forever.

Therefore, changes in the retirement systems are to be expected. There are basically two options, the first one being a reduction of the benefits; the second one, raising the effective age of retirement. This is independent from a possible change to a funded system. In the first case, the basic philosophy of the system will change. Up to now it was accepted that publicly provided pensions should provide sufficient income for all employed, except for those whose income is higher then the *Höchstbemessungsgrundlage*. If the benefits are substantially reduced, the question of a second tier will emerge immediately. If the effective retirement age is raised, the replacement ratio does not have to be lowered. In that case the pension system can keep up its basic philosophy, namely to provide sufficient income for most people. The way in which the problem will be solved is a political question and depends on political developments.

When we look at reforms in the past, we find both policies pursued. A couple of times benefits were reduced. But this was done without breaking with the basic idea of the system, namely to provide sufficient income for the retired. The reductions tried to turn the system in the direction of an insurance system. The generous minimum percentage, which was particularly important for women, was abandoned in 1984. The basis for calculating the pensions of private sector employees has been extended to the best fifteen years. Since 1988 the years of studying no longer count as years of insurance without payment, as used to be the case before that year.

There were also attempts to raise the effective retirement age. Gradual retirement has been available since 1994, and a higher replacement rate can be reached when retirement is later than at 60 (55 for women). But these benefits are too small to consider them as appropriate incentives to work longer (Holzmann, 1988). There are two reasons why the government has hesitated thus far to make later retirement attractive. Firstly, it was always afraid of increasing unemployment, or groups who were threatened by unemployment were successful in drawing the government's attention to their problems. Secondly, making later retirement comparatively more attractive by increasing benefits in case of later retirement is very expensive, and any attempt to reach later retirement by reducing benefits when retiring early did not seem appropriate. However, reducing the benefits without raising the effective retirement age cannot be seen as a solution to the problems of the Austrian pension system, as it would put the burden of providing for the contemporaneously old and building up the capital stock for its own second layer on only one generation.

The socialist-led coalition government elected in December 1995 has introduced some reforms to raise the effective retirement age. The benefit formula was slightly changed, in favour of the later years of contributions. The necessary number of years for early retirement due to long insurance was increased from 35 to 37.5 years. The deductions for earlier retirement were increased, but still are well below the deductions which would conform to an actuarially fair insurance. The *Sonderunterstützung* was abolished. The contribution to health insurance had been increased by 0.25 percentage points. These reforms were accompanied by measures to hinder dismissals of employees over the age of 50 and by granting subsidies to the employment of elderly unemployed. The firms will be experience-rated according to their employment policy. Whether these reforms will increase the effective retirement age or rather reduce pensions remains to be seen.

However, the perspective for occupational pension plans in Austria strongly depends on the development of the public pension system and the replacement ratios promised by it. Declining replacement ratios will give employed persons an incentive to accumulate assets that allow consumption smoothing. Whether this will be pursued under occupational pension plans or within private direct life insurance is open.

Up to now, efficiency wages have only played a minor role in the explanation of occupational pension plans. Small firms dominate the Austrian economy and therefore high monitoring costs will not give rise to firm pensions. Nevertheless high turnover costs may arise from a shortage in labour supply associated with the aging population. Clearly a barrier for the spread of occupational pensions is the rent sharing argument. On the one hand, state ownership is reduced in the course of privatization programmes and the reduction of public sector deficits. This will probably result in new corporate governance structures with more profit-oriented interests. On the other hand, integration into the European Union and towards Eastern Europe will result in a break-up of sheltered sectors and consequently will reduce the capability to finance occupational pension plans. The first steps in this direction were started in the late 1980s, when occupational pension plans in state-owned firms came under attack, as these firms had to be subsidized to be able to survive.

Another impulse emerged in the second half of the 1980s when a change of basic institutions of the social system seemed, for political reasons, not completely out of the question. Mixed with interests of banks and insurance companies to create new financial markets new laws have been enacted, regulating occupational pension plans and allowing the formation of pension funds for the first time. Tax incentives for firm pensions are mainly restricted to employer contributions up to 10 per cent of the wage bill. The tax deductibility of employees' contributions is restricted to tight limits. This was due to problems of the public sector deficit, and partly due to distributional problems. As it is clear that a second pension is first of all in the interest of higher income groups, any furthering of a second layer via the tax system would benefit first of all these groups (Lacina in Barazon, 1988). The trade unions do not have much of an interest in a second layer either, as it would reduce their existing influence on the public pension system.

The public interest in a second tier is mixed. On the one hand a strengthening of occupational pension plans is suggested as a solution to the financial problem of the public pensions. On the other hand, the existing occupational pension plans had come under attack. This is due to the fact that most of these plans are to be found in firms with a close relation to the public sector. This also applies to the sole sector-wide pension plan – that of the banking industry. The public stake in this sector has always been very big. Whereas these pensions were seen for quite some time as pioneer systems which should be extended to other sectors as well, they are currently seen as privileges due to monopoly position or state subsidies.

However, it never was clear which problem should be solved by furthering a funded second tier. As the saving ratio is already comparatively high in Austria, one of the classic arguments in favour of funded systems – that of furthering saving – does not apply to Austria.[24] On the other hand it is not clear how 'the Austrian pension problem', namely the too early retirement, is to be solved by a second tier.

References

Adenstedt, Erik, Juch, Josef, Lutz, Hedwig and Wagner, Michael (1990), *Einkommensverläufe. Der Einfluß der Arbeitsplatzgarantie auf das Lebenseinkommen von unselbständig Erwerbstätigen in Österreich*, Wien: Bundesministerium für Arbeit und Soziales.

Barazon, Ronald (ed.) (1988), *Pensionsfonds*. Bankwissenschaftliche Schriftenreihe. Wien: Bank Verlag.

Becker, Gary (1975), *Human Capital*, New York: Columbia University Press.

Bericht über die Soziale Lage (Sozialbericht), Herausgegeben vom Bundesministerium für Arbeit und Soziales. Annual.

Biffl, Gudrun (1992), *Ältere Arbeitskräfte auf dem österreichischen Arbeitsmarkt*. WIFO-Vorträge Nr. 58.

Gassner-Möstl, E. (1991), *Altersvorsorge unter besonderer Berücksichtigung der betrieblichen Altersvorsorge in Österreich – grundlegende Überlegungen und empirische Studie*. Diss. Wirtschaftsuniv. Wien.

Hauptverband der österreichischen Sozialversicherungsträger (1994), Statistisches Handbuch der österreichischen Sozialversicherung 1994. Wien.

Hofer, Helmut (1994), 'Über die Ursachen der sektoralen Lohnunterschiede in Österreich'. Mimeo, Institut für Höhere Studien, Wien.

Holzmann, Robert (1988), 'Zu ökonomischen Effekten der österreichischen Pensionsversicherung: Einkommensersatz, Ruhestandsentscheidungen und interne Ertragsraten', in Robert Holzmann (ed.), *Ökonomische Analyse der Sozialversicherung*, Wien: Manz.

Lindbeck, Assar and Snower, Dennis (1988), 'Cooperation, Harassment, and Involuntary Unemployment', *American Economic Review*, Vol. 78, 167–88.

Lutz, Hedwig, Wagner, Michael and Waldhör, Thomas (1993), 'Übertritt in den Ruhestand', Mimeo, Wien.

Mooslechner, Peter and Url, Thomas (1995), 'Betriebliche Altersvorsorge in Österreich', WIFO-Gutachten, Wien.

Rhein-Kress, Gabi von (1992), 'Die quantitative Steuerung des Arbeitsangebotes als Instrument der Arbeitsmarkt- und Beschäftigungspolitik', *Mitteilungen aus der Arbeitsmarkt- und Berufsforschung*, Bd. 25 Nr. 3.

Shapiro, Carl and Stiglitz, Joseph (1984), 'Equilibrium Unemployment as a Worker Discipline Device', *American Economic Review*, Vol. 74, 433–44.

Statistisches Bundesamt (1994), Löhne und Gehälter – Erhebungen über Art und

---

[24] It is not clear why the saving ratio of retired people is so high in Austria, as it contradicts all standard models of lifetime savings. If the inheritance motive is decisive for the saving decision, the small number of children should reduce savings. Maybe the recently introduced *Pflegegeld* will reduce savings.

Umfang der betrieblichen Altersversorgung. Fachserie 16 Reihe 6.1, Wiesbaden.

Stefanits, Hans and Lackner, Karin (1995), 'Wege des Übertritts in den Ruhestand', *Soziale Sicherheit*, 229–38.

Tálos, Emmerich and Wörister, Karl (1994), *Soziale Sicherung im Sozialstaat Österreich*, Baden-Baden: Nomos.

Vollmann, Kurt (1993), 'Personen- und Haushaltseinkommen von Pensionisten', *Statistische Nachrichten* (2), 82–6.

Wirtschaftskammer Österreich (1995), 'Die Arbeitskosten in der Industrie Österreichs', 1993, Mimeo, Wirtschaftskammer Österreich Abt.f. Statistik, Wien.

Wolf, Walter (1991), 'Personen- und Haushaltseinkommen von Pensionisten', *Statistische Nachrichten* (2), 158–61.

Wolf, Walter (1995), 'Personen- und Haushaltseinkommen von Pensionisten; Ausstattung von Pensionistenhaushalten', *Statistische Nachrichten* (7), 509–19.

3

France: A National and Contractual Second Tier

Emmanuel Reynaud

At first sight, the French pension system looks very diverse and fragmented. A multitude of schemes cover different occupational groups and the coherence of the overall structure is not immediately perceivable. However, some main characteristics can be stressed. First, the system is based on employment and a distinction can be made in the working population between three large groups: employees covered by the general social security scheme (68 per cent), employees covered by the so-called 'special schemes' (20 per cent) and the self-employed (12 per cent). Second, the system can be defined as a two-tier compulsory system. The vast majority of the workers have double coverage in the form of a basic pension and a supplementary pension. Members of the 'special schemes' are the principal exception to this pattern: their special scheme is usually the only compulsory arrangement to which they belong. Third, parallel to the contributory pensions, an old age minimum income is guaranteed to all French citizens from age 65 (60 in case of disability), regardless of their working record. It is a two-tier system. A means-tested minimum pension (old age and survivors' pensions) is guaranteed in all the statutory social security schemes and an additional income support allowance is paid by a special fund financed by the state, the FNS (National Solidarity Fund).

There is very little data available on the income packaging of retirees. It is fairly old (1984) and does not make any distinction between first and second tier pensions (Table 3.1). Nevertheless, the data shows that pensions do not play the same role for the different occupational groups. The major discrepancy concerns the employees and the self-employed. Pensions represent 85.2 per cent of the household income when the head of the household was previously an employee and only 58.9 per cent when he or she was self-employed. In the latter case, the household

Table 3.1 – Sources of income of retirees, for selected former occupations (1984)

Former occupation	Employ- ment %	Contribu- tory pen- sions %	Old age mini- mum %	Invest- ments/pro- perty %	Household income Francs	Household distribution %
Farmer	6.1	59.8	17.9	16.2	50 258	14.7
Self-employed	6.2	54.1	4.8	34.9	90 793	7.0
Employee	6.0	82.4	2.8	8.8	80 794	65.9
Other	6.9	65.5	12.1	15.5	53 132	12.4
Average	6.1	76.2	5.3	12.4	73 506	100.0

Note: These data are on household income, they cover households in which the head is no longer working and aged 60 and over; the former occupation is the former occupation of the household head.

Source: Enquête sur les revenus fiscaux des ménages en 1984, INSEE.

depends much more on investments and property than in the former, 34.9 per cent and 8.8 per cent of the overall income respectively.

This chapter will investigate the supplementary tier of the system. Its main focus will be on the role of work-related actors, and more precisely on the ability of employers' organizations and trade unions to set up a second-tier pension to supplement the social security programme. Therefore it will only deal with the schemes designed for employees. Moreover, it will not take into account the special schemes. For the most part, these schemes cover employees from the public sector. They are the descendants of the first pension schemes established, as in the other industrialized countries, in the civil service, the military, railway companies, gas and electricity companies, financial institutions, etc. They were maintained after the Second World War and their members were exempted from participation in the newly set general social security scheme (called general scheme for short). Today they still cover almost a quarter of the employees and provide benefits noticeably higher than the general scheme. There are fifteen of these schemes still open to new entrants, but most of them are small. The two largest cover civil servants and military personnel (2.3 million members) and local authority offi- cials (1.5 million). Together these two schemes represent 86 per cent of members of special schemes. Adding the French railway scheme and the French gas and electricity companies scheme, the proportion rises to 94 per cent.

In the civil service and the local authorities schemes the pension is set at 75 per cent of the final gross salary for a full career (37.5 years). This replacement rate, which is the result of a choice made by the state as an employer, has become a yardstick for employees' retirement provision in France. This provided a very strong incentive to establish schemes to supplement the social security programme. Public employees other than civil servants are covered by the general scheme and they have their own supplementary scheme (IRCANTEC). In the private sector,[1] a general pattern has emerged and spread to almost all employees. It takes the following shape: a basic pension is secured by the general scheme and supplementary provision is provided by two federations of pension funds, ARRCO and AGIRC (respectively, Association of Supplementary Pension Schemes and General Association of Pension Institutions for Cadres).

The general scheme is an earnings-related scheme which provides relatively low benefits. The full rate pension equals 50 per cent of average earnings (up to the social security contribution ceiling) over a given period. Under a reform programme introduced in 1994, this period is currently being extended from the best ten years to the best 25 years. This will be achieved in 2008. Besides the percentage used, the contribution ceiling is an important element of the pension formula, since it reduces the scope of earnings taken into account and consequently limits the replacement rate of the pension for the employees paid over the ceiling. It is a little higher than the average gross earnings in the private sector and it corresponds roughly to two times the national minimum wage. In other words, the maximum pension in the general scheme is more or less equivalent to the minimum wage. On the whole, the benefits provided by this scheme are far from the 75 per cent of the final salary achieved through the civil service scheme. This gap between the private and the public sectors illustrates the role played in the former by the supplementary schemes ARRCO and AGIRC.

The difference between the two organizations relates to the main distinction among private sector employees in France, i.e., the difference between *cadres* and *non-cadres*. There is no equivalent to the term cadre in English; it refers to a group covering managerial and senior technical staff. The non-cadres are all the other employees, that is those who do not have the cadre status: blue-collar workers and a fair number of white-

---

[1] The private sector, in this chapter, includes nationalized companies in the competitive sector: metallurgy, banks, insurances, airlines, etc.

collar workers. This distinction played a major role in the setting up of the pension system in France. And at the same time, the cadres created themselves as a social group through the setting up of their own supplementary scheme (Boltanski 1982, pp. 148–151). Today, the situation is as follows: all the employees in the private sector belong to the general scheme and to an ARRCO fund, and the cadres also belong to an AGIRC fund for the part of their earnings above the social security ceiling. In addition to compulsory provision, voluntary arrangements have been set up in some companies, but they involve a limited number of employees (for a detailed description of supplementary provision for private sector employees in France, see Reynaud, forthcoming).

1. Historical development

The general social security scheme was established in 1945, shortly after the Second World War. It replaced the previous social insurance scheme introduced in 1930. It was initially conceived for covering the entire working population, but several groups refused vigorously to be brought in. The self-employed very strongly opposed being included in a scheme which, they felt, had been designed for the wage-earners and would be dominated by their representatives. In 1948 they obtained the right to set up their own schemes. Besides, the members of the so-called 'special schemes', who had already been contracted out of the 1930 scheme, wanted to be left aside of the new social security programme and to keep their schemes which provided noticeably higher benefits. In 1945, the special schemes were only maintained on a provisional basis, but very quickly, in 1946, their autonomy was recognized by the law and the contracting out procedure was perpetuated. So, almost from the beginning, in spite of the will of its designers, the general scheme ended up covering employees exclusively and furthermore, only employees who did not belong to a special scheme. As already mentioned the special schemes concern for the most part the public sector and the main special schemes cover employees in the civil service and the armed forces, the local authorities, the national railways and the national gas and electricity companies. The special treatment accorded to these groups has created a strong distinction with regard to pension provision among employees. The disparity could have been reduced by improving the benefits of the general scheme, but instead there has been a widespread development of supplementary arrangements.

When the general scheme was set up in 1945, old age pensions were not considered a priority for the country. The benefit formula was set at a relatively low level. The full rate pension was equal to 40 per cent of the average earnings (up to the contribution ceiling) of the final ten years at work and it was to be paid after 30 years' contributions. In addition, the general scheme operated according to a contributory principle and, even though it did pay means-tested non-contributory benefits, it did not systematically credit the periods of service prior to its creation, it only took into account the contributions to the previous social insurance scheme established in 1930. In other words, the full pension could not be paid before 1960. Subsequently, in 1971, under the pressure of the trade unions, the government improved the benefits of the general scheme. The full rate pension was raised from 40 per cent to 50 per cent (to be paid after 37.5 years' contributions) and was to be calculated on the earnings of the best ten years instead of the last ten years. This last substitution was to take into account the case of the employees, mainly manual workers, whose earnings fall before retirement. Even after this reform, the general scheme was far from providing an adequate replacement ratio for most workers.

On the whole, the choices made concerning the general scheme left a wide space for supplementary arrangements to develop. This development started very shortly after the creation of the new social security programme. The AGIRC scheme was established in 1947 and it played a major role in the widespread introduction of second-tier pensions for all the employees in the private sector. It became a reference for other workers: an incentive to improve pension provision and a technical and organizational model.

Engineers and managerial staff reacted sharply to their mandatory affiliation to the general scheme decided in 1945 (for the creation of AGIRC see Friot, 1996). Before the war, the compulsory national insurance scheme, established in 1930, applied only to employees whose earnings did not exceed a certain ceiling. In 1938, this ceiling was raised and engineers and managerial staff who became eligible for coverage were exempted from membership when they belonged to a company or an industry-wide scheme, on condition that the latter guaranteed benefits equivalent to those of the statutory scheme. This type of employment based scheme thus operated as a substitute scheme for the national insurance programme. In 1946, this contracting out provision applied to almost 200 000 employees (Netter 1977, p. 59). That membership was compulsory for all to the new social security scheme called the existence of the employment-based schemes into question. Upper income employees objected vigorously to this compulsory membership, and demanded that their own specific schemes be maintained. The cadres found there the opportunity to be acknowledged and to exist as a specific group.

A joint committee was set up on the Minister of Labour's (communist) initiative to define the conditions for maintaining the benefits previously acquired by cadres. It comprised an equal number of cadres' and employers' representatives and it was chaired by the assistant director of Social Security. The work of this committee led to the signing, on 14 March 1947, of a national collective agreement establishing the pension scheme for cadres plus a compulsory scheme paying death-in-service benefits. For the pension scheme, the option of a single national pay-as-you-go scheme was retained. It was designed as a supplement to, rather than a substitute for, the general scheme and it covered the fraction of earnings above the social security ceiling. It was to be managed on a multi-institutional basis, but all the managing institutions had to be approved and become members of a federative body, AGIRC. This association was in charge of guaranteeing the unity of the scheme and of operating a full financial compensation between member institutions. The federation, as well as all the institutions, had to be jointly run by trade unions and employers' representatives.

As a result of the 1947 agreement, all employers belonging to the Conseil national du patronat français (CNPF), the national employers' organization who signed the agreement, were obliged to affiliate their cadres to one of the AGIRC funds. Subsequently, the obligation to join the scheme spread to include an increasing number of cadres. In 1950, the national agreement of 1947 was given by law the status of an extensive national agreement, which meant that all the employers in the sectors of industry represented in the employers' organization were brought into the scope of the agreement, whether or not they belonged to a member organization of the CNPF. At the same time, sectors not represented in the latter requested inclusion in the agreement.

The creation of the cadres' scheme paved the way to the development of supplementary schemes for other categories of employees. In the 1950s, some sectors of industry and large companies set up schemes for the non-cadres. The establishment in the beginning of 1956 of a pension scheme for the employees of Renault, the auto company, triggered in particular a multitude of actions aimed at securing the same benefits for employees of other companies. In 1957 the CNPF and the trade unions created a national scheme, UNIRS (National Association of Employees' Pension Institutions) in an attempt to rationalize and co-ordinate this development. Unlike the AGIRC scheme, membership in the UNIRS was not compulsory; nevertheless, it developed rapidly as a result of collective agreements, in particular in the metallurgical industries. It was less successful with regard to the founders' other objective, which was to co-ordinate the numerous schemes already in operation. The will to introduce a co-ordination mechanism was closely linked with the fact that the vast majority of the existing schemes were financed on a pay-as-you-go basis. Such a technique is very fragile when based on a restricted population group; it requires a wide demographic base to be viable.

Parallel to this technical aspect, there was the desire to extend supplementary pension provision to employees who were not covered. The dual objective of securing the durability of the schemes in operation and extending coverage led to the signing of the agreement of 8 December 1961 between the CNPF and the trade unions. This agreement obliged all the companies that were members of the CNPF to affiliate their non-cadre employees to a supplementary scheme. In 1962, the scope of this agreement was extended by the government to all the companies belonging to a sector of industry which was covered by the CNPF, whether or not they were members of the employers' organization. In addition, the agreement of 8 December 1961 created a federative body, the ARRCO (Association of Supplementary Pension Schemes). The employers to which the agreement applied had to affiliate all their non-cadre employees to a fund which was included in ARRCO. Unlike AGIRC, ARRCO was not a single national scheme but an association of several schemes, with their own regulations. The role of ARRCO was to harmonize these regulations and to operate financial compensation between them in such a way that members received equivalent benefits regardless of which ARRCO funds they belonged to during their career.

Supplementary provision thus developed extensively in France through collective bargaining procedures. Compulsory membership was finally made universal by the Act of 29 December 1972. The legislator extended the scope of the AGIRC and ARRCO agreements to all activities in which employees were covered by the general social security scheme. Compulsory membership was thus extended to the few sectors not yet involved (temporary employment agencies, wholesale and retail stores, employers of domestic employees, stock markets, the hotel business and bars, etc.). It was also extended to homeworkers in the sectors falling into the scope of the agreements. Only a few exceptions persisted. These concerned sectors or industries which had their own supplementary schemes; they mainly involved the public employees other than civil servants, the employees of social security bodies, airline flight staff and the cadres of banks and agricultural services.

The final important stage was an agreement in 1973 between the trade unions and the employers' organization which made it compulsory for AGIRC members also to be affiliated to an ARRCO fund, in respect of the fraction of their earnings under the social security ceiling. This agreement came in force between 1974 and 1976. By that time, supplementary pension provision for private sector employees had become complete and the current pattern of compulsory pension provision had been set up.

The universal coverage by supplementary pension schemes which had been achieved secured fairly high replacement rates for the pension in payment – all the more so since AGIRC and ARRCO schemes paid full benefits to retirees from the moment they were established. This left very little room for voluntary arrangements to develop in addition to the two-tier compulsory provision. There are in particular very few company schemes. They mainly involve, on the one hand, some large companies which have maintained their schemes after their employees were affiliated to AGIRC and ARRCO schemes and, on the other hand, special arrangements set up for senior executives and directors.

On the whole, the French employers made three main choices in the field of employment-based pensions which differentiate them noticeably from most of their European counterparts. They chose the national level to organize second-tier provision, unlike for example the British and the German employers who favoured the company level, or the Dutch employers who were involved at the industry level. They accepted that the schemes be established by means of collective bargaining procedures and be run through institutions jointly managed with trade unions, while their German or British counterparts unilaterally took the main decisions in setting up and operating employment-based schemes. And finally they favoured pay-as-you-go and not funding as a technique to finance the benefits. The reasons for these choices remain to be fully investigated and explained, but nevertheless these three features – national, contractual, financed on a pay-as-you-go basis – can well characterize the very specific way the supplementary tier has developed in France.

Table 3.2 – Benefits paid by the general scheme and compulsory supplementary schemes (1990)

Scheme	*Benefits*	
	billion Francs	*%*
General scheme	246.2	61.0
Compulsory supplementary schemes	157.7	39.0
ARRCO	96.7	23.9
AGIRC	49.4	12.2
others	11.6	2.9
Total	403.9	100.0

Source: Direction de la sécurité sociale.

2. An overview of the present situation

2.1 Benefits paid by the different tiers

The general scheme and the compulsory supplementary schemes disbursed 403.9 billion francs in benefits in 1990 (Table 3.2). Almost 40 per cent came out of the supplementary tier, in which ARRCO and AGIRC account for 93 per cent of the benefits paid. These figures are a good illustration of the major role played by the second-tier compulsory provision in providing retirement income.

In addition, the schemes acting as substitutes for ARRCO and AGIRC schemes for cadres of banks and agricultural services paid out 9 billion francs in benefits in 1990.

Data concerning voluntary provision are scarce and incomplete. Three types of organizational arrangements coexist: company or multi-employer funds, internally-funded schemes and contracts with an insurance company. Around 3 billion francs in benefits were paid by company and multi-employer funds in 1991. The amount of pensions paid directly by employers (internally-funded) is unknown, nor is there any estimate available. As regards benefits from insurance contracts, the accounts of insurance companies do not enable figures relating to company pension activities to be isolated. In addition, the surveys regularly carried out to assess these activities concern only the premiums that are collected and not the benefits paid. The figure for the benefits is probably less than one billion francs, while the amount of premiums collected can be assessed at around 7 billion francs in 1991 for group contracts.

2.2 The assets of each tier

The French retirement system relies extensively on pay-as-you-go to finance pension provision. The general social security scheme does not accumulate reserves to pay future pensions, which is quite common amongst industrialized countries, but it is also the case for most supplementary schemes. One of the main features of the French system is that the vast majority of second-tier schemes are not pre-funded. This can be illustrated by the following figures: supplementary pension funds for employees distributed a total of 167.9 billion francs in benefits in 1990, while the income they received from investment returns barely amounted to 9.5 billion francs for the same year, that is 5.7 per cent of payments (Reynaud 1994, p. 68).

As a result, the amount of assets involved in pension provision is relatively small. ARRCO and AGIRC schemes hold assets only as contingency reserves, but as their coverage is wide these reserves still represent substantial asset holdings: 168.7 billion francs at the end of 1991. Amongst the other compulsory supplementary schemes, the airline flight staff scheme, even though it does not systematically pre-fund its liabilities, holds a relatively large amount of assets: 10.1 billion francs at the end of 1991. Reserves accumulated by schemes for cadres in banks and agricultural services amounted to 26 billion francs and those of voluntary company and multi-employer funds to about 16 billion francs. On the whole, the total assets held by supplementary funds for employees in the private sector can be estimated at 220.8 billion francs at the end of 1991. This amount represents around 1.3 times the benefits paid out in a year by these funds and 3.3 per cent of GDP (6766.5 billion francs in 1991).

In addition, it is worth mentioning company savings plans. These arrangements do not fall explicitly within the field of retirement provision, but they are still long-term savings plans (the sums invested are frozen for a minimum of five years) and can be used to improve retirement income. The value of assets held in these plans was assessed at around 90 billion francs at the end of 1992. A few tens of billion francs were also invested in frozen accounts within sponsor companies.

2.3 Legal framework and design of ARRCO and AGIRC schemes

ARRCO and AGIRC schemes are defined contribution pay-as-you-go schemes (for a discussion on the different financing models for pay-as-you-go schemes see Reynaud, 1996). This type of scheme operates according to the following principle. A contribution system is established that enables members to build up credits. When the pension is calculated, these credits are assigned a value based on the plan's financial resources, which is based on the flow of contributions collected. In other words, total contributions calculated under the scheme's rules are distributed among the members in proportion to the credits they have built up. In this type of scheme, the sum of the contributions to be divided determines the level of benefits, in contrast to defined benefit pay-as-you-go schemes in which the total of benefits to be paid out determines the level of contributions.

The contribution system of ARRCO and AGIRC schemes consists of taking a given percentage of gross earnings. Contributions are turned into value units called 'pension points', which are entered into members' individual accounts. The number of points acquired over the year is calculated by dividing the amount of contributions by the point's purchase price for the year in question. Points accumulate from year to year in the member's account, irrespective of the company he or she works for (as long as the company belongs to a fund of the corresponding federation). At retirement, the annual pension is determined by the number of points in the account. It equals the total of points acquired multiplied by the value of the point when the pension is calculated. Subsequently, the pension is adjusted according to the point's value; this is fixed twice a year in ARRCO and once a year in AGIRC, but with an option to review it after six months.

In this type of financing method, the scheme's financial equilibrium is ensured in keeping benefits in line with contributions. This is achieved by the administrators of the scheme on a year by year basis through fixing the purchase price of the point and the point's value. On the whole, the sums to be distributed are equal to the total of contributions collected, and this total is proportional to the total earnings on which these contributions are levied. In other words, the level of benefits that will be paid is directly linked to changes in total salaries and earnings distributed. This is specially true for ARRCO schemes which virtually cover all employees in the private sector; the conditions are slightly different for AGIRC as it only covers a specific occupational category and thus relies on the developments within this particular category. Nevertheless, it is worthwhile to compare this characteristic with the situation that prevails in funded defined contribution schemes, where the level of benefits depends on the changes in investment returns.

ARRCO and AGIRC have developed a two-tier contribution system. A first tier corresponds to the minimum compulsory rate; and above and beyond this minimum, they offer options which allow improvements in the level of benefits. So within the compulsory schemes themselves it is possible to improve pension provision by choosing, for the company or the branch of industry, a contribution rate which is above the compulsory minimum rate. Until recently this option played an important role in second-tier provision. It is currently being phased out and this represents a major development in the French pension system to which we will come back later.

The financing technique operated by ARRCO and AGIRC schemes imposes a complete pooling of risks between the funds within each federation. A general financial compensation is applied in order to eliminate differences in demographic structure between funds. This means that members are not subject to demographic changes that affect their particular fund. The level of pension is not affected by any economic difficulties which the company, the industry, or the region covered by the fund may be experiencing. It depends on the changes in the national economy as a whole (reflected, as we saw, in changes in total salaries and wages distributed in the private sector). This solidarity between funds also means that members suffer no loss of entitlements when moving from one employer to another. Members accumulate points in their accounts regardless of the company to which they belong.

The major difference between the two federations is that AGIRC covers a single scheme, while ARRCO covers several schemes with their own regulations. This is a result of the different processes which led to their respective establishment. One of ARRCO's functions is to harmonize the regulations of member schemes in such a way that members receive equivalent benefits whatever ARRCO funds they belonged to during their working life. At the end of 1993, ARRCO covered 46 schemes managed by 111 funds and AGIRC covered 54 funds which operated a single scheme.

Several other features are worth mentioning with regard to benefits. Membership starts as soon as the work contract takes effect and it is not subject to the completion of a probationary period. This applies to all categories, including part-timers and workers employed for a very short period (seasonal workers for example). Vesting is immediate and there is a total portability of rights from one fund to another. If a member leaves the federation before retirement, the points acquired are kept in his or her account and their value will continue to increase with the point's value. Pension points are credited for periods of incapacity for work due to sickness, maternity or injury and also for periods of unemployment and early retirement. In the latter case, the contributions are paid by the unemployment insurance scheme and the state. In regard to the benefit formula, since contributions are proportional to earnings, the pension replicates movements of earnings over the member's entire working life. It is the general pattern of the whole career which is taken into account. In addition to old age pensions, the two federations also provide for survivors' pensions (60 per cent of the points acquired by the deceased spouse).

With regard to taxation, the same treatment is applied to all pension contributions. Employers' contributions to a pension scheme are fully deductible by the employer provided that the scheme applies to all the employees or to a defined category of employees and that the contributions are paid to a pension institution or an insurance company (allocations to book reserves are not deductible). Total contributions by both employer and employee to compulsory pension schemes are not taxable to the employee as long as they do not exceed 19 per cent of eight times the social security ceiling. The following pension schemes are considered compulsory pension schemes by the tax authorities: the general scheme, the compulsory supplementary schemes (ARRCO, AGIRC and the few institutions independent of the two federations) and arrangements which meet the following requirements: to be compulsory for all employees or for a specific category, to apply the same level of contribution to each employee of the specified category, to include an employer contribution, to provide for a pension (and not for a lump sum). On the whole, the threshold over which pension contributions are taxable to the employee (19 per cent of eight times the social) only concerns very high salaries, but this favourable tax treatment is associated with strict requirements. The pensions themselves are considered as taxable income.

2.4 Pension decisions in ARRCO and AGIRC schemes

ARRCO and AGIRC schemes have been set up through collective bargaining agreements which took place at national level. The state generalized compulsory second-tier provision in extending the scope of these agreements to the few branches of industry not covered by them. The two federations are considered private bodies acting in the general interest. In other words, mandatory coverage is implemented by private institutions.

At all levels of their organizational structure, ARRCO and AGIRC are run jointly by employers' and employees' representatives. A principle of equal representation, with chairmanship alternating between the two sides, is in force in all the institutions involved, from the individual funds to the federations. Moreover, all the policy decisions relating to the schemes are taken through collective bargaining procedures. The process is similar in the two federations. The basic principles are negotiated by representatives appointed by the national employers' organizations and trade union confederations involved. The interpretation and implementation of these principles are the responsibility of a joint committee, one in each federation. These committees have produced over time very precise regulations which govern the schemes. Besides, the regular decisions regarding the technical elements of the schemes, like the point's value and the purchase price of the point, are also taken on a joint basis.

The direct involvement of the state is extremely limited. The government's major role is to extend the binding power of the contractual agreements to sectors not covered by them. The legislation concerning compulsory supplementary pension provision is itself very small, just a few pages in the social security code. The schemes created in fact their own law through collective bargaining, and as there have been relatively few disputes, jurisprudential law is not developed. On the whole, we have here an example of the employers' organizations and trade unions, the so-called 'social partners', acting as virtual legislators, with their decisions having a binding power at national level.

This should of course be understood in the general context of the relationship between the state and society in France (see Rosanvallon, 1990). In particular, if the direct involvement of the state is very limited in operating and controlling the schemes, it still plays an indirect role which is far from trivial. In 1947, for example, the government created the conditions of the national agreement establishing the AGIRC scheme. It was the Minister of Labour who took the initiative to set up the joint committee which led to this agreement, and this joint committee was chaired by a senior civil servant (the assistant director of Social Security). The history of AGIRC and ARRCO has not been fully analysed yet, but doubtless the state (government and administration) has had a part in setting up these schemes which are run jointly by employers' and employees' representatives.

2.5 Coverage

ARRCO schemes now cover virtually all employees in the private sector and the competitive public sector. In 1995, there was only one exception amongst the members of the general scheme: airline flight staff, who have their own compulsory supplementary scheme (17 777 members at the end of 1991). As of 31 December 1991, the total number of members of ARRCO schemes amounted to 17.1 million, which represents approximately 14.2 million individual members.[2] By comparison, as of 1 July 1992, the general social security scheme, which also covers public employees other than civil servants, had 14.7 million members. These figures are a good illustration of the fact that almost all the general scheme's members belong to an ARRCO scheme. The difference of 0.3 million members represents the non civil servants of the public sector, who belong to their own supplementary scheme (IRCANTEC), and to a few remaining exceptions. Among ARRCO schemes' members, 41.1 per cent are women; given that membership is compulsory, this replicates the proportion of women among employees in the private sector in France. By the end of 1991, the number of beneficiaries was 5.5 million for old age pensions and 2.1 million for survivors' pensions.

The members of AGIRC are of course much less numerous, because the scheme only applies to a specific category, the cadres. As of 31 December 1991, the AGIRC scheme had 2.7 million members, including more than 2 million men (75 per cent) and 670 000 women (25 per cent). As the cadres are also affiliated to an ARRCO scheme, this means that 19 per cent of ARRCO schemes' members belong to the AGIRC scheme. The number of beneficiaries stood at 822 000 for old age pensions and 344 000 for survivors' pensions.

---

[2] Many employees are members of more than one scheme and ARRCO has great difficulties in eliminating double counting and knowing the exact number of individual members.

No accurate data are available regarding coverage by voluntary arrangements. The last estimate was less than 790 000 members during the mid 1980s. This figure is probably lower today, as many of the company schemes closed several years ago and no longer accept new members. The most accurate data with regard to beneficiaries are provided by a 1989 AGIRC survey, which only concerns newly retired cadres. Within this restricted population, only 6.6 per cent receive a company pension. They represent the category which receives the highest overall pension with the highest replacement rate. In other words, the available data show that for the most part voluntary arrangements secure a high overall pension at a high replacement rate to a limited population earning high salaries.

2.6   Income packaging: the role of second-tier pensions

Pensions represent the main source of income for former employees. As already mentioned, in households where the head was previously an employee, 85.2 per cent of the household income came in 1984 from pensions (Table 3.1). In the overall figure, second-tier pensions play a major role in supplementing first-tier pensions. The two compulsory tiers – the general scheme on the one hand, and ARRCO and AGIRC schemes on the other hand – form in fact a complete system in terms of benefits.

One of the expressed aims in establishing supplementary schemes was to bring private sector employees into line with civil servants with regard to pension provision. The available data show that second-tier schemes combine with the general scheme to fulfil this objective successfully. A survey carried out in 1988 by the Ministry of Social Affairs reveals no significant advantage on the part of civil servants as far as replacement rates are concerned (Lacroix 1993, pp. 533–5). For a full career, at an equal final salary level, replacement rates in the private sector and civil service are very similar. For medium and medium-high salaries, they are almost identical. The only discrepancy comes with high salaries for which the replacement rates are higher in the case of civil servants; this is because there are proportionally more very high salaries in the private sector and replacement rates tend to decrease as salaries increase.

The proportion of second-tier pensions in the overall pension varies widely depending on the level of earnings and the pattern of the career.

Table 3.3 – Average old age monthly pensions (1988)

Pension	ARRCO		ARRCO and AGIRC less than 15 years		ARRCO and AGIRC more than 15 years	
	Francs	*%*	*Francs*	*%*	*Francs*	*%*
General scheme	**2 815**	**71.6**	**4 170**	**55.8**	**4 834**	**36.3**
Supplementary schemes	**1 114**	**28.4**	**3 300**	**44.2**	**8 501**	**63.7**
ARRCO	1 114	28.4	2 115	28.3	2 635	19.8
AGIRC			1 185	15.9	5 866	44.0
Total	**3 929**	**100.0**	**7 470**	**100.0**	**13 335**	**100.0**

Note: Employees who have only belonged to the general scheme and to ARRCO and AGIRC schemes.

Source: SESI, Ministry of Social Affairs.

Table 3.4 – Average old age monthly pensions for employees with a full career (1988)

Pension	ARRCO		ARRCO and AGIRC less than 15 years		ARRCO and AGIRC more than 15 years	
	Francs	*%*	*Francs*	*%*	*Francs*	*%*
General scheme	**3 989**	**68.5**	**4 789**	**55.8**	**4 976**	**36.5**
Supplementary schemes	**1 836**	**31.5**	**3 786**	**44.2**	**8 673**	**63.5**
ARRCO	1 836	31.5	2 523	29.4	2 740	20.1
AGIRC			1 263	14.7	5 933	43.5
Total	**5 825**	**100.0**	**8 575**	**100.0**	**13 649**	**100.0**

Note: Employees who have only belonged to the general scheme and to ARRCO and AGIRC schemes.

Source: SESI, Ministry of Social Affairs.

A good illustration of this is given by survey data from the Ministry of Social Affairs. The distinction between cadres and non-cadres is, in particular, very clear-cut (Tables 3.3 and 3.4). For pensioners who have only been members of the general scheme and ARRCO schemes, the second-tier pension represents a total of 28.4 per cent of their overall pension, and 31.5 per cent if they had a full career (at least 37.5 years). As far as cadres are concerned, it accounts for more than 63 per cent where they had the cadre status for more than 15 years, and 44.2 per cent where their career as a cadre lasted less than 15 years. These figures show the extent to which the relative weight of supplementary pensions in the overall pension tends to grow as the level of working life earnings increases. They illustrate the way second-tier schemes play their role in supplementing the general social security scheme.

2.7   Effects of second-tier provision on income differences

ARRCO and AGIRC schemes apply a principle of proportionality between contributions and benefits and their pension formulas reproduce the movements of earnings over the entire working life. Moreover, the fraction of earnings taken into account is very wide: up to three times the social security ceiling[3] for non-cadre employees and up to eight times the ceiling for cadres.[4] Therefore, with regard to benefits paid, ARRCO and AGIRC schemes counterbalance the redistributive effects in operation within the general scheme (for these redistributive effects see Caussat, 1994). This reflects well in the replacement rates provided by the different tiers at several selected levels of earnings (Table 3.5).

For low-level earnings, the general scheme accounts for most of the replacement of final salary. Its pension formula, based on average earnings of the ten best years at work, may even lead to an overall replacement rate higher than 100 per cent for careers in which earnings had fallen. As the level of earnings increases, the fall of the replacement rate of the first-tier pension is, to a large extent, counterbalanced by the rise of that of second-tier pensions. For high-level earnings, supplementary pensions come to predominate in the overall pension, and as a consequence the total replacement rate is maintained at a fairly high level. For the highest category of earnings (16 000 F and over), for example, with a replacement rate of 46 per cent, second-tier pensions play a major

---

[3] The social security contribution ceiling is a little higher than the average gross earnings in the private sector (in October 1992, it stood for example at 12 150 F, while the average monthly gross earnings amounted to 10 816 F).

[4] For the fraction of their earnings up to the ceiling, cadres are covered by an ARRCO scheme and from one to eight ceilings by the AGIRC scheme.

Table 3.5 – Net replacement rate (%) for employees with a full career (1988)

| Final monthly net earnings | First tier | Second tier | | | Total |
		ARRCO	AGIRC	Others	
Less than 5 000 F	76	26	0	0	102
5 000 F–5 999 F	69	24	0	0	94
6 000 F–7 999 F	60	26	1	0	88
8 000 F–9 999 F	50	27	3	0	80
10 000 F–11 999 F	42	28	10	0	80
12 000 F–15 999 F	34	23	17	1	75
16 000 F and over	20	13	32	1	66

Note: Employees born in 1922 who have a total of 37.5 years' insurance or more in the general scheme and who did not belong to any other first-tier scheme.

Source: SESI, Ministry of Social Affairs.

Table 3.6 – Net replacement rate (%) for male and female employees with a full career (1988)

| Final monthly net earnings | Men | | | Women | | |
	1st tier	2nd tier	Total	1st tier	2nd tier	Total
Less than 5 000 F	86	27	113	72	23	95
5 000 F–5 999 F	75	27	102	60	19	79
6 000 F–7 999 F	63	30	93	57	22	79
8 000 F–9 999 F	52	32	84	49	26	75
10 000 F–11 999 F	43	40	83	41	33	74
12 000 F–15 999 F	34	43	77	34	35	69
16 000 F and over	20	46	66			

Note: Employees born in 1922 who have a total of 37.5 years' insurance or more in the general scheme and who did not belong to any other first-tier scheme.

Source: SESI, Ministry of Social Affairs.

role in securing an overall pension which reaches two-thirds of final net salary.

A breakdown by gender shows considerable differences between men and women (Table 3.6). For the same level of final earnings, the replacement rates are always significantly lower for women than for men. This is for the most part due to second-tier pensions. These differences replicate in fact to a large extent discrepancies between men and women on the labour market, and supplementary pensions play a major role in this as they are strictly proportional to earnings over the entire working life.

On the whole, men and employees with high salaries depend more on second-tier pensions than women and employees with low-level earnings. This means that, with regard to retirement income, men and high-salary earners rely more extensively on contractual arrangements, while women and low-salary earners depend more on schemes in which the major actor is the state.

3. Trends over time

Over the last few years, two major changes have occurred in the general framework of second-tier provision in France. On the one hand, the concentration in ARRCO and AGIRC of all the compulsory supplementary funds for employees in the private sector has almost been achieved. On the other hand, ARRCO and AGIRC schemes have decided to remove the optional arrangements they were offering above the minimum compulsory rate and to adopt a single contribution rate. These two trends play an important part in the general process of adaptation that the French pension system is currently experiencing. They contribute to a reshaping of its overall structure.

3.1 Grouping of second-tier compulsory funds in ARRCO and AGIRC

When compulsory membership of supplementary schemes was made universal by law in 1972, this mandatory coverage consisted for the most part in extending to all the members of the general social security scheme the scope of the collective agreements which govern ARRCO and AGIRC schemes. Still, few exceptions were made with regard to employees affiliated to other supplementary schemes. At the beginning of the 1990s, there were in the private sector three schemes operated by funds totally independent of the two federations: the schemes for employees of social security institutions, airline flight staff and Air France ground staff. In addition, three schemes were partially independent with regard to cadres: in the banking sector, savings bank and agricultural services.

In 1993, the Air France fund (around 26 000 members) joined ARRCO and AGIRC. In 1994, the social security institutions' staff fund (almost 190 000 members) did the same, as did the funds covering cadres in the banking sector (57 000 members).

All these funds were providing benefits noticeably higher than the ARRCO and AGIRC schemes. They were operating generous final salary schemes, but even though they covered limited population groups they had not pre-funded their commitments. Faced with unfavourable demographic trends within their respective branches of industry, they were in an extremely fragile financial situation. The funds in the banking sector are a good example of this. They were hit by the considerable restructuring of the sector in the mid 1980s: their demographic ratio had dramatically worsened and their resources in terms of contributions were affected by the shrinking of total earnings in the sector. Their liabilities were practically unfunded: they only had 14 billion francs' worth of assets to cover commitments that rose to an estimated 100 billion francs. Such a situation was not viable and the banking sector negotiated the integration of the funds within ARRCO and AGIRC federations. This has been effective since 1 January 1994. A similar process occurred for the Air France fund and the social security institutions' staff fund.

This trend illustrates the inability of pay-as-you-go schemes to operate on a long-term basis when they rely on a narrow demographic base, whether it is a company or an industry. It makes the scheme totally dependent on economic developments experienced by the company or the industry it covers. As long as their demography was favourable, the few funds which were maintained outside ARRCO and AGIRC were able to provide higher benefits than those in the two federations; but when they were faced with a reversal of the previous trend, they had to join the federations and participate in the general pooling of resources they are operating at national level. In this move, members had to accept a lowering of their second-tier provision.

In 1995, only one institution is still totally independent of ARRCO and AGIRC: the airline flight staff fund (around 18 000 members). Two institutions participate in ARRCO, but not in AGIRC: the funds for savings banks and for agricultural services (around 34 000 and 240 000 members respectively of which only a minority would be eligible for the AGIRC scheme). Besides, of these two last exceptions for cadres the latter is currently considering its integration in AGIRC.

On the whole, the process of grouping all the compulsory supplementary funds operating in the private sector in two federations has almost been achieved today. It fits in with the general trend that led to the creation of ARRCO and the achievement of universal coverage. All this development has been sustained by a double impetus: a technical necessity and an egalitarian dynamic. Both of them interacted and went in the same direction. The technical dimension relates to the necessity of extending a mechanism of full financial compensation to secure the long-term viability of unfunded schemes to the entire private sector. The egalitarian aspect refers to the establishment of pension schemes for two social groups, the civil servants and the cadres, and the subsequent process of extending similar provision to all the employees, whatever their status, conditions of employment and branch of activity.

3.2   Phasing out of optional arrangements in ARRCO and AGIRC

ARRCO and AGIRC are currently undergoing profound change. They are heading towards a single-rate contribution system. The previous situation was the following. Above and beyond the compulsory rate, the schemes within the two federations offered options which allowed improvements in the level of benefits. In ARRCO, the rate could go from 4 per cent to a maximum of 8 per cent on earnings up to the social security ceiling. In AGIRC, the minimum rate was 12 per cent on the portion of earnings between one and eight ceilings (8 per cent for companies created before 1981); the maximum rate could go up to 16 per cent. These were the prevailing conditions up to early 1993.

In February 1993, employers' representatives and trade unions signed an agreement providing for the gradual phasing out of optional arrangements in ARRCO. They fixed the single contribution rate at 6 per cent (to be implemented by 1 January 1999), halfway between the two previous limits and a little higher than the average rate (5.15 per cent in 1991). A year later, in February 1994, a similar agreement was signed for AGIRC. It provides for a gradual increase of the minimum rate up to the current maximum of 16 per cent (to be reached in 2003 at the latest).

There are two main reasons for these changes. On the one hand, from a technical point of view, to adopt a single rate system secures the long-term durability of the schemes. With optional arrangements, the viability of pay-as-you-go schemes can be threatened if the average contribution rate is on a long-term decreasing trend. This could have been the case for ARRCO and AGIRC, as employment currently increases in small companies, which tend to stay at the minimum rate, while it is falling in big firms which, for the most part, have chosen the maximum rate. On the other hand, the phasing out of optional arrangements fits in with the process of European integration. Maintaining them could have run the risk of challenges to the national monopoly of ARRCO and AGIRC, as EU institutions are putting forward the freedom to provide services throughout the Union. The two federations can all the better justify their national monopoly in compulsory second-tier provision since they no longer offer arrangements that could have been considered to fall within the scope of competitive market.

The negotiations between employers' representatives and trade unions were very tough, in particular with regard to the AGIRC scheme and the fixing of the new compulsory rate at the previous maximum. The issue at stake was to fix a limit to the extension of pay-as-you-go compulsory provision and to open a space for voluntary funded arrangements to develop. As the cadres were obviously the category which was more likely to be concerned by such provision, it was about their scheme that the negotiations were particularly hard. Trade unions unanimously supported the adoption of the maximum rate, as well as the technical staff of the scheme, but very strong tensions arose within the employers' organization, the CNPF. The insurance companies' federation, heavily involved in the promotion of funded arrangements, made strong attempts inside the confederation to try to obtain a lower rate which would have left more room for such arrangements to develop. The employers' organization finally chose to secure the durability of the scheme in accepting the principle of a progressive increase up to the previous maximum rate.

The phasing out of optional arrangements and the adoption of a single contribution rate system in ARRCO and AGIRC is an important change in the French pension system. It means that companies or industries willing to improve second-tier provision beyond the compulsory minimum will no longer have the two possibilities they previously had: to raise their contribution rates in ARRCO and AGIRC schemes or to set up voluntary arrangements. They will only have the latter. This change obviously opens a space for funded arrangements to develop. It also raises the question of what type of funded arrangements should be promoted. This issue began to be discussed in the early 1990s and has been an ongoing debate since. It developed parallel to the debate concerning the reform of the general scheme and the regular discussions which take place within ARRCO and AGIRC to maintain a balance between benefits and contributions.

4. Reforms and prospects

As in the other industrialized countries, the pension system in France is involved in a process of adaptation to socio-economic and demographic changes. Three elements are worth mentioning with respect to the relation between the two tiers of the system: the lowering of the normal retirement age in 1983, the adjustments in compulsory schemes, and the debate concerning the introduction of new funded arrangements.

4.1 Lowering of the normal retirement age

In 1983, the government (composed of socialists and a few communists) decided to lower the normal retirement age in the general scheme from 65 to 60. This move and the subsequent developments are interesting to mention here because they are a good illustration of how the two compulsory tiers are closely linked and form a system. They shed light on the interaction at work and on the relationship between the state and the 'social partners', i.e., the employers' organization and the trade unions.

After the government took its decision, the employers' organization and the trade unions decided not to follow suit in ARRCO and AGIRC schemes. This led to a long discussion between the government and the social partners which finally ended up in the creation of a special fund to finance the reduction in retirement age in the two federations (for an account of the debates and a detailed description of the fund, see Ruellan, 1983). The mechanism works as follows. ARRCO and AGIRC schemes brought their regulations in line with the general scheme by dropping their early retirement actuarial reductions for members aged between 60 and 65. The cost of this alignment is financed by an ad hoc fund, the ASF (Association for the management of the financial structure). This fund is jointly run by the employers' organization and the trade unions. It is financed by contributions levied on earnings by the unemployment insurance scheme and by a state subsidy.

The rationale behind the creation of the ASF was to transfer a proportion of the monies that had been previously allotted to an early retirement plan to the ARRCO and AGIRC schemes. This plan was withdrawn as a consequence of the lowering of the retirement age in the general scheme. The ASF pays the outstanding allowances, as well as the cost of the reduction in retirement age in ARRCO and AGIRC schemes. It is financed by the resources that were financing the former plan, that is employer and employee contributions collected by the unemployment insurance scheme and a state subsidy. The fund was set up in 1983 for an initial period of seven years; in 1990, its life was extended until 31 December 1993. At the end of 1993, a new agreement was concluded between the state and the social partners for a period of three years, ending on 31 December 1996.

Each time, the issue at stake is the financing: the level of the contributions collected and the amount of the state subsidy. The employers' organization and the trade unions stated that, if they did not have proper resources to finance normal retirement age at 60, they would have to reinstitute in ARRCO and AGIRC schemes the actuarial reductions for retirement before age 65. Until now, they have never had to carry out this threat, but have always come to an agreement with the government.

For the first seven-year period (from 1983 to 1990), the state subsidy was fixed at 10 billion francs per year and the contributions at 2 per cent of gross salary up to four times the social security ceiling (divided 40/60 between employees and employers as for unemployment contributions). This reflected the respective share of state subsidy and unemployment insurance contributions to the financing of the former early retirement plan, that is a third from the state and two-thirds from employer and employee contributions. In 1990, the agreement concerning the perpetuation of the ASF until the end of 1993 changed this ratio significantly. The state subsidy was considerably reduced to a billion francs per year, while the contribution rate was not deeply altered: it was lowered from 2 per cent to 1.8 per cent on earnings up to the social security ceiling and was maintained at 2 per cent on earnings from one to four times the ceiling. This withdrawal on the part of the state reflected the fact that the allowances of the former plan to be financed by the ASF declined drastically over the period. At the end of 1993, the ASF faced an 8.7 billion franc deficit. The agreement which was concluded in December 1993 for a three-year period set the state subsidy at 1.570 billion francs a year and raised the contributions of 0.16 points at 1.96 per cent on earnings up to the ceiling and of 0.18 points at 2.18 per cent on earnings from one to four ceilings. The contribution increase was shared equally between employees and employers, which means that the contributions to the ASF are no longer divided 40/60 as in the unemployment insurance scheme. This agreement is effective until 31 December 1996.

These negotiations concerning the financing of the reduction in retirement age in ARRCO and AGIRC schemes are a good illustration of the interdependence between first-tier and second-tier schemes. They also show how the social partners, together with the government, can be involved at national level in the decision-making process concerning the pension system.

4.2 Adjustments in compulsory schemes

The general scheme and the federations ARRCO and AGIRC made provisions to adapt to socio-economic and demographic shifts. The adjustment mechanisms in the two types of schemes are very different.

The general scheme is a classical pay-as-you-go defined benefit scheme (it provides 50 per cent of average earnings, up to the social security ceiling, over a given period). In this type of scheme, adjustments can take two forms: increasing the level of contributions to meet the cost of benefit commitments or altering the commitments themselves. To limit the increases in contributions, the government has altered the global formula for determining benefits in the general scheme. Three provisions were adopted in 1993: (1) a gradual lengthening of the contribution period before entitlement to a full pension before age 65 (from 37.5 years to 40 years), (2) a gradual extension of the earnings period taken into account for calculation of the pension (from the best ten years to the best twenty-five years), and (3) indexation of pensions and average earnings in the pension formula to price increases (for a period of five years ending in 1998). This reform came into force in 1994.

Adjustments in ARRCO and AGIRC schemes take a very different form. We have seen that the scheme's financial equilibrium is ensured, in this type of scheme, in keeping benefits in line with contributions. This is done on a year by year basis through fixing the scheme's parameters. Since the late 1970s and the early 1980s, the administrators of the schemes have implemented a policy of gradual reduction of the schemes' yield, that is, a reduction of the ratio between the value of a point in a given year and its purchase price. They did so in arbitrating between the interests involved: those of contributors (i.e., members and employers) and those of pensioners. The reduction was carried out in such a way that the burden is shared between the two sides. On the one hand, increases in the point's value have been less favourable than in the previous period and, on the other hand, increases in the point's real purchase price have been higher than the rise in members' average earnings. The latter has been achieved by using a third parameter of the schemes, the contribution collection rate or call-up rate.

The so-called 'call-up rate' was introduced to give more flexibility to the system. It enables contributions to be collected, or called up, at a different rate from the contractual contribution rate (e.g., 6 per cent in ARRCO and 16 per cent in AGIRC) without interfering in the mechanism for building up entitlements.[5] In other words, a call-up rate above 100 per cent means that an extra contribution above the contractual contribution rate which does not build up pension credits is paid to ensure the scheme's financial equilibrium. This keeps the value of the point stable while keeping the movements of its purchase price in line with the changes in members' average earnings. In 1995, the call-up rates were relatively high, reaching 125 per cent in both ARRCO and AGIRC, and it will probably be difficult to raise them significantly. Some, in particular the insurance companies' federation within the employers' organization, are even urging freezing them at their current level.

On the whole, although through different methods, the two tiers which form the compulsory pension system are involved in a reduction of their yield. The effects of this adjustment are difficult to assess. They do not automatically mean a fall in terms of overall replacement rate. The reform of the general scheme by lengthening the contribution period could for example lead to longer careers, which will improve the contribution record in ARRCO and AGIRC schemes and counterbalance in this way the reduction in yield. Besides, the adoption of a single contribution rate in ARRCO and AGIRC will increase the average contribution rate in the two federations and this will again, at least on average, improve the contribution record. So if the cost of financing pension provision will undoubtedly increase in the foreseeable future, the consequences for the level of the pensions themselves are far from being clear. The few studies that have been made to assess the effects of recent adjustments on replacement rates do not lead to definite conclusions.

---

[5] The call-up rate was introduced in 1952 in the AGIRC scheme because the collection of 100 per cent of contributions would have led to an excessive increase in the reserves of the scheme. It was kept under 100 per cent from 1952 to 1965, and it is above 100 per cent since 1979. It has never been under 100 per cent in ARRCO.

Cornilleau and Sterdyniak (1994) show for example in their analysis of a few hypothetical profiles that in some cases the replacement rate of the overall pension will not fall in 2013 and might even increase.

The adjustments in compulsory schemes also raise the question of voluntary provision. The space for new voluntary arrangements to develop depends to a large extent on the decisions taken in ARRCO and AGIRC. The adoption of a single rate system in the two federations has cleared the way: there is no longer a direct competition between pay-as-you-go schemes and funded arrangements. To go beyond compulsory provision the latter approach is now the only one available. Nevertheless, the decisions concerning call-up rates in ARRCO and AGIRC still have some implications for voluntary provision. To increase them limits the overall contributive power and reduces in proportion the amount of contributions which can be paid into funded arrangements. So the issue at stake in future negotiations concerning call-up rates will be the following alternative: to favour universal pay-as-you-go provision in sustaining the points' value in ARRCO and AGIRC schemes or to freeze or reduce the level of contribution in these schemes and favour the development of funded provision. In the near future this will probably be a main element of the French debate concerning pension provision.

4.3 Debate on funded arrangements

A debate concerning the introduction of new funded arrangements has developed in France since the early 1990s. It has two main features. One is that it has been more supply than demand oriented. It was initiated by providers of funded products (originally the insurance companies) wanting to develop a new market and not by employers eager to introduce new company arrangements. The second characteristic is that economical and financial issues became widely dominant. As the debate evolved, funded arrangements were seen by more and more players as an effective means to boost long-term savings and provide capital to French companies.

On the whole, the debate has been largely determined by the conflicting interests of the main actors involved: insurance companies, banks, large companies. Each of them made their own proposal for new legislation. Two major splits appeared. The first opposes the proponents of external funding (insurance companies and banks) and those in favour of German-type book reserves (large companies). The employers' organization (CNPF), which has supporters of both sides among its members, did not choose and its proposal is to back the two options. The second split is between insurance companies and banks. Insurance companies want the new arrangements to provide life annuities exclusively, banks want the choice between the payment of an annuity or a lump sum to be left open to members. The employers' organization has adopted a compromise solution in its proposal, which satisfies none of the parties: the member could choose between an annuity or a lump sum but only when entering the scheme.

Individual employers have not been very active in the debate. Only big firms, which for the most part already have voluntary arrangements, often unfunded, came into the discussion in expressing their preference for book reserves. By and large, employers see voluntary funded arrangements more as an increase in social security contributions than as an effective instrument of work force management. In addition, representatives of small and medium-size firms expressed serious doubts on the capacity of funded arrangements to provide capital for their type of company. On the trade union side, the emphasis has been on the defence of the compulsory schemes, and trade union officials, at least in the confederations, are very suspicious of funded arrangements and of their proponents.

The successive governments (left until early 1993 and then right) have been very cautious on the matter. The consensus concerning the pay-as-you-go technique is high in France and funding with regard to pension provision is a touchy issue. Besides, the expression of conflicting interests among the proponents of funded arrangements did not prompt the authorities to make a quick move. On the other hand, members of Parliament have been very active: four private bills have been brought in by MPs from the current majority (right and centre right) between early 1993 and mid 1994. The last one was adopted in May 1994 by the Finance Committee of the National Assembly. It tries to combine economical goals (to promote long-term savings and capital formation) with social goals (to introduce voluntary provision to supplement the existing two-tier compulsory system). This proposal has not been discussed in session as the government did not want this to happen before the presidential election (April–May 1995). Following the election, the new right-wing government seemed at first eager to have legislation passed. But after the strikes triggered at the end of 1995 by the Prime Minister's plan to reform the social insurance system, it postponed action on the question.

In any case, the debate is not over. The development of voluntary arrangements leads to tax expenditures and the general context of reduction in public deficits to meet the criteria of the Maastricht Treaty is not favourable to granting new tax incentives. Besides, several questions remain to be settled. They relate in particular to the characteristics of arrangements to be promoted, their role within the overall pension system and the advantage that employees and employers could find in their introduction. Moreover, considering the major role played by the ARRCO and AGIRC schemes, the question of what space funded arrangements really have to develop in is still open.

By and large, work is in progress within the French society to find new compromises over pension issues. It is not completed and the process of adaptation of the French pension system to the new socio-economic and demographic context will undoubtedly continue during the coming years.

5. Toward an interpretative framework and policy issues

Three elements characterize the setting up of second-tier pension provision in France: an involvement of national work-related actors, a dynamic of universalization of distinctive features, and a marked preference for pay-as-you-go. These three elements form a global coherence; they are interdependent and make up a definite configuration peculiar to France.

In short, the creation of the second tier in France is the result of a negotiation process between the national employers' organization and the trade union confederations which has been favoured by the state (government and administration). This is very much in line with the constructivist approach that the state has historically had in France in its relation to society (see for example Schnapper, 1994). More precisely, it relates to the specific effort made by the state since 1789 to produce sociability and fill up the void created by the suppression of all intermediary bodies during the French Revolution (see Rosanvallon, 1990).

The national nature of the actors involved is intimately linked with the nationwide nature of the coverage provided. This is the outcome of the following process: a social differentiation followed by a dynamic of universalization of the distinctive features that had been produced. The differentiation was in the creation of specific pension schemes for civil servants and for cadres. These schemes acted as a double reference. The civil service special scheme set the general norm. Then the creation of a new social group, the cadres, with their own pension scheme supplied a model for pension provision in the private sector: a type of scheme that can supplement first-tier provision and bring private sector employees in line with civil servants. The dynamic of universalization led to the generalization of this model to all members of the general social security scheme. The process has been carried out by the action of the national employers' organization and the trade union confederations, and completed by the state.

The third element, the marked preference for pay-as-you-go, relates to both technical and political factors. From the technical or financial point of view in France, pay-as-you-go is by and large considered safer than funding with regard to pension provision. The traditional British or American view of funding as a source of security for pension rights is somehow reversed in France: funding is widely viewed as a risky procedure, a technique that is unable to guarantee the value of pension rights over time (these opposite perceptions between Britain and France have already been pointed out by Lynes, 1985). The trust in pay-as-you-go and the symmetric distrust about funding are in part based on experience (on the one hand the level of pensions paid by pay-as-you-go schemes, on the other hand the losses French investors suffered from the First World War to the mid-century). But it probably also relates to the technical process at work.

Pay-as-you-go is a form of sharing resources. In pay-as-you-go, a community or a group distributes available resources among its members. The French word used for pay-as-you-go, 'répartition', expresses exactly such a process: it means 'sharing'. The trust in pay-as-you-go rests to a large extent on the feeling that the national community is able to distribute available resources between the working population and the retirees, and that it can do so by its own direct action and does not have to rely on capital market mechanisms. This fits in with the political aspect of the strong support of pay-as-you-go. Besides, political and technical dimensions reinforce each other. Technically, pay-as-you-go implies a pooling of risks at national level to secure the long-term durability of the schemes. In other words, a general solidarity among the national community has to be implemented: a solidarity between workers and pensioners and a solidarity among the working population. This concept of solidarity is politically essential in France with regard to pension provision.

The marked preference for pay-as-you-go is also technically very well in accordance with the two other characteristic elements of second-tier provision in France. On the one hand, national work-related actors are able, through a process of incorporation of private interests, to defend the general interest, which is a necessary condition for operating pay-as-you-go schemes on a long-term basis. On the other hand, the process of generalization of second-tier provision secured the system by extending the group of solidarity (in technical terms, the pooling of risks) to all the employees in the private sector.

The general configuration formed by the three elements above provides a framework for understanding how second-tier provision has been set up and organized in France. It is also useful when approaching the current situation and the various possibilities of evolution. This configuration has in fact been under strain for several years. All its constituent elements are raising questions, and it is in these questions that the issues which are at stake today can be seen.

The national nature of the actors who are involved in second-tier provision means that few decisions with regard to pensions are taken by or in the firm. The suppression of optional arrangements in ARRCO and AGIRC schemes has even reduced the little room for manoeuvre that the firm had previously. So a double question is raised today. Is the firm going to become a place where decisions concerning pension provision are taken? And if so what will be the roles of the different actors within the firm: the employer, employees' representatives, and individual employees?

The dynamic of universalization of distinctive features has led to a generalization of second-tier provision among employees in the private sector. By and large, this brought them in line with civil servants as regards pension provision. This is already shown by available data on current replacement rates and it has been even better achieved since the adoption of a single rate contribution system in ARRCO and AGIRC schemes. Among private sector employees, the discrepancy between cadres and non-cadres, which produced the impetus for the process of generalization, is also achieved with respect to pension provision. This double achievement raises two main issues.[6] The first one relates to the

---

[6] A third issue could be to ask whether the major reference, the special scheme for civil servants, will be questioned or not; but this falls outside the scope of this chapter. It should nonetheless be mentioned that this is a very touchy issue. The Prime Minister's plan to reform the special schemes was one of the main factors that triggered the strikes which blocked trains, public transport and the mail all over France for a month during November and December 1995.

scheme for cadres. Now that pension provision differences among employees in the private sector have been suppressed, is it necessary to maintain a specific scheme for cadres or should it be integrated in ARRCO? Some in the employers' organization have already advocated the latter approach. This fits with the project, also expressed by some employers, of suppressing the cadre status. The second issue relates to new possible differentiations among employees with regard to pension provision. This raises questions over the type of differentiation, the extent of the differences produced, the categories of employees involved, etc. Subsequently, one can wonder if the creation of new differentiations will once again lead to a process of generalization or not.

The preference for pay-as-you-go has not really been challenged by the recent debate concerning the introduction of new funded arrangements. Still, considering the rising cost of financing pension provisions, French society is faced today with few options and some entail departing from the pay-as-you-go approach. Three main options are in fact possible:

1) to supplement the existing two-tier compulsory system by introducing new funded arrangements (voluntary or compulsory),

2) to increase contributions to the pay-as-you-go schemes to offset the reduction in yield, and

3) to accumulate reserves in existing pay-as-you-go schemes.

Various combinations of these three options can of course be implemented. On the one hand, the choices relate to technical and economic aspects. This refers to the well-developed controversy concerning pay-as-you-go and funding with regard to their capacity to provide pensions and their respective effects on national savings and economic growth. On the other hand, the choices concerning the financing technique are linked to the other issues at stake and they will have retroactive effects on the actors involved and the differentiations produced. To develop arrangements at the firm level implies for example that these arrangements have to be funded; and if they are voluntary, they will doubtless create new differentiations among employees.

In certain respects the French pension system is at a cross-roads today. A new configuration is in the process of emerging from the current one. The range of the issues at stake is wide and the issues are deeply interrelated. One of the novelties of the present situation is the entry of a new set of actors and of a new logic in the debate on pension provision: the financial institutions (insurance companies, banks, investment managers, etc.) and the approach of pension schemes as instruments of financing the economy. The future of the overall pension system in France will in part depend on the importance these new actors and this new logic are given in pension issues.

References

Boltanski, Luc (1982), *Les cadres: la formation d'un groupe social*, Paris: Ed. de Minuit.

Caussat, Laurent (1994), 'Retraite et correction des aléas de carrière', INSEE, Division 'Etudes sociales', mimeo.

Cornilleau, Gérard and Sterdyniak, Henri (1994), 'Les retraites en France: des réformes sans plan d'ensemble', *Lettre de l'OFCE* 126, 26 March 1994.

Friot, Bernard (1996), 'The Origins of French Supplementary Pension Plans: The Creation of The General Association of Pension Institutions for Cadres (AGIRC), in E. Reynaud, L. apRoberts, B. Davies and G. Hughes (eds.), *International Perspectives on Supplementary Pensions: Actors and Issues*, Westport, CT: Quorum Books.

Lacroix, Jacqueline (1993), 'Eventail des retraites: logiques distinctes pour salariés et indépendants', in *Données sociales*, édition 1993, Paris: INSEE, 530–5.

Lynes, Tony (1985), *Paying for Pensions: The French Experience.* London: The London School of Economics and Political Science.

Netter, Francis (1977), 'Histoire des retraites complémentaires de salariés', *Droit social,* January, 58–63.

Reynaud, Emmanuel (with an article by Giovanni Tamburi) (1994), *Les retraites en France: le rôle des régimes complémentaires*, Paris: Documentation Française.

Reynaud, Emmanuel (1996), 'Financing Models for Pay-as-you-go Systems', in E. Reynaud, L. apRoberts, B. Davies and G. Hughes (eds.), *International Perspectives on Supplementary Pensions: Actors and Issues*, Westport, CT: Quorum Books.

Reynaud, Emmanuel (forthcoming), *Private Pension Plans in OECD Countries: France*, Paris: OECD.

Rosanvallon, Pierre (1990), *L'Etat en France de 1789 à nos jours*, Paris: Ed. du Seuil.

Ruellan, Rolande (1983), 'La retraite à 60 ans dans les régimes complémentaires', *Droit social* 7/8, July–August, 494–508.

Schnapper, Dominique (1994), *La communauté des citoyens: sur l'idée moderne de nation*, Paris: Gallimard.

4

The Public-private Mix in Pension Provision in Germany: The Role of Employer-based Pension Arrangements and the Influence of Public Activities[1]

Winfried Schmähl

1. Introduction

Structural changes in demography, economy (especially in the labour market) and society as well as changes in the political and economic environment have stimulated a new and intense debate about the future development of pension policy in Germany. As often in the past, the relative importance of public versus private provision in the area of old age security is on the agenda of political as well as scientific debates.[2] Present costs in social insurance as well as expected increasing future costs, mainly because of demographic aging, were the driving forces behind a major reform of the statutory (social) pension insurance decided upon by the (West) German Parliament on 9 November 1989. In the evening of the same day the unexpected opening of the Berlin wall occurred and the German unification was realized within less than one year. Additional problems and tasks also in pension policy were linked to this development, especially because of the differences in economic conditions in West and East Germany as well as because of structural differences in pension provision in the two parts of Germany with a separate develop-

---

[1] Sections 3, 6 and 7 of this paper are partly based on work done in collaboration with Stefan Böhm: see Schmähl and Böhm (1994a and 1994b).

[2] Thompson (1988), p. 211, mentions that the debate 'is motivated by some combination of four concerns: **1.** Future cost of the system. **2.** Impact of the system on the rate of investment. **3.** Distribution of the costs and benefits of the system. **4.** Effect of the system on retirement behavior.'

ment during more than 40 years. These differences are discussed in Schmähl (1991a and 1992b). High transfer payments from West to East Germany were necessary and took place also in the social pension insurance – financed mostly by contribution revenue and therefore resulting (ceteris paribus) in higher contribution rates and higher labour costs.

At present, the level and development of labour costs especially is a politically powerful argument in reform debate. Intensified international competition and high unemployment are very much linked in the German debate to high costs of social security. Proposals for radical reforms have been made by scientists, politicians and especially representatives of employers and industry organizations (abolishing earnings-related public pensions and introducing a flat-rate, tax-financed universal pension[3] – proposals for additional changes in the existing social insurance pension scheme as well as in shifting more towards private and funded pensions). See Schmähl 1994c. Therefore, the public-private mix in pension provision is on the agenda – as it was several times in the past, resulting inter alia from political decisions on public pensions, taxation and on regulating private pensions, but also resulting from decisions by courts of justice on the national as well as supranational level and last, but not least, from changing economic conditions on the markets for goods and labour.

This chapter tries to highlight the interaction of public and private pension provision in Germany within the complex arrangements developed over time. The chapter is organized as follows. Before dealing with the interrelation between public and private activities, some basic empirical background information is presented. The starting point is a description of the organizational and functional structure of the pension schemes in Germany (section 2). Thereafter some remarks concerning the historical development are made, showing the changing role of the public-private mix in old age protection (section 3). In addition some macro data concerning the present quantitative importance of several elements of the German pension schemes are presented (section 4), followed by an overview on data for occupational pension schemes according to branch of industry, company size and types of schemes and benefits (section 5). The next two sections present micro data concerning the frequency and level of pension benefits in occupa-

---

[3] An overview of the debate in Germany concerning flat-rate pensions – covering a period of more than 100 years – is given in Schmähl 1993b.

tional pension schemes, namely in the private sector (section 6) as well as for wage and salary earners in the public sector (section 7). As far as permitted by the present data, some information will be given concerning the question to what extent benefits from occupational pension schemes fulfil their supplementary function. For the public sector some features of the pension arrangements for wage and salary earners (- white- and blue-collar workers) are compared to the special pension scheme for civil servants (also in section 7). Thereafter the interaction of public and private activities is discussed (section 8).

All explanations will concentrate on the Federal Republic of Germany before the unification of the two German post-war states or on the situation in West Germany after unification. Special aspects which have resulted from the German unification will be dealt with only if they can be expected to endure in the future.

The final part of section 8 includes some tentative conclusions concerning recent developments and gives an outlook on future problems and possible developments. Remarks will be confined to Germany from a 'domestic' perspective. A European perspective, due to its complexity, would necessitate a paper of its own. (See Schmähl 1993a and references given there.)

2. Organizational and functional structure of Germany's system of pension provision – a short overview

In the Federal Republic of Germany there are numerous institutions operating in the field of old age security. Apart from the statutory pension insurance, which constitutes the basic pension scheme for about 80 per cent of the employees, institutions of occupational old age security play an important role for many employees with regard to their material provision for old age. As is the case for the statutory pension insurance, the range of benefits of occupational pension schemes includes not only benefits of old age protection, but also those in case of invalidity and for surviving dependants. In the frame of monetary old age protection for the employee the functions of occupational pension schemes supplement those of statutory basic schemes. Being a supplement clearly shows that public pension policy – beside tax policy, and decisions by courts and economic conditions of the firm as well as on the labour market – is among the most important influencing factors for those voluntary schemes.

Occupational old age security in the private sector is a voluntary social benefit provided by the employer and supplements pensions from the statutory pension insurance for wage and salary earners. Up to now occupational pension schemes in Germany have normally been financed entirely or to a large extent by the employer. In 1990, 97 per cent of all expenditure for occupational pension schemes in the private sector was paid by employers and only 3 per cent by employees (Heppt 1995, p. 161). Occupational pension schemes are an instrument aimed at achieving certain company goals, especially of personnel policy (only briefly mentioned here) and of financing. Here taxation of occupational pension schemes plays an important role.

There are also supplementary pension schemes in Germany for public employees which are provided by the employer and based on collective agreements that are very closely integrated with statutory pension insurance and also linked to the structure and development of the special pension scheme for civil servants. These supplementary schemes exist for both blue- and white-collar workers. Moreover, there is a special pension scheme for civil servants that combines elements of basic and supplementary old age security. The civil servants' pension scheme is not a topic of this chapter. Only some elements of it are mentioned in comparision to (and as an influencing factor for) the occupational pension scheme for wage and salary earners in the public sector.

In addition to the (old age) pension schemes there are also other pathways for exit from working life for older workers which in practice become instruments for providing income for people who are 'too old for a job, but too young for a regular old age pension'. Such pathways became more important in the middle of the 1990s because of the unfavourable labour market conditions. Benefits of former employees using these pathways (voluntarily or involuntarily) – e.g. from unemployment insurance – are sometimes supplemented by payments from firms (if a layoff of older workers is used as an instrument to reduce or restructure the work force of the firm). These elements of an income package for older people can only be mentioned briefly.

This chapter focuses on the population aged 55 and older. Table 4.1 gives some basic figures concerning the absolute number of people (male, female, in West and East Germany) in this age group. People aged 55 and older comprise about 26 per cent of the total population.

As can be seen from Table 4.1 there are remarkable differences in the socio-economic status in 1992 according to sex and 'old' and 'new' Länder of the Federal Republic. (In the following the 'old' parts of the

Table 4.1 – Population in Germany age 55 and older: absolute number and socio-economic status (1992)

	Men			Women		
	West	*East*	*Total*	*West*	*East*	*Total*
(A) Absolute number (thousands)						
55+	7 248	1 613	8 861	10 356	2 477	12 833
65+	3 485	700	4 185	6 514	1 474	7 991
(B) % of total population						
55+	8.95	1.99	10.94	12.79	3.06	15.85
65+	4.30	0.86	5.17	8.04	1.82	9.87
(C) Socio-economic status 55+ (%)						
– was never employed	0	0	0	10	1	8
– still employed	29	12	27	10	4	9
– unemployed/sick	1	1	1	0	1	0
– pensioner with labour income	1	0	1	1	0	1
– not any more employed	68	86	73	79	94	82
Absolute number of people 55+ not employed any more (in thousands)	4 929	1 387	6 469	8 181	2 328	10 523

Sources: (A) and (B): Federal Statistical Office, Statistical Yearbook 1994, Table 3.11 (p. 66), own calculation; (C): ASID '92, Overview 1-1 (p. 24), Table 2-1 (p. 32), own calculation.

Federal Republic will be called West Germany, the former 'German Democratic Republic' – the 'new' Länder (states) will be called East Germany). Because of the difficult labour market conditions in the phase of restructuring East Germany's economy after the collapse of the German Democratic Republic, many more people in East Germany are outside of the labour force. As will be shown later, the mechanisms as well as the income sources differ especially in the age group of 55–65 because of the great importance of pre-retirement provision outside the statutory pension scheme.

The following will first give an idea of those institutions aimed specifically at old age protection, although most organizations also deal with invalidity and widowhood (death of a spouse). Then the different pathways into retirement are mentioned. This is important to take into account because of attempts by public institutions or enterprises to shift costs or to look for other exits from the labour force by the employees.

Figure 4.1 gives a comprehensive overview of the structure of the different institutions dealing specifically with old age security in the Federal Republic of Germany. However, people defined as 'aged' can also have income from other sources and institutions not specifically aimed at old age security, e.g. transfer payments to subsidies to rent of flats, means-tested social assistance etc. and income from the (new) long-term care insurance in Germany (see Schmähl and Rothgang 1996). On the other hand, institutions mainly dealing with old age protection give benefits also due to other causes than being a certain age and being entitled to a pension, for example, in case of invalidity or death of a spouse.

Figure 4.1 shows that statutory (social) pension schemes form the basic pension scheme for both blue- and white-collar workers. In addition to employees, some groups of self-employed are also covered (obligatorily or voluntarily) by the statutory pension insurance.

It is also evident in Figure 4.1 that the German system of old age security is oriented towards the so-called 'three-pillar' concept, which, however, can be better described as a three-tier (or three layer) concept. Following the basic pension schemes making up the first tier, occupational supplementary schemes form the second tier. Occupational pension schemes fulfil a supplementary function for blue- and white-collar workers. Only for employees in the mining industry does the statutory pension insurance additionally have this supplementary function.[4] The special pension scheme for civil servants also integrates the first and the second tier. In Germany these are sometimes called 'bi-functional' systems. For some other groups of the population (farmers and people in professions such as medicine and architecture) special schemes give the basis of their old age protection, being supplemented by elements of the third tier.

The third tier includes all types of (additional) private savings for old age (including houses etc.). In the latter case, however, problems of definition arise, e.g. in view of the objectives of saving (other than for old

---

[4] Here special rules exist within the statutory pension insurance granting a higher level of benefits. In contrast to the statutory pension insurance in general (where employees and employers pay half of the contribution), the employers pay a higher contribution than the employees.

Figure 4.1 – Types of pension schemes for various groups of the population in the Federal Republic of Germany

Type of old age security	Total working population							
	Private sector								Public sector
	Self-employed					Employees		Civil servants[c]
	Agriculture	Professions	Crafts	Artists	Others	Blue- and white-collar workers (Mining industry)	Blue- and white-collar workers (Others)	
First tier (base)	Old age pension scheme for farmers[a]	Pension schemes of professional associations[b]	Craftmen's insurance (included in statutory insurance[d])	Artists' social insurance[d]	Compulsory or voluntary membership — Statutory (old-age) pension insurance	Miners' pension insurance	Pension insurance for other blue- and white-collar workers	Civil servants' pension scheme
Second tier (supplementary)						(part of statutory insurance)	Occupational pensions (about 50% of all employees (*voluntary*)) / Public sector schemes (for all employees) (*collective agreement*)	
Third tier (additional)	Private old age pension provisons (life insurance, savings etc)							

a Partly including family workers, as partial security, esp. beside the estate reserved by the heirs.
b Partly also for employees of the restrictive branches, with the possibility to contract out the statutory pension scheme.
c Civil servants, judges, soldiers.
d Special rules.

age provision). In this chapter only life insurance is dealt with as an element of additional provision for old age (third tier). Statistical problems exist with regard to life insurance, because this is both an instrument of private old age provision (third tier) and of occupational old age provision in the private sector (second tier).

All three tiers of the German system of old age protection are aimed at maintaining at old age what is deemed an appropriate degree of the level (standard) of living that was achieved during the employment phase. However, views differ on what 'appropriate' means when it comes to determining benefit levels. This is not only important for people who are making decisions for their old age but also for public pension policy as well as decisions made by enterprises on behalf of their employees.

According to a report submitted in 1983 by a committee of experts commissioned by the Federal Government, an appropriate level of provision is achieved, if after a long employment phase (40 to 45 years of insurance or years of service) net income in old age is maintained at 70 to 90 per cent of previous net earnings.[5]

For occupational pension schemes, concrete objectives concerning a replacement rate adequate for maintaining the standard of living were developed under the catchword 'replacement gap' (*Versorgungslücke*). Occupational pension schemes are meant to close the gap between the benefit level, achievable through the benefits from the statutory pension insurance, and the aspired overall level of net income maintenance. Overall net income maintenance, including private provision, should amount to 85 to 95 per cent of the (last) net earnings.[6]

In view of the relative importance of the two components (statutory and occupational schemes) for overall net income maintenance, it

---

[5] Cf. Sachverständigenkommission Alterssicherungssysteme 1983, p. 141. 'Net' refers to the earnings after direct levies (direct taxes and the employee's part of social insurance contributions). The Commission points out that a high benefit level is more important, the lower the insured employees' net earnings are. Cf. Sachverständigenkommission Alterssicherungssysteme 1983, p. 143.

[6] Cf. Ahrend et al. 1990, p. 6. Other authors point out slightly different values. E.g. in view of the capability of individual private provision, it makes sense to differentiate the necessary protection according to the income level. For high-paid employees (employees remunerated above the collectively agreed wage rate and senior executives) often up to 10 per cent of the disposable income is fixed for private provision. For employees covered by collective agreements, in contrast, only 3 to 5 per cent goes towards private provision. Cf. Ahrend et al. 1990, p. 6; Förster 1992, p. 117; Heubeck 1986, p. 10; Meier 1986, p. 45.

makes sense to differentiate according to earnings level. This is due to the 'contribution ceiling' in the statutory pension insurance. This ceiling amounts to about 180 per cent of average gross earnings and is linked to earnings development.[7] For those parts of earnings exceeding the ceiling no contributions have to be paid. On the other hand, since the level of benefits is determined only by those earnings being the base for contribution payments, no pension claims are acquired for this part of earnings, either. As a consequence, employees with earnings above the ceiling have a higher demand for pensions from occupational schemes to maintain their standard of living in old age. Taking this into account, the replacement gap to be closed by occupational pension schemes is estimated to be 10 to 15 per cent of the last net earnings for parts of earnings below the contribution ceiling, and 45 to 60 per cent for those earnings exceeding that amount (Förster 1992, p. 117).[8]

But there are also public institutions that give benefits before employees are eligible for an old age pension, e.g. in times of lack of opportunities for gainful employment. This may be a benefit from unemployment insurance or a benefit from special pre-retirement schemes. The latter clearly shows that in principle the same aim as an old age pension exists, namely to provide people with transfer payments instead of earnings from employment. Unemployment insurance benefits for older workers – who hardly have any chance to become employed again because of unfavourable labour market conditions – fulfil the same task. Figure 4.2 gives an overview of different possibilities for exit from the labour force for older employees in Germany.

During the last years the following pathway was used extensively especially by big firms: laying off older employees who then received an unemployment benefit, which was supplemented by payments from the former employer; thus, at age 60 the unemployed person claims an old age pension because of unemployment. Costs for restructuring the work force were thereby shifted to a remarkable extent to unemployment insurance as well as social pension insurance. In 1996 the Federal

---

[7] In 1993 the ceiling was 86 400 DM per year in West Germany (63 600 DM per year in East Germany).

[8] In the statutory pension scheme, the calculation of individual pensions is not based on last earnings (as e.g. in the scheme for civil servants) but on the relative earnings of the whole time covered by statutory pension insurance. 'Relative' means individual gross earnings compared to average gross earnings of all employees.

Figure 4.2 – Options for the transition to retirement provided for under social insurance legislation

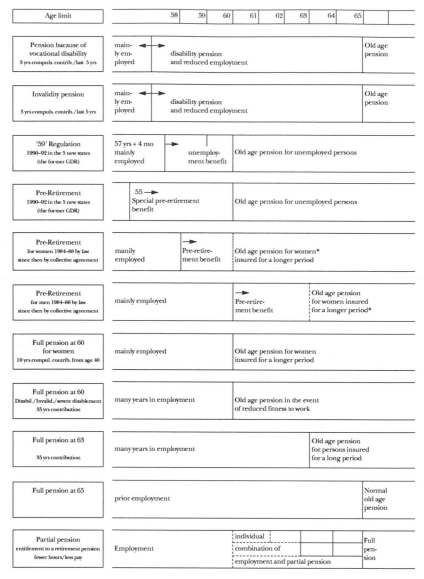

| Age limit | | 58 | 59 | 60 | 61 | 62 | 63 | 64 | 65 | | |

Pension because of vocational disability
3 yrs compuls. contrib./last 5 yrs
— mainly employed — disability pension and reduced employment — Old age pension

Invalidity pension
3 yrs compuls. contrib./last 5 yrs
— mainly employed — disability pension and reduced employment — Old age pension

'59' Regulation
1990–92 in the 5 new states
(the former GDR)
— 57 yrs + 4 mo mainly employed — unemployment benefit — Old age pension for unemployed persons

Pre-Retirement
1990–92 in the 5 new states
(the former GDR)
— 55 Special pre-retirement benefit — Old age pension for unemployed persons

Pre-Retirement
for women 1984–88 by law
since then by collective agreement
— manily employed — Pre-retirement benefit — Old age pension for women* insured for a longer period

Pre-Retirement
for men 1984–88 by law
since then by collective agreement
— mainly employed — Pre-retirement benefit — Old age pension for women insured for a longer period*

Full pension at 60
for women
10 yrs compul. contrib. from age 40
— mainly employed — Old age pension for women insured for a longer period

Full pension at 60
Disabil./Invalid./severe disablement
35 yrs contribution
— many years in employment — Old age pension in the event of reduced fitness to work

Full pension at 63
35 yrs contribution
— many years in employment — Old age pension for persons insured for a long period

Full pension at 65
— prior employment — Normal old age pension

Partial pension
entitlement to a retirement pension
fewer hours/less pay
— Employment — individual combination of employment and partial pension — Full pension

* If the respective requirements are met. If not, entitlement for pre-retirement only 3 years before the normal retirement age of 65 years.

yrs = years.

wks = weeks

Source: Viebrok (1993, p. 88) and own extensions.

government plans to change the rules in order to reduce the number of early retirees. A comprehensive overview concerning the different possibilities for exit from the labour force for older employees over time (as well as concerning the special arrangements in East Germany after unification) is given elsewhere (cf. Schmähl, George and Oswald 1996).

3. The historical development of occupational pension schemes and changes in their function – some general remarks

In Germany the beginning of social security mainly emanated from private initiatives. The origins of occupational old age security date back to before statutory pension insurance was introduced in the 1880s. Responsibility was assumed by the employer in view of a declining importance of traditional types of provision in the course of industrialization. Occupational schemes constituted the only type of old age provision for employees and their dependants besides that which was available through mutual assistance institutions organized on the basis of self-help cooperatives.[9]

After statutory old age and invalidity insurance for workers had come into force on 1 January 1891 (as the last branch of Bismarck's social legislation following statutory accident insurance and statutory health insurance), occupational pensions became supplementary benefits. At the beginning, statutory pension insurance benefit levels were very low. These benefits merely represented a cost-of-living allowance and, consequently, did not reduce the demand for occupational benefits much. Moreover the statutory pension insurance only covered some employees, namely most blue-collar workers, but not yet white-collar workers. This was one of the reasons why in the late nineteenth century white-collar workers received, to a larger extent than blue-collar workers, benefits from occupational pension schemes. This remained the case despite the establishment in 1911 of a branch in statutory pension insu-

---

[9] Early examples of occupational pension schemes are the Gutehoffnungshütte in 1832, Henschel and Krupp 1858, Siemens and Halske in 1872, BASF (Badische Anilin- und Sodafabrik) in 1878. For more details on the historical development, see Fischer (1978), Heissmann (1967), Reichwein (1965), Uhle (1987) and Koch (1988).

rance particularly for white-collar workers. Another reason why even today white-collar workers to a larger extent than blue-collar workers are covered by occupational pension schemes, will be explained below.

Occupational pension schemes were increasingly provided after World War II. Due to low levels of pension benefits from statutory pension insurance, a strong demand for additional pension benefits persisted. Moreover, in view of the high financial requirements in the reconstruction phase after the war, companies' interest in utilizing such schemes as an instrument of internal financing (using book reserves as a means of financing) grew.[10]

An important qualitative change in the development of occupational pension schemes resulted from the fundamental reform of the statutory pension insurance in 1957. The introduction of an earnings-related dynamic pension in the statutory pension insurance was based on changed objectives: the pension insurance no longer aimed to secure the insured's livelihood at a low level, but rather at a 'decent' living standard maintained throughout retirement.[11] This new objective, however, did not lead to a reduction of occupational pensions. On the contrary, companies continued to extend and/or increase coverage, the schemes being expected to contribute to the realization of the objective of 'maintaining the standard of living'.

Another effective measure was the introduction of the Occupational Old Age Protection Act (*Gesetz zur Verbesserung der betrieblichen Altersversorgung, BetrAVG*) of 19 December 1974. This Act created a binding legal framework for occupational pension schemes and has fixed minimum conditions concerning, inter alia, the vesting of pension claims in case of termination of employment before reaching retirement age, the insurance of claims against employer insolvency and the protection of benefits against inflation by a regulation on pension adjustment.

The BetrAVG guarantees a legal right to the benefit for those employees with an occupational pension commitment, who have fulfilled the respective conditions. Consequently, occupational pension schemes are only voluntary social benefits insofar as companies are not required to introduce a pension scheme (in contrast to, for example, Switzerland, where occupational pension schemes are obligatory). How-

---

[10] Tax reliefs have encouraged companies' interests in these investment opportunities. Cf. Ahrend et al. (1990, p. 3).

[11] For a discussion of objectives for pension policy in Germany cf. Schmähl (1977).

ever, once a company has committed itself to occupational pensions, it is subject to the Act's regulations.

In the last ten to fifteen years, the process of extending occupational pensions has more or less come to an end, indeed a development in the opposite direction seems to be taking place. This development is not only to be explained by increased costs for pensions due to the Act and Federal Labour Court decisions concerning the adjustment of pensions. Rather, insecurity about the economic situation of the firm in the foreseeable future is the most important factor influencing a firm's decision to introduce and/or to expand an occupational pension scheme (Ahrend et al. 1990, p. 158).

In 1972 flexibility in retirement ages was introduced in statutory pension insurance (the options can be seen from Figure 4.2) and in 1984 new rules for pensions after death of a spouse came into effect. Here adaptations of occupational pension schemes took place.

In 1992 another phase in pension reforms was enacted deciding inter alia upon a pension level in the statutory pension scheme that will remain constant over time and by introducing a 'partial pension' (combining part-time employment and a part of the full pension).[12] This is also relevant for firms' decisions about the future development of firm-based arrangements.

4. The quantitative importance of different elements of old age protection and of social expenditure by enterprises in Germany – some macro data

Expenditure of all institutions of old age protection in Germany in 1992 was about 420 thousand million DM (Table 4.2). Compared to GDP this was 14 per cent and about 25 per cent compared to private consumption.

Quantitatively by far most important is the statutory pension insurance with about 70 per cent of these expenditures, while supplementary pension expenditure in the private and public sector was about 8.5 per cent and life insurance about 10 per cent.

Table 4.2 also shows some remarkable differences in the structure of old age provision in West and East Germany today, because in the GDR

---

[12] Schmähl 1993c gives an overview of the '1992 Pension Reform' and Schmähl 1992b discusses in more detail changes concerning retirement ages.

Table 4.2 – Expenditures of institutions for old age security in Germany (1992)

Institution	Germany			West	East
	Billion DM	% of the total old age security	% of the statutory pension	West Billion DM	East Billion DM
Statutory pension insurance	290.1	68.4	100.0	241.2	48.9
Civil servants' pension	48.2	11.4	16.6	48.2	–
Farmers' pension	5.3	1.3	1.8	5.3	–
Self-employed pension	2.4	0.6	0.8	2.4	–
Occupational pension (private sector)	22.3	5.3	7.7	22.3	–
Occupational pension (public sector)	12.5	2.9	4.3	12.1	0.4
Expenditures of life insurance	42.5	10.0	14.7		
Direct insurance as old age occupational pension	0.7				
Total old age security	424.0	100.0			
Data for comparison: total expenditure of the social budget[a]	935.3			761.6	173.7
GDP[b]	3007.3			2772.0	235.3

Sources: Data on life insurance: Yearbook 1992 and 1993 of Verband der Lebensversicherungsunternehmen. Expenditure of life insurance as direct insurance are estimated according to the insured sum of the insurance contract. Other data: Revised data from Social Budget of the Federal Government (November 1993).

[a] Without tax expenditure of 70 billion DM.
[b] Statistics in Bundesamt Yearbook 1993, Table 24.2 (p. 680).

hardly any occupational pension schemes existed and neither was life insurance of any significance for old age provision.[13] Civil servants' pension schemes are currently being introduced in East Germany after unification. The same is true for the special pension scheme for farmers and professionals.

Table 4.3 gives the number of beneficiaries from different institutions. It is not surprising that the overwhelming majority of people in Germany receiving pensions at age 55+ receive pensions from statutory pension insurance. It must be noticed that official statistics only give information about the number of cases for receiving benefits. But there can be a cumulation of benefits (a) from one institution (pension being the result of one's own insurance plus a pension based on the insurance benefit of the deceased spouse), or (b) from different institutions. Therefore, judging only from the amount of one type of benefit no conclusions can be made concerning individual income or even household income.[14]

The structure of benefits for the 'stock' of pensions changes relatively slowly over time. An analysis of the benefits for new beneficiaries would, however, show remarkable changes in the structure according to type of benefit (invalidity, old age and different causes for an old age pension, as mentioned in Figure 4.2) (see Schmähl, George and Oswald 1996).

In West Germany occupational pensions in the private sector are more than a quarter of employers' social expenditure. If occupational pensions in the public sector are included, this proportion rises to more than 40 per cent.

Employers' contribution payments to the different branches of social insurance (health, unemployment, pensions, occupational accidents) is

---

[13] For differences concerning old age protection in the German Democratic Republic and the Federal Republic see Schmähl 1991a. West Germany has a relatively high savings rate of private households. Asset accumulation with insurance companies is important and is increasing: more than 20 per cent of financial assets and 25 per cent of financial asset formation and nearly 30 per cent of income from financial assets is from insurance companies (Bundesbank 1993).

[14] This is especially important to bear in mind concerning low pension benefits which are often identified with individual or household income, arguing in favour of changes in benefit formulas to avoid poverty in old age. For an early empirical analysis of low benefits compared to individual and household income see Schmähl 1977. In (West) Germany in recent years only about 2 per cent of pensioners are eligible for additional (means-tested) social assistance.

Table 4.3 – Number of beneficiaries in selected systems of old age provision

System	Number of pensioners aged 55 and older (thousands)		Percentage of beneficiaries aged 65 and older		Amount per head in DM per month	
	West	East	West	East	West	East
Statutory pension insurance pension of insured person						
men	4175	803	89	97	1859	1272
women	5312	1883	70	97	753	822
women (only childcaring)	1116	–	29	–	85	–
widow's pension	3555	862	84	93	1038	489
Total	14158	3548				
cumulation of insurance pension and widow's pension (women) (not including pensions only because of childcaring)	2141	811	55	89	1614	1247
Number of pensioners	12017	2737				
Total		14754				

	West Germany		
Occupational pension schemes			
I. Private sector			
a) insured men	1353	50	652
b) insured women	511	10	316
c) widow's pension	495		306
II. Public sector			
a) insured men	572	89	747
b) insured women	529	47	554
c) widow's pension	316		314
Civil servant's pension			
a) insured men	566	98	3428
b) insured women	98	79	3237
c) widow's pension	498	98	1870
Farmers' old age provision			
a) insured men	271	95	706
b) insured women	56		444
c) widow's pension	212		435
Professions			
a) men	33	45	3292
Veterans' scheme			
a) insured men	396	11	553
b) insured women	64	1	626
c) widow's pension	414	11	766

Source: ASID '92.

14.1 per cent of total labour costs, obligatory continued wage payments in case of employee illness is another 2.8 per cent, so the percentage of obligatory payments for social security is nearly 17 per cent of labour costs, while costs for voluntary occupational pensions are 4.1 per cent. However, it is expected that the employers' social insurance contribution payments will increase in the future, among other factors because of demographic aging. Therefore, the future development of social insurance in general, and of social pension insurance in particular, will be one of the important influencing factors for decisions by firms concerning their voluntary social expenditure.

5. The quantitative importance of occupational pension schemes by branch, company size, type of scheme and type of benefit

The availability of actual statistical information concerning supplementary pensions in Germany is far from satisfactory. The most recent official data are from the end of 1990 – referring to West Germany. Some first figures of this offical data collection were published in July 1994 (!)[15]

Concerning coverage in the private sector in West Germany at the end of 1990, 32.4 per cent of all companies (with a work force of three or more) in the West German private sector had occupational pension schemes and 46.2 per cent of all employees in the private sector had pension promises.

In companies with occupational pension schemes 70 per cent of (the 8.1 million) male employees and 53.4 per cent of (the 3.7 million) female employees had pension promises. Out of the group of all employees with pension promises 74.1 per cent were men and 25.9 per cent women.

The provision of occupational pensions in the private sector depends significantly on the company size and on the branch.

While about 95 per cent of companies with more than 1000 employees have occupational pension schemes, this ratio is only about 50 per

---

[15] The following data are taken from Heppt 1994a and Heppt 1995. The Federal Statistical Office is planning to carry out a survey for East Germany probably in December 1996 and a survey covering West and East Germany for the first time in December 2000 (Heppt 1994b, p. 769).

cent in small firms with 10 to 99 employees.[16] The figures related to eligibility are even lower: about 25 per cent of those employed in small firms have a pension promise from their present employer, while in large companies this is around 80 per cent.

In the manufacturing industry, on average, 40 per cent of the companies and 58 per cent of the employees have occupational pension schemes, in trade these ratios are less than 28 per cent and about 26 per cent respectively, and the lowest is in the service industries where only about 17 per cent of firms and 15 per cent of employees have such plans.

Differences regarding the distribution within one branch can be found between small and medium-sized companies. In large firms, on the contrary, there is a nearly equally as high level of distribution within and between the branches.[17]

If a company has an occupational pension scheme, not all of the employees in the company are necessarily beneficiaries.[18] As will be demonstrated later, occupational status and sex are of particular significance in this context. Moreover, the number of employees included in numbers of members of occupational old age pension programmes does not indicate the number of current and future claimants, since a minimum length of continuous employment at the firm is required to establish a vested claim (vesting period).

---

[16] These are official data from a survey of the Federal Statistical Office. There are, however, other sources for data. The nationwide survey by the Ifo-Institut (1990), which was based on a slightly different classification into groups of company size, comes to similar results. For a brief description of the results of this survey cf. Uebelhack 1992, pp. 31ff. Evidently, differences in provision also depend on the type of business organization. Occupational pension schemes are the most common in joint-stock companies. Cf. Ahrend et al. 1990, pp. 61ff. Concerning the empirical information reproduced in this and the following sections it has to be taken into account that the results of the surveys can only be partly compared. Thus the survey by Ifo-Institut (1990) confines itself to industry and commerce, whereas Ahrend et al. (1990) only include employees of companies having occupational pension schemes. And whereas both surveys as well as the survey of the Federal Statistical Office referred to companies, Infratest Sozialforschung (1990) and ASID '92 (1994) interviewed individuals aged 55 and over.

[17] This information is based on Ahrend et al. 1990, p. 59 (Table 7) for the state of Bavaria in 1988. These results seem to be applicable to the rest of West Germany.

[18] In 1990, 38 per cent of commercial companies with 10 to 19 employees had a pension institution. However, only 13 per cent of those employed in companies of such a size were members of this institution. Cf. Rosenberg 1992, p. 103, on the basis of the data generated by Ifo-Institut (1990).

Four different types of occupational pension schemes have been developed over time in West Germany:[19]

1) *Direct commitments* ('Direktzusagen') with pensions provided directly by the employer (the company itself being the pension institution), financed by book reserves;

2) *Pension funds* ('Pensionskassen') as legally independent institutions in the form of mutual insurance associations (Versicherungsverein auf Gegenseitigkeit, VVaG), financed through contributions to which employees can bear a part;

3) *Support funds* ('Unterstützungskassen') as legally independent institutions, mostly registered associations, financed only by payments by the employer to the fund and capital yields;

4) *Direct insurance* ('Direktversicherung'), where the employer, being the policy holder, takes out individual or group life insurance for the employee; financing is based on lump-sum payments or on regular contributions by the employer; the employee can contribute or raise the total contributions on his own (the so-called insurance by earnings conversion).[20]

There are remarkable differences concerning these four types according to company size and branch looking at the number of firms with such types and the number of employees being covered by such types. And there are remarkable changes over time. This will be discussed in connection with influencing factors.

---

[19] From the point of view of the company, several factors are considered when deciding upon the type of occupational pension scheme: besides aspects of personnel policy and the necessary administrative efforts, the timing of the financial burden, taxation policy regarding expenditures as well as the possibilities of using the funds set aside for old age provision as financial resources (within the company) are included in the calculation.

[20] An overview of the different types of occupational pension schemes can be found in Schoden 1986, pp. 161ff; Ahrend et al. 1990, pp. 19ff; Uebelhack 1991, pp. 44ff. For an overview see also Schmähl 1991c, d'Herbais 1991, and Wyatt 1992. For more details on direct commitments cf. Heubeck 1991, Blomeyer and Otto 1984, pp. 65ff; on pension funds cf. Bischoff 1991; Blomeyer and Otto 1984, pp. 186ff; Huhn and Galinat 1995; on support funds cf. Schwarzbauer and Unterhuber 1991, Blomeyer and Otto 1984, pp. 200ff; on direct insurances cf. Gehrhardt and Rößler 1991; Blomeyer and Otto 1984, pp. 163ff.

Looking at the number of employees covered by plans of their present employer, direct commitment is the most frequent type of pension arrangement (54.2 per cent), while at the end of 1990 pension funds, support funds and direct insurance were nearly of equal quantitative importance. When the survey was conducted, the possibility of additional voluntary insurance in the statutory pension insurance still existed. From an empirical point of view, however, it was insignificant.

Small companies tend to provide direct insurance most frequently, whereas this is the least frequent type in large companies. The great popularity of direct insurance with small companies certainly can be attributed to the easy administrating and the quite precise predictability of financial burden. The risks arising from benefit commitment are borne by the life insurance company.

In the case of direct commitments (which is clearly the dominating type in bigger firms), in contrast, risks are carried by the company itself. In larger companies the higher number of employees allows, according to actuarial probabilities, risks to be calculated more easily. It seems that larger companies value these risks less compared to financial advantages (resulting from the building up of book reserves being a source of internal financing and lowering tax payments).

In addition, medium-sized and large companies more often provide more than one type of scheme, not only in order to differentiate, e.g. among groups of employees, but also to spread the risk and/or to externalize part of it by reinsurance contracts with an insurance company.

Pension funds are characterized by high administrative costs (but, compared to direct insurance, low marketing costs). A relatively wide distribution of pension funds is found among small companies, since in the building industry and the ancillary building industry occupational pension schemes are covered by collective agreements and financed by the supplementary pension fund of the building and construction trade (Ahrend et al. 1990, p. 66).[21]

In 1993 from the accumulated funds of about 460 thousand million DM, about 259 thousand million DM (56 per cent) was estimated to be derived from book reserves for direct commitments, about 106 thousand million DM (23 per cent) from pension funds, while only 56 thou-

---

[21] Since the enactment of the BetrAVG, tax-effective financing possibilities of support funds have been limited, so that the use of this type of pension scheme is declining. Cf. Uebelhack 1991, pp. 48ff, demonstrating this tendency by means of various empirical investigations.

sand million DM (12 per cent) is acquired by direct insurances and about 40 thousand million DM by support funds (8 per cent).[22]

Comparing accumulated funds to GDP, Germany is far behind many other industrialized countries. Including book reserves the ratio is (1992) 15.5 per cent (without book reserves 6.6 per cent), while the ratio is 51.3 per cent in Denmark, 60.1 per cent in the UK (1991), and 75.9 per cent in the Netherlands (1992).[23] The level and structure of the basic public pension schemes seems to be an important influencing factor, when trying to explain these differences. The higher ratio of accumulated funds (assets) to GDP, however, is no indicator for a higher (macroeconomic) saving rate in these countries!

In line with their character as supplementary provision, benefits from occupational pension schemes relate to the benefits from the statutory pension insurance. The kind and the extent of this relationship, however, differ considerably. The individual pension commitments can vary significantly in design. Even within one company for different groups of employees, several parameters in the benefit formula can be combined at discretion.

To start, a rough distinction can be made between *defined-benefit plans* and *defined-contribution plans.* Under defined-benefit plans, three fundamental types are available: integrated pension schemes, earnings-related (partially dynamic) pension schemes and fixed-amount pension schemes.

The most recent official statistical survey gives some information concerning the dominating type of benefit in companies in West Germany having occupational pension plans. This survey covers all companies in all branches with three or more employees. In December 1990 fixed amount schemes (flat rate benefits) were by far the most common type (about 90 per cent, from this 60 per cent was a type independent of the duration of employment with the firm), while earnings-related schemes were hardly 8 per cent and integrated pension schemes (linked directly to stationary benefits) a bit more than 2 per cent.[24]

Also according to data from a sample survey in Bavaria flat-rate pension schemes are the most frequent type of coverage (49.1 per cent).[25]

---

[22] Cf. Urbitsch 1995, p. 35. Unfortunately, there is no data available on the distribution of vested claims and their share in the different types.

[23] Expertennetz 1994, pp. 135–6.

[24] Federal Statistical Office, Fachserie 16, Reihe 6.2 (2. Erhebung) p. 107.

[25] Ahrend et al. 1990, p. 80, Table 16.

They are most prevalent in smaller companies (52.5 per cent). These schemes involve the lowest risks of all the defined-benefit plans. Such benefits, fixed independently of earnings, primarily correspond to the idea of 'loyalty to the firm' and to a lesser extent to the remuneration character of the pension.

At 21.4 per cent, the final-pay schemes rank second place. In large firms they are the most common type. Nearly half of the companies (47.3 per cent) with more than 1000 employees provide pensions calculated on final earnings. Earnings-related fixed-amount schemes are used less often (11.4 per cent, or 15.3 per cent including reference value schemes as a specific type of fixed-amount schemes).

Integrated pension schemes are furnished in 7.5 per cent of the companies. Since the costs of the benefit plan are vulnerable to state intervention in the benefit formula of statutory pension insurance (see above), use of this type has been declining in the past years (Matschke 1989, p. 96, Ahrend et al. 1990, pp. 80ff.).

While smaller companies clearly prefer flat-rate benefit schemes, earnings-related schemes predominate in medium-sized and above all large companies. It seems that large companies attach less value to the argument according to which earnings-related plans involve uncertainty concerning the costs of benefits to be provided.

Defined-contribution plans have been scarce in small companies. In large companies, on the contrary, they are to be found more often, which may be explained by the provision of pension funds requiring contribution-oriented benefits.

A breakdown by branch of industry shows that earnings-related schemes are preferred where occupational pension schemes on the whole are widespread. Thus, in the chemical and the paper industry (44.2 per cent) as well as in the banking and insurance industry (35.9 per cent) final-pay schemes are to be found more often than average (23.0 per cent). In the banking and insurance industry integrated pension schemes are remarkably widespread with 20.6 per cent compared to 2.1 per cent as the average in the manufacturing industry (Ahrend et al. 1990, p. 82).

It must be stressed that the data concerning the distribution of certain types of benefit plans cannot be interpreted to mean that all the employees in one company of a certain size or branch of the economy are always promised the same type of benefit. Thus, it is conceivable that employees with low earnings – in line with the idea of welfare – receive flat-rate commitments, while senior executives are offered final-pay schemes and, in order to meet the provision requirements of the higher salaries, receive absolutely and relatively higher occupational pensions due to the contribution ceiling in the statutory pension insurance.

Finally we look at the relative weight of costs for occupational pension schemes in the private sector – as percentage of gross earnings.[26] The relative importance of costs for occupational pensions is higher the larger the number of employees in a firm. There is also remarkable differences according to branches of industry. This, however, does not say anything about the relative weight of occupational pension schemes in total costs of the firm because the labour intensity varies considerably between branches as well as within branches according to size of the firm.[27]

6. The frequency and level of benefits in the private sector

Very little data concerning the frequency and level of benefits of occupational pension schemes is available for the Federal Republic of Germany. The voluntary character and the large variety of types are often mentioned as main reasons for this lack of data. Up to now, in general, no regular comprehensive report of personal income distribution for Germany exists. At present the most detailed data is provided by Infratest Sozialforschung's analysis on old age pension schemes in Germany based on 1986 and 1990 data (Infratest Sozialforschung (1990) and ASID '92 (1994).[28]

In the following section of this chapter data are on pension benefits paid, not on pension claims promised. A main reason for differences between these two variables can be that the vesting requirements are not met.

In December 1990 2.4 million DM in occupational pensions was distributed. The majority was old age pensions (1.5 million DM). In addi-

---

[26] Gross earnings are not identical with total labour costs.
[27] Federal Statistical Office, Fachserie 16, Reihe 6.2 (2. Erhebung) (1995), pp. 46–8.
[28] It allows for analyses differentiating according to branch of the economy, size of company, earnings, occupational position and gender. It is not possible, however, to assign the distribution and the level of benefit to the above described types of pension schemes and benefit plans. An updating of these figures is under way, based on data for 1992.

tion to that, 0.2 million DM was invalidity pensions and 0.7 DM widows' and widowers' pensions (Heppt 1995, p. 158). In 1990 the average occupational pension was about 400 DM per month (old age 455 DM, invalidity 379 DM, widowhood 274 DM; Heppt 1995, p. 159).

The data presented in Table 4.4 is from 1986 (Infratest) and gives information for different groups of employees according to sex and last occupational status. The data show that the share of employees receiving occupational pensions and the level of benefits is differentiated. In 1986, 40 per cent of male but only 7 per cent of female pensioners in the private sector received an occupational pension. For both men and women the shares and the pension amounts were higher for white-collar workers compared to blue-collar workers. Generally speaking, women had considerably lower pensions than men, regardless of qualification. Women's average pension was 193 DM per month, which is 38.5 per cent of 501 DM paid on average to men.

The differences in pension amounts are much smaller between low-skilled blue- and white-collar workers than, for example, between senior craftsmen and qualified employees in mid-level or senior positions. A considerable number of highly qualified employees obtain occupational pensions reaching high levels, too. In relation to the total pension income from statutory and occupational pension schemes, the share representing occupational pensions has a range of approximately 9 per cent for all qualification groups of male blue-collar workers. With respect to white-collar workers occupational pensions make up nearly 13 per cent of the pension income for low-skilled workers, 21.5 per cent for qualified personnel in a senior position and up to 60.6 per cent for employees with a university degree. These data clearly reflect the target values for occupational pension schemes mentioned above.

Concerning the relative level of occupational pensions in relation to the total pension income, approximately the same shares are shown for female blue- and white-collar workers as for male, ranging from 10.7 per cent for low-skilled workers to 17.5 per cent for qualified personnel in a senior position and 36.7 per cent for highly qualified non-academics. Due to the low number of cases in the sample, the shares of qualified blue-collar workers and of academics will not be commented on. The absolute amount of pension benefits going to female employees, however, is clearly lower.

Twenty-five per cent of pensions for men but only 12 per cent for women in 1986 exceeded the amount of 400 DM per month. The share of pensioners with occupational pensions exceeding 400 DM increases

Table 4.4 – Shares of pensioners with occupational pension (OP) and pension amounts by last occupational status and sex[a]

	Share of pensioners with OP	Average OP in DM	OP as % of total pension	OP above 400 DM (%)[b]
Men				
Total	40	501	20.77	25
Blue-collar workers among them	34	173	9.24	8
Low-skilled workers	31	156	9.26	6
Qualified workers	36	178	9.16	8
Senior craftsmen	34	202	9.64	14
White-collar workers among them	51	869	28.81	50
Low-skilled workers	39	240	12.94	21
Qualified, low position	39	334	14.84	28
Qualified, mid-level	50	405	16.27	36
Qualified, senior pos.	48	625	21.57	51
Highly qual., no univ. degree	62	1436	38.77	74
Highly qual., univ. degree	73	3228	60.60	89
Women				
Total	7	193	15.73	12
Blue-collar workers among them	5	98	10.66	6
Low-skilled workers	5	102	11.49	7
Qualified workers	[4]	[64]	[5.36]	[3]
Senior craftswomen	–	–	–	–
White-collar workers among them	10	272	18.33	18
Low-skilled workers	5	107	10.66	–
Qualified, low position	8	166	14.30	5
Qualified, mid-level	12	250	16.93	22
Qualified, senior pos.	12	366	17.50	39
Highly qual., no univ. degree	32	990	36.71	60
Highly qual., univ. degree	[66]	[1705]	[43.01]	[100]

a Pensioners, employed in the private sector before retirement (mining industry excluded), with own pensions from statutory social pension insurance and own pensions from occupational pension scheme, aged 65 and over.
b Pensioners as in a, but aged 55 and over.

Source: Infratest Sozialforschung 1990.

with the level of qualification, for both blue- and white-collar workers, men and women.

Women often tend to have characteristics which combine to result in lower chances of receiving an occupational pension in the private economy. They more often work in smaller firms of trade and service industries and are less frequently found in higher qualified positions and in management. Especially for women interrupting employment for child-rearing, the vesting period of 10 years can have negative effects. The vesting period is extraordinarily long compared to other European countries; for a discussion of this aspect see various articles in Schmähl 1991d. However, some companies now guarantee reemployment after several years of parental leave, which normally is linked to a suspension and not a loss of claims. The periods of interruption are even partly taken into account for the qualifying period.

On the whole, women are covered by occupational pension schemes to a considerably lower extent than men. Not only do they receive lower statutory pensions, but this is true for occupational pensions as well. As a consequence, with regard to income distribution at old age, occupational pension schemes tend to reinforce differences resulting from unequal chances and treatment on the labour market rather than produce egalitarian effects. One central aspect that is not demonstrated here is the high share of part-time working women in the labour force. For example, in 1992 25 per cent of all working women covered by social insurance worked part-time and 92 per cent of all the employees working part-time were women (own calculations based on special evaluations of the employment statistics by the Federal Labour Office). Part-time work results in lower pensions in the statutory pension insurance as well as in the occupational pension schemes – if covered at all.

Thus, only for some of the pensioners, and for women only to a very limited extent, do occupational pension schemes fulfil their function of supplementing the statutory pension insurance and of closing the replacement gap.[29]

---

[29] Also the different taxation of benefits has to be taken into account when looking at the distributional scheme. The taxation of benefits from private pension schemes differs according to the type of scheme. Benefits from pension funds and direct insurances are taxed the same as pensions from the statutory scheme (only with the so-called 'Ertragsanteil', taking only a part of the pension as taxable income), because the employer's contribution to these schemes has been treated as part of the taxable earnings of the employee. Benefits from direct commitments and support funds, on the contrary, are liable to income tax with a tax allowance

Table 4.5 – Cohort-specific coverage and pension amounts in private supplementary pension schemes in 1986

	Men		*Women*	
	Coverage[a] *(%)*	*Pension in DM*	*Coverage*[a] *(%)*	*Pension in DM*
Age group				
65–75	26	498	5	200
75–85	20	550	3	192
85+	17	771	2	290

[a] Coverage = percentage of age group receiving a pension.

Source: Infratest Sozialforschung 1990.

A study of those who received a benefit for the first time in December 1990 shows that the average amount of the pension (568 DM/month) gives a positive 'bias', because only about one-fifth of all pensioners receive pensions that are higher than the average – typical for a frequency distribution skewed to the left.[30]

In West Germany pension benefits and not lump sum payments are most important (the latter is only 1/10 as frequent as the pension). The big differences in benefits that are received by wage and salary earners as well as for men and women are underlined by these data.[31]

Because of the tendency to reduce coverage and sometimes level of occupational pension claims especially in the 1980s and probably more pronounced in the 1990s the favourable trend at least concerning coverage – as reflected in Table 4.5 – cannot be expected in general.

The coverage rate is higher with younger cohorts for men and women alike. The decrease in pension benefits for younger cohorts, apparent among men, can be interpreted as the result of an extension of occupational pension schemes to lower income groups. But con-

---

for provision being granted. Here, the contribution payments were not subjected to income tax. The issue of tax treatment of occupational pension schemes is dealt with by Henke (1988).

[30] See Statistisches Bundesemt (Federal Statistical Office), Fachserie 16, Reihe 6.2, 2. Erhebung, p. 75.

[31] See Statistisches Bundesamt (Federal Statistical Office), Fachserie 16, Reihe 6.2, 2. Erhebung, pp. 69 and 93.

cerning coverage rates as well as pension payments, the differences between the sexes remain more or less the same.

Presumably with regard to the level of occupational pensions attainable in the future, it will continue to be necessary to differentiate according to sex and according to earnings level, company size and branch of economy.

7. Supplementary pension schemes in the public sector

The supplementary pension schemes in the public sector pursue the same objective as the occupational pension schemes in the private sector, i.e. maintaining the achieved standard of living also upon retirement. In addition a central goal is to provide equal treatment between civil servants and blue- and white-collar workers of the public sector.[32]

The supplementary schemes of the public sector are nearly as old as the occupational pension schemes of the private sector. In 1859 the Prussian state railway administration founded the first support fund for blue-collar workers. (For the historical development, see Schneider 1983, pp. 211ff).

The statutes regulating the different supplementary pension agencies in the public sector are largely identical. In the following we will take the pension agency of the Federal Government and the states (Versorgungsanstalt des Bundes und der Länder, VBL) as an example. It administers the most important public sector scheme for blue- and white-collar workers. Since new statutes came into force on 1 January 1967, the VBL has no longer been structured as an insurance scheme, but as an integrated pension scheme according to the principles of the civil servants' law and based upon collective agreements. Today, almost all employees in the public sector have a legal right to be covered, provided they have reached the age of 17 and are able to complete the qualifying period of 5 years until the age of 65.

The VBL was first financed by both employees' and employers' contributions, but since 1978, it has been exclusively financed by levies paid by the employers. Employees become eligible for supplementary pen-

---

[32] Tax and financing advantages do not play a role for the employer. However, besides a high degree of job security the supplementary pension scheme is an important factor in favour of the public sector in the competition with the private sector for scarce, qualified manpower.

sion benefits according to the same type of earnings as in the statutory pension insurance scheme, but up to a ceiling that is more than twice as high (Bauer 1991, pp. 7ff).

In the course of time the regulations on how pensions from the statutory pension insurance were taken into account when calculating the pensions from the supplementary pension scheme have been changed several times. The introduction of the earnings-related dynamic statutory pension by the pension reform of 1957 had the effect of increasing the potential total of statutory and supplementary pensions of public employees to more than 100 per cent of their last net earnings. This was due to the different taxation of earnings on the one hand, and of pensions on the other hand. Only a part of the total pension (the so-called 'Ertragsanteil') is considered as taxable income. In fact, most pensions practically remain tax-free. Several measures were meant to counteract this 'overprotection'. Since there were no changes in taxation, this required the agreement of the social partners. It was only as of 1 January 1985 that the total of statutory and occupational pension levels became limited to an amount corresponding to 89.95 per cent of net earnings.[33]

Until the end of 1991 in the supplementary pension scheme of the public sector, according to the civil servants' pension regulations, the highest possible overall replacement rate at 75 per cent of pensionable gross earnings was granted after 35 years of service. The rate by which claims increased for every pensionable year was not uniform, but graded according to years of service.[34] The amendment of the civil servants' pension act, effective 1 January 1992, involved an important change: uniform rates at 1.875 per cent per year of service, making the maximum pension of 75 per cent of the last pensionable gross earnings only attainable after 40 instead of 35 years of service. The minimum pension of 35 per cent of the last gross earnings, however, still exists. This new regulation in the benefit law has been adopted by the VBL in the 25th amendment of the statutes of 15 November 1991 (in the municipal schemes as well). Changes in the pension scheme for civil servants were a consequence of the '1992 Pension Reform' in statutory pension insu-

---

[33] Since 1 January 1992, the limit is 91.75 per cent. Net earnings are calculated, however, in a standardized manner; see Bauer 1991, pp. 46ff for details.
[34] From the completion of the qualifying period (60 months of contribution or occupational accident) up to the completion of a period of services of 10 years, there was a uniform basis of 35 per cent. From the 11th to the 25th year of service the increase rate was 2 per cent, from the 26th to the 35th year of service 1 per cent. A period of service of more than 35 years did not lead to an increase in claims.

rance. There is a political demand for more equal treatment of civil servants and other employees in times of increasing burden for old age protection (among other reasons) because of demographic aging of the population.

Figure 4.3 compares the old and the new benefit scale in the civil servants' scheme – which is also the relevant scale for calculating the supplementary pensions of the white- and blue-collar workers in the public sector – and the benefit scale in statutory pension insurance, respectively. It shows that in the future, on the whole, shorter periods of service will involve considerably lower replacement rates in the public sector compared to the former rule. Thus, after 35 years of service the gross level will be 65.625 per cent instead of 75 per cent, after 25 years of service 46.875 per cent instead of 65 per cent.

The difference of 15 percentage points, for a pensioner with 40 years of insurance (respective service), between the statutory pension insurance (60 per cent of last gross earnings)[35] and the overall income maintenance fixed in the civil servants' scheme (75 per cent of last gross earnings) corresponds to the replacement gap to be closed by the supplementary scheme (VBL) in the public sector. However, in this comparison differences in taxation of old age income have to be borne in mind. The total civil servants' pension is subject to income tax, whereas only a part of a statutory pension is considered taxable income.

Table 4.6 includes pensions from the supplementary scheme in the public sector graded according to sex and occupational status. The data reflect the broader coverage compared to private supplementary pension schemes and the fact that it is an integrated pension scheme. In 1986, 85 per cent of men and 52 per cent of women over 65, having been blue- or white-collar workers in the public sector prior to retirement, received a supplementary pension. On average the benefits were 608 DM per month for men and 502 DM for women and, consequently, especially for women were well above the respective figures in the private sector.

---

[35] This ratio is the result of the pension formula in the social pension insurance only, if the relative amount of the pensioner's earnings on average over the whole earnings career is identical with the relative amount of last earnings (relative means compared to average earnings of all employees). For a detailed analysis see Schmähl 1977. Unlike the civil servants' pension scheme and the supplementary scheme of the public sector, orientating (largely) towards the last earnings, the statutory pension insurance takes into account the lifetime earnings subject to social insurance, in relation to the average earnings of all the insured persons.

Figure 4.3 – Scale of tariffs in the pension schemes of the public sector and the statutory pension insurance

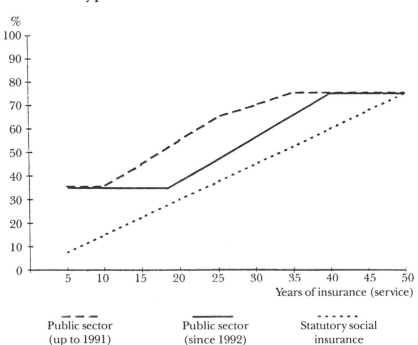

Public sector (up to 1991)	Public sector (since 1992)	Statutory social insurance

At all qualification levels the share of male pensioners receiving occupational pensions in the public sector is clearly higher than in the private sector. The only exception are employees with a university degree who, in general, also have lower earnings than their colleagues in the private sector and therefore do not receive pensions as high as in the private sector. Only with female white-collar workers do we find the same type of correlation between qualification level and share of pensioners as in the private sector. On the whole, the differences for women, compared to the private sector, are even more impressive than for men. (Figures in brackets will not be interpreted due to the small number of cases).

For all employees, but especially for male and female blue-collar workers, the share of occupational pensions in relation to the total pension in the public sector is far greater than in the private sector and for all groups it does not differ as much among qualification levels.

Interesting differences between public and private sector employees can be seen in a cohort-specific perspective. Table 4.7 shows that in

Table 4.6 – Shares of pensioners with an own supplementary pension in the public sector and pension amounts by last occupational status and sex[a]

	Share of pensioners with OP	Average OP in DM	OP as % of total pension	OP above 400 DM (%)[b]
Men				
Total	85	608	24.97	68
Blue-collar workers among them	85	452	21.95	64
Low-skilled workers	77	429	21.72	63
Qualified workers	91	455	21.59	64
Senior craftsmen	92	574	27.19	82
White-collar workers among them	86	704	26.29	72
Low-skilled workers	71	417	21.51	63
Qualified, low position	92	430	19.53	64
Qualified, mid-level	88	558	22.94	69
Qualified, senior pos.	86	919	28.88	82
Highly qual., no univ. degree	86	1455	39.19	–
Highly qual., univ. degree	63	1735	42.13	89
Women				
Total	52	502	30.33	55
Blue-collar workers among them	55	295	28.64	34
Low-skilled workers	54	274	28.63	30
Qualified workers	[57]	[406]	[30.25]	[51]
Senior craftswomen	–	–	–	–
White-collar workers among them	51	563	30.60	61
Low-skilled workers	[24]	[266]	[24.43]	–
Qualified, low position	43	414	30.20	51
Qualified, mid-level	55	556	30.47	64
Qualified, senior pos.	58	626	26.74	59
Highly qual., no univ. degree	[87]	[1104]	[40.51]	–
Highly qual., univ. degree	[82]	[1374]	[50.15]	–

[a] Pensioners, employed as blue- or white-collar workers in the public sector before retirement, with own pension from statutory social pension insurance and own pension from the occupational pension scheme of the public sector, aged 65 and over.

[b] Pensioners as in a, but aged 55 and over.

Source: Infratest Sozialforschung 1990.

Table 4.7 – Cohort-specific coverage and pension amounts in public supplementary pension schemes in 1986

	Men		*Women*	
	coverage[a] *(%)*	*pension in DM*	*coverage*[a] *(%)*	*pension in DM*
Age group				
65–75	12	672	7	536
75–85	8	458	3	300
85 +	6	271	2	80

[a] Coverage = percentage of age group receiving a pension.

Source: Infratest Sozialforschung 1990.

contrast to private pension schemes, the pensions in the public sector are higher for younger cohorts, especially for women. This can be interpreted as a result of the strong increase in benefit levels due to the shift towards an integrated pension scheme in the mid 1960s.

To sum up, with this type of pension arrangement, explicitly closing the replacement gap, public employees are far better off in retirement than their colleagues in the private sector. This remains true even after the introduction of the new benefit scale that will affect the benefits of future cohorts of pensioners. These favourable pension arrangements financed on a pay-as-you-go basis made e.g. the privatization of Lufthansa and the railways complicated as well as privatization of public utilities on the local level.

Projections concerning the average pay-as-you-go financing rate of supplementary pension schemes of public employers show a remarkable increase from 4.4 per cent in 1992 to about 7 per cent in 2010 and about 11 per cent in 2040.[36] This possible development has not really been recognized in Germany up to now in the public discussion on pension policy.

---

[36] Cf. Prognos 1995, p. 189. These projections do not take into account structural changes such as more privatization.

8. Interaction of public activities and private supplementary pension provision in retrospect and some reflections concerning future developments

8.1 Main elements of interaction

If we try to put together some central elements relevant for design and development of supplementary pension schemes and decided upon by public authorities, the following four factors (discussed in previous sections) can be mentioned:

1) The main basic public pension scheme, namely the statutory pension insurance, is an important factor for occupational pension schemes in the private sector, and the pension scheme for civil servants is a benchmark for the design of the supplementary pension scheme for wage and salary earners in the public sector – the design of the schemes, its financing, level and structure of benefits.

2) Taxation is relevant especially for decisions by employers and employees concerning pension schemes in the private sector.

3) Regulations like the law specifically regulating occupational pensions in the private sector (vesting, supervision, indexation, protection of pension claims and benefits in case of insolvency of the firm) as well as other regulations like rules and agencies for supervision of the activities e.g. concerning asset holding are important.

4) Jurisdiction, decisions by national and supra-national courts (European Court of Justice) concerning especially social, labour and tax law influence the occupational pension schemes.

In the following some examples of interaction relevant in the German context will be highlighted. Reference, however, should also be made to section 3 of this chapter on the historical development of occupational pensions in Germany.

8.2 The Occupational Pension Act - especially rules on indexation and vesting

Legislation introducing the Occupational Pension Act (BetrAVG) in 1974 was primarily aiming to increase protection of employees. Employees were looked upon as being the weaker partner in negotiations in this area. The rules, however, were mostly based on prior decisions of courts on labour law and looked upon as being more or less a consolidation of the existing situation (Beyer 1994b, p. 11). This resulted in additional costs for the employer because of vesting rules and the necessity to adjust occupational pensions. On the other hand more favourable rules on taxation were implemented. When introducing the BetrAVG the opinion was that 60 percent or more of the costs for occupational pensions should be covered by tax expenditure, i.e. by taxpayers (Beyer 1994b, p. 11).

A crucial point in the discussion about occupational pensions in the private sector was and is from the point of view of employers the adjustment of pensions according to inflation (based on a price index, but also taking into consideration the economic situation of the firm). But it was not so much the result of legislation but of jurisdiction that the rules for indexation of occupational pensions became more restrictive over time.

In principle the employer is obliged to increase the pension payment every three years according to the increase of the price index (of a household of four persons with medium income).[37] The adjustment rate can be lowered or can even become zero if the economic conditions of the firm are bad. In 1992 the Federal Court of Labour (Bundesarbeitsgericht) decided that in case of a lower or completely absent pension adjustment this has to be compensated later if the economic situation of the firm becomes better. This is a topic much discussed today in Germany and mentioned – inter alia – as being one of the important factors for the tendency to reduce occupational pension provision for new labour contracts.

The rules and rates of pension adjustment are of great importance for pensioners. Different rules in four different pension schemes can have significant impact on the development of income in old age, especially in the light of increasing life expectancy. A different mix of pensions (statutory and occupational) with different rules of adjustment in the overall pension package can have important effects for real and relative income development, even if the amount of pension e.g. for two pensioners is identical at time of retirement. Since 1992, in the statutory pension insurance, pension adjustment rate is linked to the develop-

---

[37] In the beginning of the 1970s firms wanted to have an indexation only based on 50 per cent of the inflation rate. This proposal was made again recently.

ment of average net earnings increase. This means that over time the role of an occupational pension – even if price-indexed – will decrease (assuming that during retirement the increase of average net earnings is higher than the inflation rate).

But of course it is relevant, how much occupational pensions were adjusted in the past. It is remarkable, however, that up to now there has not been any really convincing data available on this in Germany. The Federal Statistical Office recently published some information on firms (not the number of pensioners) having adjusted occupational pensions during the last years for the majority of their pensioners. Only 36.2 per cent of all firms adjusted pensions (and only a minority regularly). However, the bigger the firm (measured in number of employees), the higher the percentage of firms who adjusted pensions and did it regularly (e.g. of companies with 1000–4999 employees 87.2 per cent adjusted pensions and thereof 82.3 per cent regularly).[38] Therefore, the percentage of pensioners with adjustment of occupational pensions is much higher than the 36.2 per cent of firms who made pension adjustments. However, there is a great lack of information on how many pensioners had regular pension adjustments and how much.

8.3 Reform measures in public pension schemes

As mentioned already, reductions in the pension level of the statutory pension insurance were the main reason for mostly abolishing integrated occupational pension schemes granting a fixed replacement rate based on public and occupational pension.

Because occupational schemes supplement the public pension scheme, firms adapted their schemes when major changes in public schemes took place. In 1973 in the statutory pension insurance retirement ages became flexible (e.g. men could now retire under certain conditions at age 63 instead of 65, without actuarial deductions from the pension). The occupational pension schemes followed concerning the flexibility but introduced in most cases actuarial deductions.[39]

---

[38] For more detailed information cf. Heppt 1995, Table 11.

[39] However, employers are not legally bound to pay an occupational pension in case of early retirement. They may also make actuarial deductions (§6 BetrAVG). In 1988 almost 2/3 of the employers granting occupational pensions calculated actuarial deductions in case of early retirement. Cf. Ahrend et al. 1990, pp. 87f.

The Federal Constitutional Court (Bundesverfassungsgericht) decided that the existing different rules for men and women concerning widows' pensions were against the constitution. Therefore, in 1984 widowers' pensions were introduced in the statutory pension scheme. This became relevant in occupational pension schemes as well.[40] Costs for pensions would increase. Therefore, in the public scheme as well as in many occupational schemes other measures were decided upon trying to compensate additional costs because of granting now also widowers' pensions. New legal rules in case of divorce also stimulated changes in public as well as in private pension schemes.

Of great importance for private pension plans is also the 1992 Pension Reform Act. The main reasons for the 1992 Pension Reform Act were projections on the development of the contribution rate necessary to balance the budget in the future because of changes in demography and the economy, especially the labour market. Projections showed that the contribution rate of the statutory pension insurance would increase from 18 per cent to about 36 per cent in the year 2030 if nothing were changed concerning calculation of pensions etc.

Based on a broad political consensus between the governing coalition parties in the German parliament and the major opposition party as well as between employers' organizations and trade unions some remarkable changes were decided upon.[41]

The pension adjustment procedure was to be changed by linking the adjustment rate from 1992 to the growth rate of average net earnings of all employees instead of average gross earnings. This measure was based on a political objective concerning income distribution. In principle the ratio of individual pensions and (average) net earnings of employees will remain constant over time (i.e. a constant net pension level). This gives employees as well as employers more reliable information concerning the 'gap' to be filled by other arrangements for old age security. Compared to the 'old' pension formula, based on pension adjustment linked to gross earnings development, the 'pension level' will be lower with the new formula. Therefore, the necessity to supplement statutory pensions for many employees is increasing, if the level of living of the last phase during employment is to be maintained. The new political objective makes it easier, however, to design pension plans to cover the replacement gap.

---

[40] Cf. Ahrend et al. 1985.
[41] For a detailed discussion see Schmähl 1992a.

Moreover, this political decision concerning the stability of a net pension level of the statutory scheme makes it easier to calculate the contribution rate necessary to balance the budget of the statutory pension insurance, while giving firms more reliable information about the development of an important element of labour costs.

In contrast to (most) private occupational pension schemes, supplementary pensions in the public sector automatically fill the replacement gap because of the existing integrated pension scheme.

The Pension Reform Act also addresses issues of retirement age. (For an extensive discussion, see Schmähl 1992b). This is of direct importance for the firms, too.

1) Deductions from the pension are to be introduced in case of retirement earlier than a reference retirement age. This reference retirement age will be increased step by step up to age 65, starting in 2001. Early retirement (from age 62, for both men and women) will be possible in the future, too, but after the turn of the century it will become more costly for employees to retire earlier. The deduction will be 3.6 per cent a year before a certain reference retirement age that will increase step by step up to age 65, for men and women alike. The aim is to increase the average retirement age. Occupational pension schemes (as well as the supplementary pension scheme in the public sector) are often linked to retirement ages of the statutory pension insurance. Whether this will remain the same in the future, however, will depend very much on labour market conditions. As can be seen in the United States, occupational pension schemes can be an important instrument to influence the date of retirement at the company level (Burkhauser and Quinn 1989).

2) Since 1992 a partial pension exists in the statutory pension insurance, making it possible to combine part-time employment and claiming only a part of an (otherwise full-time) old age pension. This new option, however, has rarely been used up to now mainly because there are alternatives for an exit from the labour force that are much more attractive. Therefore, it is not surprising that so far, no information has been available on how firms will react to this in their occupational pension schemes. But there are some reflections on introducing a partial occupational pension, too. This is also linked to the most recent debate (1995) on measures to reduce early retirement options.

One feasible strategy in the future concerning occupational pensions could be that occupational pensions will only be paid when the full statutory pension is claimed. Employers and employees are free to find individual or collective agreements concerning partial occupational pensions for those who receive a partial pension from the statutory pension insurance.

While in the past – starting in the nineteenth century – civil servants' pensions gave a guideline for demanding better pension provision for other groups of employees, this seems to have ended. Today the development of the statutory pension insurance serves as the model for measures aiming at a reduction in the field of pensions. This became obvious in 1989 when political decisions concerning the statutory pension insurance were prepared (most of them becoming effective in 1992). A precondition for acceptability of measures reducing pension payments in the future for wage and salary earners in social insurance will be that for civil servants also some measures in the same direction are decided upon. This, however, will have effects on the supplementary pensions for wage and salary earners in the future, too.

It must be mentioned, however, that reduction in pension level etc. in occupational pension schemes in the past affected mostly employees being hired, while claims and pension benefits of employees with already existing pension promises were not affected (having a protected property right) or they were even the 'winner' of new rules as a consequence of court decisions.

8.4   Taxation

Favourable tax treatment is obviously an important factor for a decision to introduce an occupational pension scheme or to choose a specific design of the pension plan. As already mentioned, after World War II internal financing of firms by building up book reserves in case of direct pension commitments was favoured because of economic policy reasons. Firms could reduce tax payments on profits as long as the book reserves were not dissolved. The rules for building up book reserves were, however, changed from time to time, e.g. by increasing the relevant interest rate allowed for calculation of book reserves: the higher the rate, the lower the book reserve allowed to build up for a pension promise and the higher the taxable profit of the firm. In 1982 this interest rate was increased from 5.5 per cent to 6 per cent. Also changes in income taxation in case of direct insurance made occupational pensions of this type less attractive in 1988 and 1996.

8.5 Decisions by courts and measures of deregulation in the European Community

Decisions by courts were important in the past as already mentioned concerning pension adjustment. There is a tendency to strengthen the protection of those already having pension claims. In the national context a higher degree of regulation had to be taken into account by firms. One reaction seems to be to shift risks, either by using other methods of occupational pension arrangements – namely direct insurance, shifting risks to insurance companies – or by shifting risks to employees by changing from defined-benefit to defined-contribution schemes and also having more financing directly by employees. These seem to be recent tendencies in Germany.

In particular, decisions concerning equal rights for men and women led to abandoning the practice of only covering full-time employees. This practice was looked upon as indirect discrimination, because most part-time employees are women.

Measures of deregulation in the European Community affected pension funds and life insurance companies; decisions by the European Court of Justice (for example, the Barber case) stressing the view that occupational pensions are part of earnings and that there has to be equal pay for men and women stimulated discussion in this area as well as proposals of the European Commission towards a directive aimed at reducing barriers for mobility of labour because of the design of supplementary pension schemes. This, however, is in the process of discussion, but may influence the German occupational pension landscape (see below).

8.6 Possible tendencies for the future

Looking at the development of recent years, lower tax incentives, increased costs especially because of decisions by the courts, increasing unemployment and therefore less necessity to use occupational schemes to attract productive workers, changing conditions in international competitiveness with the consequences of looking for possibilities to reduce (especially labour) costs were important factors resulting in a tendency to reduce occupational pensions in West Germany. This mostly affects newly hired employees. For example the percentage of employees being covered by occupational pension schemes is decreasing. This tendency can be seen by comparing the surveys of the Federal Statistical Office of 1976 and 1990 as well as the sample survey of the Ifo-Institut (the latest is from 1993, cf. Beyer 1994a). This is true regardless of the size of the firm. Looking at the amount of money for occupational pension commitments in the private sector, 1993 shows for the first time a (however small) absolute reduction (less than 1 per cent), while this sum increased in 1991 and 1992 by about 5 per cent per year (Urbitsch 1995, p. 34).

As already mentioned, there is also a shift in the type of pension schemes by firms: a reduction of direct commitments and an increase in pension funds and especially in direct insurance. However, if we look at the number of employees being covered by schemes of different types, then the percentage of employees covered by direct commitments remained relatively stable from 1976 to 1990, while the percentage of employees covered by pension funds and direct insurance increased. This is mainly because big firms often have direct commitment schemes based on book reserves. But direct insurance seems to become more attractive. This is combined with a tendency to more defined contribution schemes.

The future development of pensions in general and occupational pensions in particular and the mix of pensions from different sources will be influenced by many factors. Above all the demographic and economic development will have a significant impact. Labour market conditions and political decisions – as mentioned in the previous sections – on the development of the basic pension schemes (statutory pension insurance and civil servants' pension scheme) and taxation will constitute main parameters shaping future development of occupational pension schemes. Here only a few reflections concerning the very complex relationship resulting from the interplay of influential factors can be given.

Firstly, company decisions concerning their occupational pension schemes are influenced in particular by expectations regarding future labour market development. In Germany this is now additionally complicated by the extremely different situation in East and West Germany following German unification. Since in the process of German unification the decision was to transfer the entire West German economic and social system to the former GDR, the supplementary function of occupational pension schemes in East Germany should in principle follow West German standards. For a discussion of the transformation process concerning the statutory pension scheme, see Schmähl (1992b). Only a very small number of occupational pension schemes were provided in the former GDR. In the meantime most of these schemes have been terminated, entitlements and claims have expired or have been transferred to the statutory pension insurance scheme. The current economic situation in East Germany is extremely difficult and a severe hindrance for the introduction of new occupational pension schemes. Only economically successful firms with a good economic outlook can take over long-term commitments such as pensions. In the process of transformation especially those branches of industry in East Germany have problems or are already closed down, which in West Germany have high coverage rates (e.g. large companies in the iron and steel industry, electrical industry and automobile industry). Large administrative organizations in the banking and insurance industry, another branch with high coverage rates in West Germany, do not yet exist. It is only in a few prospering branches like the building and construction trade that the situation is better. But even here, not all employees are covered (Niermann 1993, pp. 21f). Therefore, the process of convergence in unified Germany in the field of occupational pensions will only take place gradually and will need a rather long period of time. In addition, the demographically induced aging of the German labour force may encourage adaptive measures. In case the problem of a lack of qualified manpower arises, it can be expected that firms will extend or improve occupational pension schemes as an instrument to attract workers. But estimates concerning the development of the labour market for the next 10 to 15 years are controversial. Increased immigration or the shift of production to other countries could be reactions as well.

At present (1995), retirement schemes in the public and private sector are again very much discussed, mainly the statutory pension insurance, but increasingly also the pension scheme for civil servants. Because the occupational pension scheme for wage and salary earners in the public sector is very much in line with the civil servants' scheme, occupational pensions in the public sector will get more public attention than in the past, when pension schemes of the public sector were hardly a topic in the public discussion on pensions (being financed from public budgets without a specific levy as the contribution rate for statutory pension insurance).

A new pension reform debate has started, pointing at the increase in (earnings-based) contribution rates necessary in the future even after taking into account the effects of the 1992 Pension Reform Act. Projections show that the contribution rate necessary to balance the budget will increase up to 26–28 per cent by the year 2030. (This, and different strategies by which to cope with future problems are discussed in Schmähl 1994a and 1994b. See also Prognos 1995).

If a strategy for the future would be – as sometimes proposed in the German debate – to generally reduce the level of pensions in the statutory scheme, this would result in insufficient provision at least for some groups of pensioners. As one solution to this problem it has been suggested that the supplementary pension schemes could and/or should compensate for these losses in order to keep the overall pension level constant. This would be a rather unsatisfactory solution as long as a considerable portion of employees, as was indicated above, is not covered by a supplementary pension scheme. (It has been pointed out as well that often those groups of employees not covered in occupational schemes get low pensions from the statutory scheme, too). Therefore, one might consider an expansion of occupational pension schemes to hitherto non-covered groups. The fact that in Germany no influential political proposals for changing occupational pension schemes from voluntary to mandatory schemes are made, is mostly due to the fact that the statutory pension insurance has thus far fulfilled its function of stabilizing the standard of living to a remarkable degree after retirement for a great number of employees. Therefore, in my view, proposals for a radical reduction of the pension level in the statutory pension scheme would lead to demands for making a second tier (e.g. occupational pensions) mandatory. This is a clear tendency in most of the countries that have introduced flat-rate (tax-financed) pension schemes. (See Schmähl 1991c).

The current trends, however, go in the opposite direction. In the present economic environment occupational benefits as a whole are seen as a disadvantage in competition because of (labour) costs. Many firms cut back these benefits in order to reduce their non-wage labour costs. Occupational pensions are, however, only cautiously cut back because of their significance for the employee's own long-term planning of old age provision and because of the precautionary measures stipulated by the BetrAVG. But – from a present-day perspective – in the near future, further reductions and the closing down of schemes for new employees will be more likely than a further expansion.

Because of the downward trend in occupational pensions and in the light of prospects for the future, the government announced after parliamentary elections in October 1994 that the conditions for occupational pensions were to be improved. One of the most effective instruments in stimulating expansion of occupational pensions is tax policy. However, at present it is unclear what the government intends to do, especially if one takes into account the difficult situation of public budgets because of high costs in the process of restructuring the East German economy after the German unification and the general economic conditions with high unemployment etc.

A factor which can reduce the willingness of firms to become more engaged in occupational pensions could emerge from the European environment, if a draft of a new directive of the European Commission concerning protection of supplementary pension schemes were to be decided upon. The proposal of the draft is aiming at an obligatory indexation not only of pension benefits but also of pension claims according to price increase and is demanding a reduction in vesting period. Both would increase ceteris paribus costs of occupational pension schemes. Not surprising, there is resistance against such a directive in Germany.

However, there is a tendency in the German discussion aiming at a reduction of the (relatively long) vesting period. The price to be paid by the government could be that there will be a clear condition in the occupational pension act that there is no need to catch up on indexation that was not carried out in the past because of unfavourable economic conditions of the firm.

From a social policy point of view, the present coverage rate of only about half of the employees in the private sector can become a problem, if the pension level in the statutory scheme would be reduced. In addition, cohort-specific differences in coverage have to be taken into account. A political task is to avoid a situation – such as is often complained about in the UK – of 'two nations in retirement', one group mainly receiving only a low statutory pension (in the UK the basic pension is even below the poverty line), while the other receives supplementary pension payments in addition. This also has to be avoided because there might be a tendency in the labour market of shifting jobs from labour contracts to self-employment.

Changing labour market conditions in the future, growing demand for (qualified) labour, and a favourable economic outlook may increase the coverage rate because occupational pensions again become an instrument in personnel policy to attract productive workers. The fact that occupational pensions are a voluntary social benefit can be used as an advantage, because this principle allows for more flexibility in the design of occupational pension arrangements to take into account the situation of the employees as well as of the firms, in contrast to strongly regulated systems. This might make it easier to find a satisfying solution. Whether this will be enough, however, can be questioned.

There are several possible ways for stimulating an increase in coverage. One may be more collective agreements on at least (relatively low) minimum standards giving the firms a chance to increase pension commitments according to their specific economic situation. In Germany trade unions do not seem to be interested in occupational pension arrangements. In principle they are demanding a universal coverage of all employees. Collective agreements, also linked to proposals of trade unions for a broader distribution of assets in the economy, could be a way to achieve this. Another way would be possibilities for offering direct insurance with fixed contributions only for a limited number of years (say the next five years), to be extended if the economic conditions of the firm allow it. Here the period of binding agreements can be limited while the risk is borne by an insurance company.[42]

There is a growing demand for flexibility in many areas. This can also be introduced into the occupational pension scheme, i.e. by linking pension claims to the development of profits.

There may also be more substitution of direct wages by financing pension claims by the employee personally (earnings conversion, deferred compensation), if, for example, tax rules make this attractive. This can supplement the financing of the employer for occupational pensions. This would increase the role of defined-contribution plans. The borderline between the second and the third tier of old age protection would be blurred.

In the future the different approaches just mentioned may result in a multi-tier (pillar) concept in occupational pension arrangements: a base of collectively agreed pension arrangements, topped up by pensions linked, for example, to the development of profits of the firm or as a special award for productive activities of the employee and supplemented by, for example, earnings conversion respective contributions by the employee. The broad tendency points in the direction of more

---

[42] Cf. Niermann 1993, pp. 22f, and Rößler 1992 for a special version of direct insurance recommended for East German firms.

defined-contribution arrangements. Ahrend, Förster and Rößler (1995) point especially at advantages for the firms by choosing the way of direct pension commitments based on defined contributions instead of – as has largely been the case up to now in Germany when using direct pension commitments – defined benefit plans.

Finally, when looking at the interaction of public and private activities it must be underlined that an important factor for future decisions of firms is the stability of rules because of the long-term aspect of pension policy. This points at political decisions concerning public pension policy (especially for the future development of statutory pension insurance) but also at other rules based on political decisions being relevant for the firms' decision to establish, design and develop supplementary pension schemes. Therefore, a comprehensive approach to pension policy is needed. Researchers especially have the obligation to bring this topic into the political arena again and again.

References

ABA Arbeitsgemeinschaft für betriebliche Altersversorgung (ed.) (1991), *Handbuch der betrieblichen Altersversorgung, Band I Grundlagen und Praxis*, Wiesbaden: Forkel.

ABA Arbeitsgemeinschaft für betriebliche Altersversorgung (1995), *Memorandum zur Sicherung und Förderung der betrieblichen Altersversorgung in Deutschland*, Heidelberg.

Ahrend, Peter, Beucher, Doris and Förster, Wolfgang (1985), 'Die Reform der Hinterbliebenenversorgung in der gesetzlichen Rentenversicherung und ihre rechtlichen und belastungsmäßigen Auswirkungen für die betriebliche Altersversorung', *Der Betrieb*, Beilage 22.

Ahrend, Peter, Förster, Wolfgang and Walkiewicz, Norbert (1990), *Die betriebliche Altersversorgung in Bayern. Situationsanalyse – Anregungen*, München: erstellt im Auftrag des Bayerischen Staatsministeriums für Arbeit und Sozialordnung.

Ahrend, Peter, Förster, Wolfgang and Rößler, Norbert (1995), 'Effizienzgewinne bei gleichzeitiger Kostenreduktion in der betrieblichen Altersversorgung', *Betriebs-Berater*, Beilage 10.

Andresen, Boy-Jürgen (1995), *Betriebliche Altersversorgung im Umbruch – Die zweite Säule auf verändertem sozialen und wirtschaftlichen Fundament*, Vortrag 5. Speyerer Sozialrechtsgespräch, mimeo (in print).

ASID '92 (1994), *Alterssicherung in Deutschland 1992* Vol. 1 and Vol. 2, Bonn: Bundesministerium für Arbeit und Sozialordnung.

Bauer, Uwe (1991), 'Die zusätzliche Alters- und Hinterbliebenenversorgung für die Arbeitnehmer des öffentlichen Dienstes', in ABA (1991).

Beyer, Jürgen (1994a), 'Betriebliche Altersversorgung: Insgesamt rückläufige Tendenz', *Bundesarbeitsblatt,* 3/1994.

Beyer, Jürgen (1994b), '20 Jahre Betriebsrentengesetz: Wo stehen wir heute?', *Bundesarbeitsblatt* 12/1994, 10–18.

Beyer, Jürgen (1995), 'Perspektiven der betrieblichen Altersversorgung', *Betriebliche Altersversorgung,* Vol. 50, 261–4.

Bischoff, Hans-Albrecht (1991), 'Pensionskassen', in ABA (1991).

Blomeyer, Wolfgang and Otto, Klaus (1984), *Gesetz zur Verbesserung der betrieblichen Altersversorgung. Kommentar,* München: C.H. Beck'sche Verlagsbuchhandlung.

Bundesbank (1993), 'Zur Vermögenssituation privater Haushalte in Deutschland', in Deutsche Bundesbank (1993), *Monatsbericht* Oktober, 19–32.

Burkhauser, Richard V. and Quinn, Joseph F. (1989), 'American Patterns of Work and Retirement', in Winfried Schmähl (ed.), *Redefining the Process of Retirement: An International Perspective,* Berlin, Heidelberg, New York: Springer.

Expertennetz (1994), *Ergänzende Altersversorgungssysteme in der Europäischen Union. Bericht des Expertennetzes für Ergänzende Altersversorgungssysteme der Europäischen Kommission,* Brüssel, V/864/94-DE (mimeo).

Fischer, Wolfram (1978), 'Die Pionierrolle der betrieblichen Sozialpolitik im 19. und beginnenden 20. Jhdt.' in Hans Pohl (ed.), *Betriebliche Sozialpolitik deutscher Unternehmen seit dem 19. Jahrhundert,* Wiesbaden, Beiheft der Zeitschrift für Unternehmensgeschichte, 12, 34–51.

Förster, Wolfgang (1992), 'Möglichkeiten eines betrieblichen Versorgungssystems', in Förster and Rößler (1992).

Förster, Wolfgang and Rößler, Norbert (eds.) (1992), *Betriebliche Altersversorgung in der Diskussion zwischen Praxis und Wissenschaft.* Festschrift zum 60. Geburtstag von Peter Ahrend, Köln: Dr. Otto Schmidt.

Gehrhardt, Heinz and Rößler, Heinz (1991), 'Versicherungsverträge mit privaten Versicherungsunternehmen', in ABA (1991).

Heissmann, Ernst (1967), *Die betrieblichen Ruhegeldverpflichtungen,* Köln: Schmidt-Verlag.

Henke, Klaus-Dirk (1988), 'Die betriebliche Altersversorgung aus einkommensteuer-systematischer Sicht', *Finanzarchiv* N.F. 46.2, 268–82.

Heppt, Ehrenfried (1994a), 'Neueste Ergebnisse der Erhebungen des Statistischen Bundesamtes über die betriebliche Altersversorgung 1990', *Betriebliche Altersversorgung,* 179–86.

Heppt, Ehrenfried (1994b), 'Methode der Erhebungen über Art und Umfang der betrieblichen Altersversorgung 1990', *Wirtschaft und Statistik,* 763–9.

Heppt, Ehrenfried (1995), 'Betriebliche Altersversorgung 1990 im früheren Bundesgebiet', *Wirtschaft und Statistik,* 155–65 and 137*–41*.

d'Herbais, Pierre-Guillaume (1991), *A Guide to Pensions in the E.E.C. – A Comparative Analysis of the Basic and Supplementary Pension Plans for Salaried Employees and Civil Servants,* Paris: European Pension Committee.

Heubeck, Georg (1991), 'Die Pensionsrückstellung', in ABA (1991).

Heubeck, Klaus (1986), 'Betriebliche Altersversorgung – heute und morgen', in *Wegweiser für die Altersversorgung,* 3–16.

Huhn, Harald and Galinat, Withold (1995), 'Die Pensionskasse – Vorurteile und Vorteile', *Betriebliche Altersversorgung*, 50, 267–9.

Ifo-Institut (1990), *Befragung der Bereiche Industrie und Handel zur Situation und Entwicklung der betrieblichen Altersversorgung*, München: Ifo-Institut für Wirtschaftsforschung im Auftrag des Bundesministeriums für Arbeit und Sozialordnung.

Infratest Sozialforschung (1990), *Alterssicherung in Deutschland 1986, Vol. III: Rentner mit Zusatzsicherung and Vol. Z: Zusammenfassender Bericht*, München.

Koch, Peter (1988), 'Zur Geschichte der betrieblichen Altersversorgung', in ABA – Arbeitsgemeinschaft für betriebliche Altersbersorgung e.V. (ed.), *50 Jahre für die betriebliche Altersversorgung*, Heidelberg.

Matschke, Manfred Jürgen (1989), 'Betriebliche Altersversorgung', *WISU*, 1/89, pp. 31–4; 2/89, pp. 95–9.

Meier, Herbert (1986), 'Die Netto-Versorgungslücke bzw. der Brutto-Versorgungsbedarf aus betrieblicher Altersrente bei Eintritt des Arbeitnehmers in den Alters-Ruhestand', in *Wegweiser für die Altersversorgung*.

Niermann, Udo (1993), 'Betriebliche Altersversorgung in den neuen Bundesländern', *Betriebliche Altersversorgung*, 1/1993, 20–3.

Prognos (1995), (Konrad Eckerle, Michael Schlesinger, unter Mitarbeit von Gudrun Blaha), 'Perspektiven der gesetzlichen Rentenversicherung für Gesamtdeutschland vor dem Hintergrund veränderter politischerund ökonomischer Rahmenbedingungen', Schlußbericht für den Verband Deutscher Rentenversicherungsträger – Textband, Basel, mimeo.

Reichwein, Roland (1965), *Funktionswandlungen der betrieblichen Sozialpolitik*, Dortmunder Schriften zur Sozialforschung, Bd. 26, Köln and Opladen: Westdeutscher Verlag.

Rosenberg, Peter (1992), 'Wie leistungsfähig ist die 'zweite Säule'?', in Förster and Rößler (1992).

Rößler, Norbert (1992), 'Spezielle Versicherungslösungen für die betriebliche Altersversorgung von Arbeitnehmern im Beitrittsgebiet', *Betriebliche Altersversorgung*, 5/1992, 169–73.

Sachverständigenkommission Alterssicherungssysteme (1983), *Gutachten der Sachverständigenkommission Alterssicherungssysteme, Berichtsband 1, Vergleich der Alterssicherungssysteme und Empfehlungen der Kommission*, Bonn, veröffentlicht durch die Bundesregierung, der Bundesminister für Arbeit und Sozialordnung.

Schmähl, Winfried (1977), *Alterssicherung und Einkommensverteilung*, Tübingen: Mohr.

Schmähl, Winfried (1991a), 'Alterssicherung in der DDR und ihre Umgestaltung im Zuge des deutschen Einigungsprozesses', in Gerhard Kleinhenz (ed.), *Sozialpolitik im vereinten Deutschland I*, Berlin: Duncker & Humblot.

Schmähl, Winfried (1991b), 'Coordination and Integration of Old Age Pension Schemes – Some Experiences from a German Point of View', in Werner Puschra and Jae-Sung Min (eds.), *Policy Issues in National Pension Schemes: Korea and Germany*, Seoul: Friedrich Ebert Stiftung.

Schmähl, Winfried (1991c), 'On the Future Development of Retirement in Europe

Especially of Supplementary Pension Schemes – An Introductory Overview', in Schmähl, Winfried (ed.) (1991d).

Schmähl, Winfried (ed.) (1991d), *The Future of Basic and Supplementary Pension Schemes in the European Community – 1992 and Beyond*, Baden-Baden: Nomos.

Schmähl, Winfried (1992a), 'Changing the Retirement Age in Germany', *The Geneva Papers on Risk and Insurance*, pp. 81–104.

Schmähl, Winfried (1992b), 'Transformation and Integration of Public Pension Schemes – Lessons from the Process of the German Unification', in Pierre Pestieau (ed.), 'Public Finance in a World of Transition, Proceedings of the 47th Congress of the International Institute of Public Finance, St. Petersburg 1991', *Public Finance 47*, Supplement, 34–56.

Schmähl, Winfried (1993a), 'Die europäische Dimension der Alterssicherung', *Hamburger Jahrbuch*, Vol. 38, 137–54.

Schmähl, Winfried (1993b), 'Proposals for Flat-rate Public Pensions in the German Debate', in Jos Berghman and Bea Cantillion (eds.), *The European Face of Social Security*, Aldershot: Avebury.

Schmähl, Winfried (1993c), 'The "1992 Reform" of Public Pensions in Germany: Main Elements and Some Effects', *Journal of European Social Policy*, Vol. 3(1), 39–51.

Schmähl, Winfried (1994a), 'Perspektiven der Alterssicherung in Deutschland', *Wirtschaftsdienst*, 390–5.

Schmähl, Winfried (1994b), 'Strategien und Maßnahmen künftiger Alterssicherungspolitik in Deutschland', *Wirtschaftsdienst*, 507–514.

Schmähl, Winfried (1994c), 'Umbau der sozialen Sicherung im Alter? Zur Diskussion über die weitere Entwicklung der Alterssicherung in Deutschland', *Staatswissenschaften und Staatspraxis*, Vol. 3, 331–65.

Schmähl, Winfried and Böhm, Stefan (1994a), 'Occupational Pension Schemes in the Private and Public Sector in the Federal Republic of Germany – An Overview', Zentrum für Sozialpolitik, University of Bremen, Working Paper No. 5/94.

Schmähl, Winfried and Böhm, Stefan (1994b), 'Les régimes de retraite complémentaires du secteur privé et du secteur publique en République Fédéral d'Allemagne: vue d'ensemble', *La Revue de l'IRES*, No. 15, Les Retraites Complémentaires – Acteurs, Enjeux, Perspectives.

Schmähl, Winfried, George, Rainer and Oswald, Christiane (1996), 'Gradual Retirement in Germany', in Lei Delsen and Geneviève Reday-Mulvey (eds.), *Gradual Retirement in the OECD Countries*, Aldershot: Dartmouth, 69–93.

Schmähl, Winfried and Rothgang, Heinz (1996), 'The Long-Term Costs of Public Long-Term Care Insurance. Some Guesstimates', in Roland Eisen and Frank A. Sloan (eds.), *Alternatives for Ensuring Long-Term Care*, Dordrecht: Kluwer.

Schneider, Hans-Peter (1983), 'Zusatzversorgung der Arbeitnehmer im öffentlichen Dienst. Einzelgutachten', in *Gutachten der Sachverständigenkommission Alterssicherungssysteme, Berichtsband 2, Darstellung der Alterssicherungssysteme und der Besteuerung von Alterseinkommen*, Bonn: Bundesregierung, Bundesminister für Arbeit und Sozialordnung.

Schoden, Michael (1986), *Betriebliche Altersversorgung. Leitfaden und Kommentar für die Praxis*, Köln: Bund.

Schwarzbauer, Fritz and Unterhuber, Hans (1991), 'Unterstützungskassen', in ABA (1991).

Sozialbericht (1990), *Sozialbericht*, Bonn: Der Bundesminister für Arbeit und Sozialordnung.

Thompson, Lawrence H. (1988), 'Altering the Public/Private Mix of Retirement Incomes', in Susan M. Wachter (ed.), *Social Security and Private Pensions*, Massachusetts/Toronto: Lexington.

Uebelhack, Birgit (1991), 'Die betriebliche Altersversorgung', in ABA (1991).

Uhle, Carlhans (1987), *Betriebliche Sozialleistungen. Entwicklungslinien und Ansätze einer Erklärung ihrer Bereitstellung*, Reihe Märkte – Branchen – Unternehmungen Bd. 7, Köln: Müller Botermann Verlag.

Urbitsch, Christian (1995), 'Neue Zahlen zur betrieblichen Altersversorgung', *Betriebliche Altersversorgung*, pp. 34–5.

Viebrok, Holger (1993), 'Kriterien zur betrieblichen Ausgestaltung des Übergangs vom Erwerbsleben in den Ruhestand', Zentrum für Sozialpolitik, University of Bremen, Working Paper 5/93.

Wegweiser für die Altersversorgung (1986), *Wegweiser für die Altersversorgung – aus dem Kreise seiner Mitarbeiter Georg Heubeck zum 75*, Stuttgart: Fachverlag für Wirtschaft und Steuern Schäfer.

Wyatt Company S.A. (1992), *Benefits Report Europe USA*, Brussels.

5

The Retirement Provision Mix in Italy: The Dominant Role of the Public System

Rita Di Biase, Aldo Gandiglio, Maria Cozzolino and Gaetano Proto[1]

1.   Introduction

Italy has a pay-as-you-go public pension system, which under the latest reform law of August 1995 will gradually switch from the earnings-based award formula to one based on contributions. Public pension expenditure is proportionally higher in Italy than in any other Western country (14 per cent of GDP in 1993), while the fertility rate is among the lowest (1.3 children per woman of childbearing age). Moreover, spending on pensions as a proportion of total social spending (57 per cent in 1993) is very high by international standards. This public scheme is far and away the dominant form of retirement provision. The recently introduced supplementary pension funds are as yet insignificant, and their diffusion is outstripped by personal supplements.

As regards the first pillar, the problems afflicting Western pension systems in general are compounded by the peculiar development of the Italian system. There is a lack of transparency and of uniformity in pension rules between classes and categories of workers. In short, Italy's public pension system is compulsory, but it is universal only in appearance. The original organization based on occupational categories still makes

[1] This report has been prepared at the Institute for Studies on Economic Planning (ISPE-Rome-Italy) by a group of researchers coordinated by Rita Di Biase. The sections on the first pillar were drafted by Rita Di Biase and Aldo Gandiglio, those on the second and third pillars are by Maria Cozzolino and Gaetano Proto. The authors are very grateful to Gino Faustini for his invaluable suggestions, to Roberto Malizia (National Statistical Institute, Istat) and Laura Bardone (Eurostat) for their useful information on data, and to Roger Meservey for observations on the English draft. The views expressed in the paper are those of the authors and do not involve the responsibility of the Institute.

itself felt: in practice, the principle of universality is violated by many exceptions, which are not only the source of inequities but also help undermine the financial sustainability of the whole system. Until there is a radical break with this organization, it is only too understandable that new forms of supplementary retirement provision are discouraged.

Although efforts at adjustment have been made in recent years through comprehensive reforms, the effects of the corrective measures will make themselves felt only in the medium term. In fact, both the 1992 and the 1995 reforms are very gradual, and entail a long period of transition. Not many estimates have yet been projected for the ultimate effects of the latest reform, i.e. beyond the transitional period ending in 2036. Comparison with the previous system is greatly complicated by the fact that those with 18 years of covered employment at the end of 1995 continue to be treated under the old rules, while those with less than 18 years enjoy pro rata treatment. Nor can one ignore the numerous exceptions to application of the new rules and the equally numerous relevant areas in which the government has been mandated by enabling acts to issue regulations in the near future. For this reason we have chosen to concentrate on the existing pension system, though taking into account what has been changed, and bearing in mind that our aim is to describe the evolving relations among the three pillars of the retirement system.[2]

The process of revision of the first pillar recently started in Italy is accompanied by measures aimed at modifying the mix between the first and the second pillar. Comprehensive legislation to encourage and regulate supplementary and private retirement provisions first passed in 1993, in an effort to compensate for the presumed reduction of the coverage offered by the compulsory public system stemming from the 1992 reform, proved ineffective. More favourable measures were included in the 1995 social security reform: these include mainly fiscal incentives and the use of severance pay to finance pension funds.

Severance pay is a form of deferred wage to which the worker is entitled upon termination of his employment relationship and could thus be seen as a kind of supplement to the public pension system. Italian severance pay is now at quite high levels as a share of non-wage labour costs by European standards as well. Given its size, it should come as no surprise that the 1995 reform assigns a primary role among sources of

---

[2] The reform of August 1995 goes into effect as of 1 January 1996. In this chapter, reference to the 'present' or 'existing' rules indicates the system in being *prior* to this latest form.

financing of pension funds to the severance pay funds. However, under this respect, the 1995 reform has chosen a very gradual approach: only in the long term will supplementary pension funds take the place of severance pay.

The chapter is organized as follows: sections 2, 3 and 4 describe the public pension system since its institution, including the main issues to be resolved, the recent trends in outlays and the factors which undermine the financial sustainability of the system; section 5 describes recent developments in the area of company pension plans, also providing some evidence on individual retirement provisions.

2. The origins and the basic features of the Italian public pension system

Retirement, disability and survivors' benefit programmes were first instituted for public sector employees in the second half of the nineteenth century. Later, old age and disability pension programmes for private sector employees were created and administered by voluntary funds. In 1919 these two programmes were made compulsory. As a result of reorganization in 1919 and 1933, the different funds were first merged and then placed under the management of the newly created Social Security Administration (INPS, founded in 1933). Survivors' benefits were introduced in 1939.

A brief account of the history of the Italian pension follows, considering three of its main aspects: the model of coverage, the benefit formula, and system financing.

First, the model of coverage and solidarity of the system has been imbued from the outset with an employment-based philosophy. Since the end of the Second World War there have been several attempts to move from the occupationally-based system to a universal one, in order to overcome the 'occupational particularism' inherited from Italy's previous political regimes, the liberal and then the Fascist (Ferrera 1993). These attempts mainly failed because of the lack of solidarity among the different categories of insurees. Furthermore the universal pension system was considered difficult to support financially. There was also a broad consensus in favour of the mutualistic-occupational definition of social security, and finally the conviction that the pension should be considered as 'deferred wages' and consequently a kind of benefit due only to workers, not extended to the citizenry at large. In 1968 a comprehensive reform of the pension system confirmed the occupational model and accentuated its categorical disparities. In the 1970s Italy was left with one of the most chaotic retirement systems in the western world, which an influential study described as 'the labyrinth of pensions' (Castellino 1976).

The second aspect related to the evolution of the Italian pension system is the calculation of benefits. Until 1968 the award formula was based on the amount of contributions paid; in 1969 it went over to an earnings-related method, which was also extended to self-employed workers. For new registrants at the beginning of 1996, according to the reform of August 1995, benefits will be based on contributions.

The third key point is the financing of the retirement schemes. Originally the system was a funded one. From 1945 on this was flanked by a pay-as-you-go system, which soon became predominant. In 1970 the original funded system was definitively abandoned and even the reform of 1995 maintains the pay-as-you-go mode. The main reason for the triumph of the pay-as-you-go approach was the difficulty in protecting the real value of accumulated reserves, which had been massively eroded by inflation. Nor should we underestimate the importance of the political pressure exerted by the generations already entitled to pensions and by the beneficiaries of the more recently created schemes (such as self-employed workers, whose plan was born in 1957). Both, in fact, stood to gain with the pay-as-you-go system, under which retirement pensions were granted immediately to all present retired, regardless of their contribution history.

3.   The present situation

The total number of pensions paid in Italy rose from 12.5 million in 1970 to 16.5 million in 1980 and over 20 million in 1992. (Bear in mind that many retirees are eligible for more than one type of benefit, so that the number of pensioners is significantly lower). Of these pensions, 17.6 million, or 85 per cent of the total, went to private sector retirees. The bulk of these private sector pensions (14.1 million, or 80 per cent) are retirement, disability and survivors' benefits; 14.5 million, or 82 per cent of the private sector pensions were disbursed by the Employee Pension Fund, the general retirement scheme for private sector employees administered by the Social Security Administration (Istituto Nazionale della Previdenza Sociale, INPS). Another 1.4 million (7.9 per cent) came from the National Industrial Accident Insurance Institute (Istituto Nazionale Assicurazione Infortuni sul Lavoro, INAIL) and the remaining 1.7 million are essentially welfare benefits administered by smaller institutes outside INPS. In 1992, civil servants' pensions numbered about 3 million, accounting for 15 per cent of the total (ISTAT 1994).

Total expenditure by the public pension system in 1992 was 215 trillion lire, or 14.3 per cent of GDP. Government retirement provision outlays (disability, retirement, and survivors' benefits and occupational accident benefits) have risen rapidly – from 7.5 per cent of GDP in 1970 to 10.2 per cent in 1980 and 13.8 per cent in 1992 – far outstripping the growth in other kinds of social spending, which just increased from 6.5 to 6.9 and 7.6 per cent (*Relazione Generale sulla Situazione Economica del Paese* for 1994). Essentially, in part because short-run savings on pension outlays are impracticable, efforts to curb social spending have concentrated more heavily on health services, unemployment benefits and family allowances.

3.1   The sources of funding

Table 5.1 shows the main sources of funding of the social security system in 1992, the ratio of active workers to pensioners and the net financial impact of the main pension schemes. For the private sector employee fund run by INPS, social contributions and state transfers accounted respectively for 83.6 and 13.3 per cent of total revenues. In 1980 they had accounted for 88.6 and 9.3 per cent.

If the increase in outlays for pensions is not accompanied by a corresponding rise in contributions and/or general revenues, then a larger deficit will be produced and public debt increased. And this is what has happened in Italy, stemming from the rules and the 'perverse incentives' of the public pension system.

However, the achievement of balance between contributions and benefits (the financial sustainability of the system) also depends on economic and demographic dynamics, on the structure and evolution of the productive sector and the labour market and on social and fiscal policy. These constraints help to explain the deficit of the INPS private sector Employee Pension Fund (the bottom rows of the first two columns), in particular the net imbalance in stock terms.

Similar constraints apply to the management of those pension benefits paid directly by government or government agencies not linked to previous contributions and to the allocation of additional public transfers to some pension funds. The increase in these outlays, when not accompanied by a corresponding rise in general revenues, produces larger budget deficits and swells the debt, which is already at an alarming level.

Specifically, Table 5.1 (the first two columns) excludes all INPS funds and programmes that are different in nature from social security. These provide benefits that may be complementary, subsidiary or instrumental to the general scheme (social pensions; family allowances; tax relief; unemployment benefits; maternity and sick leave). In these cases, the state takes over the financial burden of the pension benefits and of special support granted by the various agencies.

Overall, the social security imbalance, which includes not only the welfare benefits mentioned above but also outlays for the pensions of government employees and other non-contributory benefits (war pensions and disability benefits run outside INPS), accounted for 3.7 per cent of GDP in 1980 and 6 per cent in 1992.

Given that the burden on general government is now very heavy indeed, the problem of financing the public pension system (or, better, sharing the cost between general revenues and social contributions) cannot be solved simply by separating 'welfare' from 'social insurance', as some participants in the present debate have proposed. By itself, of course, reclassification of expenditure according to purpose does nothing to increase the financial resources at the disposal of government.

In seeking to balance pension expenditure and contribution revenue, an essential standard must be that of ending disparities of treatment on both the benefit and the contribution sides.

3.2 The various schemes within the Italian pension system

The Italian public pension system has a number of different retirement schemes for different occupational categories, with enormous disparities both in terms of benefit provisions and in compulsory contribution rates. Recent reforms (Legislative Decree 503 of 30 December 1992 and Law 335 of 8 August 1995) were intended to reduce these differences. The current system is formally universal and compulsory, thanks to its origins in a compulsory employment-based public system, but it has

Table 5.1 – Italian public general pension scheme: sources of funding in 1992

	Private sector employee schemes	of which INPS Employee Pension Fund	Self-employed schemes	Professionals' schemes	Public[a] employee schemes	Total
Total revenues (% composition)	100.00	100.00	100.00	100.00	100.00	100.00
of which: Social contributions	82.80	83.63	90.98	68.41	81.17	83.14
– paid by the employers	56.96	57.13	–	–	55.54	48.19
– paid by employees	25.84	26.50	–	–	25.63	21.92
State transfers	12.06	13.29	1.51	0.29	2.76	9.28
Other[b]	5.14	3.08	7.51	31.31	16.07	7.58
Total outlays (% of GDP)	6.91	6.14	1.25	0.20	1.04	9.40
Number of insured workers/ number of pensioners	1.59	1.54	1.60	5.83	2.88	1.69
Net flow balance (% of GDP)	–0.92	–0.97	–0.26	0.05	–0.02	–1.14
Net stock balance (% of GDP)	–4.25	–4.78	–2.46	0.34	1.21	–5.16

a   Only local government employee schemes (INPDAP).

b   Recovery of benefits improperly paid, collection of back contributions, fines and penalties, voluntary supplementary contributions to reconstruct career, contributions in correspondence to years of study. Voluntary contributions are largest among professionals and public employees, as the table shows.

Source: Relazione Generale sulla Situazione Economica del Paese, 1994, vols II–III.

Table 5.2 – Italian public general pension schemes in 1992 (billion lire)

First Pillar – basic coverage schemes	*Old age + seniority*	*Disability*[a]	*Survivors*	*Total*	*(Percentage composition)*	*(% of GDP)*
Private Sector	83 216	35 864	25 069	144 149	75.13	9.58
Employees	72 660	23 879	21 910	118 448	61.73	7.87
INPS	69 763	23 702	21 430	114 895	59.88	7.64
– *Employee Pension Fund (FPLD)*	65 226	23 374	20 143	108 743	56.68	7.23
– *Other funds (electrical, transport, telephone)*	4 537	328	1 287	6 152	3.21	0.41
INPDAI	2 222	114	363	2 699	1.41	0.18
INPGI	137	2		139	0.07	0.01
ENPALS	537	60	117	715	0.37	0.05
Special funds for occupational groups						
INPS special schemes	111	19	149	279	0.15	0.02
(group insurance, housewives, clergy)						
Self-employed workers	10 446	11 966	3 010	25 422	13.25	1.69
INPS	9 562	11 885	2 538	23 985	12.50	1.59
– Farmers	4 491	8 003	901	13 395		
– Artisans	2 425	2 230	989	5 643		
– Shopkeepers	2 647	1 652	649	4 947		
Professionals	884	81	472	1 437	0.75	0.10

Public Sector[b]	38 040	9 681	47 721	24.87	3.17
Public employees	26 295	6 976	33 271	17.34	2.21
– Central government	21 774	5 437	27 211		
– Public enterprises	4 521	1 539	6 060		
INPDAP (Local government and health service)	11 745	2 705	14 450	7.53	0.96
TOTAL	**121 256**	**35 864**	**191 870**	**100.0**	**12.75**

a   National Accounts figures on disability pensions are lower than those of Table 5.1 (i.e. in 1992 amount just to 4.795 billion lire as against 35.864 billion in the table). The reason for this large discrepancy is that most disability pensions are included by National Accounts data in old age benefits, according to the age of the beneficiaries.

b   For the public sector the distinction between disability and old age pensions is not available.

Source: Relazione Generale sulla Situazione Economica del Paese, 1994, vols. II–III; ISTAT, Statistische sui trattamenti pensionistici al 31 decembre 1992, Roma 1994.

remained far from general or uniform in terms of benefit entitlements and contributions. Table 5.2 shows Italy's principal pension schemes in 1992 for the private sector (employee, self-employed and special occupational schemes) and also provides the amount of pensions for civil servants' schemes.

Within the general earnings-related scheme, administered by INPS, which provides basic compulsory coverage for private sector employees, we focus on the main pension programmes: retirement (old age and seniority), disability and survivors' benefits. These three basic programmes are the core of the system, accounting for 80 per cent of the pensions paid and 90 per cent of pension expenditure in 1992. We exclude the retirement provisions administered by INAIL (occupational accident benefits), the welfare components of the system such as so-called 'social' pensions (old age welfare benefits), benefits to the blind and deaf-mutes, and disability pensions dispensed outside INPS.

INPS runs these general schemes through its largest pension plan, the Employee Pension Fund (FPLD) and three separate schemes for self-employed workers (artisans, 'shopkeepers' and the like, and farmers). These four schemes provide the overwhelming majority of pensions: 13.4 million in 1992, 10 million disbursed through the Employee Pension Fund and 3.4 million through the three self-employed schemes, with total retirement outlays of 133 trillion lire, or 70 per cent of the total pension expenditure.

This general basic pension scheme for the private sector is complemented by numerous special schemes for special occupational categories of employees and professionals. A dozen of these are fairly sizable. They are divided into two types, which may be called 'alternative' and 'supplementary' with respect to the general social security system. *Alternative* public pension schemes run by INPS include some special occupational categories of employees, the most important being funds for electrical power workers, railway and urban transit workers, and public telephone service employees. In 1992, 161 000 pensions were paid by these funds (3.2 per cent of the total pension outlays, as shown in Table 5.2).

Other alternative schemes are run outside INPS, by the occupational groups themselves, including the schemes for industrial managers administered by Istituto Nazionale di Previdenza per i Dirigenti di Aziende Industriali (INPDAI), that for journalists administered by Istituto Nazionale di Previdenza per i Giornalisti Italiani (INPGI) and that for entertainment workers run by Ente Nazionale di Previdenza per i Lavoratori dello Spettacolo (ENPALS). These non-INPS alternative schemes paid 794 000 pensions in 1992, accounting for about 2 per cent of outlays.

Special smaller voluntary schemes within INPS exist for other categories of workers and citizens, such as funds for voluntary group enrolments, housewives and clergy and voluntary basic insurance: these disbursed 125 000 pensions in 1992, making up 0.1 per cent of total benefits.

A large number of professional associations operate pension schemes for their members outside INPS, paying 171 000 pensions in 1992 (0.8 per cent of expenditures).

Supplementary compulsory pension schemes, within INPS, provide additional coverage to specific segments of the labour force. These will be briefly treated later on in describing the second element in the triad of retirement income maintenance.

Public sector pensions are given to two broad categories of civil servants: central and local government employees (including part of the health service, some parts of the school system and the judicial system). Central government has no independent administration of pensions: pensions paid are directly charged to the current account of the Treasury and of independent state agencies. Local government pensions, which were formerly administered by four separate funds, merged in 1993 into a national social security institute for public sector employees (INPDAP). In 1995, INPDAP became the main public employee pension institution, with a special section for central government employees. Overall, 2.2 million civil service pensions were paid in 1992, compared with about 4 million active workers in the sector. Total expenditure came to almost 48 trillion lire, or 25 per cent of the total pension expenditure and 3.2 per cent of GDP.

3.3   Pension entitlement age and the pension formula

Law 421 of October 1992 and Legislative Decree 503 of December 1992 operated to curb the growth in government retirement outlays by raising the retirement age, lengthening contribution requirements for eligibility and extending the reference period for the calculation of pensionable earnings. The reform should also gradually harmonize the treatment of different groups of workers. Moreover, a general revision of the means tests for the welfare components of the pension system has been planned. The objectives were to stabilize the ratio of social security spending to GDP and to create uniform pension benefits for all categories.

Other partial changes have been effected as part of the annual Finance Acts. Law 335 of 8 August 1995 enacts a new reform of the pension system that will be operative from January 1996. The central innovation is the shift from an earnings-based system to one based on contributions. New registrants after 1 January 1996 will be covered by the new system. A mix of the two will apply to workers with less than 18 years of contributions, the so-called pro rata method. The first share of the pension, related to the years of contributions paid up to 1995, is earnings-based; the second, related to the following years, is contribution-based. Workers with more than 18 years of contributions maintain the current earnings-based system. Both these latter two groups, however, may opt for the pure contribution-based formula.

The main aims of the reform are to improve the infra and inter generational redistribution of income and ensure the system's financial and macroeconomic sustainability. Naturally, judgment concerning attainment of these objectives requires long-term projections beyond the transitional phase that ends in 2036. Any such projections require great caution.

The main characteristics of all recent reforms will be examined from the standpoint of their impact on the principal pension schemes.

Private sector employees

One must always distinguish between two types of pension entitlements: the standard *old age* pension and the seniority pension.

Within the general private sector employee retirement scheme, for the *old age* pension, retirement age was 60 for men and 55 for women; Legislative Decree 503 gradually raises these thresholds by five years. The Finance Act for 1995 accelerates the process.

The reform of August 1995 retains the provision raising the retirement age from the present 62 for men and 57 for women to 65 and 60 in the year 2000.

Under the reform new registrants in 1996 will be covered only by the new award formula, which is no longer earnings-based but contributions-based. Accordingly, this will also supplant the old seniority pension mechanism, as pension entitlement age will range from 57 to 65, provided that the worker has at least five years of contributions under the new system providing entitlement to a pension at least 20 per cent larger than the social allowance for indigent persons over 65. Alternative requirements are age 65 with at least five years' contributions under the new system or 40 years of contributions, regardless of age.

For those beginning work in 1996, the award formula is based on career contributions, revalued each year at an 'interest rate' that takes account of GDP growth in the previous five years. The amount so obtained is converted into an annuity, using coefficients that reflect life expectancy and thus increase with the age at which the pension is first drawn.

For workers who have 18 years of covered employment by 31 December 1995 and do not opt for the contributions-based formula, the pension benefit is computed by the present formula; for those with under 18 years of contributions, the portion of the pension accrued by that date is fixed by the present award formula.

The basic characteristics of the pension award formula pre-1992, post-1992 and post-1995 are depicted in Box A; they will be commented on in more detail later, with discussion of the impact on the various pension schemes.

Under the pre-1995 system, the accrual rate is 2 per cent of average assessed earnings in the entire working life (only for new registrants), multiplied by the number of contribution years with a ceiling of 80 per cent of pensionable earnings.[3] The ceiling thus corresponds to 40 years of contributions.

The minimum contribution requirement for eligibility was 15 years, but this is now being gradually raised to 20. Under the 1995 reform these adjustments have been accelerated.

More favourable rules on pensionable earnings and pension benefits are enjoyed by some private sector employees inside and outside INPS, such as electrical power workers, railway and assimilated workers, industrial executives and journalists.

Until the 1992 reform a worker with, say, 20 years of contributions would have an *income replacement* rate of 37.7 per cent; with 40 years, this rose to 76.4 per cent. Following the reform, it is estimated that in 2010 these replacement rates will be diminished by about 4 and 5 percentage

---

[3] For workers with more than 15 years of contributions at the moment of the 1992 reform, the reference period for calculating pensionable earnings is gradually extended to 10 years, instead of 5 years under the pre-1992 rules; for workers with less than 15 years of contributions the reference period has been gradually raised up to the entire working life.

Box A

Basic pension benefits formula (P), according to different reforms

Before 1992 reform $P = 2\% \cdot n \cdot E$

                                2% = the accrual rate

                                n = years of contributions

                                E = pensionable earnings (average earnings in the last 5 years)

1992 reform $P = 2\% \cdot n \cdot E$

                                2% = the accrual rate

                                n = years of contributions

                                E = pensionable earnings (average lifetime earnings)

1995 reform $P = \beta(e_p) \cdot C_t \cdot \sum_{j=0}^{n-1} \dfrac{(1+r)^j}{(1+w)^j}$

                                β = conversion coefficient, varying with age of retirement (e_p), hence life expectancy (from 4.720% at age 57 to 6.136% at age 65)

                                n = years of contributions

                                C_t = contributions in year t

                                r = average change in nominal GDP over 5 years preceding the adjustment

                                w = average rate of growth of nominal wages

---

points, respectively; in 2030, by 4 and 15 points (CER 1994). It is evident that as the end of the transitional period approaches, which is overlong for the 1992 reform, the replacement rate sharply decreases.

Estimates of the effects of the 1995 reform show that assuming rates of economic growth comparable to those recorded in the past, the replacement rate for wage and salary earners would be higher than under the previous legislation (Banca d'Italia 1995a). However, the replacement depends on the relative increase in GDP and earnings: the higher the former with respect to the latter, the higher the replacement rate.

In addition to the standard old age pension, Italy also recognizes a seniority pension, to which the employee is entitled, according to the current rules, after 35 years of contributions, regardless of age, and he may draw it immediately upon retiring.

The 1995 reform maintains the seniority pension (except for new registrants) but raises the 35-year requirement to the ceiling of 40 years from 2008 onwards; alternatively, it simply raises the minimum age from 52 in 1996 and 1997 to 57 in 2008. The intention is to gradually eliminate the seniority pension de facto encouraging people to retire later, as well as to equalize benefits between groups of workers.

Self-employed workers

A major reform of self-employment pensions was enacted by Law 233/1990. For self-employed workers, the schemes for the largest groups, which are those run by INPS, allow retirement at 65 for men and 60 for women, with a minimum of 20 years of covered employment to achieve gradually. At present the self-employed schemes administered by INPS determine pension awards by multiplying amounts 2 per cent of average earnings over the last 10 years by the number of years of contributions (ceiling of 40). Pensions are revalued by the same indexation rules as in the private sector schemes, which will be described below.

The 1995 reform extends the reference period for the calculation of pension formula for self-employed workers to the last 15 years. Also, they will be eligible for the seniority pension only with 35 years of contributions and at least 56 years of age. The age will gradually increase to reach 57 years in 1998.

As a result of the 1992 reform the *income replacement rate* for self-employed workers with, for example, 20 years of contributions will diminish by 2.3 percentage points between 1992 and 2010, while it will be steady in 2030. For a worker with 40 years of contributions this replacement rate will be cut by about 2 percentage points from 1992 to 2010 and by a further 7 points in 2030 (CER 1994). It is evident that from 2010 onwards the effects of the reform will be more pronounced (less generous in terms of benefits) for private sector employees than for self-employed workers. However, this pattern may change in the years to come, as the 1995 reform is less favourable to the self-employed.

Public sector employees

Finally, in the public sector a hotly debated issue in Italy has been the disparity in pension rules between private and public sector employees, widely perceived as producing unwarranted privileges for civil servants in many key areas. For example, the distinction between old age and seniority pensions is similar to that for the private sector, but prior to the 1992 reform there were major divergences in rules. Some important differences still exist.

First of all, in the public sector pension payments are granted from the moment of retirement, while in the private sector workers with less than 35 years of contributions must wait until retirement age to start drawing their benefits. Until 1992, the minimum contribution requirement for *central* government workers was 20 years for men and women; for *local* government employees it was respectively 25 years for men and 20 for women. However, including imputed contributions based on such factors as family status, military service and university education, this could actually be reduced to a minimum of 15 years for women. (This minimum, which sometimes produced 'baby pensioners' in their thirties, is now being gradually raised to 20). The 1992 reform cancelled all these preferential treatments for employees with less than 8 years of seniority at the end of that year, setting a 35-year minimum as in the INPS schemes. For those with more than 8 years' service, the previous minimums were raised proportionally to the number of missing years. Naturally, this differential observance of vested rights means unequal treatment to the disadvantage of younger civil servants.

In the public sector there is mandatory retirement at 65 years for men and women. This can be extended to 70 years for employees falling short of the minimum contribution requirement. There are exceptions in some categories: university professors and judges have higher age limits; whereas military personnel, the police, firemen and railway workers have lower ones.

Until 1992 the basis for the calculation of the pension was the last monthly salary received by the civil servant. With 15 years of contributions, the *replacement rate* was 35 per cent, reaching a ceiling of 94.4 per cent for central government and 100 per cent for local administration after 40 years of service. With the 1992 reform, for civil servants having under 15 years of seniority, pensionable salary is now calculated over the full career, as for private sector workers; for those with more than 15 years' service, it is the average of earnings over the last ten years. Both these rules will be gradually reached. The indexation mechanism has also been adjusted to that covering private sector employees.

With the latest reform, the pension award and entitlement rules for new workers in the public sector are the same as in the private sector. For those with under 18 years of contributions, the new rules are applied on a pro rata basis. Those with 18 years' service by the end of 1995 have, in addition to the two private sector formulas (35 years of contributions, but with a rising age requirement; or a gradually rising contribution requirement), a third possibility: no minimum age, only a service requirement, with the size of pension being diminished for every year of contributions under 37. The 35-year entitlement rule cited above is only putative, however; the effective minimums are those of the present rules, i.e. 20 years for women and 25 for men; there is a decrease for every year under 35, however.

Let us now briefly review the mechanism of *indexation* of pensions. Prior to the 1992 reforms, the initial pension was revalued over time with the rise in consumer prices and according to an indicator of the divergence between real wages for active workers and consumer prices, which meant that pensions could generally be kept in line with changing living standards. The less favourable indexation mechanism installed by the 1992 reform only safeguards pensioners' purchasing power, in that retirement benefits are now linked only to prices and not to the earnings of employed workers, although the Decree does allow for optional adjustment to wages in the framework of the annual Finance Act. From 1985 to 1990, under the old mechanism of indexation the value of pensions in the private sector actually outpaced inflation, rising by 6.6 per cent per year compared with an average inflation rate of 5.7 per cent. Subsequently the less favourable formula covered only about half of the rise in the cost of living (2.5 as against 4.2 per cent in 1993–94).

Under the 1995 reform, benefits are indexed to prices only. Additional increments of 1 per cent of GDP are envisaged starting in 2009, but only for pensions below 10 million lire a year.

3.4 Main issues and problems

The 1992 law is unquestionably important and comprehensive and the August 1995 reform seeks to cope with the unresolved problems, but their effects will be felt only in the medium term. Consequently some issues are still debated and require solutions. Among them we have analysed the following.

Firstly, there are the redistributive effects of the present threshold level of 57.58 million lire a year for pensionable earnings, above which the accrual rate is diminished in a series of steps. Originally covering only the private sector employees' plan, this cap (indexed to annual rises in the cost of living) has been extended to the self-employed and civil service schemes. It is relevant to the benefit formula but has no effect whatever on contributions, as all earnings, even above the threshold, continue to be subject to the social security contribution. Exceptions are industrial managers and self-employed workers, for whom the cap also applies to contributions. The two caps are respectively 195 and 93.3 million lire.

Some analysts contend that under the 1992 reform alone (fully in effect), the implicit yield of contributions for the typical worker will still be positive, but considerably less than at present. Even in the future, however, and despite the cap, the present high accrual rate will make the public pension system more advantageous than supplementary pension funds or the other possibilities offered by the financial market, thus discouraging the development of such alternatives (Castellino 1994).

In the meantime, under the present system, the public pension system will have very limited redistributive effects stemming from the rules determining minimum benefits and maximum pensionable earnings. Although the 1995 reform does introduce modifications in this regard, a look at the effects under the current legislation is nevertheless revealing. Table 5.3 shows the accrual rates at various earnings levels and their effects on pension amounts, based on the legislation in force until 1995. Below the minimum benefit (Table 5.3, section a), where government compensation tops pensions up to the minimum level, the lower one's average earnings or, alternatively, the fewer one's contribution years, the higher the effective accrual rate. Figures shown in the first two columns, both for 25 and 40 years of contributions, are provided as examples of different gross pensionable earnings which generate the same level of pensions, the so-called minimum pensions, owing to the government compensation.

This minimum is 8.1 million lire a year and corresponds to gross pensionable earnings of 10.2 million lire and 40 years of contributions or to 16.3 million lire for 25 years. From the minimum to the maximum (Table 5.3, section b), the accrual rate of 2 per cent generates benefits ranging from 8.1 to 46.1 million lire a year, considering 40 years of contributions.

166

Table 5.3 – Accrual rates in 1995

a) Under the minimum				
Years of contributions	25	40		
	Ge = Pe	*Ge = Pe*	*P*	*ar*
		(thousands of lire)		
	11 424	7 144	**8 144**	2.85
	14 688	9 154	**8 144**	2.22
	16 320	10 200	**8 144**	2.00

b) From the minimum to the maximum			
Years of contributions	40		
	Ge = Pe	*P*	*ar*
	10 200	**8 144**	2.00
	46 062	**36 850**	2.00
	57 578	**46 062**	2.00

c) Above the maximum				
Years of contributions		40		
	Ge	*Pe*	*P*	*ar*
	76 579	72 750	58 223	1.90
	109 398	92 988	74 564	1.70
	123 217	101 654	**81 440**	1.65

Ratio of max. to min.	**12.1**	**10.0**	**10.0**

Ge = gross earnings of employees (thousands of lire)
Pe = gross pensionable earnings (thousands of lire)
P = pension amounts (thousands of lire)
ar = accrual rate (as percentage)

Source: Senato della Repubblica (1995).

Above the earnings cap of 57.58 million lire a year, where the redistributive effects of the public retirement provisions should be especially pronounced, the table shows that with earnings of 123.2 million lire and 40 years of contributions a retiree achieves an average accrual rate of 1.65 per cent and a pension of 81.4 million lire, which is 10 times the minimum.

The corresponding gross earnings ratio is 12.1 to 10 (see the last row of Table 5.3). The closeness of these two high ratios indicates that the redistributive effect of the pension minimum and the earnings cap, i.e. the extent to which the public pension system narrows the gap, is very limited indeed, especially by comparison with the impact in other countries' systems. This situation confirms the effect of Italian legislation of conferring primacy on the public system and discouraging high-income occupational groups from turning to the other two pillars.

The new law eliminates the cap of 57.58 million lire on pensionable earnings. As the new regime embodies incentives to keep working, the elimination of the cap means that the contributions-based award formula could actually result in an income replacement rate of over 100 per cent. The repercussions on financial stability, equity, and incentives for private retirement plans should be obvious.

On the other hand the new law institutes an income ceiling of 132 million lire a year for both contributions and pension benefits. Above this amount, those investing in supplementary private pension plans receive fiscal and contribution relief. One purpose is to encourage the growth of private pension plans. The fiscal and contribution benefits must be promulgated by the government before the end of 1995; they will apply only to workers beginning their careers in 1996 and to those opting for the new system, providing they have at least five years of contributions under it (and could thus enjoy the benefits no sooner than 2001). The effects of the ceiling, clearly, will not be felt in the near future. Moreover, the new ceiling does not apply to industrial managers or the 16 privatized special funds (that of journalists, for example), which retain the present ceiling of 195 million.

In short, the high level of the cap, the gradualness of the reform and the exemption of the higher-income categories suggest that this measure will be ineffective in spurring the takeoff of private pension plans. The impact of using the existing severance pay funds, discussed below, will undoubtedly be more significant.

Although vertical redistribution will be slight in the future as in the past, the cumulative reforms have improved the other aspects of redistribution (the harmonization of public sector with private sector employees and the gradual reduction of the advantages enjoyed by the self-employed). The main innovations of the 1995 reform, the contributions-based formula, is more favourable to workers with long careers (not those with steeply rising earnings).

Secondly, there is the great importance of the *minimum retirement benefits* for low-income workers until 1995. The yearly pre-tax minimum is 7.5 million lire (about $4500 at the exchange rates of June 1995). Sub-minimum benefits requiring state compensation numbered about 6 million in 1992 (51 per cent of all the pensions administered by INPS within the Employee Pension Fund and the three main self-employed schemes). In the future, moreover, the number of beneficiaries of sub-minimum compensation is expected to increase rather than decrease. The average number of years of contributions remains quite low (just 18 years for women in 1993 and 25 years for men). Moreover, projections based on employment trends and the size of the underground economy indicate an accentuation of the phenomenon. Raising the contribution requirement from 15 to 20 years will mean that a larger number of workers will fail to reach the minimum, which gives them an incentive to work off the books and evade the contributions altogether.

The 1995 law eliminates the sub-minimum allowance for benefits determined exclusively by the contributions-based formula. Instead, a 'social allowance' for those over 65 and under a minimum income will be introduced in 1996.

Thirdly, there is the question of *seniority pensions.* Instituted in 1965, these are considered an Italian anomaly and a prime source of disparity of treatment and inequity between the beneficiaries of different retirement programmes (especially vis-à-vis regular old age pensions) and between the various pension schemes. In 1993 the seniority pensions accounted for 16 per cent of the outlays of the main retirement programmes (old age, disability and survivors' benefits), 14 per cent going to men and 2 per cent to women.

While the award formula for the two benefits is the same, the disparity of treatment consists in the seniority pensioner's enjoyment of the retirement benefit during the years before standard retirement age. For a worker retiring at 50 with 35 years of contributions, for example, the advantage amounts to 130 monthly cheques (ten years of retirement benefits, including the 'thirteenth' month), assuming a regular retirement age of 60.

As noted above, the inequities inherent in the seniority pension provision are still more severe when it comes to public sector employees, for whom the 35-year requirement may be cut to just 20. Some correctives were instituted in 1995, as we have seen, but seniority pensions have not been abolished, as had been proposed by some analysts.

Fourthly, there is the problem of *cumulability,* another Italian anomaly, whereby the system allows a retiree to draw more than one pension. Furthermore, pensions may also be combined with earned income (both salaried and self-employment), with reductions in the pension benefit of at most 50 per cent of the non-pension income. Especially privileged treatment is accorded to pensioners with self-employment income (craftsmen, shopkeepers, farmers). Until the end of 1994 these groups enjoyed 100 per cent cumulability of pension and earned income; and this possibility is retained for those who by 31 December 1994 had satisfied the pension eligibility requirements.

The 1995 reform restricts cumulability with other salaried income and sets coefficients reducing cumulability with self-employment income for those retiring under the contributions-based formula.

Fifthly, there are *survivors' benefits*, whose number accounted for 35 per cent of total retirement and disability pensions in 1992. That year, within the four largest INPS funds 78 per cent of the total number of survivors' benefits were paid by the Employee Pension Fund and 22 per cent by the three schemes for self-employed workers. Originally intended to provide a subsistence for families deprived of all means of support with the death of the breadwinner, survivors' benefits have gradually deviated from this pattern over the years and taken on a largely auxiliary role. In fact, they are now frequently paid to persons with other sources of income, both earned and other. This raises problems of equity, in that often the condition of economic hardship for the beneficiary is not fulfilled; indeed, it can actually happen that the survivor is better off economically than when the original pensioner was alive. Prior to the 1992 reform only the pensioner's own income was counted in the means test for sub-minimum compensation; now the spouse's income is also included.

The new law retains the percentages of revertibility, depending on the survivor's income; survivors' benefits are increased for families with dependent children. Some restrictions on the cumulability of disability pensions were introduced.

Sixthly, many rules, some of them highly advantageous, govern pensions for women. Today, 53 per cent of all Italian pension recipients (including survivors' benefits) are women; it rises to 72 per cent for holders of two pensions and 81 per cent for triple-pensioners (as shown in Table 5.4, section a). Women's share of employment is rising (now 35.3 per cent), and in the public sector is nearly equal to that of men (47.5 per cent).

As noted, women enjoy certain privileges under the current pension system (above all, the effective reduction of 4 or 5 years in the seniority eligibility requirement for public employees); some other provisions are mainly used by women (survivors' benefits, causing problems of cumulability and sub-minimum allowances).

The reform law of 1995 introduces some provisions explicitly affecting women and others that will apply mainly to them. First, women's retirement age (for old age pensions) during the transition is raised to

Table 5.4 – Pensioners in 1991: number, type of pension, and values

	Single	*Double*	*Triple*	*Total*
a) Number of pensioners (% values)				
Pensioners	**87.8**	11.8	0.4	100.0
of which: – women	52.4	**71.6**	80.6	54.8
– under 60 years	29.2	13.4	4.6	27.3
b) Typology of pensions (% values)				
old age + seniority	**67.2**	16.2	15.6	61.0
disability	13.5	17.0	**33.8**	14.0
survivors	13.4	**54.4**	23.0	18.3
occup. accident	0.7	2.2	18.5	1.0
others (*)	5.2	10.2	9.1	5.7
total	100.0	100.0	100.0	100.0
c) Average value of pensions (million lire)				
multiple pensions	**10.77**	**14.66**	**20.82**	11.26
1st pension	10.77	8.65	10.72	10.52
2nd pension		6.01	4.06	5.94
3rd pension			6.04	6.05

(*) 'social pensions' (old welfare benefits), war pensions and other welfare components of the system.

Source: Itaxmod data on 1991.

60 in the year 2000 for all pension plans (though later, as we have seen,
the contributions-based formula will allow retirement at 57). In the public sector women will enjoy, paradoxically, a relative advantage compared with the private sector, as the standard retirement age becomes
flexible, dropping from the present 65 to 60 and to as low as 57. Second,
the new system abolishes the sub-minimum allowance, which 'tops up'
retirement benefits for the indigent to the minimum pension. The
allowance had benefited mainly women, with their more irregular
careers, lower earnings and lower contributions. Third, survivors' benefits are made to depend on the beneficiary's income and may be cut by
as much as 50 per cent of the cumulative pension. Clearly, this affects
women more than men. Fourth, the special labour market position of
women is recognized with the confirmation of some existing provisions
(the option of a lengthy period of unpaid maternity leave) and imputed
contribution years for child-rearing (enhanced for handicapped children), up to one year's early retirement per child or else a higher award
coefficient than that corresponding to the woman's age of retirement.

Table 5.5 – Households' sources of income in 1991

1) Number of households	North-Centre	South	Italy
	(% by area)		
Households with:			
a) only pensions of which:	1.3	2.7	**1.8**
retirement, disability and survivors'	1.1	2.5	1.5
b) pensions plus other incomes	26.2	26.6	**26.3**
c) pensions plus labour incomes	21.0	16.5	**19.5**
a) + b) + c)	48.5	45.8	**47.6**
d) other households	51.5	54.2	**52.4**
Total	100.0	100.0	**100.0**

2) Incomes			
	(index: average = 100)		
a) only pensions of which:	29.4	30.5	**29.9**
retirement, disability and survivors	30.6	30.6	30.6
b) pensions plus other incomes	62.2	47.2	**57.3**
c) pensions plus labour incomes	138.2	112.6	**131.1**
a) + b) + c)	94.2	69.7	**86.5**
d) other households	153.7	106.7	**137.7**
Total	108.8	81.7	**100.0**

Source: Itaxmod data on 1991.

Fifth, an enabling act gives the government the possibility of instituting a pension for housewives.

Finally, there are a number of additional problems with the pension system that do not appear to be receiving adequate treatment even in the latest reform. These concern the *age* of beneficiaries (are they really the elderly?), *multiple* pensions and the size of pension benefits in proportion to total household incomes. Microdata on individual and household income for 1991 (Di Biase et al. 1995) provide some information on these issues and have been exploited at the individual and household level (Tables 5.4 and 5.5).

Table 5.4, section a, shows that 88 per cent of pensioners have just one pension; of these 'single pensioners', more than half are women and nearly 30 per cent are younger than 60. The remaining 12 per cent of pensioners draw two or even three pensions. These are even more heavily female, women accounting for 72 per cent of the multiple pensioners. Section b breaks down pension benefits by type. The majority of 'single pensioners' (67 per cent) are drawing retirement pensions;

among double pensioners, the largest group is survivors' benefits (54 per cent); and for triple pensioners, retirement pensions become the least significant category (under 16 per cent). The most frequent combination is survivors' plus disability benefits. By age, 80 per cent of disability pensioners are older than 55, and 40 per cent are aged 55–64 (figures not shown in the table).

Section c shows that the average yearly value of single pensions is 10.8 million lire. Recipients' income from double pensions averages around 15 million (36 per cent higher than single pension) and from triple pensions, 20.8 million (42 per cent more than double pensions). According to this source, the number of pension entitlements in 1991 was 1.83 times the over-65-year-olds.

The number and size of pension benefits have also to be considered in relation to the overall earnings of the household, to assess the standard of living of beneficiaries. It could be useful for this purpose to use microdata at the household level. Table 5.5, in fact, breaks down households by source of income (section 1) and supplies the average value of the different sources (section 2). There are great differences among households whose incomes include pensions, which account for 47.6 per cent of total Italian households. In particular, households totally dependent on pensions make up just 1.8 per cent of the total and their income is modest (29.9 per cent of the national average household income). Households with pensions plus other incomes (unearned income) account for 26 per cent of the total and have incomes 57.3 per cent of the average. Households with pensions plus labour incomes are 19 per cent of the total and their income is above the average (131 per cent). The remaining Italian households (52 per cent) with no pension have income (labour income) which is well above the average (137.7 per cent).

More homogeneous assessments which take into account the number of members show that the standard of living of households deteriorates as the number of members increases both for households totally dependent on pensions and for those with pensions plus other incomes.

The problems listed in the foregoing are the main issues to be resolved. The 1992 reform began to deal with them, but the adjustments made must be judged as too gradual, hence of insufficient efficacy. Accordingly, it comes as no surprise that these same problems were dealt with again in August 1995. It is evident that first and foremost these problems have set constraints on the financial sustainability of Italy's public retirement provisions, and will continue to do so. The 1995 law is

173

more incisive than the previous reform but still gradual. Moreover, one cannot ignore the numerous areas in which the government has been mandated to issue future regulations on important aspects of the reform. This would make it very complicated indeed to compare the two systems. Second, the present system is so ordered as to make it over-generous to some groups of beneficiaries, with a munificence that poses serious problems for the success of supplementary private pension plans. Certainly the elements of equity introduced by the latest reform improve the redistributive effects and open up possibilities for the growth of private retirement plans.

For the less generously protected income brackets, meanwhile, the option of a large-scale shift into private retirement schemes is unthinkable; for these groups, the government inevitably must be the ultimate guarantor of the pension promise.

3.5 Severance pay: social protection benefit or deferred wages?

Some consideration must also be given to the institution of severance pay in Italy, whose inclusion as part of the old age function is questionable but whose possible role in discouraging supplementary retirement schemes warrants discussion. Here we examine the importance of Italian severance pay funds in quantitative terms, seeking to define them within the classificatory systems adopted internationally while noting their national peculiarities. We supply examples concerning typical workers in the private and public sectors to bring these quantitative questions out. The issue of the severance pay entitlement's presumable damping effect on the growth of supplementary retirement plans will be discussed further in section 5.

First of all, let us recall that severance pay as such was legally instituted at a time of mass unemployment as a termination benefit and acted as income support for dismissed workers during job search. With the expansion of employment and more importantly with the increase in job stability (low inter-firm mobility), severance pay turned into nothing but a kind of deferred wage, which takes the form of a lump-sum payment upon termination of the employee's relation with the employer. Severance pay funds are mandatory for all employees (public and private) and can be considered as a 'supplement' to the state pension for Italian workers. According to Eurostat (1992a), severance pay benefits represented 10.9 per cent of old age cash benefits and 10.7 per cent of total old age benefits in Italy in 1988; in 1992 these shares were 12.6 and 12.4 per cent. This type of scheme is not available to employees in other EU member states. However, Eurostat maintains that 'the inclusion of this benefit in the old age function is questionable. Firstly, because part of the amount that is paid to a beneficiary can be granted at any age after the termination of employment. Secondly, and more importantly, such payments may be considered not as social protection benefits, but as enforced saving or deferred wages.' Eurostat accordingly concludes that in evaluating old age benefits in Italy these considerations need to be taken into account. As regards the enforced saving function of severance pay, it is worth recalling that after eight years' service the law grants the employee the possibility of an advance, amounting at most to 70 per cent of severance pay entitlement, for extraordinary health expenditures or for house purchase. However no more than 4 per cent of a company's employees may use this facility each year. A rather widespread fringe benefit is the concession of advances at more favourable conditions than those provided by the law (Cozzolino and Proto 1994).

Severance pay is significant in size when viewed from the financing side as well. It is charged to employers in both the private and public sectors, though in the latter a small employee contribution is also levied. In 1992, according to National Accounts data, severance pay accounted for 6 per cent of total labour costs in all of industry and 12 per cent in banking and insurance (shares that have held steady for the past decade).

European labour cost statistics (Eurostat 1992b) put these severance pay benefits under the heading of 'payments for days not worked', i.e. as so-called non-wage labour costs. In 1988 these 'payments for days not worked' accounted for 11.4 per cent of the total cost of labour in all industries, and for Italy this figure was largely due (more than half the total) to the inclusion of severance pay.

Going by the generally accepted classifications of labour cost components most widely used internationally, the features of Italian severance pay qualify it as a *statutory* contribution, because it is imposed on firms by government regulation. Its compulsory nature distinguishes it from ordinary fringe benefits. For even though a good portion of fringe benefits consists, like severance pay, of deferred payments, they are generally classed as *non-statutory* social welfare contributions, in that in most cases they are paid by firms under collective bargaining agreements, or voluntary commitments between employers and employees.

To put it simply, the amount of non-statutory contributions in Italy is small because statutory contributions include severance pay. As a consequence, firms' ability to control non-statutory social welfare contributions is limited and their role in the development of welfare programmes, including supplementary pension programmes, is accordingly insignificant.

Now let us briefly examine the rules governing Italian severance pay, as regards financing, award formula and hence the amount of the benefit. As we shall see, the institution reflects earnings disparities, which are thus added to those already discovered in the pension system, namely that between the public and private sectors and those within the public sector.

In the *private sector* the employer must set aside 6.91 per cent (7.41 per cent minus 0.5 per cent additional employer social security contributions) of the employee's gross annual salary; the fund is revalued yearly with a real rate of return equal to 1.5 per cent plus 75 per cent of the inflation rate. This formula provides decreasing real yields up to a 6 per cent inflation rate and negative real yelds above that rate. In substance, the fund so created reflects the employee's entire earnings history; the influence of wage increases concentrated in the last few years is accordingly slight.

In the *public sector* there are innumerable disparities between agencies both in the size of the employer and employee contributions and in the reference salary. To summarize, for the central government the total effective charge is 6.67 per cent, for local government and health service it is 5.33 per cent, and for other public agencies, 8.33 per cent. For the latter no contribution is levied on employees; the others require a 2.5 per cent contribution. However, these differences are offset by tax advantages when benefits are received. Unlike the private sector, here the size of the severance pay benefit depends heavily on the last year's earnings. The base for calculating the severance pay award consists of an amount ranging from 80 to 100 per cent of the last monthly pay cheque (less certain pay packet items that are excluded, varying with the employing agency), multiplied by the number of years of service, effective and imputed.

Here again the 1995 law moves towards harmonization, equalizing severance pay as between private and public sector employees. For those already in service, the transition to the new rules will be defined by collective bargaining.

The reader may find it a useful aid to consult Table 5.6, which gives figures on severance pay for a number of typical employees (private and

Table 5.6 – Yearly earnings, pensions and severance pay in 1995* (gross and net values in thousand lire**)

Government agencies	High level manager (grade I)	Middle manager (grade IV)	Clerical employee (grade VII)
Gross earnings	101 000	52 000	33 100
Gross pension	57 800	32 800	24 500
Gross severance pay	263 500	75 700	59 500
Net severance pay	183 300	62 500	50 500

Central government	High level manager (grade I)	Middle manager (grade IX)	Clerical employee (grade V)
Gross earnings	92 000	51 000	32 700
Gross pension	52 700	30 000	22 000
Gross severance pay	184 300	70 400	49 500
Net severance pay	150 400	62 800	45 500

Metal and engineering industry	High level manager (grade I)	Middle manager (grade VII)	Production worker (grade IV)
Gross carnings	125 000	73 100	30 200
Gross pension	70 623	39 000	17 200
Gross severance pay	312 500	122 800	66 300
Net severance pay	209 289	91 200	55 300

(*)   Assumptions: for managers, at least 10 years' service at managerial level; for other grades average salary for each grade and 30 years' service.

(**)   10 million lire correspond to about $6000 at exchange rates of June 1995.

Source: Based on data from Ministry of the Treasury and Federmeccanica.

public sectors, production and clerical workers, managers and executives) with 30 years' service. The table also shows the last year's salary and presumable pension benefits, to show the relative importance of severance pay as deferred wages.

Given these figures, it is easy to see why, under the pre-1995 rules, Italy is unlikely to witness any substantial development of supplementary retirement schemes for middle and higher levels, who have little incentive to supplement the basic public retirement scheme, or for the lower income brackets, who can hardly be expected to allocate an additional share of their income to such purposes.

4.   Recent trends in pension expenditure

The number of retirement, disability and survivors' benefit entitlements rose from 9.6 million in 1970 to 13.2 million in 1980 and more than 16.3 million in 1992. In the 1970s most of the increase (2 million) was accounted for by INPS disability pensions, whereas in the 1980s the steepest rises were recorded for retirement benefits (over a million), disability pensions (800 000) and civil servants' pensions (500 000).

This expansion reflects employment trends, lengthening life expectancy, and such reforms as the extension of social security to the self-employed and to needy elderly or disabled persons and the introduction of seniority pensions. Eligibility requirements for certain benefits were also relaxed: first the INPS disability pension and later the civil disability pension. In the 1980s the number of beneficiaries was also swollen by early retirement programmes, used as social shock absorbers, which by the end of the decade covered some 200 000 workers below the regular retirement age.

The size of retirement benefits has also increased greatly. The average pension rose from 27 per cent of employees' average gross earnings in 1970 to 29 per cent in 1980 and 39 per cent in 1992, owing to the increase in contribution years as the system matures and steadily more generous rules governing both initial awards and indexation. In the late 1980s benefit payments were further increased by measures raising 'social' pensions (old age welfare benefits) and the minimum pension for low-income workers, bringing the minimum self-employed pension up to that for employees and recalculating earlier pension awards. Finally there has been a steady relative increase in the numbers of retirees with larger pensions, such as civil servants, and a reduction in groups with comparatively small benefits (self-employed farm workers and the recipients of 'social' pensions) (Banca d'Italia 1991).

The importance of retirement benefits increased progressively from 1970 to 1990, coming to account for over half of total expenditure in 1992. Conversely, the share of disability and survivors' benefits declined. Starting with Law 222/1984, the rules governing disability pensions were progressively tightened, mainly by abrogating the consideration of socio-economic distress on an equal footing with medical condition as

Table 5.7 – Average pension amounts (thousand lire) and economic ratios based on pre-reform rules*

(a)	*Old age + seniority*	*Disability*	*Survivors'*	*Weighted average*	*Percentages*		
	(o)	*(d)*	*(s)*	*(w)*	*o/w*	*d/w*	*s/w*
1960	183	158	146	171	107.0	92.4	85.4
1970	526	355	379	439	119.8	80.9	86.3
1980	3 539	1 972	1 993	2 677	132.2	73.7	74.4
1990	13 630	7 400	7 668	10 279	132.6	72.0	74.6
1995	15 049	8 170	8 466	11 661	129.1	70.1	72.6
2000	16 615	9 021	9 347	13 132	126.5	68.7	71.2
2010	20 253	10 996	11 394	16 403	123.5	67.0	69.5
2040	36 686	19 918	20 639	31 014	118.3	64.2	66.5

(b)	*No of pensions* *P*	*Pension expend.* *(% of GDP)*	*Other Estimates** on pension expend.* *(% of GDP)*		
	(thousands)		pre-1992	post-1992 (1)	post-1992 (2)
1960	5 786	4.3			
1970	9 639	6.7			
1980	13 225	10.5			
1990	15 349	12.0			
1995	17 170	14.4	12.7	12.4	12.4
2000	18 691	15.4	13.9	13.2	12.5
2010	21 101	17.1	16.0	14.9	13.0
2040	26 011	23.0			

*   Projections for 1995 and the following years are based on the rules in effect prior to the 1992 reform, including indexation to prices and to earnings.

** These estimates are based both on pre-1992 and post-1992 rules. The latter are differentiated according to indexation to prices and earnings (1) or only to prices (2).

Source: Senato della Repubblica (1995); CER (1994).

an eligibility requirement. Essentially this approach curbed use of disability benefits as a pathway to early retirement, a way of getting a pension without working or to cumulate it with earned income. Retroactive medical checks to uncover anomalies and irregularities in awards were stepped up. The 1995 reform introduces still more rigorous rules for checks and controls.

In the past, the generous award of disability pensions was used as the functional equivalent of unemployment benefits (beneficiaries were concentrated in the South). This sustained consumption well above output and helped contain the potentially devastating repercussions of unemployment. The budgetary effects, however, were substantial.

Let us recall, finally, that the rise in pension outlays has greatly improved the economic status of old people. Today the poverty rate for households headed by elderly does not differ much from the national average. Elderly people are thus comparatively better off in Italy than in many other countries (Franco 1993).

Table 5.7 shows the average size of each type of pension and its ratio to the overall average pension (section a), the number of pensions and pension expenditure (section b). The projections in relation to GDP, under the pre-1995 rules, are based on different sources and assumptions. These rules are of interest because they will continue to cover many workers for many years. We do not know how many will opt for the new system and it is too early to make any reliable projections.

The growth in the number of pensions was projected to drive pension expenditure from 14.4 per cent of GDP in 1995 to 17.1 per cent in 2010. The projected further rise in this ratio to 23 per cent in 2040 has to be ascribed to demographic factors, as will be discussed later on.

Notwithstanding the structural reform measures enacted in 1992, then, in the absence of the 1995 reform pension expenditure would have continued to outpace GDP growth. This trend poses serious problems of sustainability and makes measures to contain pension expenditure unavoidable. There is nothing to be surprised at; in fact, on the basis of the projected increase of the elderly population from 17 to 29 per cent of total population between 1995 and 2040, it is reasonable that the ratio of pension outlays to GDP should also increase. Moreover, the projections given in Table 5.7 consider both pre- and post-1992 rules to highlight the moderating effect of indexation only to prices (Senato della Repubblica 1995).

Other estimates based on the 1992 rules are also available (CER 1994). They take into account alternatively indexation to prices and earnings and to prices only, comparing both with pre-reform estimates. The last three columns of Table 5.7 show that under the first type of indexation, which is more generous, the rate of pension expenditure increases will be faster, reaching nearly 15 per cent of GDP in 2010. With indexation to prices only the growth will obviously be slower, and the proportion of GDP in that year will be 13 per cent.

Over the same period, according to the CER estimates, the pre-1992 rules would push the ratio up from 12.7 per cent to 16 per cent, confirming the growth of nearly three points shown by the figures in the second column, which are based on a different source.

Recent assessments (CER 1995) of the effects of the reform of August 1995 show the ratio of pension outlays to GDP stabilizing after the transitional period, i.e. from 2036 onwards. In general, all estimates in this field depend crucially on the different assumptions concerning the key macroeconomic variables; in the case of the pension system the role of demographic variables is decisive. CER, for example, assumes no change in the existing preferences of Italians on the distribution of income and the constancy of the ratio of active workers to pensioners. Demographics, however, projects the relative growth of the elderly with respect to the working-age population, as we shall see. CER itself stresses the absolute necessity of instituting mechanisms for monitoring and adjusting the key variables, to make adjustments of pension system parameters swifter, more frequent and more flexible, not left up to the annual government budget as at present. In a word, the CER estimate is a cautious one.

In any case the stabilization of the ratio of pension expenditure to GDP should be favoured by indexation to prices, not to real GDP, while turnover between old and new pension awards should push the ratio upwards. The outcome should be relative stabilization, especially if the reform succeeds in raising the effective age at which people retire.

5. The other pillars of the welfare mix

5.1 Some overall data

The development of the second pillar in Italy is both a fairly recent phenomenon, and a still unexploited potential. Historically, supplementary pension schemes have been discouraged by the quite comprehensive coverage of the public system, including severance pay, as described in the previous sections. The reduction of this coverage, announced in the second half of the 1980s and begun in the 1990s, has directed attention to private group social security: so far, however, resources have not followed it. The first comprehensive legislation regulating the field came only in April 1993, and did nothing to end the continuing stagnation. In the meantime, individual life insurance has grown fast, capitalizing among other things on a tax advantage relative to pension funds. As a consequence, the second pillar appears to be the weakest in the welfare mix in Italy. The effects of the new regulation of integrative pension funds included in the August 1995 social security reform will begin to be felt in the next few years.

Precise data are hard to obtain, mainly owing to the lack of a consolidated tradition of institutional investment and – until recently – to uncertainty regarding the regulatory role of the state. Data on the number of participants and the amount of benefits paid are very difficult to reconstruct in full. However, data from the Bank of Italy's Survey on Household Income and Wealth show that the percentage of families contributing to pension funds rose from 5.4 per cent to 7.3 per cent in 1989–1993, while in the same period families paying premiums to life insurances grew from 14.0 per cent to 18.6 per cent. On the other hand, a reasonable estimate of the total assets of the non-state pillars can be derived by assembling data from a variety of sources (Table 5.8). This reconstruction improves considerably over previous estimates circulated at European level (see for example European Commission Network of Experts (1994), reporting an estimate of 11.25 trillion lire in 1991 based on Pace (1993), and *The Economist* (1995), reporting the estimate of 19.90 trillion lire in 1993 by the European Federation for Retirement Provision). Obviously, the numbers given in the table are far from totally reliable, nor could it be otherwise in view of the inconsistencies and discrepancies between sources.

The table leaves out a few compulsory supplementary pension plans, established since the 1960s for special occupational categories (miners, tax collectors and private gas company employees, administered by INPS, and business agents). These plans are typically unfunded and therefore lack proper asset management. Compared to the first pillar, these plans are very small, paying benefits of 1.175 trillion lire in 1992 (about 0.6 per cent of total first-pillar benefits).[4]

From 1991 to 1993 the assets of the third pillar grew rapidly, while those of the second stagnated, largely because people were waiting for a law governing private pension plans. And the standstill has continued since, as expectations of further reform correcting the 1993 decrees were disappointed until August 1995. Pension funds managed by banks, representing roughly two-thirds of second pillar assets, are mainly the

---

[4] This figure can be incremented only by a partial official estimate of benefits paid by supplementary pension funds in banking and some professions, totalling 1.66 trillion lire (0.1 per cent of GDP).

Table 5.8 – Assets of the second and third pillars (billion lire and percentages of GDP)

	1991	%GDP	1992	%GDP	1993	%GDP
Second pillar						
a) pension funds						
– managed by banks	21 410	1.5	19 070	1.3	21 450	1.4
– managed by insurance companies	2 460	0.2	3 230	0.2	4 090	0.3
– other (1)	1 850	0.1	1 950	0.1	2 000	0.1
b) other group insurance schemes (2)	4 050	0.3	4 970	0.3	5 160	0.3
total (a + b)	29 770	2.1	29 220	1.9	32 700	2.1
Third pillar						
total (2)	42 830	3.0	53 750	3.6	60 840	3.9

Sources: Bank of Italy, National Association of Insurance Companies (ANIA), Centro Europa Ricerche (CER), 'Relazione Generale sulla Situazione Economica del Paese', own estimates.
(1) Estimate.
(2) Assets have been divided between individual and group insurances on the basis of the composition of premiums.

banks' own special pension funds. In some cases, they date back to a time when bank employees were not entirely covered by the public pension system, a situation that lasted until 1990. Pathbreaking surveys of pension funds in the mid 1980s found that the banks had the lion's share. The uneven diffusion across sectors is a distinctive characteristic of the second pillar in Italy, along with their company-based rather than industry-wide nature.

Additional structural data are furnished by a partial survey by Centro Europa Ricerche (CER) in 1991, covering 1,078 funds with 1,440,000 members and 11.25 trillion lire in assets (see Pace 1993). Owing to the virtual halt to the establishment of new funds in recent years, the survey is probably still fairly up-to-date: however, its representativeness is limited, since it is not based on a statistical sample. 42.9 per cent of sampled funds belonged to banking or insurance, and they accounted for 61.7 per cent of members and a full 91.4 per cent of assets. Independently funded schemes, often managed by insurance companies, prevailed over book reserves, the former representing 88.5 per cent of funds, 82.8

per cent of members and 59.5 per cent of assets. Defined-contribution funds were preferred to defined-benefits in 88.4 per cent of cases, covering 76.9 per cent of members but only 46.6 per cent of assets. Exclusive employer contribution was the most frequent source of financing (66.3 per cent), followed by joint employer and employee contribution (30.6 per cent) and, very marginally, exclusive employee contribution (3 per cent). Average contributions ranged from 4 per cent of gross earnings in financial services to 6 per cent in industry.

A survey undertaken by the Italian association of credit institutions (Assicredito, not including savings banks and rural and artisan banks) in 1994 shows that 96 per cent of bank employees, concentrated in 68 per cent of associates, are covered by some supplementary pension scheme. A specialized survey of compensation in financial institutions (banks, factoring and leasing companies and hire-purchase companies), in 1992 found a smoother distribution across occupational categories than in industry, with 50 per cent of the sample offering a pension scheme to managers and 35 or 40 per cent to other white-collar workers. As regards industry and some selected non-financial services, the 1992 Hay Compensation Survey reported that 40 per cent of firms offered a pension scheme to managers, but just 10 per cent had one for other white-collar workers. These figures refer to an atypical subset of firms, the Hay surveys being strongly biased towards large and multinational companies. Nevertheless, they reveal a further distinctive characteristic of the second pillar in Italy to date, namely its uneven distribution across occupational categories, with the partial exception of banks (Cozzolino and Proto 1994).

5.2   Why is the second pillar lagging?

The comparative underdevelopment of supplementary pension schemes in Italy is widely attributed to the high coverage offered by the compulsory social security system. Of course, this explanation does not refer specifically to the second pillar, as a reduction in public coverage could perfectly well spur the growth of individual rather than group retirement plans. Indeed, this appears to have been the case in Italy since the mid 1980s.

The role of the state as regulator is also at issue. Until 1993, the modesty of the second pillar was blamed in part on the lack of specific legislation. At that time supplementary pensions were governed by various provisions in a number of areas; the net result was favourable (but somewhat uncertain) tax and contribution treatment.

The 1993 decrees were preceded by the presentation of several reform projects that reflected the growing interest in private retirement provisions. Typically, these projects formed part of broad proposals for reform of the entire social security system. In the early 1990s, reform bills specifically devoted to supplementary pensions started to appear, among them the Amato-Rosini proposal of 1991. Since the mid 1980s, many analysts in Italy too have come to see the 'three-pillar model' as a possible solution for the financial crisis of public social security. The development of the second pillar has been authoritatively considered not only as a way of reconciling the need to reduce the budget deficit with that of maintaining an adequate pension coverage, but also as an instrument for the revitalization of the financial market.[5] At the same time, pension funds in the industrial sector started to develop, particularly in large firms operating multinationally. For instance, in 1987 Montedison and the trade unions reached agreement on establishing the firm's supplementary pension fund; the same year welfare funds for IBM employees and Olivetti managers were also established. At the beginning of the 1990s this trend slowed in expectation of systematic legislation.

The 1993 decrees fell short of expectations. Generally, the existing pension funds responded to the 1993 Decrees by suspending the admission of new employees (for instance this countermeasure was decided officially by Assicredito on behalf of its associated banks). After two years, there has still been no significant growth in supplementary pensions, although the available data are scant. Indeed, the existing pension funds immediately complained that the decrees raised difficulties, and the new regulation came to be considered as provisional in expectations of a further reform, eventually fulfilled in August 1995.

It is often argued that a basic reason for the comparative underdevelopment of supplementary pensions in Italy is inadequate fiscal incentives. Certainly the tax treatment under the 1993 decrees was less favourable than previously, as the need to minimize the public financial burden was stressed. On the other hand, favourable tax treatment in itself does not seem to be a sufficient stimulus to the growth of supplementary pensions, as is shown by the experience prior to 1993.

---

[5] In his 'Concluding Remarks' to the Annual Report for 1991, the Governor of the Bank of Italy cited pension funds as a potential key to the development of the stock market, historically the weakest of Italian financial markets (Banca d'Italia 1992).

At least as great a contribution would come from the application of companies' severance pay provisions (see section 3.5) to funding pension plans. This would amount to a transfer of resources across the frontiers between the first and the second pillar, at a point where the distance between the two is minimal. In fact, severance pay can be looked upon as a kind of forced saving for supplementary social security purposes, with the payment of a lump-sum benefit upon termination of employment. Severance pay has long played an important role in the Italian social security system, and the use of these provisions now seems to be the only way to develop pension funds without increasing labour costs. However, severance pay funds take the form of book reserves, and as such are managed by the firms themselves, whereas pension funds would be run by independent institutional investors. The link between social security saving and firms would be provided by the financial markets. It is obvious, then, that the key issues are what share of severance pay will be utilized for pension funds and what the consequences for firms will be.

The use of a company's severance pay provision to finance a pension plan is not automatic but must be established by collective bargaining. For the employees, this solution is highly convenient, yielding a higher return than they could otherwise obtain.[6] Moreover, this source of financing creates no additional costs for the public budget, as severance pay is already exempt from taxes and contributions until it is paid out. However, firms would suffer an increase in financing costs, as severance pay is an important source of low-cost financing.[7] Severance pay benefits are disbursed only upon termination of employment, and at the low interest rate provided for by the law. Meanwhile, firms' yearly allocations to the provision and the interest accrued are tax deductible. This lowers the tax burden on the firms, and increases internal financing.

Finding a satisfactory mix between severance pay and the other two sources of financing, namely employer and employee contributions, is not easy. As noted, turning severance pay to this use would benefit

---

[6] Specialized publications have generally estimated that in recent years the statutory return on severance pay has been only about half the market return on comparable saving for social security purposes.

[7] Recent studies have found that external finance is particularly costly to small and medium-sized firms, which have little chance of raising funds by share issues and must therefore resort to short-term bank loans (see Aronica and Pittaluga 1993). On the other hand, company accounts show that severance pay represents a higher share of net capital in large firms than in small and medium-sized firms (Aronica 1993).

employees but not employers. For firms, contributions would be attractive as an alternative to wage increases because of their favourable contribution treatment, but would mean lower direct salary, severance pay and public pensions for employees. Finally, for employees the economic advantage of contributions depends on the difference between the income tax allowance or credit on contributions and the actual value of taxes paid on the future benefits (for a model of the respective advantage to employers and employees, see Ministero del Tesoro – Ragioneria Generale dello Stato, 1994).

In recent years, other sources of difficulty have been added. The 1993 Decrees provided for differential treatment between the newly and the already employed, and between old and new members of funds, greatly complicating bargaining over supplementary pension plans. Further segmentation of the work force stems from the reform of the first pillar, as different rules depending on seniority result in varying income replacement rates among employees. In particular those near retirement find it less convenient to join a private fund, being still entitled to high public coverage. For them, contributions to pension funds as an alternative to wage increases would mean greater losses in terms of public pension forgone, and smaller gains in terms of private pension.

5.3   Recent developments

The 1993 decrees first tackled the problem of severance pay, assigning it a primary role as a source of financing of pension funds. The decrees envisaged a transition to a system in which supplementary social security would ultimately take the place of severance pay. The trade-off between supplementary pensions and severance pay was made explicit by the provision that the entire severance pay allocation for new employees be invested in the pension fund. Given the limit of total payments into the funds (10 per cent of earnings) and the net severance pay allocation of 6.91 per cent, very little room would be left for financing by employer and employee contributions. For workers already in service, the allocation of severance pay to the pension fund was made a requirement for the deductibility of employer contributions, in the ratio of two to one. As a partial compensation for this constraint, firms were offered the possibility of obtaining a lower overall allocation rate for severance pay through bargaining.

As regards the other two sources, in some important respects tax treatment under the 1993 Decrees was less favourable than the previous regime. Contributions to the pension fund, previously exempt, were taxed at a rate of 15 per cent. This special levy, unknown to the tax codes of the other developed countries, would be reimbursed to the pension fund only at the time of benefit payment, with an abatement of the tax on benefits. Also, employer contributions were no longer fully deductible but were limited to 50 per cent of the amount transferred from severance pay to pension funds. The tax allowance on employee contributions was turned into a tax credit, subject to a value ceiling pooled with life insurance premiums and other voluntary social security contributions. However, rather surprisingly, existing members of pension funds at the date of issue of the first decree were allowed to retain the previous tax and contribution treatment.

On the whole, the tax treatment of supplementary group pensions thus much more closely resembled that of personal retirement saving than the treatment of public social security. As a consequence, the three-pillar model rooted in the constitutional law collapsed into a strict public-versus-private (personal or collective) schema (Visentini and Marchetti 1995). Indeed, it was estimated that individual life insurance policies were now a more profitable investment for employees than contributions to pension funds, thanks to the more favourable tax treatment of annuities and lump-sum benefits (Banca Commerciale Italiana Research Office 1993).[8]

The result, hardly surprising, was a halt to the establishment of new funds and a freeze on admission of new employees to existing funds. A fair sample of the general opposition to the 1993 decrees can be found in the preliminary agreement on the establishment of a national supplementary fund as part of the 1994 metalworking industry contract, traditionally the bellwether in industrial bargaining. This document explicitly stated that 'the parties ... consider as a necessary prerequisite a substantial modification of Decree 124/93, which at the moment makes unfeasible a private pension system adequate to the needs of workers and firms.

To end the standstill, the August 1995 social security reform law modifies the 1993 Decrees. It reforms both the use of severance pay and the fiscal incentives for employees, employers and the funds themselves. In

---

[8] Life insurance annuities are taxed at 60 per cent of their value, while lump-sum benefits are taxed at 12.5 per cent, applied only to the amount exceeding the total sum of premiums paid.

addition it seeks to increase competition among fund managers and enhance the transparency and oversight of management.

As regards severance pay, its key role is confirmed: full investment into the fund for new employees is retained, although small firms are excepted for the first four years of the law's application. However, the mix between incentives and constraints is changed. A special untaxed reserve of 3 per cent of the severance pay provision allocated to the fund is introduced to offset the higher financing costs incurred by firms. The amount of employer contributions deductible is raised from 50 per cent to 100 per cent of the severance pay invested, up to a maximum of 2 per cent of gross wages. However, the same ratio and percentage limit are now applied to employee contributions as well. These combined requirements will presumably give rise to a de facto upper limit of 6 per cent of gross wages for total payments into the fund for the already employed, replacing the statutory 10 per cent limit provided for by the 1993 decrees, now abolished.

As regards fiscal incentives, the most controversial aspect of the 1993 decrees, a more favourable treatment is established. First of all, the special 15 per cent levy, suspended in August 1994, is abolished outright. The proportional capital tax on the funds is replaced by a lump-sum tax liability, thus favouring the largest funds. The tax credit on employee contributions is transformed into a tax allowance, although subject to a double ceiling. The 2 per cent ceiling with respect to gross wages is instituted alongside the value ceiling of 2.5 million lire, now dedicated exclusively to contributions to the fund.[9]

This restores a basic difference in the tax treatment between the second and the third pillar, enhancing the competitiveness of pension funds. On the other hand, the taxability of the annuities paid out by the funds, although lowered to 87.5 per cent, is still higher than the 60 per cent in force for life insurance annuities.

On the whole, the reduced constraints on the use of severance pay and the increased incentives should make the institution of new funds easier, enabling bargainers to find an acceptable mix among the three sources of financing. Still, the segmentation between old and new employees outlined by the 1993 Decrees remains, both regarding the use of severance pay and the tax and contribution treatment.

---

[9] Special tax and contribution treatment is foreseen for contributions to the fund paid by employees out of wages exceeding the ceiling for pensionable earnings. To date, the details are still to be specified by the government.

The probable development of supplementary pensions in Italy is as yet difficult to forecast. A first attempt was made in the technical report attached to the government reform bill from which the law originated. New membership in pension funds in the next decade was estimated assuming that the advantage of joining decreases with seniority, depending on the different replacement rates provided by the public pension system and on the different returns to pension funds investments due to length of capitalization. From 1996 to 2005, 3.2 million new members of pension funds are forecast among employees in the private sector, amounting roughly to 27 per cent of employees in the final year. Forecasts are lower for the self-employed (0.7 million and 16 per cent) and for public sector employees (0.4 million and 12 per cent).

However, the technical report underlines that hypotheses used to estimate the number of new members are affected by a high degree of uncertainty. Factors influencing the propensity to join a pension fund are many, and interact one with the other. Surely, seniority is a key variable, as assumed in government estimates, but other factors also play a role. For instance, the advantage is greater, the greater the difference in returns between the pension fund and severence pay, and the greater the fiscal appeal of employee contributions to the fund, which depends on the individual's marginal tax rate. More accurate forecasts will have to take account of these and other factors.

6.   Conclusions

The public system continues to dominate the Italian retirement provision mix even after the two latest reforms. It is only too understandable that the high coverage offered by the public system should discourage workers from turning to the other forms of retirement provision. The public compulsory, pay-as-you-go system will switch over in 1996 from an earnings- to a contribution-based award formula. It is still flawed by countless exceptions to the principles of universality and social solidarity, being overgenerous to some occupational categories, with disparate rules governing both benefits and contribution rates. The reforms will reduce such disparities, but over an excessively long period of transition. Many other problems that threaten the financial sustainability of the pension system also have to be resolved.

The reform of August 1995 was designed primarily to bring the pension system under control from the financial standpoint. Its budget effects have been estimated by some observers as very substantial even in the relatively short run, with savings of significant size already in 2000 and rising until final stabilization of the outlay/GDP ratio in 2036. However, the projections offered beyond the transitional period must be handled with great caution, because they depend crucially on the different assumptions concerning the key macroeconomic variables; in the case of the pension system the role of demographic variables is decisive. What is more, under the flexible eligibility formula it will be possible to begin drawing one's pension at an earlier age than in other countries, and the income replacement rate will be higher.

Analysts generally concur, however, that without the 1995 reform Italian public finances were headed for eventual collapse, and that from the viewpoint of sustainability the finances of the system should now be considered under control, although the projections produced so far are few in number and not exactly concordant. In any case, the basic concern stems from demographics. The working-age population is projected to shrink and the old-age dependency ratio to rise steadily in the decades to come, with significant impact on the ratio of pension entitlements to employment, whose repercussions in a system retaining the pay-as-you-go principle could be drastic. Thus the generic call to caution in assessment should be accompanied by a certain pessimism in consideration of the interplay of demographic trends with the pay-as-you-go scheme.

Meanwhile, supplementary, private pension plans face serious difficulty in really getting off the ground, owing in part to some of the undesirable effects of the public system. These stem in particular from its very limited impact on income distribution, which offers little incentive to the higher-income groups to make alternative provisions, and in part from the lack of harmonization between different schemes, although this should be somewhat attenuated in the future. All in all the configuration of the system, even after the 1992 reform, confirms the legislative intention of conferring primacy on the public retirement system.

The development of the second pillar in Italy is still limited and seems to be inferior to that of the third pillar, judging from available data on respective assets (2.1 and 3.9 of GDP in 1993 respectively). Two distinct elements have hampered the development of the second pillar: the high coverage of the public system and the severance pay mechanism. It should come as no surprise, then, that the new regulation of supplementary pensions has coincided with the lowering of the public replacement rate and has relied on use of severance pay funds.

191

The first comprehensive legislation regulating supplementary pensions came just one year after the 1992 social security reform. However, it stimulated no significant growth in supplementary pension. On the contrary, the new regulation resulted in a standstill in the development of pension funds, owing in the first place to a less favourable fiscal treatment than the previous one, mirroring the priority granted to public finance considerations. Moreover, the utilization of severance pay was pursued using constraints rather than incentives.

The section of the August 1995 social security reform law devoted to supplementary pensions aims at overcoming the standstill in the development of pension funds. In the first place, it provides for a more favourable fiscal treatment. It also changes the mix between incentives and constraints in the use of severance pay. On the whole, the new measures should make the establishment of new pension funds through bargaining easier. Still, a source of difficulty lies in the strong segmentation between the newly and the already employed and between old and new members of funds, adding to the segmentation of workers according to seniority caused by the reform of the public pension system. Even taking account of different joining rates according to seniority, one existing official projection forecasts 4.3 million new members of pension funds in the whole economy from 1996 to 2005.

It is clear that the more successful the 1995 rules are in harmonizing treatment of different groups and providing for more significant redistribution of income, the greater will be the possibilities opened up for private plans.

In any case, the success of the reforms depends to a large extent on a fundamental change of course as regards the purposes that the system is meant to serve. In Italy, public retirement provisions have often been used to achieve ends more properly relating to labour market stimulus, industrial policy, anti-poverty income support and unemployment more generally. It was for these ends, in fact, that Italy instituted its generous rules on disability pension eligibility, early retirement, cumulability and social security tax relief.

In the process, the purposes of retirement provisions as such were distorted. The pension system was burdened with improper, extraneous tasks, and the alarming rate of increase in social security system spending was one of the results. Unquestionably the latest reforms have begun to redress this anomalous situation and narrow the range of tasks assigned to the system, but action in this regard needs to be made still more incisive.

In closing, let us underscore that correction of the defects need not deprive the public system of one of its essential features, namely a certain orientation to social solidarity, i.e. towards some redistribution of income. It is inconceivable that the basic welfare-state provision for old age income maintenance, which has been so successful in eliminating extreme poverty, should be abandoned.

References

Aronica, Alessandro (1993), 'Il TFR: dall'autofinanziamento al mercato finanziario', in D. Pace (ed.), *Il risparmio previdenziale ed i fondi pensione,* Milan: Franco Angeli.

Aronica, Alessandro and Pittaluga, Giovanni B. (1993), 'L'abolizione del trattamento di fine rapporto e la struttura finanziaria delle piccole imprese', *La trasformazione difficile. Sesto rapporto CER/IRS sull'industria e la politica industriale italiana,* Bologna: Il Mulino.

Banca Commerciale Italiana (1993), 'Le prospettive di sviluppo dei fondi pensione e i possibili effetti sui mercati finanziari', *Tendenze Monetarie,* No. 69, June.

Banca d'Italia (1991), *Economic Bulletin,* October, No. 13, Rome.

Banca d'Italia (1992), *Annual Report for 1991: The Governor's Concluding Remarks,* Rome.

Banca d'Italia (1995a), *Annual Report for 1994: The Governor's Concluding Remarks,* Rome.

Banca d' Italia (1995b), *Economic Bulletin,* October, No. 21, Rome.

Camera dei Deputati (1994), *Decisione e Relazione della Corte dei Conti sul Rendiconto Generale dello Stato,* Vol. III, Tomo I, Rome.

Castellino, Onorato (1976), *Il labirinto delle pensioni,* Bologna: Il Mulino.

Castellino, Onorato (1994), 'La riforma del sistema previdenziale ovvero il rapporto che non fu scritto', *Moneta e Credito,* pp. 515–40.

Centro Europa Ricerche (1994), *Pensioni: e ora la riforma,* Rapporto no. 6, Rome.

Centro Europa Ricerche (1995), Rapporto no. 3, Rome, 63–81.

Cozzolino, Maria and Proto, Gaetano (1994), 'I benefici accessori nei maggiori paesi della CEE: rapporto di sintesi', *Lavoro e Relazioni Industriali,* No. 4, October–December, 161–83.

Di Biase, Rita (1990), 'Spesa sociale e suo finanziamento nei Paesi della CEE', *Rassegna di Statistiche del Lavoro,* no. 1, 35–55.

Di Biase, Rita and Di Marco, Marco (1995), 'The Redistributive Effects of the Tax Wedge in Italy', *Labour,* No. 2, Volume 9, 377–401.

Di Biase, Rita, Di Marco, Marco, Di Nicola, Fernando and Proto, Gaetano (1995), 'ITAXMOD: A Microsimulation Model of the Italian Personal Income Tax and of Social Security Contributions', *Documenti di lavoro,* No. 16, Rome: ISPE.

Economist (1995), 'When George Soros Meets Granny Smith', 22 April.

European Commission Network of Experts (1994), *Supplementary Pensions in the European Union. Development, Trends and Outstanding Issues,* Brussels.

Eurostat (1992a), Digest of Statistics on Social Protection in Europe, Old Age, Volume I, Statistical Document, Luxembourg.

Eurostat (1992b), *Labour Costs 1988*, Theme 3, Series C, Statistical Document, Luxembourg.

Ferrera, Maurizio (1993), *Modelli di solidarietà*, Bologna: Il Mulino.

Franco, Daniele (1993), *L'espansione della spesa pubblica in Italia*, Bologna: Il Mulino.

Hannah, Leslie (1992), 'Similarities and Differences in the Growth and Structure of Private Pensions in OECD Countries', in *Private Pensions and Public Policy*, OECD, Social Policy Studies, No. 9, Paris: OECD.

ISTAT (1994), *Statistiche sui trattamenti pensionistici*, Collana d'Informazione, No. 9, Rome.

Ministero del Bilancio e della Programmazione Economica, *Relazione Generale sulla Situazione Economica del Paese* (various years), Rome.

Ministero del Tesoro – Ragioneria Generale dello Stato (1994), *La previdenza complementare: problemi e prospettive per il decollo*, Rome, May.

Pace, Daniele (1993), 'La previdenza complementare in Italia: un'analisi quantitativa', in D. Pace (ed.), *Il risparmio previdenziale ed i fondi pensione*, Milan: Franco Angeli.

Senato della Repubblica (1995), *Profili di Documentazione sul Sistema Pensionistico*, Rome.

Visentini, Gustavo and Marchetti, Fabio (1995), 'Riforma della previdenza complementare: riflessioni sul trattamento fiscale', *Economia Italiana*, no. 1 (January–April), 95–112.

6

The Role of the Japanese Company in Compensating Income Loss after Retirement

Yoko Kimura

1.   Introduction

Japanese companies are reputed to have a well-established welfare policy for their employees. They have been eager to compensate the employees' loss of income after retirement on the basis of retirement pay and their employment policy. Retirement pay consists of three parts: lump sum payments, tax qualified plans and employee pension funds (details are discussed in section 3.1). Together these programmes represent the aggregate of company pension funds. Employment policy consists of the practice of reemploying older workers in daughter firms after workers have reached the retirement age. However, today this practice has become increasingly problematic as pressure from the state to deal with public pension costs has lead to a policy of progressively raising the *teinen* (age of retirement from 'life-long' job) from 55 to 65. This practice has increased the cost to the firm of both retirement pay and the policy of reemployment. One early sign of this increased burden is seen in data on labour costs. In 1989, non-wage labour costs amounted to 22.5 per cent of the total cash wage, while they amounted to 19.4 per cent in 1980. It was due to the increase in social insurance contributions and retirement pay. Aging will push the total labour cost further. At the same time, the financial problems of the public pension plans are becoming serious. So, the pension reform of 1994 was aimed at raising the pension age of the Employees' Pension Plan from 60 to 65 by 2018. How have companies reacted to the recent reform of the public pensions?

One way that companies have been able to deal with the growth of pension costs is through the practice of contracting out. Contracting out has been widely adopted in Japan as in the United Kingdom, and the provision of the earnings-related benefits to all employees may be made through either Employees' Pension Funds or the Employees' Pension Plans. However, contracting out is limited to the non-indexed part of the benefit replaced, the increase due to indexing remaining with the social security system. About 30 per cent of the employees are in contracted out Employee Pension Funds. But analysts believed that future expansion was unlikely. Consider the analysis of Dyer (1977) writing in the late 1970s:

> It is not difficult to visualize the contracted out benefits becoming so insignificant in relation to the whole that there remains little justification for continuing the option. In the absence of a complete overhaul of the Japanese social security system, the need for which is widely recognized quite apart from the question of coordination with private benefits, there are indications that contracting out has a very limited future in Japan.

In this chapter, I analyse two issues: (1) changing company policy in response to recent public pension reforms; more specifically, the impact of the aging of the population on retirement pay and employment policy; (2) the background of the Japanese government encouraging contracting out by deregulating the Employees' Pension Funds while the contracted out benefits are becoming so insignificant. Section 2 explains the pension reform of 1994 and analyses the reaction of companies to the reforms. Sections 3 and 4 discuss their historical backgrounds and some features of public pension and retirement pay of Japanese companies, respectively. Sections 5, 6 and 7 analyse the interrelation between the public pension and company pension and the effect of the pension mix on income distribution, savings, and labour supply, respectively. Section 8 concludes the chapter.

2. The pension reform of 1994 and the reaction of the firms

In 1994, amid the financial crisis, the Japanese government decided to reform the public pension system. The reform consisted of three main parts: a rise in the pension age, a rise in the contribution rate, and a reduction in the level of public pension benefits. The impacts of raising the pension age on private arrangements for retirement income are strong.

2.1 Pension reform of 1994

One of the basic ideas behind this reform is to discourage people in their early sixties from leaving the labour market. This aims at mitigating the tight labour market conditions and also decreasing financial burdens on younger generations. The Ministry of Health and Welfare has estimated that contribution rates of the Employees' Pension will rise from 14.5 per cent in 1994 to 34 per cent in 2025 if the pension age remains at 60. To solve the problem of financing, the reform emphasizes cutting expenditure for pension benefits and also strengthening the financial basis of the Employees' Pension Scheme. Specific points in the reform are as follows.

1) The pension age will be raised from 60 to 65 in the next century. It will rise from 60 to 61 in 2001 for men and in 2006 for women, thereafter it will rise a year at a time every three years until it will be 65 in 2013 for men and in 2018 for women. To compensate the loss due to this change, partial pension will be provided at the same rate as earnings-related pensions.

2) A net wage index will soon replace the wage index, thus creating a new rule of distribution between beneficiaries and contributors.

3) The contribution rate from monthly earnings of salaried workers was raised from 14.5 per cent to 16.5 per cent in 1994, and it will go up by 2.5 percentage points every three or five years.

4) Tax on bonus has been introduced, though the rate is only 1 per cent for the time being.

5) To stimulate labour supply of the elderly, the conditions for pension benefits for working pensioners have been relaxed. Before 1994, benefits were cut for the working elderly so that a higher marginal tax rate was imposed on them than otherwise was the case. This is now corrected and the marginal tax rate is lower than before.

This reform will decrease the peak contribution rate for salaried workers drastically, to 28 per cent in 2025, yet this still is quite high. The contribution of the self-employed insured will also become large: about 20 000 yen per month in 2025 (in 1994 prices) compared to 11 000 yen per month in 1994.

2.2 The effect of the recent reform of the public pensions on the private company

Raising the retirement age and cutting the retirement pay because of aging became urgent both in public pension plans and retirement pay. Aging increased the cost of retirement pay based on the seniority-oriented wage system. Here we define retirement as exiting from the lifetime job. In Japan, most workers leave their company at the mandatory retirement age (teinen) and continue to work in a subsidiary company. In the past, the teinen age was 55, while the pension age of the Employees' Pension Plan was 60. With life expectancy increased, more workers noted a disadvantage of the gap between the pension age and the teinen age and demanded a filling of this gap. As a result, 80 per cent of the companies raised the teinen age to 60 by 1990. In 1982, 36 per cent of companies set teinen age at 55, and 43 per cent set it at 60. This changed markedly by 1990; only 3 per cent set it at 55, while 80 per cent set it at 60.

However, since the salary and position of employees rise in accordance with length of service in many companies, the extension of the teinen age increases the financial burden for companies and also prevents the promotion of younger people. Thus, most companies have altered their personnel management, the wage systems and retirement pay. Seventy-four per cent of the companies attempted to depress the growth of retirement pay after the teinen age was raised from 55 to 60. Many of them now fix the retirement pay at 55.

Along with raising the teinen age, the companies changed formulas for calculation of retirement pay in order to reduce it. Normally, retirement pay is determined according to the length of service and the wage. Many companies decreased the wage used in calculation of retirement pay. Figure 6.1 shows that the ratio of retirement pay to the final monthly salary gradually is decreasing. The ratio decreased from 53 per cent in 1969 to 40 per cent in 1990.

An increasing number of companies entrusted funds to trust companies and insurance companies, thus securing the financial base of the payment at retirement.

Japanese companies encourage employees to invest in personal pensions. Nearly 50 per cent of the companies have introduced and 5 per cent of the employees are covered by the scheme. On average, each employee invested 150 000 yen in 1990 (see p. 207).

The government subsidizes companies hiring employees over the

Figure 6.1 – Retirement pay of high school graduates at 55 to the final monthly salary

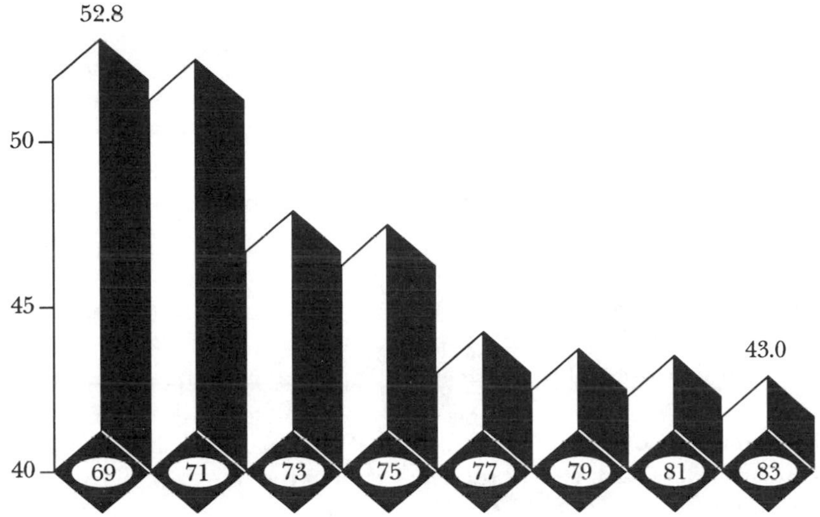

Source: Murakami (1990).

age of 60 through the unemployment insurance. For the pensioner who earns less than 85 per cent of their previous wage at the age of 60, the employment insurance compensates the loss, up to 25 per cent of the wage. The companies whose teinen age is 60 try to hire the retired again at their subsidiaries up to 65.

3.   Historical background

Japanese employees rely largely on private arrangements for retirement income. Retirement pay has two functions: first, as a reward for the employees' long services and loyalty to their companies; thus dismissed employees are usually not entitled to this benefit; second, as compensation for the loss of income after retirement. Today, the latter has increased in importance. Retirement pay is composed of three parts: (1) the lump sum on retirement, (2) the Tax-qualified Pension Plan and (3) the Employees' Pension Funds, with which the employers contract out of the Employees' Pension Plan.

Let us look at the history of retirement pay.

3.1   Development of retirement pay

In Japan, the lump sum on retirement has a history of over a hundred years and was the only retirement pay from the companies until occupational pensions were introduced in the early 1960s. The lump sum on retirement was created first for white-collar workers. As the economy grew and heavy chemical industry was developed after the First World War, the lump sum on retirement became popular in Japan.

At the same time, to prevent skilled workers from leaving, many companies adopted the system of the lump sum on retirement for blue-collar workers. After the boom, the Japanese economy fell into recession in the 1930s. A high unemployment rate stimulated labour movements and workers demanded better lump-sum payments. The Interior Office reported that over 30 per cent of the companies hiring more than 30 employees adopted the lump sum on retirement in 1935. The Act of Retirement Allowance, introduced in 1936, stipulated that employees and employers each contribute 2 per cent of the monthly salary for the lump sum on retirement or a death allowance. In 1936, the Workers' Pension Act was introduced and this was developed into the Employers' Pension Act in 1944. At the same time the Retirement Allowance Act was merged into the Employees' Pension Act.

After the Second World War, the lump sum on retirement rapidly developed and the union got a say in the wage bargaining also on the lump sum system. The Ministry of Labour reported that 83 per cent of the companies hiring more than 30 employees adopted the lump sum on retirement system in 1951. Unions began to include the lump sum on retirement in wage negotiation. In the 1960s, their main target was introducing the company pension because, according to the unions, the lump sum on retirement had already been increased sufficiently. The Tax-qualified Pension Plan and the Employees' Pension Funds were introduced in 1962 and 1966, respectively. Yet, monthly benefits of the Employees' Pension Plan, a public pension scheme, were on average only 3000 yen, which fell very short of the retirement income (see Fujii 1978 and Murakami 1984). In 1961, the National Pension Scheme for self-employed and farmers was introduced, and all citizens were covered by the public pension schemes.

Figure 6.2 – Structure of employees' pension funds and national pensions

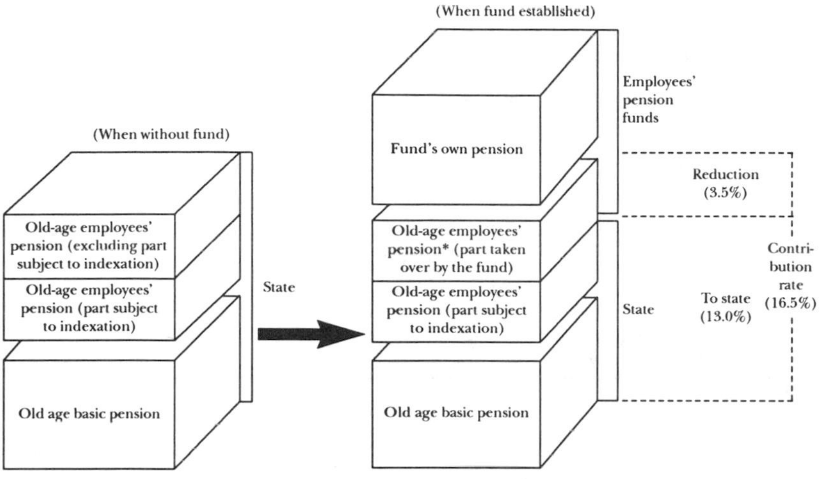

(When fund established)

Employees' pension funds

(When without fund)

Fund's own pension

Reduction (3.5%)

Old-age employees' pension (excluding part subject to indexation)

Old-age employees' pension* (part taken over by the fund)

Contribution rate (16.5%)

State

Old-age employees' pension (part subject to indexation)

Old-age employees' pension (part subject to indexation)

State

To state (13.0%)

Old age basic pension

Old age basic pension

* Instalment payments to the state are exempted.

Source: Annual Report on Health and Welfare 1991–92.

3.2 Development of the public pension plans

The public pension scheme was substantially expanded in the 1970s and this contributed to making the income distribution more equal. Important reforms were made in 1973. This, first, set the replacement ratio of the public pension benefits to monthly earnings of younger generations at about 60 to 70 per cent for the people with 40 years' employment (40 per cent of annual earnings). Second, it introduced price and wage indexation. The reform affected the Employees' Pension Funds largely, and contracting out was limited to the non-indexed part of the benefit replaced, the increase due to indexing remaining with the social security system (see Figure 6.2). Company pensions were managed on the basis of a funded system, while the public pension schemes were changed to a pay-as-you-go system. The reform of 1985 introduced a two-tiered pension plan. The National Pension provides a basic pension for every resident in Japan and the Employees' Pension and various mutual aid pension plans provide earnings-related pensions.

Table 6.1a – Public pension schemes

National Pension Schemes:

	Division	Insured persons	Insurer
A	No.1 Insured person	Self-employed	
B	No.2 Insured person	Salaried workers	State
C	No. 3 Insured person	Wives of salaried workers	
D	Total	——	——

Employees' Pension Schemes:

	Division	Insured persons	Insurer
E	Employees' Pension Insurances	Private salaried workers	State
F	National Public Service Employees etc. MAAs	National public service employees	National Public Service Employees etc. MAAs
	Federation Japan Railways	Employee of passenger railway companies etc.	Japan Railways MAA
	Nippon Telegraph & Telephone	Employee of Nippon Telegraph & Telephone	Nippon Telegraph & Telephone MAA
	Japan Tobacco Corporation	Employees of Japan Tobacco Corporation	Japan Tobacco Corporation MAA
G	Local Public Service Employees MAAs	Local government employees	Local public service employees MAAs
H	Private School Teachers and Employees MAA	Private school teachers and employees	Private School Teachers and Employees MAA
I	Agricultural, Forestry, and Fishery Cooperative Employees MAAs	Employees in agriculture, etc.	Agricultural, Forestry, and Fishery Employees MAAs
J	Total	——	——

Table 6.1b – Public pension schemes (as of end of March 1992)

	No. of insured persons (1000 persons) (1)	Persons eligible for old age pension (1000 persons) (2)	Degree of Maturity (2)/(1)%	Average Monthly (Retirement) Pensions (in 1000 yen)	Contribution rates % (1992)	Pensionable Age (Fiscal 1992)
A	17,580	7,730	——	32	(From April 1992) Insured persons: 9700 yen	65 years old
B	11,960					
C	36,780	4,270				——
D	66,310	11,990	18.1	——	——	——

					Male 11.5% Female 14.3% Miners and seamen: 16.3%	Male: 60 Female: 57 (60 by 1999) Miners and seamen: 55
E	31,000	4,760	15.4	146		
F	1,130	500	44.3	189	15.2	59 (60 by 1995)
	200	340	173.8	175	19.09	Self-defence personnel: 57
	280	110	40.1	192	14.02	Japan Railways
	20	30	104.1	176	17.07	Tobacco Corporation: 60
G	3.920	1,040	31.8	205	14.06	Police officers, etc.: 57 (60 by 1991)
H	370	30	7.8	180	11.8	
I	500	110	22.5	146	16.3	
J	36,780	6,920	18.8	——	——	——

N.B.   1. The National Pension Scheme also includes the old-age welfare pension. The number of the pension is 960,000.

2. The number of No. 2 insured persons eligible for old-age (retirement) pension is equal to the number of that of employees' pension over 65 years old.

3. The contribution rates are double as much as their share based on the standard renumeration.

4. Pensionable age of MAA is adopted from July 1, 1992 police officers etc. is adopted from April 1, 1992.

Source: Annual Report on Health and Welfare 1991, 1992.

Figure 6.3 – Structure of the pension schemes

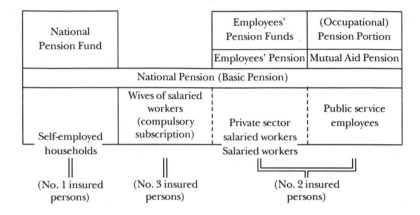

Source: Annual Report on Health and Welfare 1991–92.

4. Characteristics of the Japanese public pension scheme

The characteristics of the Japanese public pension scheme managed by a social insurance system are summarized in Table 6.1 and Figure 6.3.

Before the pension reform of 1985, the National Pension did not cover salaried workers insured by the Employees' Pension and MAA Pensions. The Employees' Pension and MAA Pensions were two-tier pensions, where the first tier consisted of the lump-sum benefit and the second tier of the earnings-related benefit which was proportional to duration. Financially, each pension scheme had its own independent account.

The basic National Pension insures every resident aged from 20 to 59. This was introduced in 1961, and fundamentally reorganized in 1985. By the pension reform of 1985, the National Pensions became a basic pension for every Japanese resident. It is a universal, flat-rate pension, proportional to number of years employed. A minimum of 25 years is needed to qualify for this pension. The maximum qualifying period is 40 years of gainful employment leading to a pension of about 65 000 yen per month as of 1994.

The Employees' Pension covers the private employees, and the various mutual aid pension plans cover the public employees and private school teachers and employees. For instance, Local Public Service Employees' MAAs is for local government employees. They provide pensions supplementary to the basic pension, proportionate to earnings, and based on average earnings over working years, although a ceiling exists. They have the same pension benefit formula and pension age. Normally 40 years of gainful employment is required for full pension (on average, full pension is 84 000 yen per month for male workers and the average wage rate of male workers is presently 280 000 yen per month). Pension benefits are price-indexed every year and wage-indexed every few years. A net wage indexation will replace a wage indexation in a few years as a result of the pension reform of 1994.

The National Pension, the Employees' Pension, and each MAA pension plan all provide three kinds of pensions: the old age, the disability and the survivors' pension.

The pension age is 65 for the National Pension. The pension amount is adjusted for early or late retirement between 60 and 70. The pension age is 60 for the Employees' Pension but the reform of 1994 raised it to 65 starting in the first decade of the next century.

The Japanese public pension scheme is managed by a social insurance authority. The Japanese public pension schemes have enormous reserves at present: the National Pension and the Employees' Pension together totalled 110 trillion yen in 1994. The amount of the reserves of the Employees' Pension is equal to five times pension payments in 1994. However, the government estimates that the reserves of the Employees' Pension will decrease to twice pension payments by 2025. All the reserves are deposited at an institution affiliated with the Ministry of Finance and yield interests at a going rate in the market of the national bonds. They are spent mostly for constructing social overhead capital. Public pension schemes on the basis of a funded system have been changed to a pay-as-you-go system.

The insured in the National Pension scheme are composed of three groups: (No. 2) salaried workers, (No. 3) dependent spouses of salaried workers and (No. 1) self-employed workers, farmers, students and all other residents aged from 20 to 59 except No. 2 and No. 3 insured.

The annual basic pension expenditure is financed out of grants from each pension scheme, the amount of which is proportional to the total number of their own insured and their dependent spouses. State grants are limited to one-third of the basic pension benefits. They are run on the basis of the pay-as-you-go system.

Self-employed and farmers pay lump-sum contributions (11 400 yen per month). The lump-sum system is adopted because it is quite difficult for the government to grasp all income sources for these persons and to impose contributions according to their incomes. This is markedly different from the payroll fee system for the contributions of employees. The contributions of employees insured are proportional to their earnings, with a ceiling. Private sector salaried workers pay 16.5 per cent and public service employees pay 19.0 per cent of their earnings, of which half is borne by the employers. Dependents do not contribute to the National Pension.

5. The retirement pay of Japanese companies

The state influences the companies by providing public pension schemes, regulating pension plans and the lump sum on retirement, giving them favourable tax treatments, encouraging the companies to hire workers over 60 years of age by giving them allowances from the employment insurance, and financing the public pension plans.

Japanese company pension plans are different from their counterparts in, for example, France and Sweden. The financial base of the latter covers the whole of the private sector for collective provision for retirement. In Japan, company pension plans are not collective provision while being based on a funded system and defined-benefit plans.

The Japanese Tax-qualified Pension Plan aims at providing pension benefits on retirement and contributions to it are funded outside the firm. They are different from the Tax-qualified Pension Plan in the United States in two respects. First, the employees have a lump-sum option which is almost always chosen. Second, the benefits of public pension plans and the Tax-qualified Pension Plans are not necessarily complementary, though those in the United States have three kinds of integration: the offset plan, the excess plan and the step-up plan.

Contracting out is done widely in Japan, and the provision of the earnings-related benefits to all employees may be made through either Employees' Pension Funds or the Employees' Pension Plans. The Funds provide some funds for the benefits of the employees' pension (that is, the part of the old age benefits not subject to price or wage indexation) and for their own supplementary benefits which are more than 43 per cent of the employees' pension benefits.

There are advantages for the companies to establish the Employees' Pension Funds. First, the increase in retirement pay due to aging gives companies a strong incentive to introduce company pensions and also to make funds outside the firms. The Employees' Pension Funds are exempted from special corporate tax on pension funds, though the Tax-qualified Pension Plans are not. Second, a part of interest income of the pension funds can be used for the improvement of the pension benefits and of other welfare policy for the employees. Third, the company can cut the contribution rate under the Employees' Pension Funds when the average age of employees is low. Fourth, the company can design pension benefits more flexibly. Fifth, an equivalent or better-paying company pension can be substituted for the earnings-related pension. Sixth, the accumulation of pension funds activates investments.

The Employees' Pension Funds is an alternative to the Employees' Pension Plans, and it is regulated more strictly than the Tax-qualified Pension Plans. Most employees covered by them work in big companies. The Funds provide three kinds of pensions, the old age, the disability and the survivors' pensions, as alternatives of the Employees' Pension. Their own supplementary benefits provide the old age pensions and the survivors' lump-sum pay.

The lump sum on retirement is taxed at a lower rate than the benefits from company pension plans. This is a main reason why the retired choose the lump sum on retirement. The lump sum is used partly for purchasing their own houses and partly for higher education for their children.

Japanese companies encourage employees to invest in personal pensions, that is, workers' tax-free pension-making deposit founded in 1982. The condition for this investment is that the employees must be under 55 years of age, and also be covered by the scheme for over five years. Contributions are collected under the PAYE system.

Japanese companies bear almost all the costs of retirement pay and half of the cost of the public pension plan. In 1989, the ratio of the contribution for retirement pay to the total cash wage was 8.1 per cent on average, and the ratio of the employer contribution to it for public pension was 4.3 per cent.

Almost 30 per cent of employees were covered by the Employees' Pension Funds (34 per cent of male workers and 27 per cent of female workers). Insured of the Employees' Pension Funds were 9.8 million in number, while those of the Employees' Pension Plan were about 30 million. The Tax-qualified Pension Plans covered almost 30 per cent of the employees. Insured of the Tax-qualified Pension Plans were 9.4 million in 1990 (see Figure 6.4).

Yoko Kimura

Figure 6.4 – Distribution of coverage 1980–90

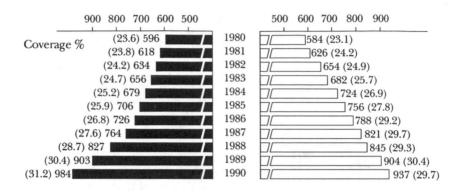

The insured of the Employees' Pension Funds (10 000 persons)

The insured of the Tax-qualified Pension Plans (10 000 persons)

Source: White Paper on Occupational Pensions (1992).

Figure 6.5 – The balance of the pension funds

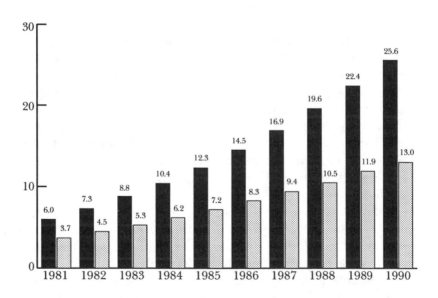

Source: White Paper on Occupational Pensions (1992).

208

The benefits from the Funds depended on the length of service and the average wage. The benefits of the Employees' Pension Funds were on average 302 000 yen (for males 347 000 yen, for females 159 000 yen) in 1991, while the benefits of the Employees' Pension Funds were 1.6 million yen on average. The total cost of the benefits of the Employees' Pension Funds was 403 billion yen and the pensions of the Employees' Pension Funds amounted to 13 per cent of the total pensions of the Employees' Pension Plans. The benefits are 50 per cent larger than social security benefits replaced. The balance of the Funds was 26 trillion yen, while the balance of the Employees' Pension Plan was 70 trillion yen in 1990. See Figure 6.5.

Benefits of the Tax-qualified Pension Plan were on average 800 000 yen in 1990. Today, the employees, on average, receive pension benefits for ten years from the age of 60. Most employees do not contribute to the plan. The balance of the funds of the Tax-qualified Pension Plan amounted to 13 trillion yen in 1990. Those benefits also depend on the length of service and the wage, though some companies adopt flat-rate pensions.

The Tax-qualified Pension Plans are supervised by the National Tax Agency. Companies can choose between term certain and life annuities, and can also decide the pension age, and levels of benefits. To establish pension plans, over 15 employees are needed in a company. Usually 15–20 years' duration is needed to get benefits. Benefits are not wage or price-indexed.

The Employees' Pension Funds are supervised by the Ministry of Health and Welfare. Life annuities are essential and the pension age must be the same as that of the Employees' Pension Plans. They are limited in a number of ways. Firstly, replacement benefits are required to be at least one-third higher in value than the social security benefits they replace; secondly, the option is available only for employers or employer groups with 500 or more employees; thirdly, employee and union consent are required; fourthly, the reduction in employee and employer contributions from contracting out is only about one-third; fifthly, lump-sum commutation of part of the replacement benefits can be permitted; and sixthly, in case of termination of the plan providing the replacement benefits, the actuarial value of accrued benefits must be turned over to the social security reserve fund (Dyer 1977, pp. 32–3).

Fringe benefits include privileges for using company-owned recreational and health and welfare facilities, insurance against sickness, joblessness and aging, and social insurance contributions. In 1990, the ratio

Table 6.2 – Distribution of the ratio of fringe benefits to the total cash wage

| | The ratio of fringe benefits to the total cash wage | | | |
	A Fringe benefits	B Non-legalized fringe benefits	A + B	Retirement
1980	8.2	5.5	13.7	5.7
1981	8.7	5.3	14.0	5.7
1982	8.7	5.2	13.9	5.9
1983	8.7	5.2	13.9	6.9
1984	8.7	5.2	13.9	6.9
1985	9.1	5.1	14.2	8.1
1986	9.3	4.9	14.2	7.9
1987	9.2	4.9	14.1	8.5
1988	9.4	5.0	14.1	7.6
1989	9.1	5.0	14.4	8.1

Source: White Paper on Occupational Pensions (1992).

of retirement pay to the total cash wage was 8 per cent, while that of public pension contribution was 2.7 per cent, that of social insurance contribution 9.1 per cent and that of the total fringe benefits was 22.5 per cent in 1989 (see Table 6.2).

The Japanese government has encouraged individuals and companies to save for retirement and, for this, provides various favourable tax treatments. The employer contributions for the lump sum on retirement are tax-free. Less than half of the lump sum on retirement is taxable. Employer contributions for the Tax-qualified Pension Plan are entirely tax-free, while employee contributions are partly tax-free. The income of the pension funds is taxed at 1 per cent (corporation tax). Pension benefits are taxed after deducting the public pension benefits and employees' contribution. Employer and employee contributions to the Employees' Pension Funds are tax-free. The income of the pension funds in excess of official contributions is also taxed at 1 per cent (corporation tax). Pension benefits are taxed after the public pension benefits deduction. Contributions of the employer and the employee and the income of the pension funds for the Employees' Pension Plans are also tax-free. Their pension benefits are taxed after some deductions.

When the employee changes his job, the amount that he has accu-

Figure 6.6 – Company pension plans

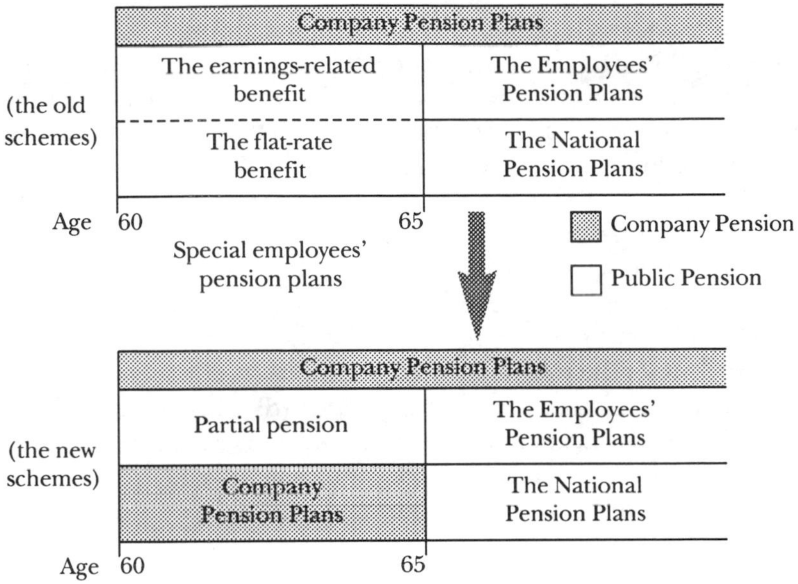

Company Pension Plans		
(the old schemes)	The earnings-related benefit	The Employees' Pension Plans
	The flat-rate benefit	The National Pension Plans

Age 60 65

Special employees' pension plans

▢ Company Pension

☐ Public Pension

Company Pension Plans		
(the new schemes)	Partial pension	The Employees' Pension Plans
	Company Pension Plans	The National Pension Plans

Age 60 65

mulated for the Employees' Pension Fund is transferred to the Employees' Pension Fund Association, guaranteeing portability.

Personal pensions are a novel financial good and not yet very popular among Japanese. Only 10 per cent of people are covered by personal pension plans supplied by insurance companies.

6. How have changes in the first tier influenced the design of the second tier?

6.1 Deregulating the Employees' Pension Funds

The Japanese government provided the funds with more flexibility in the benefits packages by combining the limited pension (it is possible to pay pensions for more than ten years) and the lifetime pension in 1984. As the government is raising the pension age of the public pension plans, the combination will become popular among Japanese employers. For example, the employers can receive both the limited pension for five years between 60 to 65 and the lifetime pension from 60 years of age to compensate the loss of the National Pension benefits (Figure 6.6). At the same time, lump-sum commutation of the replacement benefits was not permitted in the past. However, today, lump-sum commutation of a part of the replacement benefits is allowed by the government.

Recently, the schemes of the Employees' Pension Funds have been deregulated significantly. For instance, the number of employees needed to establish a fund was reduced from 700 to 500 in 1989. The Funds engage the services of an actuary to determine annual contributions to the plan and had to employ a trust company or an insurance company to serve as trustee. As a result of the pension reform of 1990, advice can be purchased from an investment consultant, who becomes the effective manager of the assets, and at the same time the Funds whose balance of the pension funds is over 0.5 trillion yen are allowed to invest one-third of the total funds at their own discretion.

Each Fund can set the contribution rates (that is, reduction from contributions of the Employees' Pension Plan) between 3.2 and 3.8 per cent according to their financial situation from next year. The contribution rate for the funds has been fixed and today it is 3.5 per cent (see Figure 6.2).

The number of Funds and of employees covered with the Funds increased remarkably between 1986 and 1991. The increase in the Funds took place for the following reasons. Firstly, as a result of deregulations, smaller companies can establish Employees' Pension Funds. Secondly, a high growth rate in the economy brought huge amounts of profits to companies, which enabled them to introduce the Employees' Pension Funds. Thirdly, shortage of workers encouraged companies to introduce Funds. Figure 6.7 shows the trends of the coverage under the Employees' Pension Funds. When the Employees' Pension Funds were planned in 1966, the employers intended to cut the lump sum on retirement. Yet, this was actually not retirement. Furthermore, they insisted that retirement pay and public pension plans should be independent and also the former should be incorporated into welfare policy for the employees of the company, and the latter into the social policy of the government.

When the Employees' Pension Funds were introduced in 1966, the coverage of the employees under the Funds was less than 10 per cent. In 1971, the coverage was about 20 per cent. The Employees' Pension Funds became dominant in Japan for the following reasons. First, the Japanese economy enjoyed a boom, and Japanese companies not only faced a shortage of workers but also had enough profits for establishing the Funds. Second, the employers encouraged the employees to retire

212

Figure 6.7 – Coverage of the employees' pension funds

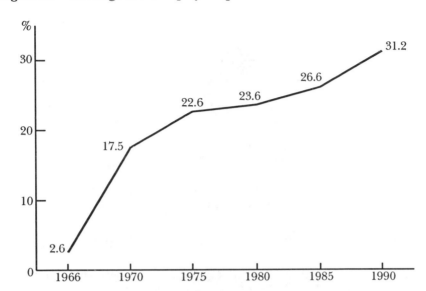

Source: White Paper on Occupational Pensions (1992).

with pensions in lieu of the traditional lump sum on retirement. The Tax-qualified Pension Plans were not sufficient for retirement income on several points; for example, they were not life annuities.

Today a high internal rate of returns cannot be expected because domestic interest rates are low and the stock market has shrunk. Usually the Funds are expected to earn a rate of return higher than 4.5 per cent, but because of the recession, most Funds fail to do so at present. Managers of the Funds want the Ministry of Health and Welfare to lower the expected minimum yield from 4.5 per cent to 3.0–3.5 per cent.[1]

However, in the long run, the world economy may face a lack of capital, and in that case the interest rate in Japanese markets will become higher. The sum of the pension funds of the Funds and the Tax-qualified Pension Plans amount to 39 trillion yen (the development of the balance of the pension funds is shown in Figure 6.5), while the balance of the public pension funds amounts to 110 trillion yen. In the future, under the pay-as-you-go system, the balance of the public pension funds

---

[1] The expected rate of return decreased from 5.5 per cent to 4.5 per cent in 1994.

213

Figure 6.8 – Distribution of retirement pay by types

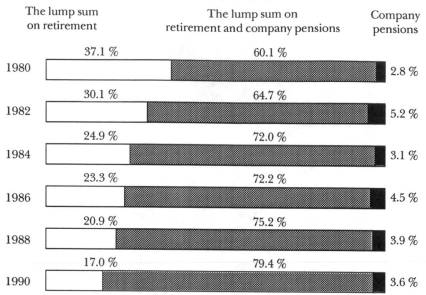

| The lump sum on retirement | The lump sum on retirement and company pensions | Company pensions |

Source: White Paper on Occupational Pensions (1992).

will be reduced dramatically and the private pension plans will then become main providers of funds into the capital market.

7. The effects of the pension mix on income distribution, savings and labour supply

The income of a household consisting of a husband and a wife both of whom are 65 years old or older is on average distributed as follows: 67 per cent benefits of public pension, 16 per cent earnings, 13 per cent income from business and farms, and 2 per cent others, according to the Census of 1990. On the other hand, according to the survey of the Ministry of Health and Welfare in 1989, retirement income of the household having a husband at 65 and over and his wife at 60 and over is distributed as follows: 50 per cent benefits of public pension, 24 per cent earnings, 10 per cent income from business and farms, 3 per cent income from assets and 2 per cent private pension benefits and others.

Almost 90 per cent of the employees in Japanese companies receive retirement pay based on lifetime employment and seniority systems.

The remaining 10 per cent are mainly employees in small companies. Retirement pay was the only source of retirement income for employees before the 1970s, but today public pensions represent a main source of this income. The average retirement pay at 60 is 42 times as much as the final monthly salary, while the present value of public pension benefits at retirement is 90 times as much as the final monthly salary.[2]

Percentage distribution of the employers by type of retirement income in 1990 was as follows: about 17 per cent only the traditional lump sum on retirement, 4 per cent only the company pension and 79 per cent both the lump sum on retirement and the company pension. About 56 per cent of the employees receive only the lump sum payments at their retirement and 7 per cent only the company pensions. About 28 per cent receive both. The rest (9 per cent) receive no retirement pay. Because the retired can receive the lump sum on retirement instead of the company pension as mentioned above, most retired choose the lump sum on retirement (see Figure 6.8 and also Japanese Association of Company Managers, 1990).

Table 6.3 shows the average amount of retirement pay classified by education and types of retirement income in 1990. It shows that university graduates get larger retirement pay than high school graduates, while the ratio of retirement pay to the final monthly salary of high school graduates is larger than that of university graduates, and that the present value of company pensions amounts to 80 to 90 per cent of the lump sum on retirement. People still prefer the latter form.

A rise in the pension age and a decrease in the pension benefits will result in an increase in the saving ratio of the household. In the capital market, the balance of both the public pension funds and company pension funds will continue to play an important role in the capital market as a supplier at least for the time being.

The pension age for female employees was 55 in 1985. It was raised to 59 in 1996 and will be further raised to 60 in 1999. On the other hand, the pension age for male employees has been fixed at 60 for these 15 years. The rise in both the pension age for women and the retirement age increased the labour participation ratio between 55 to 59 for women by 7 per cent for these 10 years, while that for men has been stable for the same period.

---

[2] The present value of public pension benefits will be gradually reduced according to the estimates. While a person born in 1946 gets 80 times the final salary, a person born in 1976 gets 50 times the final salary of the Employees' Pension.

The labour participation ratio of the elderly aged 60 to 65 in Japan is relatively high among OECD countries: for females, about 40 per cent, and for males, about 75 per cent; for females over 65, about 15 per cent and for males, less than 40 per cent. These figures have been stable for the past 15 years. The Japanese pension age is 60 today and 60 per cent of workers aged 60 to 65 are pensioners and more than 90 per cent of workers aged over 65 are pensioners.

The labour participation ratio of the elderly will decrease because the number of farmers will continue to decrease in the future. On the other hand, for employees, the pension age will be raised. Thus, the labour participation ratio for people aged 60 to 65 will probably rise in the future.

8. Conclusion

In Japan, retirement pay has played an important role in providing income for the retired. An increasingly older work force forced Japanese companies to reduce the amount of their retirement pay, and also to raise the mandatory retirement age, hiring people aged over 60. Furthermore, the Japanese government has encouraged companies to contract out by deregulating the Employees' Pension Funds.

Today, after the economic boom has ended, many of the Employees' Pension Funds are faced with financial difficulties. In 1994, the Employees' Pension Funds for the small spinning companies went bankrupt; for the first time a pension solvency insurance programme – the Pension Guarantee Programme – which was established in 1989, was terminated due to insolvency. In 1996, some contracted out pension funds went bankrupt even though the insured firms did not.

With the decrease in the interest rate and asset prices, some companies filled the deficit which had resulted from the poor investment to guarantee the defined-benefit plans, with their profits.

Furthermore, most of those who are on the boards of directors of the Funds are former governmental officials and not experts in the management of pension fund assets and thus do not have adequate knowledge of investment policy.

In the past the high economic growth rate and the high interest rate contributed to the good results which were reached by the Funds without the portfolio policy. This situation has changed.

The Japanese government is considering changing the defined-

Table 6.3 – Retirement pay by education and length of service

Education	Length of service	Age	Total			Lump sum on retirement			Lump sum on retirement and company pensions					Company pensions		
	Years		A	B	C	A	B	C	A	D	E	B	C	A	B	C
University graduate	30	52	213	19 446	33.8	105	18 580	32.9	105	12 020	8 041	20 061	34.5	3	28 169	35.5
	33	55	193	22 211	37.4	91	20 587	35.5	99	13 104	10 247	23 351	29.2	3	33 862	38.5
	35	57	145	23 622	39.2	68	21 258	36.3	75	13 475	11 766	25 241	41.9	2	43 299	39.9
High school graduate	30	48	205	14 809	32.6	104	14 758	32.9	98	10 125	4 523	14 648	32.3	3	21 843	34.5
	37	55	166	20 039	39.5	83	19 056	38.4	80	12 195	8 331	20 526	40.5	3	34 250	42.4
	39	57	122	20 455	40.3	63	18 999	38.2	57	11 784	9 351	21 135	42.2	2	46 959	45.8

A   The number of companies
B   Retirement pay (1000 yen)
C   The ratio of retirement pay to the final monthly salary
D   The lump sum on retirement (1000 yen)
E   The present value of company pension (1000 yen)

Source: White Paper on Occupational Pensions (1992).

benefit plans to the defined-contribution plans under the Employees' Pension Funds. Some critics are opposed to contracting out because it entails larger management costs, and also involves inconsistency of the financing system between the Employees' Pension Funds (based on a funded system) and the Employees' Pension Plans (based on a pay-as-you-go system), along with inequality between the insured of the Funds and the Plans.[3] In my view, contracting out has advantages by increasing flexibility in the benefit packages for employers and also in stimulating investments. Deregulation, clarification of the responsibility of the investment and mandatory reporting, disclosure requirements and an appropriate investment strategy are necessary for the Funds to make progress in Japan.

References

Aaron, Henry J., Bosworth, Barry P. and Burtless, Gary (1989), *Can America Afford to Grow Old?*, Washington, DC: The Brookings Institution.

Bodie, Zvi, Marcus, Alan J. and Merton, Robert C. (1988), 'Defined Benefit versus Defined Contribution Pension Plans: What are the Real Trade-offs?', in Zvi Bodie, John B. Shoven and David A. Wise (eds.), *Pensions in the U.S. Economy*, Chicago: The University of Chicago Press.

Dyer, John K. Jr. (1977), 'Coordination of Private and Public Pension Plans: An International Summary', in Dan A. McGill (ed.), *Social Security and Private Pension Plans: Competitive or Complementary?*, Pension Research Council.

Fry, V.C., Hammond, E.M. and Kay, J.A. (1985), *Taxing Pensions*, The Institute of Occupational Studies.

Fujii, Tokuzo, (1978), *A Primer on Retirement Pay*, Tokyo: Nihon Keizai Sinbunska.

ISSA (1987, 1990), *Conjugating Public and Private: The Case of Pensions*, Tokyo: Tokyo University Press.

Japanese Association of Company Managers (1990), *Statistics of Retirement Pay*.

Kimura, Yoko (1988), 'Taxation on Retirement Pay', *Kikan Shakai Hosho Kenkyu*, Winter.

Ministry of Health and Welfare (1992), *Annual Report on Health and Welfare 1991–2*.

Murakami, Kiyoshi (1984), *A New Introduction to Company Pension*, Tokyo: Shakai Hoken Junpousha.

Murakami, Kiyoshi (1993), *Pension Reform*, Toyo Keizai Sinpousha.

OECD (1988), *Reforming Public Pensions*, Paris: OECD.

OECD (1992), *Private Pensions and Public Policy*, Paris: OECD.

Research Institute of Life Design (1992), *White Paper on Occupational Pensions*.

---

[3] See Murakami (1993), pp. 133–91.

Rix, E. Sara and Fisher, Paul (1982), *Retirement-Age Policy. An International Perspective.* Pergamon Press.

Takayama, Noriyuki (1992), *The Idea of the Pension Reform,* Tokyo: Nihon Keizai Shin-bunsha.

Turner, John and Watanabe, Noriyasu (1995), *Private Pension Policies in Industrialized Countries: A Comparative Analysis,* Kalamazoo: W.E. Upjohn Institute for Employment Research.

7

The Netherlands: Growing Importance of Private Sector Arrangements

Martin Blomsma and Roel Jansweijer

1. Introduction

Studying social protection at the end of the labour career generally means addressing the pension system. In the Netherlands, however, things are not as simple as that. With respect to social protection of older people there are two Dutch stories to tell. One of them consists of income maintenance for those who have passed the statutory retirement age of 65. These people receive their benefits from the Dutch pension system. The other comprises social protection for those between 55 and 64 years of age who have left the labour market and who will not return into paid employment. They are considered as being retired, although they don't receive a benefit from the pension system. Their income maintenance has been organized in a different way.

A major reason for the distinction between retirement and early retirement is the inflexibility of the Dutch pension system. This is in contrast to the systems in other countries. As a rule it is impossible to enter the Dutch pension system before the statutory retirement age of 65. While in many countries early retirement options have been created within the pension system, this does not hold for the Netherlands where early retirement is only possible by way of using separate regulations outside the pension system.

The present Dutch system of social protection for early retirement (55–64) consists of disability, unemployment and pre-retirement arrangements. They have been brought about by both the public and the private sector. These arrangements generally produce benefits that cover a certain percentage of the final wage. As a rule, the amount and the duration of the benefits are sufficient to allow older workers to withdraw early from the labour market, i.e. five to ten years ahead of the statutory pension age of 65. Upon reaching the age of 65 older workers and early retirees will be transferred to the pension system. This guarantees them a flat-rate, basic state pension. In addition, for most employees the state pension is supplemented by private sector pension plan benefits.

Dutch social protection is based upon tiers rather than pillars both with respect to retirement and early retirement. Before the age of 65 the public disability and unemployment benefits (first tier) are often supplemented by company-related benefits (second tier). However, the private, pre-retirement so-called VUT-schemes (approximately 300) are more pillar than tier because there is no basic scheme in a first tier. There has been a tendency recently to transform these schemes into flexible and individualized pre-retirement programmes which makes them a mix of a second- and third-tier plan.

After 65 the three tiers consist of the basic state pension (first tier), the supplementary company-related pension plans (second tier) and the individual pension or life insurance plans (third tier).

The portions of the tiers in old age social protection have not been stable over time. In the nineteenth century we only encounter private sector initiatives to establish company-related income maintenance arrangements for those in old age. In the twentieth century, with a growing penetration of the state into socio-economic life, the initiative gradually shifts to the public sector. After the Second World War, with the unfolding of the welfare state, this process accelerated.

In the last two decades, however – and this is our central thesis – the importance of the second tier in the income provision of older people in the Netherlands has increased remarkably: since the 1970s the welfare state arrangements (first tier) gradually lost ground with respect to both the income of early retirees (55–64) and of those in the pension system (65 and over). There even seems to be a tendency right now for the third tier to become more important.

In our view this shift away from the first to the second and even a third tier is mainly a consequence of declining options and benefits in the public sector. This decline has been compensated by the creation of new private sector arrangements as well as the adaptation of existing ones.

This chapter has been organized as follows: section 2 will address part of the history of the institutions that play a role in old age social protection. In this we will especially focus on the 1970–95 period. We will systematically distinguish between retirement and early retirement and between first and second tiers. In section 3 we will illustrate the changing pension mix in the last two decades. We will relate developments in expenses and assets of the social protection arrangements to changes in the institutional framework described earlier in section 2. Section 4 addresses the pension mix of the future. It presents the current discourse about changes in old age social protection with respect to the near future and in the long run. Finally, there will be some concluding remarks.

2. The development of the institutional framework for old age social protection

2.1 Late nineteenth century till the early 1970s

Until the late nineteenth century there were hardly any insurances against old age, disability or unemployment. Public sector involvement in social protection – aside from local community poor relief – was completely absent. In as far as old age arrangements had come into existence, the initiatives had been taken by the private sector (Veldkamp 1978, pp. 51–8). The history of Dutch company-related pension arrangements (OPFs) starts in the mid nineteenth century. These early funds were few and mostly charitable ad hoc arrangements of employers. In general, they didn't offer much protection. Between the two World Wars some hundreds of them were added. Especially since 1945 the number of company pension schemes grew rapidly. In addition to the company-related pension funds, the employer and employee organizations established sectoral pension funds (BPFs). They also developed especially after 1945: in 1987 there were 80 of them.

Civil servants as a group were the first to have a regulated and legally enacted pension arrangement (since 1798). Gradually its coverage was extended. Eventually, in 1966, the Civil Servants' Pension Act was replaced by the ABP Law (Civil Servants' Superannuation Fund), which regulated the inclusion of the basic state pension (AOW) into the civil servants' pension (Kuné 1987, pp. 17–18).

In the late nineteenth century, one of the central demands of the rising labour movement became the right of the people to an old age pension. Labour argued that the thinly spread and often underdeveloped private sector old age arrangements could not satisfy the needs of the time. According to Gales (1986, pp. 70–3) the labour movement concluded that the private sector would not come up with a substantial insurance for employees upon retiring. Therefore the state should be involved in old age social protection.

Public pension laws started in the early twentieth century. In 1919, the Law on Disability and Old Age was implemented. It established a mandatory public pension for employees and their survivors based on insurance. There was the option of a voluntary old age insurance for the self-employed. The statutory pension age was set at 65. The benefit amount was fixed and non-indexed. In the inter-war years many of those over 65 could not claim a benefit under the Old Age Act of 1919. Moreover, the receipt of a public pension was definitely not a guaranteed escape from poverty. In 1920 the maximum benefit was by no means impressive. Ever since, its real value has declined (Verbon 1988, p. 244). Winters (1990, pp. 78–95) states that only a tiny fraction of the retirees received an additional company pension benefit.

In 1947 Parliament accepted – as a temporary measure – the Old Age Emergency Act, which was designed to secure a basic level of income for the aged in anticipation of a definitive settlement (Veldkamp 1978, p. 95).

In 1957, the Old Age Emergency Act was replaced by the General Old Age Act (AOW), which is still in function. The new Act created a compulsory old age insurance for all inhabitants, independent of the source or size of their income. Payment of the flat-rate AOW-pension benefit would start at 65. The benefit amount would depend primarily upon the period of insurance (though not on the amount of contributions). A full public pension would be paid to those continuously insured for 50 years. However, at the introduction of the law, fictional years of insurance were given away as if the law had always existed. This was made possible by the choice to replace the former funding system by a pay-as-you-go (PAYG) financing method.

Everyone was to pay contributions at a specified rate of their income up to a maximum amount. Contrary to the 1919 Act, the employers would not contribute to the system. The benefits would be index-linked to (regulated) wages in the market sector. Single persons would receive 62 per cent (later raised to 70 per cent) of the benefit of a married couple. Married women were independently insured and built up their own pension rights, but were not entitled to a benefit independent of their husband (Ministerie van Sociale Zaken en Werkgelegenheid 1990a, pp. 20–7). Some years later (1959) the General Widows' and Orphans' Act (AWW) was added, which regulated a survivors' pension and was structured in much the same way as the AOW.

The AOW Act ended a political debate which lasted more than sixty years. It created a public pension system that has basically survived till the present day. Ever since, the political debate has hardly touched upon the structure of public pension legislation and has focused primarily on the level of the flat-rate AOW-benefit.

The public pension legislation of 1956 did not only improve the income position of the aged, it also changed the position of the private sector pension funds. A peculiarity of the AOW Act has been that private sector pension schemes are obliged to take into account the size of the public pension benefit. Thus, a salary-related private pension benefit scheme has to include the AOW-pension in its benefit structure. This is in order to prevent a possible future 'unreasonable accumulation of pension income'.

The AOW-pension was meant to be a basic tier to which private pension schemes should be supplementary. It has never been the intention to push out the private funds. On the contrary, the absence of any means test was to encourage private plans. Pension arrangements were to remain primarily a responsibility of the employers and employees. This explains why AOW-benefits were, initially, rather moderate and could certainly not cover the costs of living.

However, over the years the state pension became more important because the benefit level was increased several times on top of the automatic adjustment mechanism prescribed by law. Over the course of time the AOW-benefit reached the level of the social minimum. In 1976 even a formal relation between the public pension and the statutory minimum wage was established ('net-net coupling'). Until now the original expectation of a mature, highly developed system of private pension arrangements on top of the basic public pension has not yet been realized. The relative increases of the AOW-benefit meant that the public pension grew along with (and maybe even stronger than) the private arrangements (Verbon 1988, pp. 24–5; Oversloot 1986, p. 14; Winters 1990, p. 113, 118).

After the Second World War the state created a legal framework for private sector (company and sectoral) pension schemes to protect the interests of the workers participating. The Act regarding Obligatory Participation in a Branch of Industry Pension Fund (1949) created the possibility for the Dutch Minister of Social Affairs to declare the pension arrangements of one particular collective labour agreement (CAO) in a given branch of industry generally binding for all employees within that branch (administrative extension).

In 1954 the Pension and Saving Funds Act (PSW) was enacted. Its first aim was to control and supervise the soundness of private pension funds' investments. The Act ordained that private sector pension plans should be funded and that the pension funds' money should be completely separated from the capital of the enterprise. The supervision on the soundness of the investments of all private pension funds was entrusted to the Insurance Chamber.

Finally, in 1972 regulations were enacted regarding the obligatory participation in professional pension funds for groups of self-employed professionals.

As stressed before, not only retirement provisions are significant in the Dutch pension system. Income maintenance arrangements for older workers (under 65) are also important. In this respect the establishment of some compulsory social security regulations was important, i.e.: the Unemployment Insurance Act (WW-1949), the Unemployment Provisions Act (WWV-1964) and the Disability Insurance Act (WAO-1967). Together with the General Disability Benefits Act (AAW-1976) this created a legal framework which played a prominent role in early retirement of older workers in the last two decades.

2.2 Early retirement arrangements (55–64) 1970–95

The first tier in early retirement arrangements

In the last decades the labour force participation of older workers in the Netherlands has drastically declined. In 1971, 74 per cent of the 60-to-64-year-old males participated, while in 1994 the rate had fallen to a mere 19 per cent (Centraal Bureau voor de Statistiek 1995, p. 87). Even from an OECD perspective the decline has been rather extreme. Figure 7.1 shows the sharp decline in the average retirement age since the mid 1970s.

Many different factors help explain the trend, not least the fact that the Dutch system of social security has been highly accessible to applicants: it offers a number of pathways into early retirement; flexible and gradual options have been very limited. On top of this, institutional policy has generally been directed at offering income replacement instead of employment opportunities for older social beneficiaries. So in fact these beneficiaries have retired.

When older workers have been granted social security benefits, in most cases this forebodes a premature termination of their working life. This is remarkable, because the system of social security was originally not intended to create possibilities for early retirement. The primary purpose was to realize, if possible, a reintegration into paid labour for

Figure 7.1 – Average retirement age (men and women)

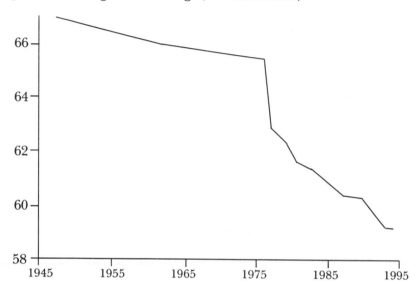

Source: Jansweijer (1996, p. 28).

beneficiaries of all age groups. However, in the course of the 1970s it became clear that a number of social security regulations – separately or in combination – could function as pathways into early retirement. In practice these regulations were partly transformed into instruments of early retirement, without the official (but with informal) consent of the Dutch government. Of crucial importance has been the role of the social partners, i.e. the organizations of employers and employees. They had a serious interest in promoting early retirement of older workers, while at the same time they were highly involved in the implementation of the social security regulations concerned (den Broeder 1987).

The main exit-routes based on social security have been the disability pathway (I) and the unemployment pathway (II). These will be discussed below.

(I) Since 1970 the disability pathway predominantly had the following characteristics. Employees unable to work due to ill health, whatever the cause, could receive a Sickness Act benefit (ZW-1967). This guaranteed them an 80 per cent benefit for at most one year. Thereafter, if still incapable of working, they could receive a disability benefit emanating from the Disability Insurance Act (WAO-1967) and the General Disability Benefits Act (AAW-1976). A separate, but largely

226

similar, disability pathway existed for civil servants (based on AAW- and ABP-benefits).

The WAO Act offers a compulsory insurance for all employees with a wage related benefit. Initially, the highest level of incapacity (80–100 per cent) guaranteed a near 80 per cent benefit of the final wage (up to a fixed maximum). The General Disability Benefits Act (AAW-1976) extended coverage for the risk of disability to virtually the entire Dutch population under 65, though actual loss of income through disability was generally a condition for claiming a benefit. The level of an AAW-benefit depends on the degree of incapacity and the statutory minimum wage.[1] Since 1976 the WAO-benefit for employees includes AAW-entitlement.

The conditions for claiming a disability benefit have been lenient. Both acts offer integral coverage of all disability risks (i.e. 'risque social'). Disability benefits would be awarded for an indefinite period. Moreover, a person was considered disabled if unable to earn his final wage in 'suitable work'. Since the mid 1970s, it was also – officially – taken into account whether this work was actually available. If not, a person was considered fully disabled. So, unemployment was partly labelled as disability. This accounts for much of the fall in the average retirement age in Figure 7.1.

The institutions of the disability pathway are public, but they are financed by the private sector. Until recently they have been administered by the 26 Industrial Insurance Boards, governed by organizations of employers and employees. These boards were supervised by the Social Insurance Council (SVR), representing government, employers and employees.

In 1987 the Dutch system of social security was reconstructed. Ahead of this in 1985, the sickness and disability benefit rates had already been reduced from 80 to 70 per cent. Among other things the reconstruction established that the actual availability of suitable jobs should no longer be taken into account when assessing the level of incapacity. This was in order to clearly distinguish between disability and unemployment and to limit the new AAW/WAO-entrance with a full benefit. Partially disabled workers in need of additional income replacement should have to apply for a supplementary – temporary – unemployment benefit (WW).

---

[1] For a fully disabled person it amounts to 70 per cent of the minimum wage (Ministerie van Sociale Zaken en Werkgelegenheid 1990a, pp. 34–9, 55–62).

In the early 1990s the policy climate in the Netherlands changed in favour of a generally higher labour force participation. In the wake of the debate a number of rule changes were introduced with the aim to reduce sickness and disability costs. This affected the disability pathways of both private sector employees and civil servants.

In 1992, with respect to the Sickness Act, financial incentives to both employers and workers have been inserted (TAV-Act) in order to reduce the number of beneficiaries. The contributions, which used to be the same for all companies in a given industrial sector, have become company-differentiated. From January 1994 (TZ-Act) employers have been made responsible for the payment of employees in the first six weeks of sickness absence.[2] According to Civil Code these employees then are entitled to a 70 per cent income replacement (but at least the statutory minimum wage). Re-insurance of supplementary benefits will only be tolerated through private insurance companies. After six weeks the Industrial Association takes over control and provides a Sickness Act benefit (70 per cent of the last wage) for the remainder of the sickness year.

With respect to the disability Acts a number of rule changes were introduced from 1992. First (TAV-Act-1992), financial incentives were created for employers to hire (partially) disabled workers or to retain them. At the same time the employer had to pay a penalty for each employee entering disability for whatever reason.

In 1993 (TBA-Act) more radical measures were taken. The disability status has become temporary, with periodic re-assessments of the level of incapacity (every five years); however, current older beneficiaries escape re-assessment. The wage-related part (WAO) of the disability benefit too has become temporary, dependent upon the age of the claimant.[3] A fully disabled average production worker of 55, with a wage of 1.8 times the statutory minimum wage, will receive 1.26 times the social minimum for 2 1/2 years, and then 1.15 times the social minimum. Moreover, the concept of 'suitable work' has been widened to 'common labour' in

---

[2] The first two weeks for companies with less than 15 employees.

[3] The 70 per cent benefit (of fully disabled) is granted for two and a half years (age 53–7) or up to the age of 65 (58 and over). After the 70 per cent benefit, a follow-up benefit may continue up to the age of 65. For this benefit (instead of the former wage) the statutory minimum wage, supplemented with 2 per cent of the difference between the former wage and the minimum wage for each year the claimant is over 15, is taken as the basis for the benefit-formula.

order to extend the range of possible jobs. As a corollary, a much larger share of the claimants is considered partially disabled.[4] Finally, older (50 and over) and long-term disability beneficiaries are stimulated to continue a search for a job by way of a specific financial incentive.

Due to these rule changes – apart from compensation in second-tier supplements – the disability pathway into early retirement has much deteriorated especially for younger workers. New disability beneficiaries (40–50 years), for instance, may lose between 12 and 20 percentage points of their benefit income compared to the previous situation. For older workers (58 and over), however, comparatively little has changed: after a first year of sickness benefit they are still entitled to a 70 per cent AAW/WAO-benefit till the official pension age (65). The new method of benefit calculation is going to cost them at most about 5 percentage points benefit income (Kroon and Meijnen 1993).

(II) The second most important social security exit-route has been the unemployment pathway, initially consisting of the Unemployment Insurance Act (WW-1952) and the Unemployment Provisions Act (WWV-1964). The first is premium-financed and administered by the private sector; the second budget-financed and publicly administered. Initially WW guaranteed benefits of 80 per cent of the last wage (up to a maximum) for at most six months. Then WWV would provide a follow-up benefit of 75 per cent for two years. In 1985 the benefit rates have been reduced to 70 per cent.

At the outset, WW and WWV were not designed for a period of massive and prolonged unemployment. However, with unemployment rapidly growing in the 1970s, specific unemployment provisions were developed to counteract the difficulties older job-seekers faced on the labour market. Thus, unemployed aged 57 1/2 years and above were given a prolonged period of WWV-entitlement to prevent a relapse into means-tested welfare benefits. Unintentionally this induced the use of unemployment regulations for early retirement (de Kemp 1992, pp. 33–5, 54). The issuance by the state in 1975 of the Older Workers Directive also furthered the use of the unemployment pathway. It facilitated the disproportionate dismissal of older workers at collective discharges. One of the

---

[4] In re-assessment, 47 per cent of the younger disabled lost (part of) their disability status (College van toezicht sociale verzekeringen 1995a, p. 6). The tendency of a declining disabled population will probably continue (but slow down) in 1996 with a 3 per cent lower volume, while demographic change alone would have caused an increase (ibid. 1995b).

stipulations was that the older workers concerned had to accept their early retirement voluntarily (Ministerie van Sociale Zaken en Werkgelegenheid 1984a, p. 71)

Using the unemployment pathway with an extra-legal supplement from the enterprise, the number of in fact collectively subsidized company reconstructions increased strongly. In 1983, the state decided to curtail the appeal of the unemployment pathway slightly: employers were no longer allowed to pay supplementary benefits for more than two and a half years.

The reconstruction of social security in 1987 drastically changed the Unemployment Insurance Act (WW) and abolished the Unemployment Provisions Act (WWV). As a consequence, the original unemployment pathway was closed. Its current participants were nearly all transferred to the New Unemployment Insurance Act (nWW-1987). Older WWV-beneficiaries (58 and over) would stay in there until the normal pension age of 65.

The New Unemployment Insurance Act is premium-financed and administered by the private sector. Insurance is mandatory for employees. The Act provides three consecutive types of unemployment benefit: first, the loss of earnings benefit, which amounts to 70 per cent of the final wage (up to a maximum) and is paid up to six months; second, the extension of loss of earnings benefit, the duration of which is determined by a claimants' age and work history and may range from three months to four and a half years; and third, prolonged benefit, which provides a benefit of 70 per cent of the statutory minimum wage for one year. A special clause guarantees the older unemployed (57 1/2 and above) a longer duration of the prolonged benefit until the normal pension age of 65. It means they do not have to claim benefit from Social Assistance, which is income- and means-tested (Ministerie van Sociale Zaken en Werkgelegenheid 1990a, pp. 50–2).

In fact, since 1987 the unemployment pathway into early retirement has remained much the same. Older workers, with generally a long work history, are entitled to a relatively long-term nWW-benefit. For instance, those who worked 35–40 years may expect up to 4 years' nWW (loss of earnings)-benefit; those with 40 years and over up to five years. On top of this those aged 57 1/2 and over may receive prolonged benefit till the normal pension age.

However, an essential difference between the initial and current unemployment pathway is that the level of public benefit in the last stretch has been reduced. Nevertheless, this pathway has retained its popularity in the private sector. Restructuring companies consider the nWW- and prolonged benefits substantial ingredients of a so-called company social plan for older employees (57 1/2 and over). Until recently, the state furthered the private sector social plan policy for older workers with its Older Workers Directive. Since January 1994 this directive is no longer effective.

The second tier in early retirement arrangements

The first-tier sickness, disability and unemployment benefits in the Netherlands may be topped up by second-tier entitlements. This has been done across the board, but the possibility has been especially of interest with respect to the disability and unemployment pathways into early retirement. Also, alongside these social security pathways, a private sector pre-retirement route (VUT) has developed since the late 1970s. Both second-tier supplements and the VUT-schemes will be the subject of this section.

The disability and unemployment exit-routes to a certain extent have always included second-tier supplementary benefits. These have been negotiated in collective bargaining between the social partners. So benefit conditions may differ considerably by industrial sector or company.

Within the disability pathway the Sickness Act benefit (ZW) has generally been supplemented to 100 per cent of the final wage. The follow-up disability benefits (AAW/WAO), already fairly generous themselves, have often been supplemented with interesting sweeteners, in order to tempt older workers to cooperate with the employer concerning their early withdrawal from the labour market.

Due to the reconstruction of social security (1985/7) the benefit levels have been reduced 10 percentage points. The loss of sickness benefit has been nearly fully offset in collective bargaining through adjustment of the terms of collective labour agreements. The loss of disability benefit has only partially been repaired, depending upon company- and sector-specific conditions (Ministerie van Sociale Zaken en Werkgelegenheid 1989, pp. 5–9, 31–5).

The recent changes (1993) in the disability system have created the perspective of a decline over time of the first-tier AAW/WAO-benefit, especially for younger workers. In the current discourse the difference between the original and the present benefit is known as the WAO-gap.

More explicitly than before, the purpose of this change was to discourage the use of social security by employees and to raise labour participation.

However, employers were using social security as much as employees were. They provided a relatively cheap sweetener upon the publicly financed social security thereby making it easier to lay off older workers. In most industrial sectors, the income-effects of the 1993 rule changes have been fully repaired: in collective bargaining the second-tier (sector and company) pension schemes have been adjusted to the new situation. In a few cases, however, this has implied some reduction of the total first- and second-tier benefit. So far the costs of repairing the WAO-gap seem to have been shifted mainly to the employees.[5]

The Dutch government, trying to raise labour force participation and reduce the costs of social security, has strongly opposed the idea of sealing the WAO-gap through collective bargaining. In 1994 it even attempted to discourage private sector agreements on this subject by law. It introduced a bill stipulating that provisions in Collective Labour Agreements (CAO) concerning supplementary disability benefits in private sector pension schemes can be excluded when CAOs are extended by the state to a whole industrial sector (Tweede Kamer 1994).

In the unemployment pathway, likewise, first-tier benefits have generally been supplemented by second-tier benefits agreed on in collective bargaining. This also in order to increase the attractiveness of the exit-offer to older workers. Very often to those aged 55 and over second-tier supplements have been paid for up to $7^1/_2$ or 10 years. Generally, the amount of supplementary benefit depends upon the expected duration of payment (Ministerie van Sociale Zaken en Werkgelegenheid 1990b, pp. 17–19).

Interesting here are also the so-called social plans at collective discharge of employees. These practically always contain special clauses concerning second-tier supplementary benefits for older workers who are to be dismissed (Trommel and de Vroom 1994, p. 56). Since the unemployment rule changes of 1987 (i.e. for the $57^1/_2$ and over after five years of unemployment benefit no more than a social minimum

---

[5] Already in 1993 approximately 85 per cent of the employees under larger Collective Labour Agreements (i.e. each relating to more than 3000 employees) had been covered by a 'WAO-gap repair clause'. On average the employees pay an additional premium of 1.4 per cent of their gross wage; the employers pay 0.2 per cent (Ministerie van Sociale Zaken en Werkgelegenheid 1994, pp. 35–40).

benefit) these private sector supplements are especially meant to top up first-tier benefits in the last years before the official retirement at 65.

Apart from these private sector supplements to social security pathways a specific second-tier pre-retirement route (VUT) has developed. In the mid 1970s, in a context of rising unemployment, the idea gained ground in policy circles that older workers should be entitled to a well-earned retirement before the normal pension age. In addition, it was thought, their pre-retirement would create vacancies on the labour market, which could be filled by unemployed younger workers. To a certain extent the first VUT-schemes have been initiated and subsidized by the Dutch government. The basic idea, however, has always been to create sector- and/or company-specific preretirement programmes negotiated through collective bargaining between the social partners, without public sector interference and entirely financed by the employers and employees.

Since 1976 these private sector pre-retirement arrangements have boomed. VUT has become a standard issue in collective bargaining over labour conditions. Already in 1980 VUT-regulations had been included in 191 Collective Labour Agreements. That year also the state, in its capacity of employer, enacted a VUT-programme for its civil servants. In 1988 the total number of VUT-schemes amounted to 471. By then VUT-schemes covered about 70 per cent of employees in the private sector, and nearly all civil servants and workers in the subsidized service sector. Ever since, coverage growth has slowed down somewhat.

VUT-eligibility typically requires a work history of ten years. The benefit conditions of the many VUT-schemes range from 75 to 85 per cent of the final gross wage (net results being better). Between 1983 and 1990 the average age of entitlement to a VUT-benefit gradually came down from 62.5 to 59.9 years, or even younger for employees with a job-tenure of at least 40 years. In recent years, however, this process of a continuous improvement of VUT-conditions seems to have halted (Ministerie van Sociale Zaken en Werkgelegenheid 1984b, pp. 52–68; ibid. 1990c, pp. 44–54, 58–61; ibid. 1993).

VUT-arrangements are not just regulated but also financed by the private sector. The implementation of the schemes is highly decentralized and done by a variety of rather different corporate bodies. In principle VUT-benefits can be derived from three sources: VUT funds, pension funds and direct payments by employers. Most VUT-financing has been organized on a PAYG-basis (Ministerie van Sociale Zaken en Werkgelegenheid 1990c, p. 66). The level of contributions is a matter of collective bargaining. As a rule the premiums are split between employers and employees. Distributive codes may differ considerably by scheme.

Since the early 1990s researchers and policy-makers in the public and private sectors have begun to voice their doubts whether VUT really contributed to a redistribution of labour. At the same time worries started to come up about the impressive cost growth of the schemes. Demographic projections added to the fears that a continuation of VUT in its current shape would be out of the question in a few years from now (Wetenschappelijke Raad voor het Regeringsbeleid 1993, pp. 206–14).

This situation has furthered a tendency in many collective bargaining rounds in the last few years to change the design of VUT-programmes fundamentally. The outcome seems to be a transformation of the second-tier, collective (PAYG), standardized VUT-schemes into a mixture of second- and third-tier, highly individualized and flexible pre-retirement programmes, mainly financed out of personal savings accounts of employees. An additional effect may very well be that the financial burden of these programmes will be shifted increasingly towards the employees (Blomsma 1996).

2.3 Pension arrangements (65 and over) 1970–95

The first tier in pension arrangements

The General Old Age Act (AOW-1957) provides a first-tier flat-rate benefit for any citizen, regardless of labour history, wealth or other income. Since the basic pension does not depend on the former wages and only provides a minimum, second-tier supplements are more important in retirement than in the public pathways into early retirement. Moreover, the level of the first-tier benefit determines at least partly the expenditures within the second tier.

Until the mid 1970s the level of all minimum social security benefits (from old age to social assistance) increased at a higher rate than the growth of wages negotiated through collective bargaining. The resulting benefit levels were rather high compared to those in surrounding countries. At the end of the 1970s it became increasingly clear that it would not be possible or desirable to continue the prevailing growth rate of the index-link between social minimum benefits and the negotiated wages. This index-link had already been institutionalized into the AOW-legislation. However, the index-linking policy became the subject of public discussion. This resulted in an Act (WAM-1980) which formalized the practice of the preceding years: all minimum benefit-levels and the statutory minimum wage should be index-linked to wage growth. However, as the economic situation deteriorated this law was seldom enforced, thus showing the illusionary safety of formalization.

The frustrating lack of enforcement produced a new piece of legislation: the so called 'Law on linkage with options not to link' (WKA-1991). Its name already shows how social desirability of index-linking conflicted with economic conditions. The WKA specified two main conditions under which index-linking was to take place: wage growth has to be moderate; the ratio of the inactive to active population should be below the level of 1991.

In the last four years wages did not grow much. But the ratio of the inactive to the active population has been rising due to demographic changes. Since the benefit-structure of AOW has become individualized, the number of AOW-recipients grows stronger than before, when a couple receiving AOW-benefit counted only one time. This obviously affects the second criterion and makes it the more important one. From the beginning it was rather clear that index-linking to the negotiated wages under WKA was not to be implemented most of the time. Nevertheless, the law institutionalized the desirability of raising benefits while the realization of this desire became a matter of policy decision rather than an automatism.

The WKA has contributed to a situation in which the volume-ratio of the inactive to active population deteriorated while the expense-ratio (total costs to contributions base) improved, due to (almost) frozen benefits and a relatively higher weight of cheaper – individualized – old age basic pension benefits. Only recently, with a harsh reduction of the sick and disabled population, is the volume-criterion about to be met. The government that entered office in 1994 promised index-linking to half the wage growth. In 1995 benefits remained unchanged; in 1996 index-linking will be resumed for at least one year.

Figure 7.2 shows the result of the developments described above. At equal growth rates of the net minimum benefits (including the AOW basic pension) and the net wage of an average worker, the curve would follow the X-axis. The growth of the benefit-level compared to the growth of wages rose steeply during the 1970s. This was especially due to the fact that net benefits were set equal to the level of the net minimum wage. In the 1980s by contrast, the minimum benefit-level hardly grew, although the purchasing capacity of the lower income-groups was partly

Figure 7.2 – Differences in growth rate between the net minimum benefits and the net average negotiated wages since 1970

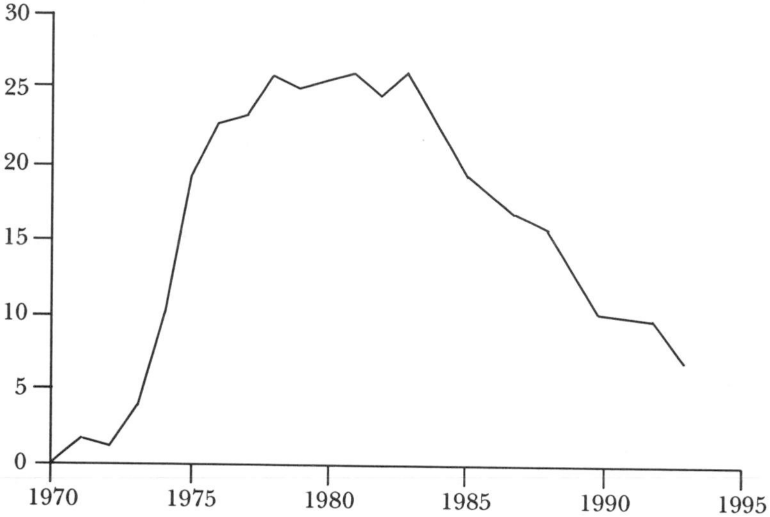

Source: Sociaal en Cultureel Planbureau (1994, p. 202).

repaired by special government measures. From 1990 there was a partial index-linking. In summary, the relative level of minimum social security benefits, compared to net wages, is now back at where it stood at the beginning of the 1970s.

We may conclude a growing collective responsibility for the first-tier basic state pension from the 1950s until about 1980. After that, however, the relative level of the AOW-benefit structurally decreases.

Not just the benefit level but also the benefit structure has changed. The AOW-benefit is granted regardless of labour history, but initially married women were excluded. When the AOW was introduced in 1957, this was a simple way to create a broad insurance for the working population, in which married women hardly took part. However, this exclusion could not stand under the pressure of EC-regulations, stipulating equal rights regardless of sex and marital status.

Between 1985 and 1987, in order to comply with EC-regulations, equal rights were created for men and women and the differentiation of benefits by sex and marital status was replaced by a differentiation by type of household. The benefit of the married man was split into two halves, one for each spouse. Since most women are some years younger than their husband, splitting created a gap in the benefit during the years in which the husband was entitled but the wife was not. For this period the benefit of the first pensioned spouse was supplemented with an allowance up to the former level of 100 per cent of the net minimum wage. After some years the provision of the allowance has become conditional on the labour market income of the dependent spouse, but there are no conditions on the income of the first pensioned (mostly male) spouse. First (1987) the rate was 70 per cent of the AOW-benefit of a couple for the first spouse and 30 per cent supplement; in 1994 this was changed to 50:50.

The splitting of the AOW-benefit raised the number of beneficiaries but not the budget. Married women gained rights previously paid directly by their husband. In fact, the entitlements of married couples to basic pension declined if women were active in paid work or receiving a social security benefit. The supplementary allowance to the first pensioned spouse introduced a strong incentive for older women to quit the labour market. Nevertheless the effect was modest, because only a tiny fraction of older women was actually employed.[6]

The basic pension contributions changed in accordance with the benefits. Until 1985 married men paid contributions on both their own and their wives' income (if any) up to a certain maximum. Since 1985 both spouses pay contributions separately up to the same maximum amount. This has created a heavy extra burden for married women with a substantial income, while their future entitlements have in practice decreased due to the splitting of the benefit. This again meant an incentive for some to quit the labour market.

In 1990 the contributions to the General Old Age Pension have been integrated into the tax system. In this process an exemption like in the tax system has been given to Old Age Pension contributions and the maximum income basis for contributions has been lowered. This reduced the macro basis for contributions and as a consequence the contribution rate rose from 10.8 in 1989 to 14.3 per cent in 1990. The integration of the tax system and part of the social security system gener-

---

[6] The supplementary allowance was challenged before the European Court of Justice, but the government won the trial with the argument that the allowance was to guarantee a minimum level of existence. Still, it can be demonstrated that the supplement creates bigger rather than smaller differences in wealth since it is mostly claimed by married men, who generally receive more supplementary income from second-tier pensions (Jansweijer 1996, p. 151). Just recently the government has announced the intention to abolish the allowance by the year 2015.

ated upward changes of the gross benefit levels, in order to compensate for the changes. The net basic pension level, however, was not affected.

The result of the above mentioned changes has been that any remaining link between the labour history of the claimant and the basic state pension benefit, has now been cut. Initially, AOW was meant to be a broad insurance for the working population. At this moment AOW is a – de facto – budget-financed pension benefit for the whole Dutch population, albeit with a reduced (split) benefit (Jansweijer 1990).

In the near future it may become clear that the differentiation to household types is not enforceable since there is no workable definition of a household. A government committee that studied the future of the pension system (Commissie Drees 1987) thought it unavoidable to dispose of this differentiation, thus creating a benefit of 50 per cent of the net statutory minimum wage for singles and 100 per cent for couples. This, however, would create marked inequalities in wealth among the aged (Jansweijer 1996, pp. 152–5).

The second tier in pension arrangements

The flat-rate basic pension (AOW) can be supplemented by second tier pension income. This applies to private sector employees as well as civil servants. Because second-tier pension plans have to take into account the first-tier benefit, accrual of pension rights usually starts way above the statutory minimum wage. Thus a total result from first and second tier in relation to the former salary is aimed at (typically 70 per cent). This goal can be reached by means of: (a) inclusion of the first tier benefit, or (b) using a franchise. When the first tier is built in, the benefit will be calculated in relation to the (final) salary; then an amount for the basic state pension is subtracted (even when the claimant has no entitlement to AOW). Under the franchise system, an exemption corresponding to the basic pension is subtracted from the salary to calculate the basis for the pension-formula. In the course of time, inclusion of the AOW-benefit is being replaced by the franchise system.

Traditionally, the franchise was geared to the situation of the male breadwinner and was set at 10/7 of his first-tier benefit. In some plans different franchises have been applied for married men and others. In these cases the franchise for married men is higher than for singles since the first tier generates lower benefits to singles than to couples. Thus, in these plans the second tier compensates differences in income from the first tier.

Under the franchise system a 70 per cent benefit creates a total pension result of first- and second-tier benefits at 70 per cent of the final salary. Many second-tier plans had their franchise directly related to the level of the first-tier benefit of a married man. So, after the splitting of the first-tier benefit in 1985 halved this benefit, many second-tier plans would be obliged to fill in the other half of the first-tier benefit in order to meet the promised pension targets. The enormous costs of this operation were prevented by the insertion of a clause which permitted pension funds to use the fiction that the married man was still entitled to both his own and his wife's benefits.

Since the splitting of the benefit in the first tier there is no longer an integrated system of first- and second-tier plans which produces a total pension result in direct relation to the final salary. In fact, the system was never really integrated except for the male breadwinner and (mostly) singles, since married women were excluded from first-tier benefits while most pension plans used the fiction that they were not.

The novelty of the changes in the mid 1980s was that the lack of integration then became widely recognized. Ever since, there has been a trend to lower the franchise and to abandon any differences in franchise by marital status. This creates more pension rights for married men and less for others. It has also started the development to a situation where there is no longer a direct relation between the final wage and the total pension result. And important in the frame of this study, the loosening of the integration of the first- and second-tier pension income may announce a shift of responsibility from the state to the enterprise concerning the total pension result.

Since the benefit level of the first tier is rather low, an abundance of over 1000 second-tier plans has come into existence. It has always been an explicit aim of state policy that the first tier would create an incentive for supplementary pension plans. Over the years the number of participants in these plans has grown far more than the dependent labour force. In 1992 65 per cent of the labour force aged 25–64 took part in a plan.[7] According to research of the Pension Chamber (Pensioenkamer 1987) 82 per cent of the employees in this age group participated in a

---

[7] Pension plan participants counted by the Insurance Chamber as a percentage of the labour force according to the Central Bureau of Statistics labour force survey (EBB). In general, pension rights are accrued to those aged 25–64.

pension plan. The difference between these figures may be explained by the exclusion of the self-employed and the more stringent definition of the labour force in the Pension Chamber report.

Most of the non-participants are working in the profit service-sector, especially part-timers and people with low wages. Women have a smaller chance to participate in a plan, but if they do they are likely to take part in one of the two biggest plans: ABP (civil servants) or PGGM (medical and welfare). These plans offer a relatively high quality pension, although PGGM excluded part-timers (working less than 40 per cent of a full-time job) until 1991. After the recent (1994) European Court of Justice ruling that the exclusion of part-timers is illegal, PGGM repaired the pension rights of part-timers back to 1976. PGGM could do this easily because the fund reserves by far exceed those necessary for the directly accrued rights. The ABP-plan did not exclude part-timers but did not offer them equal rights until 1986.

There has been a long history of discussion about the desirability of a mandatory second-tier system. Mandatory in this case means that the employer is obliged to offer a plan. In 1973, the FVP-fund (Fund Advance Payment to Pension Insurance) was created to facilitate the establishment of such a mandatory system. At the beginning of the 1980s a mandatory system seemed to become feasible, but when the Pension Chamber in 1987 showed that most employees already participated in a plan the urgency was disputed again. In 1991 the government finally decided not to introduce a mandatory system (Ministerie van Sociale Zaken en Werkgelegenheid 1991). In fact, the decision was already taken earlier: since 1985 the capital yields of the FVP-fund (by now about dfl 4 billion) have been used to prolong the participation of the older unemployed in a pension plan. Also other ideas have blossomed to use this fund to repair deficiencies in the second tier, but until now to no avail.

The second-tier plans can be divided into three main groups: (a) the ABP for civil servants (0.9 million active participants), (b) some 80 sector-wide pension plans (2.5 million) and (c) over 1000 company plans (0.7 million). These will be discussed below.

The civil servants' pension fund (ABP) is organized in much the same way as the sectoral funds as far as the benefit-formula and the relation between second and first tier are concerned and the fact that the financing method is capital funding. Nevertheless, it has a special relation to the state. It is exempted from supervision by the Insurance Chamber. The state heavily influences the setting of its own contributions and the investment of the assets (to a large extent in state bonds).

240

The ABP (together with the first tier) offers 70 per cent of the final salary after 40 years of service. Until 1986 the first tier was built in, which accounts for the less than equal rights for part-timers. Since 1986 the franchise system is used. From 1995 ABP has abandoned the differentiation in franchise to marital status and cut the link with the benefit-level in the first tier. Now, the franchise is set to the uniform and substantially lower level of dfl 26 500, about the gross minimum wage (Lutjens 1994).

Until recently the ABP-plan has been the only scheme which offered a pension with a prescribed index-link to the wages (of civil servants). Most other plans try to index-link to the wages in their sector, but do not guarantee. In spite of this comparative advantage, de Kam and Nypels (1995) state that the prescribed ABP index-link did not help retired civil servants much over the last fifteen years, since the wages of civil servants were not raised for many years and were even lowered in the beginning of the 1980s. Also, the ABP-plan could only offer an index-linked pension because ABP was not subject to the Pension and Saving Funds Act (PSW, which ordains supervision by the Insurance Chamber). Ever since it has been the state which guaranteed the pension; the funds of the ABP can only account for the now accrued (not to be indexed) rights.

From the second half of the 1980s there has been a trend in politics to reduce the size of the public sector. In accordance with this public enterprises have been privatized (e.g. postal services, railways). As a corollary, workers in these enterprises have been moved from ABP to different private pension funds.[8] As of 1996, the ABP-fund itself will be privatized. This will bring the fund under the rule of the PSW and will give the government the status of a normal employer. Henceforth, pension arrangements for civil servants will be a theme in collective bargaining between employer (state) and employees. However, the state keeps two identities, being employer as well as decision-maker on the budget of ABP.

The privatization of the ABP is a very complex process in which tendencies of the last decade will become structural. Since 1982 the government has paid less than the required contributions for a funded pension. According to Petersen (1994) this created a deficit of up to dfl 32 billion (on a total reserve of dfl 152 billion) in 1992. Since civil service disability- and VUT-benefits are capital funded (in contrast to the

---

[8] Railway personnel already had their own pension fund.

corresponding benefits in the market sector) these specific funds of ABP are now used to cover the old age pension deficit. The foreseen change in the financing method of disability and VUT means that current civil servants will lose their secured rights to early retirement. In recent negotiations the state has tried to curtail the civil servant VUT-programme. The gradual evaporation of funds for early retirement will help employees to accept the necessary changes. This because the alternative of an unchanged programme would require a considerable rise in contributions.

Already the disability-benefits of civil servants have been lowered to bring them in line with the first tier arrangements in the market sector. The ABP-disability-pensions will now be financed in a mixed way. The part of the disability insurance that is mandatory for all workers will be financed on a PAYG basis as in the market sector. The supplementary benefit will continue to be funded.

Moreover, the index-link of ABP-pensions becomes conditional on the financial strength of the fund. This is sound by now, thanks to the recent changes (including the conditionality).

The privatization of the ABP confirms a long-term process of under-financing of civil servants' pensions. It frees the government budget of a large claim by retired civil servants. The costs of the pensions are shifted to future ABP-participants. To civil servants it means a deterioration of their pension rights, although this is not widely recognized due to the complexity of the issue. In the end the privatization of ABP is accepted by the unions in collective bargaining. They saw it as a possibility to cut their losses, since it was very unlikely that the government would ever pay its debts.

The following component of the second tier comprises the sector-wide pension plans (BPFs). These have changed much over the years. Until the beginning of the 1980s, many of the plans offered a flat-rate benefit for each year of service or a benefit related to the average wage during participation. However, the final-salary-related ABP-benefit of the civil servants and some big company schemes was the goal to strive for. Since there was a steady entrance of cheap young participants and relatively low wage growth, while over the years the profits of pension funds soared because of high interest rates,[9] it was possible to improve the plans rapidly in the 1980s. This process is still going on.

---

[9] Until now, Dutch pension funds have a preference for bonds; this is changing, however.

By now over two-thirds of the participants in sector pension plans have a civil-servant-type final-wage scheme. As a corollary, a large number of the current participants now have rather little by way of accrued rights, but they will strongly increase them in the coming years. At the moment the accrued rights per participant in the sector-wide plans are only about one-third of those in the civil servants' plan and the company plans. The differences between the various sector-wide schemes are huge: of the sixteen biggest plans the richest quarter shows a ten times higher reserve/participant ratio than the poorest quarter (Het Financieele Dagblad 1991, 1993).

The sector-wide plans created portable rights within the sector. Notwithstanding this fact, especially these plans carry a tremendous amount of so called sleepers' rights. These are based on the accrued rights of participants at the moment they changed jobs to another sector and for that reason left the plan. Sometimes even firms moved from one sector-wide plan to another, thereby creating collectively broken pensions. From 1987, according to the PSW-Act, job-leavers are entitled to pension rights equivalent to their years of service. Until recently, however, it was quite common not to raise these sleepers' rights. As a consequence they have been eroded by inflation. The decision not to raise sleepers' rights may be attributed partly to the chosen method of financing. This often implicated that the financing of the pension was moved to the last stretch of the career.[10] So, in mid career not even the rights that had been accrued by that time were funded, let alone the future backservice for indexation. In fact, the contributions of the young, not staying participants were used to finance the pensions of those who kept with the plan.

Since the sector-wide plans are mandatory there is not much competition. Firms that do not receive value for money cannot opt out unless they create a (far) better company-based pension plan. Recently, efforts have been undertaken to create more of a market, but up to now not much has been achieved.

PGGM (medical and welfare) is the biggest sector-wide plan. It offers a benefit of 70 per cent of the final salary with a relatively low franchise of dfl 23 000 (1993). This makes it a better plan than the ABP civil servants' scheme. Also, PGGM has a funded early retirement pro-

---

[10] Funding is mandatory. However, most funding systems have incorporated PAYG financing concerning the backservice.

gramme and a more than sound financial basis. In all this, it contrasts with most other sector-wide plans.

The third large group of pension plans consists of the company plans (OPFs). These vary from very small and administered by insurance companies to very big and administered by pension funds. Again there is a great diversity, albeit less than in the sector-wide plans. The richest quarter of the 24 biggest plans produce a three times higher reserve/participant ratio than the poorest quarter (Het Financieele Dagblad 1991, 1993). On average the company-based plans offer a much better pension than the sector-wide plans and are comparable to the ABP civil servants' scheme, or sometimes even better.

The portability of company-based pension plan rights has improved much over the years. Although job-leavers do have entitlements these are mostly eroded by inflation. Portability was hampered for a long time, since two different pension-systems coexisted that differed in the way backservice was given for the accrued rights with former employers. The representative organizations of employers and employees were much in favour of the 'years of life' pension system in which the indexation of accrued rights with a former pension plan was taken care of in the current plan. Within this system indexation of sleepers' rights would not be necessary. However, two big pension plans (ABP and PGGM) practised the 'years of service' system, in which indexation is related only to the actual years of service and consequently to the level of accrued rights after leaving the plan. The 'years of life' and 'years of service' principles are not compatible with regard to portability of pension rights.

Until the beginning of the 1980s portability to another plan was not possible. During the 1980s several portability circuits were created by the employers' and employees' organizations. In 1987 37 per cent of pension plan participants in the market sector enjoyed portable rights, but since the giving as well as the receiving scheme had to support the same circuit, options for portability were in practice much more restricted. Nevertheless, a tendency to further portability was clear. By the end of 1988 already 79 per cent of the participants enjoyed portable rights (Pensioenkamer 1989a, p. 139). And since 1994 a portability clause is legally required. So, in a long debate the 'years of service' system has prevailed; 'years of life' is now rapidly disappearing.

As such, the developments concerning the pension portability are an illustration of the Dutch consensus-economy in which the social partners (employers' and employees' organizations) generally agree 'voluntarily' on system improvements, although the actual realization may take a rather long stretch of time. After these improvements have become widely accepted in the various sectors, they may or may not be confirmed by a completing law.

Vesting has never been a problem in the Dutch pension system. In most cases rights are accrued within a year.

Portability does not help those who become long-term unemployed or leave the labour market, since in these cases there is no receiving scheme for pension rights. In order to protect this type of sleepers' rights, in 1991 a law was passed that requires the same index-linking for sleepers' rights and pension benefits alike. Especially in the 1980s most funds raised the benefits of the retired with inflation or sometimes the wage index. However, in itself no index-linking is required. It is a matter of choice to the fund managers whether or not to raise entitlements. The decision largely depends on the financial situation of the fund. Since the backservice burden of sleepers' rights is heavy, it may be expected that the index-linking of sleepers' rights and benefits incurs the same risk as soon as inflation or wage growth return into the economy.

3.   A changing pension mix

In the introduction to this chapter we advanced the thesis that the importance of second-tier provisions in the income of older people has increased remarkably in the last two decades. In section 2 it was shown how welfare state arrangements (first tier) gradually lost ground both with respect to the income of early retirees (55–64) and the income of pensioners (65 and over). Recently, even third-tier income arrangements seem to gain prominence in old age. In the course of time the deterioration of first-tier benefits has been counterbalanced by the creation of new as well as the adjustment and maturation of existing private sector arrangements. Until now the emphasis has been on the institutional changes.

This section intends to picture the effects of the institutional changes on the pension mix. First we will focus on pension expenditures and assets within the various tiers. Then we will consider the sources of income for the elderly. Finally we will try to locate the changes in the composition of the labour costs.

3.1 Pension expenditures in the three tiers

First we will address the early retirement-system (pre 65) and the pension system (post 65) separately. Then the information will be integrated.

In 1975 virtually all 55-to-64-year-old early retirees were in the disability or unemployment early retirement pathways, both routes essentially having a first-tier character with only small second-tier supplements, especially for disability. This picture has gradually changed since the introduction in 1977 of the first second-tier VUT pre-retirement schemes. In 1993 already 30 per cent of the 55-to-64-year-old early retirees participated in VUT-schemes while the percentage of those in the disability or unemployment pathways had dwindled to less than 70 per cent. The growing significance of the VUT-schemes can be illustrated even more clearly with respect to retirees aged 60–64: in 1993 nearly 50 per cent of them received a second-tier VUT-benefit. To some extent the VUT-schemes have been supplementary to the already existing first-tier exit-routes. This especially applies to the 55–59 age group. But for the 60–64 age group the picture is rather different. New entrance figures of pathways into early exit clearly indicate a substitution between the public pathways and the private pre-retirement route for those aged 60–64.[11] So, in terms of volume first-tier arrangements have yielded here to the private pre-retirement route.

Figure 7.3 shows the gradual shift in pathway participation of the 55–64 age group in terms of expenditures in the first and second tiers; third-tier income components have hardly played a role so far. The first tier includes the statutory sickness and disability (ZW and AAW/WAO), unemployment (WW, WWV) and social assistance programmes. The second tier concerns private sector sickness and disability supplementary arrangements and the VUT pre-retirement schemes. Unfortunately second-tier data on supplementary unemployment arrangements are lacking.

Between 1980 and 1993 the real value of total first- and second-tier benefit outlays rose, at an average annual growth rate of 3.2 per cent,

---

[11] Between 1975 and 1992 in the 60–64 age group the total yearly new entrance to the disability exit-route (including the civil servants' ABP disability programme) gradually declined from approx. 17 000 to approx. 3800, while new entrance to the VUT-route increased from zero to approx. 24 000 (sources: CBS and SVr (Sociale Verzekeringsraad); figures not corrected for demographic changes).

Figure 7.3 – Social protection expenditures in the first and second tier, age 55–64

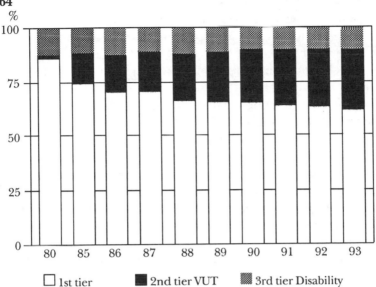

Sources: CBS, SVr and ABP (Algemeen Burgerlijk Pensioenfonds).

from dfl 9 billion to dfl 13.6 billion. In this period real value growth was much stronger in the second tier than in the first: the average annual second-tier growth rate was 11.8 per cent against a mere 0.5 per cent first-tier rate. This indicates the proportional decline of the first tier in social protection expenses for the 55–64 age group.

The part of second-tier expenditures for the 55–64 age group increased from about 13 per cent in 1980 to almost 38 per cent in 1993. As Figure 7.3 shows, this was exclusively the result of a steep growth in expenditures of the VUT pre-retirement schemes. Outlays of the first and second tiers as a percentage of GDP confirm the growing importance of the second tier. Between 1980 and 1993 first tier expenditures fell from 2.4 to 2.0 per cent GDP. Especially the (sickness and) disability programme lost ground (from 2 to 1.5 per cent GDP). In the same span of time, second-tier expenditures increased from 0.4 to 1.2 per cent GDP. So declining first-tier expenditures have been offset by a growth of second-tier outlays.

Generally, retirees aged 65 and over have several sources of income that together constitute the pension benefit. This contrasts with the majority of pre-pension retirees, who may collect their income from one tier or the other. As a rule retirees over 65 receive a first-tier basic state pension. On top of this they may receive second-tier supplementary sector and/or company pensions and possibly third-tier individual retirement benefits. Between 1975 and 1994 the total number of retirees (excluding survivors aged 55–64) has grown from about 1.2 to 2.1 million. Only a small part of this may be attributed to demographic changes. The most important growth was the splitting of the first-tier benefit to both spouses in 1985, in accordance with the EEC-directive concerning equal treatment of the sexes in social security.

Between 1980 and 1993 the real value of the total first-, second- and third-tier social protection expenditures for retirees (65 and over)[12] increased at an average annual growth rate of 3 per cent, from about dfl 30 billion to dfl 44 billion. As in early retirement, the growth rate was much more striking in the second tier than in the first (5.3 versus 1.3 per cent). In 1993 even a real value decline of first tier expenditures for retirees occurred (from dfl 26.6 billion to dfl 25.9 billion).

The third-tier old-age income expenditures have been comparatively small. Nonetheless, they displayed the highest average annual growth rate (7 per cent). This may be partly explained by the fact that a substantial share of the third-tier expenditures has never been paid out to the aged, because many of the individual savings accounts were never destined to finance income in retirement.[13] For this reason we may properly assume that first- and second-tier expenditures by far have been the most important sources of social protection for retirees in the last two decades. Still, there seems to be a tendency currently to enrol into (third-tier) individual retirement savings plans. In due course this may generate a larger share of the third tier in retirement income.

We conclude that the raise in social protection outlays for retirees aged 65 and over has been mainly the result of growth in the second and third tier.

Figure 7.4 displays the effect of the growth in the second and third tier for the composition of the expenditures. In 1980 the first tier still accounted for 72 per cent, while in 1993 this percentage had declined to approximately 59 per cent of the total expenditures. Between 1980 and 1989, the growth in second-tier supplementary pensions was slightly

---

[12] Including survivors aged 55 and over.

[13] The popularity of mortgage contracts based on life insurance has grown rapidly over the past ten years due to fiscal facilities. Available statistics do not permit a distinction between these contracts and real pension savings.

Figure 7.4 – Social protection expenditures in the first, second and third tier, age 65 and over

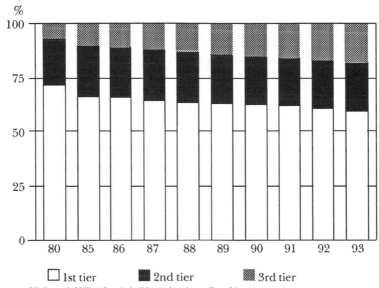

□ 1st tier   ■ 2nd tier   ▒ 3rd tier

Sources: CBS and SVB (Sociale Verzekerings Bank).

faster than in third-tier outlays. Since the early 1990s, however, this situation has reversed.

The growing importance of the second tier in social protection of retirees also becomes clear when expenditures are related to GDP. Between 1980 and 1993 the second tier increased from 1.6 to 2.6 per cent of GDP. At the same time the first tier declined from 6.5 to 6.2 per cent of GDP. With a total rise of 8.1 to 8.8 per cent of GDP this suggests offset between the two tiers. The reasons behind these trends, however, do not suggest interdependence: in the first tier cutbacks were most important, while in the second tier system maturation prevailed.

In an aggregate picture of the total retirement and early retirement outlays, Table 7.1 shows the tiers as a percentage of GDP. Since 1980 the total payments for social protection of the aged has risen from 11.7 to 13.8 per cent of GDP in 1993, at an average annual growth rate of 1.3 per cent, which is small compared to the changes in the separate tiers.

Growth has essentially occurred in the second tier, at an average annual growth rate of 5 per cent. Approximately the same growth rate pushed the third tier, though only part of this should be considered as retirement income. In contrast to second- and third-tier developments, the first tier either stagnated or declined. The clear upswing from 1989

Table 7.1 – Total payments from the three tiers for those aged 55 and over, as a percentage of GDP, 1980–93

	First tier	Second tier	Third tier	Total
1980	8.8	2.0	0.9	11.7
1985	8.5	2.8	1.2	12.5
1986	8.1	2.8	1.2	12.1
1987	8.2	3.1	1.3	12.6
1988	8.0	3.3	1.3	12.6
1989	7.8	3.3	1.4	12.5
1990	8.4	3.4	1.5	13.3
1991	8.4	3.5	1.5	13.4
1992	8.4	3.6	1.6	13.6
1993	8.2	3.8	1.8	13.8

Sources: Central Bureau of Statistics (CBS), Sociale Verzekeringsraad (SVr), Sociale Verzekerings Bank (SVB) and Algemeen Burgerlijk Pensioenfonds (ABP).

to 1990 has been a mere consequence of the major 1990 tax reforms, which hardly affected the net income of (early) retirees.

The growing importance of the second tier in social protection of the aged (55 and over) can also be demonstrated by the booming of second-tier assets over the past 25 years: between 1970 and 1993 these have increased from 18 to 90 per cent of GDP, at an average annual growth rate of 7 per cent. In contrast the assets of first-tier provisions have always been very modest, due to the PAYG system. In the last 10 years these have oscillated between 4 and 6 per cent of GDP.

The Netherlands is one of the countries with the highest per capita pension savings in the world. Nevertheless, it also stands out with a rather high level of PAYG provisions with respect to old age income.

3.2 Composition of incomes of retirees

As in the former section, we will address people in retirement and early retirement separately.

Research on income sources of people aged 60–64 is only very sparsely available. Information for 1983 and 1985 (Pensioenkamer 1989b) suggests an increase of the share of the VUT pre-retirement benefit in the total average income of the 60-to-64-year-olds ('Occupational pensions, annuities and VUT' rose from 28.9 to 35.2 per cent). It also indi-

Table 7.2 – Composition of income for people aged 65 and over

	1970	*1975*	*1980*	*1985*
Public pensions	47	55	58	57
Contractual pensions	21	21	22	26
Other sources	32	23	21	18
Total	100	100	100	100

Sources: Timmermans (1993); Sociaal en Cultureel Planbureau (1990).

cates a moderate decline (0.5 per cent) of the first-tier pathway benefits. In contrast there was a sharp proportional drop of 'earnings and other income', from 48.9 per cent to 43 per cent. This information essentially illustrates that between 1983 and 1985 quite a few of the people aged 60–64 left paid work and entered a VUT-scheme.

This change may also explain the simultaneous decline of the average gross income within the 60–64 age group between 1983 and 1985: corrected for inflation it boiled down to a 6.6 per cent drop in real value. For our purpose here, it is important to note that the available information on income levels of the 60–64 age group does not suggest that the people concerned have suffered because of declining first-tier involvement in social protection. The drop in income levels has basically been a consequence of the rising popularity of early retirement. In our view this also applies to the years after 1985.

Research on income sources of retirees over 65 indicates a growing share of the basic state pension (AOW) and a declining part of 'earnings and savings' in income for the 1970s, while the share of second-tier supplementary pensions remained fairly constant (Timmermans 1993). Then, in the 1980s the share of the state pension stabilized and the 'earnings and savings' part continued to decline, while the portion of the supplementary pensions started growing, especially till 1985. Table 7.2 illustrates the changes over time.

In the 1980s, as shown in section 2, the level of the first-tier basic pension declined in relation to the average earned wage in the labour market. At the same time the share of second-tier occupational pensions in the average retirement income increased. Unfortunately, information with respect to the average gross income of pensioners before 1986 cannot be compared to figures for later years due to rule changes in the first-tier basic pension and in the tax system in 1985 and in 1990.

There has been a modest growth of the average gross retiree income

Table 7.3 – Average gross incomes of people aged 65 and over as a percentage of average earnings for those aged 25–64

	Male	Female
1987	66.1	84.2
1988	71.7	86.5
1989	70.9	86.0
1990	55.5	69.1
1991	57.8	69.9

Sources: Various sources.

in the last decade. However, the interpretation of the figures in Table 7.3 is difficult. The ratio of pension income to average earnings is much higher for women than for men, because working women have lower incomes than working men due to part-time work and lower payments. When women receive their half of the split first-tier benefit of the basic state pension, it is large compared to their last earned wage, even when their second-tier supplements are lower than those for men. Especially the retirement income of women has hardly grown, because the increase of the basic state pension has lagged behind growth of the average earned wage in the labour market in the past decade.

Retirees with second-tier pension(s) have generally been in a more comfortable position: in this category the gradual deterioration of AOW-benefit has in most cases been fully compensated by the growth of company and/or sectoral pensions. This has been mainly caused by 'system maturation' within the second tier. Table 7.3 shows an increasing pension result especially for men. The dip after 1989 is explained by major tax reforms. These changed gross incomes, however, without seriously affecting net incomes.

More recent figures (CPB 1995) show that in the 1990s the rise in the second-tier supplementary retirement benefits still outgrows the lack of increases in the basic state pension. As a result the average yearly rise in total pension income per head is 2 to 3 per cent, while social benefits below 65 remain at best stable.

In the income both of retirees and early retirees, second-tier benefit provisions have come to play a more prominent role while the importance of first-tier benefits dwindled. With respect to early retirees, the first-tier decline may essentially be attributed to the introduction of private sector pre-retirement programmes with more favourable benefit conditions than first-tier provisions offered. The VUT-schemes explicitly intended to promote early retirement. They both supplemented and substituted first-tier provisions for the 55–64 age group. With respect to retirees the first-tier decline in their personal income may be explained by a maturation of second-tier provisions as well as by the state decision not to raise the basic state pension in accordance with the growth of the general standard of living since the early 1980s.

Despite the decline of first-tier income provisions for the aged (55 and over) there are no signs that their income position on average has deteriorated. On the contrary, in 1993 the average (early) retiree probably fared better financially than he did in the years before. This, however, is not to say that all retirees have been well off. Especially those who have to rely completely on the basic state pension noticed a loss of purchasing capacity.

3.3   The composition of labour costs

It would be interesting to see how the growing importance of company-related social protection of the aged compares to developments in social protection at large. For that reason we have examined the public and private components of Dutch social security. We have focused on shares of social security premiums in the total labour costs.

Table 7.4 presents the composition of labour costs in the Netherlands. As a rule the Eurostat labour cost study only distinguishes the employer premiums to 'statutory' and 'customary social security'.[14] This leaves aside the mandatory contributions paid by employees, which in the Netherlands are part of the 'gross earnings'.[15] We have corrected the Dutch labour cost data for this, in order to get a more realistic impression of the share of social security in the total labour costs. Also the state contributes to statutory social security. For practical reasons, however, this comparatively small part has been left out of Table 7.4.

Statutory social security premiums as a portion of the total labour cost increased until the early 1980s (from 31.8 per cent in 1978 to 38.0

---

[14] 'Social security statutory expenditures' concern first-tier programmes; 'social security customary expenditures' relate to second-tier schemes.

[15] The 'gross earnings' consist of: 'direct earnings', 'special bonuses' and 'paid non-working hours'. Taken together this accounted for 75 per cent of the 'total labour costs' in 1992.

Table 7.4 – Social security premiums (statutory and customary) paid by employers and employees, as a percentage of the total labour costs (1978–92)

	1978	1981	1984	1988	1992
Total labour costs	100	100	100	100	100
Gross earnings	73.0	72.7	73.3	72.7	74.8
Social security statutory premiums	31.8	33.8	38.0	36.7	31.5
– Unemployment Act (WW)	0.8	1.2	1.8	2.4	1.7
– Family Allow. Act (AKW)	2.1	1.5	3.0	1.5	0.0
– Sickness Act (ZW)	6.6	6.3	4.9	5.2	5.7
– Health Insur. Act (ZFW)	5.0	5.3	6.2	5.7	3.7
– Special Health Insur. and Disab. (AWBZ/AAW)	4.0	5.6	7.9	8.7	8.1
– Disab. Insur. Act (WAO)	5.1	5.4	4.0	3.0	2.9
– Basic Pension (AOW)	8.2	8.5	10.1	10.1	9.4
Social security customary premiums	9.1	9.2	9.8	9.4	8.7
– Occupational Pensions	7.6	7.2	7.2	5.3	4.8
– Early Retirement (VUT)	0.0	0.6	1.1	1.8	2.3
– Sickness benefit	0.3	0.3	0.2	0.6	0.4
– Health Insurance	1.0	0.6	0.6	0.7	0.6
– Retirement Donations	0.0	0.0	0.0	0.2	0.2
– Other	0.2	0.5	0.7	0.7	0.4
Total social security premiums (excl. state contributions)	40.9	43.0	47.3	46.1	40.2

Sources: Central Bureau of Statistics (CBS) and own calculations.

per cent in 1984). Then, after an initial stabilization a decline ensued in the late 1980s. The sharp downfall between 1988 and 1992, however, does not indicate serious cutbacks on the welfare state in these years. Rather this has to be explained by the major tax reform of 1990. As a consequence both gross wages and tax-burden increased. At the same time the state enlarged its share of the total contributions to social security drastically (from 3.8 per cent in 1988 to 12.8 per cent in 1992). If corrected for this 'responsibility shift', the total social security statutory premiums moderately declined between 1988 and 1992 (from 38.1 per cent to 36.1 per cent).

The share of customary social security premiums in the total labour costs also increased between 1978 and 1984, albeit at a much lower rate than statutory social security (from 9.1 per cent in 1978 to 9.8 per cent in 1984). Likewise the share of customary social security premiums declined between 1984 and 1992 (to 8.7 per cent in 1992). These trends do not support the supposition that the second tier is replacing the first tier in Dutch social security at large.

Until 1992 customary social security premiums have been paid for the most part to old age income maintenance. Although the portion of customary premiums to old age income remained fairly stable over time (83.5 per cent in 1978; 81.6 in 1992), within this section a significant shift occurred between the two types of programmes for old age income maintenance (occupational pensions and VUT-schemes). Until 1978 all premiums went to occupational pensions. Then in a relatively short span of time its share declined to 67 per cent (in 1992) of the total customary premiums to old age income maintenance. At the same time the portion of VUT-premiums rose to 33 per cent (in 1992).

These trends can be largely explained by the booming growth of PAYG-financed VUT pre-retirement schemes since 1978. Equally important has been that the social partners in quite a few sectors, due to high capital yields and low wage growth in the 1980s, have lowered the level of premiums to the funded occupational pensions in collective bargaining. They assumed that the capital accumulation of the occupational pension funds would be sufficient to meet (near) future pension commitments.

Due to statistical constraints the share of statutory social security premiums devoted to old age income maintenance to the 60+ age group is hard to assess. Therefore we restrict ourselves here to the share of basic state pension premiums (AOW for the 65+ age group) in the total statutory social security premiums. Despite some fluctuations this share has been relatively stable since 1978 (about 26 per cent of the total).

The growing share of AOW-premium contributions in the total Dutch labour costs until 1984 can be explained both by the constantly rising number of AOW-pensioners over time and the rise in the benefit level in the early 1970s. A stabilization of this share in the second half of the 1980s was followed by a decline in the early 1990s. The recent trend may be explained by the gradual deterioration of the AOW-benefit level.

4.   The future pension mix

4.1   The near future

The Dutch welfare state is confronted by three main problems. First, the labour force participation rate (in full-time years) is low compared to the surrounding countries. This is due to the still large number of house-wives, the high incidence of part-time work and the high level of disability and early retirement.[16] In the past decades, unemployment in the Netherlands has been diminished by reducing the labour force. This resulted in generous early retirement provisions and a lenient disability insurance (WAO/AAW). The high disability frequencies have created a large army of disabled of 13 per cent of the working population, 2 to 2.5 times the percentage in other Western industrialized countries.

The second problem is not unique. The aging process is progressing in all Western countries. In comparison the Netherlands still has a rather young population. However, after the year 2010 the ageing process will accelerate even more than in other countries.

The third problem is a result of the first two: until recently, a high level of social security spending. It is a result as well as a cause: the difference between gross and net income makes it increasingly expensive to hire labour.

The state's solution to the problems seems to be to reduce the level of spending in social security. Its ambitions have been twofold. Firstly, less generous benefits will reduce the costs directly. Secondly, cost savings may result from improvements in the administration of social security schemes. It is expected that the market will create the right incentives for a good management of the social insurances. Over the last year or two, privatization and cutbacks have resulted in public social security expenditures comparable to surrounding countries.

In 1992 the Parliament created a Committee of Enquiry (Enquête-commissie 1993) to deal with the steep growth of the number of disability beneficiairies. A report of the Scientific Council for Government Policy (Wetenschappelijke Raad voor het Regeringsbeleid 1994) further

---

[16] In the past thirty years women have increasingly entered the labour market, but also choose to work part-time to an increasing extent. As a result, the female labour force participation (measured in labour years) did not increase since the 1960s. At the same time, the labour force participation of men declined (Wetenschappelijke Raad voor het Regeringsbeleid 1990, p. 65).

analysed how interest groups had influenced the administration of social security. The Parliamentary Committee concluded that the organizations of employers and employees had used the public disability insurance to reorganize the firms in the private sector. The employers' organizations' interest was to shed less productive older workers; the interest of employee organizations was to guarantee obsolete workers a good pension. The public sector would pay for it all.

While the disability-assessment procedure was designed to prevent able persons from entering the disability insurance, in practice the administration of the social security had been largely given away to the representative organizations of employers and employees. The physicians who did the medical examinations were not independent. In fact, they had incentives to be lenient. Their clients just wanted to be labelled as disabled, for in most cases they saw this as the preferred way into inactivity. Denying cooperation could mean that applicants would have to settle for a less favourable unemployment benefit. If the physician were to judge them healthy, the applicants would be likely to appeal. Those appeals would bring a lot of extra work to the physicians and were for that reason highly unpopular. Very often the employer was not interested in reintegration and also opted for disability status for his former employee. With a small income supplement from the company, this was a cheap way to reorganize the firm. An appeal on behalf of the interest of the state was not possible.

The agency supervising the system of social security (SVr) was, like the administering Industrial Boards, dominated by employer and employee representatives and has failed to perform its function adequately. Consecutive governments thought it was acceptable to create jobs for the younger unemployed by sending older workers into early retirement. Moreover, Parliament also hesitated to take action because societal opposition to a major reform of the system of social security was very strong. As a result the process of misusing first-tier social security programmes, which had started somewhere in the mid 1970s, could continue for a long time.

The reports of the Parliamentary Committee and the Scientific Council have resulted in a process of reorganization of the administration of public social security. The implementation of the programmes now occurs under direct supervision of the state: the Ctsv has replaced the SVr. Furthermore, financial incentives have been introduced for the administration agencies to raise their effectiveness and efficiency. To this end a limited set of competitive measures has been introduced:

firms are allowed (within limits) to choose their favourite administrative agency and now (more extensively) have a free choice of agencies that cover the process of reintegration of potentially disabled workers.

Like the premium contributions to the Sickness Benefits Act (ZW), those to the Disability Insurance Act will be differentiated by rating the firms with respect to their disability incidence. These measures are directed at aligning costs to benefits at the enterprise level. The public Sickness Insurance (ZW) has been abolished from 1996. Instead, the firm will be obliged to continue payment of 70 per cent of the wage during the first year of sickness (Fase 1995a). This liability can be insured in the private market.

There is a continuous discussion about the possible privatization of the public disability insurance itself. A private and funded insurance has the advantage that the incentives for efficient behaviour will be maximal.

Privatization of the disability insurance, however, is not that simple. The main obstacle is that the present insurance is financed on a PAYG basis. A private insurance is feasible only on a funded basis, administered by insurance companies. The switch-over will at least require a temporary doubling of the contribution. The premiums related to the current disability beneficiaries (on a PAYG basis in the public insurance) will drop only gradually since the current AAW/WAO-volume is rather large. The separate contribution concerning the funded insurance of the new entrants will have to cover present as well as future benefits and remain more or less stable over time. As a consequence opting out of the collective, PAYG-financed disability insurance is supposed to be unattractive in the short term.

The possibility of contracting out could introduce an unstable system in the long run. This is because the good risks opt for private insurance while the bad risks have to stay in an ever more expensive publicly PAYG-financed disability insurance (Fase 1995b). As soon as this process starts, it will inevitably result in the abolishment of the public insurance.

The strategy chosen in the recent past has been to reduce the level of the PAYG-financed first-tier social benefit. The benefit structure of the disability insurance is thus made less attractive. However, in reaction the second-tier supplements from the enterprise increased. The risk remains that the second-tier supplements will prove to be too cheap to create a powerful incentive for prevention and reintegration. So this option carries the danger that the misuse of public social security by the social partners will continue.

The recently proposed and introduced changes in social security produce a shift of responsibilities from the state to the enterprise. The representatives of employers and employees in collective bargaining tend to accept that the enterprise at least partly takes over the social security burden, and that the outcome of negotiations should be mandatory for all enterprises in a sector. In this way, again some sort of first-pillar-like system will be created under the collective responsibility of the social partners.

Apart from the efforts to create an efficient administration of social security through privatization, there is also a general tendency to increase the responsibility of the enterprise and the individual. Adherents of this philosophy stress that the primary task of the state is to safeguard against poverty. Whenever possible, the enterprise or the individual should take their responsibility to insure anything that goes beyond a social minimum benefit. We consider two examples.

With the ongoing tide of more private responsibility, the new General Widows' and Orphans' act is designed to further limit the survivors' benefits. According to the new act, benefits are given to men and women alike, but the criterion of age over 40 is replaced by 'being born before 1950'. Moreover, the proposed new benefit is partly income-tested.[17] This will transfer the survivors' insurance largely to the enterprise and the individual.

Private pensions in the second tier generally include pensions for widows and orphans. The private survivors' benefit is supplementary to the first-tier benefit, largely in the same way as the private old age pension supplements the General Old Age Pension, i.e. both private benefits presuppose a basic pension in the first tier at a minimum level. Beginning in the year 2000, the new Pension and Savings Act (PSW) ordains that participants will be free to choose whether to include the widowers' pension or to opt for a higher old age supplementary pension in their second-tier package. So far, pension fund managers are reluctant to grant this free choice. They prefer to restrict the free choice to the moment of retirement, so that the risk of widowhood before retirement will be shared collectively. Also, they are reluctant to accept the fair rise in the old age pen-

---

[17] The basic benefit is set to the social minimum of a single person. Of any labour income, the first 50 per cent of the minimum wage is left to the worker. Above that amount, 1/3 of the labour income is subtracted from the benefit. For single parents, the basic benefit can be supplemented with the difference between the social minimum of a single parent and that of a single person. This supplement is not income-tested (Eerste Kamer 1995).

sion in exchange for the exclusion of the widowers' pension. The perspective of free choice to the participant in the second tier will confer on the occupational pension traits of an individual third-tier insurance.

The second example is a tendency to delegate responsibilities to the third tier. This can be illustrated clearly with respect to pre-retirement. The costs of the present private VUT-programmes will rise strongly when the post-war baby boom reaches the age of eligibility to pre-retirement. Therefore, in collective bargaining the VUT-programmes will be gradually transformed from collectively PAYG-financed arrangements into individually funded ones. Accrued second-tier rights to pre-retirement will be individually portable then. Through this route third-tier old age pensions insurance has grown. Although the perspective is clear, the process is still moving rather slowly into this direction. The unions are well aware of the unavoidability of this reform. Nevertheless, they often oppose changes, not wanting to give away established rights in collective bargaining.

4.2   The distant future

In the long term the second-tier costs are expected to rise strongly for two reasons (Jansweijer 1996). One reason (even though not the most important) is the rapid growth of the pension basis in the second tier. There are two causes for this: firstly, the gap created by the slower growth rate of the first-tier benefit as compared to the average wage; secondly, the fact that the first-tier benefit is still tailored to the old breadwinner situation which is increasingly becoming obsolete.

In the current system a franchise is subtracted from the wage to calculate the pension basis. Many schemes still have the franchise directly linked to the first-tier AOW-benefit of a two-person household. If this benefit does not grow at the same pace as the wages, the second-tier pension basis will increase more rapidly than the wages. Coopers & Lybrand (1994) in a recent report have warned Dutch employers of the growth of the second-tier pension burden that will result from this mechanism.

Fund managers try to immunize their schemes by setting the franchise at an amount that is not defined by the benefit in the first tier. However (second cause), these franchises are generally lower than before. Thus they create a higher pension basis, because the splitting of the first-tier benefit (in 1985) has made it increasingly clear that in the future most workers will not be entitled to the high benefit of a couple. Especially working spouses are supposed to integrate their own as well as their partner's first-tier benefit in their total pension result. Due to this mechanism a growing number of people will notice a gap in their pension, as the labour market participation of women increases.

Even if the pension basis is no longer directly defined by the first-tier benefit, it may still be indirectly defined because of the set goal of final-wage pensions. When the dependency is not automatic, though, it will be easier for fund managers to adjust not only the franchise but the pension-formula as well.

The second reason why expenditures on second-tier pensions will rise strongly in the future is the marked improvements of the schemes in the past two decades. As the accrued rights mature, ever more contributions will be necessary to finance these rights. It may be thought that as second-tier pensions in the Netherlands are funded they should be free of these effects. That is only partly true. Only the nominally accrued rights are funded. The backservice, caused by the raising of formerly accrued rights, is grossly PAYG-financed, because it is suspended to the end of the career. Especially for civil servants the (ABP-)pension costs will rise rapidly, due to the rather high average age of participants. For the sector-wide plans the more important cause is that these plans have much improved over the past two decades.

The forecasted rise in costs of the second tier makes it very unlikely that occupational pension plans will remain unchanged. As long as inflation is low, wages do not increase much and capital yields are favourable in the years ahead, there is no immediate urge to reform. In that case only the early retirement opportunities will be curtailed. However, only some years of inflation or more than average wage increase will suffice to press the urgency of pension reform clearly. Two forces will contribute to this process.

Firstly, it may be expected that the raising of benefits and sleepers' rights will be ended, because such cuts do not directly affect the rights of the currently contributing participants. This strategy is highly probable because the organizations of employers and employees decide on the quality of the occupational pension schemes. However, once participants enter into retirement they may hope to have benefits that are at least price adjusted.

Secondly, because the final wage system implicates vast income transfers from low wages to high wages and from sleepers to careerists, this system may be amended as well. It will probably be replaced by an average wage system that is less subject to backservice. Also the flexibility of the pension rights may be used to reduce the overall costs. Early retirement will be paid by the retirees themselves at the cost of personal savings or the second-tier pension rights. Several pension funds have already created daughter companies for life insurances (for instance PGGM).

If benefit formulas in the second tier are adjusted in order to reduce the mounting costs, the inequalities in wealth between young and old and also within the retired population may even grow stronger than anticipated from just the intended state policy with respect to the first tier. Prospective retirees may be wealthy according to current norms but poor in relation to future standards. In turn this may induce a shift back to public pensions because these then are considered as a necessary basis that the second and third tier cannot provide. So there is no reason to believe that the current shift from first to second and third tier will cumulate indefinitely. Second-order mechanisms will correct such trends.

5. Concluding remarks

Until the late 1970s, the importance of the public arrangements for retirement was growing. Especially the public pathways into early retirement have boomed. From the early 1980s however, there has been a shift from the state to the enterprise. This has occurred after the social security was used by the (representatives of) employers and employees to reconstruct the firms at the expense of the public sector. The shift in responsibility has been mainly the result of the two following mechanisms.

Firstly, the benefit structure in the public social security has been made less attractive to claimants, for instance by lowering the benefit rates. The social partners have reacted with the creation of alternative pathways into early retirement and the promotion of pre-retirement (VUT). In order to create a maximum collective good and minimal competition, they have aspired to create mandatory sector-wide provisions.

After the Parliamentary Enquiry Committee in 1993, the state has introduced other incentives than lowering benefit levels, in order to curb the volume of beneficiaries. In some areas public social security is, or will be, replaced by enterprises' to insure social risks. Also, a rating of risks is introduced in relation to the level of contributions to the Disability Insurance. Furthermore, prevention of disability and reintegration of disabled workers is delegated to the private sector.

The second mechanism of shifting responsibility to the firm and to the individual has been a creeping lowering of the social minimum benefit level as compared to the average standard of living. This process has been going on now for about ten to fifteen years and has resulted in a marked correction of the minimum benefit levels. This is especially important in relation to the post-retirement (65 and over) pensions, where the first tier only provides a flat-rate minimum. Continuation of this state policy may prove a necessary condition for a sustainable first-tier pension. In the long run, however, its cumulative effect will result in an eroded first-tier old age income benefit and in a remarkable shift to the second tier. This will safeguard the public old age pension from bankruptcy, but may also contribute to a lowering of the expected level of second-tier pensions. As such, the process of maturation in the second tier will already cause serious financial problems without the aging process, although it is likely that the shift from the first to the second tier and the aging process will press the urgency of pension reform.

References

Blomsma, Martin (1996), *VUT-bepalingen in CAO's, 1990–1995; Veranderende opvattingen en regelingen*, The Hague.

Bovenberg, Lans and Petersen, Carel (1991), 'Pensioenen en de internationale vergelijking van overheidsschuld', *Economisch Statistische Berichten*, 28 augustus, 863–7.

Broeder, Arie den (1987), 'Zeggenschap over werknemersverzekeringen', *Sociaal Maandblad Arbeid*, juli/augustus.

Centraal Bureau voor de Statistiek (1995), *Enquete Beroepsbevolking 1994*, Voorburg.

Centraal Planbureau (1995), *Waar blijft de groei van het nationaal inkomen?* Werkdocument no. 76, 's-Gravenhage.

College van toezicht sociale verzekeringen (1995a), *Volume-effecten van het gewijzigde arbeidsongeschiktheidscriterium*, Zoetermeer.

College van toezicht sociale verzekeringen (1995b), *Ontwikkeling ziekteverzuim en arbeidsongeschiktheid 2e kwartaal 1995*, Zoetermeer.

Commissie Drees (1987), *Gespiegeld in de tijd; de AOW in de toekomst, rapport van de Commissie Financiering Oudedagsvoorziening*, The Hague: Ministerie van Sociale Zaken en Werkgelegenheid.

Coopers & Lybrand (1994), *Bezuinigingen op de AOW; financiële verkenning van de gevolgen voor de aanvullende pensioenregelingen door bezuinigingen op de AOW*,

Utrecht.

Dijkshoorn, M.W. and ter Welle, H.I. (1995), 'Een alternatief voor model D', *Economisch Statistische Berichten*, 13 september, 818–20.

Eerste Kamer (1995), Algemene Nabestaandenwet, 1995–96, nr. 24169.

Enquêtecommissie uitvoeringsorganen sociale verzekeringen (1993), *Rapport enquêtecommissie; Samenvatting*, The Hague: Sdu Uitgeverij.

Fase, Wil (1995a), 'Privatisering van de Ziektewet', *Sociaal Maandblad Arbeid*, juni.

Fase, Wil (1995b), 'De beoogde arbeidsongeschiktheidsverzekering van werknemers', *Sociaal Maandblad Arbeid*, october.

Financieele Dagblad, Het (1991, 1993), *Pensioenfondsen*, 6 september 1991, 3 september 1993.

Gales, B.P.A. (1986), *Werken aan zekerheid; een terugblik over de schouders van AEGON op twee eeuwen verzekeringsgeschiedenis*, The Hague: Aegon Verzekeringen.

Jansweijer, Roel (1990), 'De AOW en het einde van de alleenverdienerstoeslag', *Economisch Statistische Berichten*, 21 februari, 186-8.

Jansweijer, Roel (1996), *Gouden bergen, diepe dalen; de inkomensgevolgen van een betaalbare oudedagsvoorziening*, Wetenschappelijke Raad voor het Regeringsbeleid, reeks voorstudies en achtergronden V92, The Hague: Sdu Uitgeverij.

Kam, Flip de and Nypels, Frans (1995), *Tijdbom*, Amsterdam/Antwerp: Uitgeverij Contact.

Kemp, A.A.M. de (1992), *Ouderen tussen pensioen en bijstand*, SCP-studies 95, Rijswijk.

Kroon, J. and Meijnen, J. (1993), 'Het WAO-gat', *NRC/Handelsblad*, 25 maart.

Kuné, Jan (1987), *Pensioen en economie; Enige financieel-economische aspecten van pensioenvoorzieningen*, University of Amsterdam (dissertation).

Kuné, Jan, Petit, W.F.M. and Pinxt, A.J.H. (1993), *The Hidden Liabilities of Basic Pension Schemes in the European Community*, Working Document no. 80, Brussels: Centre for European Policy Studies (CEPS).

Lutjens, Erik (1994), 'Point of no return bereikt bij complexe privatisering van ABP', *NRC-Handelsblad*, 15 mei.

Ministerie van Sociale Zaken en Werkgelegenheid (1984a), *Rapportage Arbeidsmarkt 1984*, The Hague.

Ministerie van Sociale Zaken en Werkgelegenheid (1984b), *Vervroegde uittreding in CAO's*, The Hague.

Ministerie van Sociale Zaken en Werkgelegenheid (1989), *Bovenwettelijke uitkeringen na de stelselwijziging sociale zekerheid*, The Hague: Loon Technische Dienst.

Ministerie van Sociale Zaken en Werkgelegenheid (1990a), *Social Security in the Netherlands*, Deventer/Boston: Kluwer Law and Taxation Publishers.

Ministerie van Sociale Zaken en Werkgelegenheid (1990b), *Bovenwettelijke uitkeringen bij collectief ontslag*, The Hague: Loon Technische Dienst.

Ministerie van Sociale Zaken en Werkgelegenheid (1990c), *Vervroegde uittreding in CAO's*, The Hague.

Ministerie van Sociale Zaken en Werkgelegenheid (1991), *Pensioennota*, Tweede Kamer 1990-1991, nr. 22167.

Ministerie van Sociale Zaken en Werkgelegenheid (1993), 'Gemiddelde VUT-leeftijd niet gedaald in 1992', *SZW-Nieuws*, 10 juni.

Ministerie van Sociale Zaken en Werkgelegenheid (1994), *CAO-afspraken 1993*, The Hague.

Oversloot, Johannes (1986), *The Development of the Old Age Pension: The Dutch Case*,

Leiden University (unpublished paper).

Pensioenkamer (1987), *Witte vlekken op pensioengebied,* The Hague.

Pensioenkamer (1989a), *Pensioenkaart van Nederland,* The Hague.

Pensioenkamer (1989b), *Inkomens personen 60–1 en 65–70 in 1983 en 1985,* The Hague.

Petersen, Carel (1994), 'Verzelfstandiging van het ABP: gevolgen voor de overheidsfinanciën', *Openbare uitgaven,* nr. 3, 114–8.

Sociaal en Cultureel Planbureau (1990), *Sociaal en Cultureel Rapport 1990,* Rijswijk.

Sociaal en Cultureel Planbureau (1994), *Sociaal en Cultureel Rapport 1994,* Rijswijk.

Timmermans, J.M. (1993), *Rapportage Ouderen 1993,* Sociaal en Cultureel Planbureau, Rijswijk.

Trommel, Willem and de Vroom, Bert (1994), 'The Netherlands: The Loreley-Effect of Early Exit', in Frieder Naschold and Bert de Vroom (eds.), *Regulating Employment and Welfare,* Berlin/New York: W. de Gruyter.

Tweede Kamer (1994), Aanhangsel van de Handelingen, 1993–4, nr. 519.

Veldkamp, G. (1978), *Inleiding tot de sociale zekerheid en de toepassinger van in Nederland en België; Deel I, Karakter en geschiedenis,* Deventer: Kluwer.

Verbon, Harry (1988), *On the Evolution of Public Pension Schemes,* University of Amsterdam (dissertation).

Wetenschappelijke Raad voor het Regeringsbeleid (1990), *Een werkend perspectief; arbeidsparticipatie in de jaren '90,* rapport nr. 38, The Hague: Sdu Uitgeverij.

Wetenschappelijke Raad voor het Regeringsbeleid (1993), *Ouderen voor ouderen; Demografische ontwikkelingen en beleid,* rapport nr. 43, The Hague: Sdu Uitgeverij.

Wetenschappelijke Raad voor het Regeringsbeleid (1994), *Belang en beleid,* rapport nr. 45, The Hague: Sdu Uitgeverij.

Winters, W. (1990), *Die staatshulp wenschen wij...; pensioenstrijd in Nederland,* The Hague: Sdu Uitgeverij.

8

The Welfare Mix in Pension Provisions in Sweden

Eskil Wadensjö

1.   The pension system in transition

Several changes or proposed changes in social insurance schemes have recently been introduced in Sweden. One of the intentions behind the changes has been to influence labour market participation. The most important changes or proposed changes will be listed here and briefly commented on.

1)   The principles for a new old age pension system were decided on in 1994 and the new scheme will be instigated from 1999 (the year of commencement has been advanced gradually from 1996 to 1999). The main principles of the new system are the following:
  i) In the present system the 15 years with highest earnings when aged 16 to 65 are the basis for the calculation of the pension and 30 years with earnings are enough to get a full pension. In the new system the pension is based on lifetime earnings. All years with earnings for those aged 16 or more will influence the pension, even years with earnings after the age of 65. These changes increase the incentives to work at higher ages.
  ii) The formal retirement age will continue to be 65 but there are changes in the new pension scheme that are intended to raise the actual retirement age.[1] According to the job security law the

---

[1] A change of the ordinary retirement age from 65 to 66 was decided by an agreement involving the government and the major opposition party in the fall of 1992. The change was planned to take place gradually during the next few years. The time schedule was changed in spring 1993, however, and when the pension agreement was decided on, the idea was finally abolished in principle.

seniority rule is valid at layoffs for people up to the age of 67, but collective agreements lower this age to 65 (and still lower in some occupations – there is no law against mandatory retirement agreements in Sweden). Therefore, in most cases, people aged 65 and older are not protected by the law. According to the new pension reform, that age will be raised in two steps to 67 either by collective agreement or by law (if the social partners do not reach an agreement).

iii) The earliest age of eligibility for an old age pension (partial or full) changes from 60 to 61 when the new pension system replaces the old one in 1999.

iv) The disability pensions will be transferred from the old age system to the sickness benefit system.

2) Since 1 October 1991 disability pensions are no longer granted for labour market reasons only, and from 1 January 1997 they will not be granted for medical and labour market reasons combined, leaving medical reasons as the only ground for granting a disability pension.

3) The liberal/conservative government that was in power 1991–94 tried to abolish the partial pension scheme or lower the replacement rate. The *Riksdag* voted against such proposals twice. But as a part of the new pension system which was agreed upon in spring 1994 between the government and the Social Democratic party, the partial pension system was changed from 1 July 1994. The replacement rate was lowered, the number of hours that are compensated was reduced, and the minimum age raised from 60 to 61. According to the agreement the law will be changed later so that no new partial pensions will be granted from the year 2000. The intention is that part-time pensioning should continue, but through partial early old age pensioning instead.

4) In 1991 legal changes were made to further the rehabilitation of long-term sick employees. The rules that have been in force from 1992 oblige the employers to conduct a rehabilitation investigation for employees who have been sick-listed for more than four weeks, who have had many short spells of illness, or who themselves demand an investigation. The examination is to be reported to the social insurance society within a defined time limit. The social insurance society has to make an assessment and also devise a plan for rehabilitation. In the period after the introduction of the new system its main effect was probably to identify cases where rehabili-

tation efforts were not likely to have positive effects and a surge in disability pensions in 1992 and 1993 may partially depend on this programme. The long-run effects may be different.

5) In 1993 several changes were made in the occupational injury scheme. The most important was a stricter definition of an occupational injury and a lowering of the compensation level from 100 per cent to the same as for sickness cash benefits. The number of new annuities that are granted has also decreased drastically as a result of the changes in the law. The changes made it more difficult to leave the labour market by that exit-route.

6) As mentioned the disability pension will not be a part of the new scheme for old age pensions. According to the proposal in the final report of the committee on the disability pension and occupational injury system,[2] the main principle will be that the disability pension scheme will be integrated with the sickness benefit scheme instead. After a sickness benefit period of one year a monthly compensation should be paid out if the work capacity is expected to be reduced for at least one more year. For those with low earnings a guarantee compensation of 2.1 base amount should be paid (the same as in the old age pension scheme). For others the compensation should be based on the average earnings of four of the last six years (the year with the lowest and the year with the highest earnings are left out of the calculation).[3] The compensation should be 65 per cent of the amount calculated that way. According to the proposal the ceiling should be increased from 7.5 to 10 base amount.

There are also other changes to be expected. One example is that a governmental investigation in 1996 put forward a proposal for changes in the unemployment insurance scheme, making it more difficult for older workers to exit from the labour market by that system. Decisions regarding that scheme will probably be made in 1997.

---

[2] See SOU 1996:113, Chapters 11 and 15.
[3] There will be a second alternative way of calculating the compensation at disability.

2. The present pension system and its origin

2.1 The first pillar[4]

A social security pension scheme was introduced in 1913 that provided compensation at old age and disability. The new pension system covered everyone, not only employees but even those who were self-employed such as farmers, for example. The retirement age was set to 67. The pension consisted of two parts – one which was funded and a supplementary part which was not. The funded part was financed by earnings-related fees paid by the individuals (at maximum 13 kronor a year), the pension was 30 per cent of the total fees paid for men and 24 per cent for women. With a maximum of 50 years of payments of the fees, the maximum yearly pension became 195 kronor for men and 156 kronor for women. The supplementary part, which was introduced directly, was tested against income and wealth. The maximum supplementary pension was 150 kronor for men and 140 kronor for women plus 0.08 per cent of the sum of the fees paid (the supplementary pension was reduced by 50 per cent of earnings higher than 50 kronor). The supplementary pensions were financed by 3/4 from the state budget, 1/8 from the counties and 1/8 from the municipalities.

The social security pensions were low in the first decades after their introduction; the fee-based part of the pension was low since there were few qualifying years. The pensions (the non-supplementary part) were changed in 1935 to 70 kronor plus 10 per cent of the fees paid (the same for men and women). The maximum fee was raised to 20 kronor for an unmarried person and 40 kronor for a married couple. The maximum of the supplementary pensions was set to 250 kronor (and the rate of reduction 70 per cent of earnings higher than 100 kronor). In practice the new system did not mean an increase of the pension, but the change was a step in the direction of a basic pension that was equal for everyone. Another change was that the supplementary pensions became financed to 7/8 from the state budget and 1/8 from the counties.

In 1937 the pension became differentiated according to regional differences in living costs – it meant that on average the pensions were increased.

The pensions were enhanced considerably from 1948, and the old

---

[4] See Schmidt (1974) for the long-term development.

age pensions were no longer tested against earnings and wealth. The old age pension became 1000 kronor for unmarried old age pensioners, and 800 for married. Disability pensions were still tested against earnings and wealth. The disability pension consisted of a basic part of 200 kronor and a supplementary part of 800 for unmarried pensioners, and 600 for married. The differentiation according to regional differences in living costs was abolished, and was replaced by a housing supplement which varied according to regional differences in housing costs.

The pensions became indexed from 1950, and from 1957 by being calculated in base amount (see above).

In the 1940s a long political process started for the establishment of a supplementary social security pension system which ended with the decision to establish the ATP-scheme by the *Riksdag* in 1958 after a referendum in 1957 and an extra parliamentary election in 1958.[5] The first fees to the new pension scheme were paid in 1960 and the first pensions paid out in 1963.

The pension consists of two parts: the national basic pension and the national supplementary pension (the ATP-pension).

The basic pension has been the same for everyone except in the case of married couples, where both have old age pensions. The sum of their two pensions combined is less than twice that of a single person or a married person whose spouse does not have an old-age pension. From 1993 a new requirement was introduced. For a full basic pension 40 years of residence in Sweden between the ages of 16 and 64 years or 30 years of earnings are required (only years with earnings with one base amount or more are included). If the requirements are not fulfilled the pension is reduced proportionally.

The ATP-pension scheme supplements the old age pensions as well as the disability pensions. Participation is mandatory. Supplementary pensions, which are consumer price indexed, depend on the number of years worked (30 years are required for a full pension) and the income during the 15 years with highest income. Incomes up to 7.5 base amounts a year are the basis for calculation of the pension. (The base amount is a consumer indexed unit which is used in most social insurances. In 1996 a base amount was 36 200 kronor.) The total compensation from the national basic and the national supplementary pension

---

[5] See Molin (1965) for a detailed study of the political process that lead to the new pension system.

schemes for most persons is about two-thirds of the average income during the 15 best years.

The age for receiving an old age pension was 67 years up to 1 July 1976 and thereafter 65 years. However, both before and after 1976, there have been several options to leave the labour market at another age without a pension from the social security system.

Until July 1976 it was possible to receive an early old age pension from the age of 63, or to delay the pension up to the age of 70. In the former case, the pension amount was reduced by 0.6 per cent times the number of months (maximum 48) taken prior to the pension age of 67, that is, up to 28.8 per cent monthly for the duration of the pension (continuing after the age of 67). If the retirement was delayed, for each month of delay the pension was augmented by 0.6 per cent, that is, up to 21.4 per cent monthly for the duration of the pension.

The rates were changed in 1976 when the retirement age was lowered to 65. The new interval became 60 to 70 years. If a person retires earlier than 65 his pension is now reduced by 0.5 per cent a month, that is, up to 30.0 per cent monthly for the duration of the pension. A delayed pension is still compensated by an increase of 0.6 per cent a month, that is, up to 36 per cent monthly for the duration of the pension.

Disability pensions can be calculated by the same method as for old age pensions. This method of calculation gives low pensions for those who have worked only a few years. Another possibility for calculation exists, however, if the person has been working or has received sickness cash benefits in the years before being disability pensioned. In that case assumption points (expected income) are calculated for the years up to 65.

The pension is calculated using the assumption points and pension points from earlier years. Those who fulfil the conditions of 30 years' employment (or employment plus assumption point years) will receive income compensation equalling approximately 2/3 of their average gross income for the 15 years with highest income. The exceptions, as with the old age pension, are those with the highest income (the scheme has a ceiling). The earnings testing of the disability pensions was abolished from 1962.

A disability pension is much more generous than an actuarially-reduced old age pension. An actuarially-reduced pension drawn at the age of 60 gives a 30 per cent lower pension than a disability pension. The difference is the same even after the age of 65.

The requirements for obtaining disability pensions gradually became easier in the 1970s. From 1970 older workers could receive a disability pension where labour market considerations were weighed together with medical ones (those 63 years or more were considered to be 'older'; from 1 January 1974 the age was changed to 60). They no longer had to meet the same requirements regarding occupational and/or geographical mobility as younger persons.

From 1 July 1972, medical reasons were no longer a necessary requirement for unemployed persons 63 years of age and older (changed to 60 from 1 January 1974). If an older worker has used up his compensation rights from the unemployment benefit society (or has had cash unemployment assistance for a minimum of 450 days) and cannot support himself with the same work that he did earlier or other suitable types of work he is eligible for a disability pension.

From 1 January 1977 the law was changed so that only the disablement per se and not the cause of the disablement is of relevance for the decision about disability pension. This means that alcoholism, for example, is accepted as grounds for granting a pension.

In the 1990s the trend towards easier access to a disability pension has been reversed. Disability pensioning for labour market reasons was discontinued from October 1991 and from January 1997 pensioning for medical and labour market reasons combined will be discontinued. It means that the regulation for granting a disability pension is more or less the same as before 1970.

An important difference between Sweden and most other countries is that in Sweden it is possible to combine part-time work with a part-time pension, thus facilitating gradual withdrawal from the labour force.[6] There are three possible ways to do this:

1) Between the ages of 60 and 65 a partial early old age pension may be drawn, i.e. one may combine part-time retirement with part-time work. Between 1960 and 1993 the only alternative to a full-time early old age pension was a half pension. From July 1993 onwards, however, it has been possible to draw 1/4, 1/2 and 3/4 of a pension. An early partial drawing of the pension means that the latter is reduced, a reduction that continues after the official retirement age of 65. Conversely, a delayed drawing of part of the pension, i.e. starting or

---

[6] See Wadensjö (1996) for a more detailed presentation.

continuing part-time work after that age until 70 years, increases the pension.

2) Combining a disability pension with work is also possible. Between 1970 and 1993, three forms of disability pension were possible: full pension and, for those retaining some work capacity, a 2/3 and a 1/2 pension. As of July 1993, two new forms were added: the 3/4 and 1/4 pensions, and no new 2/3 pensions were granted.

3) A partial pension scheme was launched in July 1976 with the following eligibility requirements: the candidate had to be between 60 and 65 years of age; work time had to be reduced by at least 5 hours a week; remaining work time had to amount to at least 17 hours a week; the candidate must have worked at least 10 years since the age of 45; and the candidate had to reside in Sweden. Provided the employer's consent had been obtained, a partial pension would be awarded on application by a candidate. The income replacement rate under the scheme was 65 per cent up to 1981, when it was lowered to 50 per cent until 1987, after which it was restored to 65 per cent. In 1994 the starting age for entitlement to a partial pension was raised from 60 to 61 years, the replacement rate was lowered from 65 to 55 per cent, and the maximum reduction compensated for was set at ten hours per week.

2.2 The new old age pension scheme

The pension system has been in the focus of an intense debate during the last decade and parliamentary and governmental committees have investigated all aspects of it. The main worries have been that the decline in economic growth, longer life expectancy, increased frequency of disability pensioning and other forms of early exit from the labour market and the pensioning of the baby-boom generation of the 1940s will lead to very high payroll fees in the first decades of the next century if the system is not changed.

A parliamentary committee which had examined this problem for several years presented its final report in 1990 (SOU 1990:76). The lively discussion and criticism of the committee's proposals resulted in the government not putting forward a proposal for a change of the old age pension system but instead appointing a governmental committee composed of members from all the political parties that were represented in Parliament. This committee presented a report in 1994 with a proposal for a radically reformed pension system (SOU 1994:20). The proposal was supported by the four liberal and conservative parties that formed the government at the time, and also the main opposition party – the Social Democratic party. The government presented a proposition for guidelines for a reform of the pension system based on the report. The proposition was accepted by Parliament in June 1994.

Only the general principles, no legal changes, were decided on by Parliament in June 1994. A third committee was appointed with members from those political parties in the Parliament which supported the reform. This committee was to work on transforming the guidelines into proposals for legislation. There were (and still are) some unresolved questions, the main ones being how to divide the financing between employee and employer fees, the organization of the premium reserve part,[7] and the design of an index for calculation of the pensions.

A renewed debate within the Social Democratic party on the principles of the pension reform started in spring 1996. The consequences of this debate are unclear but it may lead to a new round of negotiations between the political parties on some details of pension reform.

Another important issue which is still unresolved is how to organize disability pensions. The disability pension system will no longer be a part of the same system as the old age pension system. A special committee has presented a report with suggestions for changing that system but not all the details are worked out as regards the disability pension scheme.

According to the decision by Parliament in June 1994, the new pension system should have been implemented from 1 January 1996 as regards the payment of fees and the accumulation of pension credits. This date has later been changed in two steps to 1 January 1998 and will probably be changed once more to 1 January 1999. The first pensions in the new system will start to be dispensed in January 2000.

The main principles

The main idea behind the new pension system is to increase work incentives by making the pension system actuarially fair and by that making

---

[7] A special governmental investigator was appointed in September 1994 to study the design of the premium reserve part of the new pension system. A report, SOU 1996:83, was published in 1996 and a final report is expected in 1997.

the pension system viable. The system should be more an insurance system and less a system for income redistribution. A second aim of the reform is that the pension system should guarantee a basic income for everyone at old age.

The determination of the pension

The pensions will be based on earnings for every year beginning at age 16 and including earnings after the age of 65. An amount corresponding to 18.5 per cent of the earnings will constitute the pension credits accrued during a year (the same as the fee, see below). Besides earnings, military service, care of one's own children up to the age of four, years of study (to some extent) and years with disability pensions will be taken into account when calculating the pension. In general, hypothetical earnings are calculated, for example for those who are at home caring for their children, and pension credits which correspond to 18.5 per cent of the hypothetical earnings are added to the person's account. For transfer payments, the earnings upon which the transfer payments are based are called the hypothetical earnings. Pension credits are calculated on the transfer payments enhanced by 13.3 per cent which generally does not mean the full hypothetical earnings (85 per cent of the earnings if the replacement rate is 75 per cent).

The pension credits are indexed to the development of the total earnings in the economy.

Each year the accumulated pension credits of those who reach 65 years of age that year are transformed to a pension. It is done by using a partition rate, a rate which is decided anew for every cohort upon reaching 65. The size of the partition rate, and therefore the pension, depends on the expected period for which those who turn 65 will receive a pension. As the expected remaining life-time increases with each cohort, the partition rate will gradually increase. The earnings-related pension will be indexed to a price- and growth-related index.

Secondly, there will also be a guarantee-pension for those with low or no earnings. For a full guarantee-pension the applicant must have resided in Sweden for at least 40 years between 16 and 65 years of age. A full guarantee-pension is 2.1 base amount for an unmarried pensioner and 1.87 base amount for a married pensioner. The guarantee-pension is reduced if the pensioner receives an earnings-related old age pension. If the total pension is 3.0 base amount or more for an unmarried pensioner or 2.655 base amount or more for a married pensioner, the pension will consist of only the earnings-related pension. The guarantee-pensions will be indexed to the consumer price index by the base amount.

The financing of the system

The new pensions will be financed by fees which amount to 18.5 per cent of earnings. As mentioned earlier, not only earnings but also military service, child care etc. will give pension credits. The state will pay fees covering the pension credits acquired in this way. The costs for the guarantee-pensions will also be paid over the state budget.

The system will mainly be a pay-as-you-go system but part of it will be a premium reserve system. 16.5 percentage units of the fees are paid to the pay-as-you-go system and 2 percentage units to the premium reserve system. Payments to the premium reserve system started already from the fiscal year 1995 (1 per cent employee fee). Both parts of the new pension system will be defined-contribution and not defined-benefit schemes.

The present plan is that half of the fee will be paid by the employer, half the fee by the employee. The supplementary pensions of the old system are financed by an employer fee. The new system will be implemented in the following way: the employee fee will be raised to 9.25 per cent of the earnings in one step. At the same time the employer fee will be decreased by the same percentage and the wage rate increased by the same percentage. Thus neither the employees nor the employers should gain or lose from the change of financing system. The idea behind turning employer fees into employee fees is that employees will be made more aware that they are gaining the right to a pension by paying for it and therefore the work incentives should be strengthened.

Dividing the pension credits between spouses

Married couples where both of the spouses were born 1954 or later are offered the possibility of dividing their pension credits. A requisite is that both spouses apply and that the application is made before 31 January of the year in which the couple want to divide the pension points. After the application is made, the dividing of the pension credits continues until an application is made for a discontinuance. If both spouses apply for a discontinuance it becomes valid from the year the discontinuance application is made. If only one of the spouses applies, it becomes valid from the following year.

According to the proposal, when dividing pension points an adjustment should be made regarding the difference in life expectancy between men and women. This part of the proposal has been much criticized.

Age at retirement

The change to actuarial pensions is intended to increase labour supply and delay retirement. There are other steps which have been taken with the same intention. In the present scheme, a reduced old age pension can be received from the age of 60, but in the new pension system 61 will be the lowest age (this change will take place from 1999). It is only possible to receive an early old age pension as regards the earnings-related pension. It will only be possible to receive a guarantee pension from the age of 65. In the case of early old age pension of the earnings-related pension, the guarantee pension will be calculated as if the earnings-related pension is what it would have been if the person had retired at the age of 65 (it will not be possible to get a higher guarantee-pension by retiring early).

The committee proposed that job security according to labour market legislation should be changed so that collective agreement could not influence the age limit and that this limit should be raised first to 66 and later to 67. Instead, the government wanted to propose that the social partners change their collective agreements in the same way and only if they did not, propose that Parliament should change the job security law.

Part-time pension

The partial pension system, which has been the most popular way of combining work and retirement between 60 and 65, will be abolished. No new partial pensions will be granted from the year 2000. The remaining combination of work and retirement in that age group will be partial old age pension from the age of 61 or over. As in the present pension system it will be possible to draw 1/4, 1/2 or 3/4 of an old age pension.

The transition from the present system to the new one

The pensions of those who were born in 1934 or earlier will be completely based on the old system and the pensions for those who were born 1954 or later, completely on the new system. For those who were born between 1935 and 1953 the pension will be based on both systems. For those born in 1935, the pension will be based 19/20 parts on the old system and 1/20 parts on the new system, for those born in 1936, 18/20 parts on the old system and 2/20 parts on the new system, etc.

To be able to calculate the new pensions for those who enter the labour market before 1997 the pension points acquired in the ATP scheme have to be translated into pension credits in the new scheme. This is done by adding one base amount (for the basic pension) to the ATP-base amounts and thereafter converting them to pension credits and using the same indexation as in the new pension scheme. The pension credits for child care will be calculated from 1960 on, the pension credits for military service and studies from 1995 on, and those for other non-earnings based credits from 1997 on.

2.3   The development of the occupational pension systems[8]

Central government employees

Occupational pension schemes have existed long before the social security pensions. The first ones were established in the public sector more than 200 years ago. The general principle was that the public servant had the right to his salary independent of sickness, disability or age. The *Riksdag* granted civil servants the right to retire at the age of 70 but continue to be paid their salary already in 1770. Since no special funding was granted to the authority from which the person retired, it could not pay a salary to a person who replaced the retiree. In 1825 a special pension fund for civil servants made it possible to pay a salary for the person succeeding the retired person (a fund for the military with the same intent had already been established in 1756). The funds did not cover the total costs but direct governmental subsidies covered the rest of the pension costs.

---

[8] See especially Schmidt (1974) for the development of occupational pension schemes other than those for employees of the counties and the municipalities.

In the nineteenth century a system developed that divided the salary in two parts, 2/3 of the salary being the remuneration for the position, 1/3 for actually carrying out the work related to the position. It meant that 2/3 of the total salary constituted the pension – the remuneration of the position (but no work carried out by the retiree). The retirement age was 65 or 70 and 30, 35 and some instances 40 years of public employment were required in order to be eligible for a pension.

In 1907 a major overhaul of the system was made and a new pension scheme for those employed by the public sector was established. A special fund was constituted, which was financed 1/3 by employee fees (proportional to the salary) and 2/3 by the government. The pension was set to 2/3 of the salary – the same as in the earlier system.

Only those with a formal position as a public servant were paid a pension in the 1907 system, not those with a non-tenured position. Even if most with a non-tenured position got a tenured position before retirement it meant that many people with very long service for the government did not receive a public servant pension at retirement. Those with non-tenured positions were included in the system from 1934 (53 per cent of those employed by the central government had non-tenured positions at that time). In 1938 the fund was abolished and also the employee fee.

With the introduction of the ATP-scheme, the pensions for those employed by the central government were coordinated with the social security basic and supplementary pensions. The total pension level was set by the central government pension scheme and the difference between the pension set by that system and that set by the social security scheme was paid out. The majority of the central government employees had a lower pension age (65 or lower) than that of the national schemes (67), and the central government pension scheme covered the total pension costs from that lower retirement age up to the age of 67.

From 1992 the pension scheme was changed so that instead of guaranteeing the total level it became an addition to the pension from the social security schemes.

Local government employees

The pension schemes for those employed by the local government (counties and municipalities) were modelled after the pension schemes of the central government sector. For some groups employed by the local government, for example teachers and policemen, the pensions were regulated by the state and paid out by the authority paying out the central government pensions but the pensions were in fact financed by the local governments. Also several other groups had pensions of the same size as those who were employed by the central government, but their pensions were paid by a special pension authority, Sveriges Kommunalanställdas Pensionskassa (SKP). A governmental committee made an investigation of the pension schemes in the local government sector in the mid 1940s. See SOU 1946:26. According to that study almost all counties and towns and most of the other (250) larger municipalities had pension plans. In the majority of cases the replacement rate was 60–70 per cent and the pension paid out by SKP. In the counties the retirement age was 65 for men and 60 for women and in the municipalities 65–67 for men and 60–62 for women.

With the introduction of the ATP-scheme, the pensions for those employed by the local government (counties and municipalities) were coordinated with the social security basic and supplementary pensions. The total pension level was set by the local government pension scheme and the difference between the pension set by that system and that set by the social security scheme was paid out. The majority of the local government employees had a lower pension age (65 or lower) than that of the national schemes (67), and the public sector pension scheme covered the total pension costs from that lower retirement age up to the age of 67.

White-collar workers in the private sector

The private sector did not have a coordinated pension scheme at the beginning of this century, but many of the larger companies had pension schemes for white-collar employees. This group of employees also took initiatives for the organization of a more general system of occupational pensions for them. One of their organizations took the initiative so that a special pension fund was started in 1917, Svenska Personalpensionskassan (SPP). It was started with the support of some of the major companies. The employees were called active members and the employers passive members of the SPP and both sides were represented on the board. The number of passive members increased from 19 in 1917 to 1635 in 1937, and the number of active members from 1137 to 36 397 in the same period. Specific for SPP pensions compared with other occupational pension schemes in the private sector was that the pension rights were not lost if an employee moved to another company.

In the early 1950s SAF conducted a survey among its members. See SAF (1954). The survey was answered by most members of SAF, and the employers who answered had in their employ 90 per cent of the white-collar workers in SAF companies. Of those employed in the answering companies 93 per cent of the white-collar workers had a pension. The white-collar workers mainly received their pensions through the insurance company SPP (79 per cent of white-collar workers with a pension) or from other insurance companies or a combination of SPP and another insurance company (11 per cent).

The fees for pensions that were paid by SPP were in most cases paid partly by the employer, partly by the employee. The size of the fee paid to SPP varied. In the 1950s a common size was 24 per cent of the salary, 1/3 paid by the employee and 2/3 by the employer.

With the introduction of the ATP-system in 1960 a new pension scheme – the ITP-scheme – was established for white-collar workers in the private sector. The ITP-pension was constructed as an addition to those from the national pension schemes. It is administered by the SPP, which, as mentioned, administered most of the pensions for the white-collar workers already. Another possibility that was introduced was that the firm guarantees the pension by a fund of its own, and secures it by insuring itself in a special insurance company in order to protect against insolvency – the FPG-PRI scheme.

The costs for the occupational pensions declined as a result of the ATP reform and therefore the fees were reduced and as a result the salaries were raised.

The retirement age for white-collar workers in the private sector was 65 for men and 60 for women in 1960 (the retirement age for women was raised to 62 in the 1960s and to 65 from 1971). For the period between the ages of 65 and 67 for men and 60 and 67 for women the pension was 65 per cent of the salary for the part of earnings up to 7.5 base amount and 32.5 per cent for the part of earnings exceeding 7.5 base amount. From the age of 67 the corresponding replacement rates were 10 per cent and 32.5 per cent.

With the change of the retirement age in the social security scheme from 67 to 65, the replacement rates were also changed to the rates which are valid at present (see section 2.3).

Blue-collar workers in the private sector

At the beginning of the twentieth century, pensions for blue-collar workers in the private sector were much less common than for white-collar workers. In some companies, especially in some industries, a worker could continue to receive a wage at old age even if his work capacity was low and his contribution to the production of the firm was low or none – in practice a form of pension. See Olsson (1996).

The share of blue-collar workers with pensions and the levels of the pensions gradually increased but both the share with pensions and the levels of the pensions continued to be much lower than those of the white-collar workers. LO, the trade union federation of blue-collar workers, conducted a study regarding the prevalence of pensions in 1953.[9] It showed large differences between unions, that means in practice between industries. For example, 91.2 per cent of the workers in the mining industry but only 6.4 per cent of the workers in agriculture had pension plans. In some cases – as mentioned above – the differences could be explained by the existence of pensions paid out as wages.

As a part of the debate on the introduction of a national supplementary pension scheme, SAF (the employer association covering most private sector employers) conducted a study in the 1950s of the existence of occupational pensions among their members with the intention to establish an occupational pension scheme for blue-collar workers. See SAF (1954).

The survey was answered by most members of SAF; the employers who answered employed 87 per cent of the blue-collar workers in SAF companies. Of those employed in the answering companies 72 per cent of the blue-collar workers had a pension.[10] The pensions for the blue-collar systems were arranged in other ways than by through an insurance company for the large majority of workers (92 per cent), in most cases by direct payment of the pension from the company.

The retirement age for getting a full pension for the majority of male blue-collar workers was 67 (70 per cent), which was the retirement age in the social security system at that time. 24 per cent had 65 as the retire-

---

[9] See Olsson (1996) for a presentation of results from that survey.

[10] The share with a pension was higher in larger than in smaller companies, and the response rate was higher among the larger than among the smaller companies. This means that the prevalence of occupational pensions is most likely somewhat overestimated.

ment age. For women 25 per cent had a retirement age of 60, 19 per cent had 62, 14 per cent 65 and 39 per cent 67. In companies with both male and female blue-collar workers, the retirement age was the same for men and women in 54 per cent of the companies and lower for women in the rest. For most workers with a retirement age below 67 the pension was the same before and after 67, but in some companies the pension was higher before the age of 67 (somewhat compensating for the fact that no social security pensions were paid out before 67).

The variation in the size of the pension for blue-collar workers was considerable. Many, however, had a pension of 600 kronor a year (38 per cent of married men, 24 per cent of unmarried men, 27 per cent of married women and 28 per cent of unmarried women) or 400 kronor (9 per cent of married men, 37 per cent of unmarried men, 35 per cent of married women and 37 per cent of unmarried women). The old age pension from the social security scheme was at that time 2800 kronor a year. The requirement for getting a pension from the firm in most cases was an employment period of at least 25 or 30 years in the company.

The recommendation from the committee was to start an occupational pension scheme covering all SAF companies. The report was sent to LO, the trade union federation of blue-collar workers, but no agreement was reached. Instead the ATP pension scheme was decided on, a unified system for both blue-collar and white-collar workers in both the private and the public sector.

For the blue-collar workers an occupational pension scheme was not established at the time of the introduction of the ATP-scheme as for the other three major groups and the existing pension schemes (which had a much lower replacement rate than the ATP scheme) were dismantled. In the early 1960s the blue-collar workers were the major group of employees without an occupational pension scheme. Also as regards other forms of occupational insurances or extra pay from the employers this group had less income protection than other groups. Among the LO-members this was widely felt as being unfair and LO started to try to change the situation in the beginning of the 1960s and gradually succeeded. In the decades after the establishment of ATP, a whole system of occupational insurances were formed for blue-collar workers. All together seven contractually-determined insurances have been agreed on between the LO and SAF. Five of them still exist: the TGL (occupational group life insurance) established in 1963; the AGB (severance pay insurance) in 1965; the AGS (supplementary sick pay insurance) in 1972; the STP (supplementary old age pension) in 1973; and the TFA (supplementary work injury insurance) in 1974. Two schemes were established and later discontinued – at least for the time being. The PLE (temporary layoff compensation) was established in 1985 as a complement to the social security scheme established at the same time and discontinued when the social security scheme was discontinued; and TUFS, compensation at early exit caused by layoffs, started in 1993 and was discontinued in 1995.

The AGS, which went into effect as of 1 September 1972, provides a supplement to the sickness cash benefits or to a (temporary) disability pension. A person who has a disability pension/temporary disability pension receives a monthly compensation which depends on his/her sickness cash benefit-based income.[11]

The occupational insurance scheme for blue-collar workers, STP, established in 1973 (see below for details) was initially both a method for lowering the retirement age to the same as that for other groups in the labour market, i.e. 65, and a method for raising the total pension level for blue-collar workers. After the lowering of the retirement age in the social security system in 1976 it became a supplement to the old age pension from the social security schemes.

As mentioned, the establishment of those insurances can be viewed as an attempt on the part of the workers to achieve the same benefits as white-collar workers, and by doing so, to decrease the social differences. The choice of central contractual solutions cannot be fully explained without mentioning the solidaristic wage policy and its attendant central negotiations. The solidaristic wage policy became effective in the 1960s, at the same time as the first contractual insurances. The goal behind such a wage policy is to achieve a 'fair' and equal wage structure. Job-connected social benefits are also included in the concept of 'wage'. One basic tenant of a solidaristic wage policy is thus equal social benefits for employees. Solutions other than those which are built upon central negotiations tend to result in unequal social benefits, as does an uneven wage structure in general, depending, among other things, on the groups' different negotiation abilities and strengths.

From the point of view of the employer organization, there are advantages in coordinating fringe benefits in the form of contractual insurances: the competitive relations between the companies on the

---

[11] For the other three major groups the occupational pensions were coordinated with the occupational insurance for the old age pensions.

labour market become more comparable. Wage drift in the form of increased insurance benefits for a company's employees becomes less common. In earlier periods (for example, the 1950s), SAF strongly emphasized restraint regarding pension rights from the companies to the blue-collar workers.

2.4   The present occupational pension system[12, 13]

At present there are four main occupational pension schemes: ITP for white-collar workers in the private sector; one scheme for blue-collar workers in the private sector (STP, replaced by a new scheme in 1996); *kommunal tjänstepension* for those employed by the counties, municipalities and parishes; and *statlig tjänstepension* for those employed by the central government. There are many similarities but also important differences between the four systems. A short presentation of each of the four schemes is given below.[14]

White-collar workers in the private sector

A pension scheme for white-collar workers in the private sector existed before the introduction of the national supplementary pension scheme (ATP) in 1960 but it covered less than half of all employees in that category. The system was changed as a result of the introduction of the ATP-system to be a complement to that system.

The retirement age for white-collar workers has been 65 for many decades. Up until the lowering of the retirement age in the national schemes from 67 to 65 in 1976, the ITP paid the total pension for those

---

[12] See e.g. Edebalk and Wadensjö (1989), SOU 1990:76, SOU 1990:77, Wadensjö (1990), Sjuk- och arbetsskadekommittén (1995) and Edebalk, Ståhlberg and Wadensjö (1996) for more detailed descriptions of various aspects of the schemes.
[13] Collectively bargained schemes also supplement disability pensions paid by the national pension scheme and the national supplementary pension scheme. See e.g. Wadensjö (1984 and 1991) and Kruse and Söderström (1989). This part of the schemes is not dealt with in this chapter.
[14] There are a few other schemes, for example for people employed in the insurance, banking, and consumer cooperative sectors. The construction of the schemes closely follows that of the ITP-scheme.

aged 65 and 66. Now only a few percent of those covered by the ITP-system have a formal retirement age lower than 65.

The ITP pensions depend on the number of qualifying months which must have been worked between the ages of 28 and 65 years. In general, 360 months (30 years) are required for full ITP. The right to receive ITP requires a minimum of three ITP years. Further, at least three ITP years must have been earned between the ages of 55 and 64, or at least 0.25 ITP years between age 63 and 64.

The size of the pension depends on the size of the salary during the year before retirement. Full ITP constitutes 10 per cent of the pension wage for the part of the salary which is below 7.5 base amount, 65 per cent for the salary between 7.5 and 20 base amount, and 32.5 per cent for the salary between 20 and 30 base amount. The pensions are only guaranteed in nominal terms but the surplus of the funds are used to index-regulate the pensions.[15]

To this should be added a special supplement, ITPK, a premium reserve defined contribution supplement. This means an increase of the compensation by between 2.5 and 3 per cent of the salary.

The ITP system is a defined benefit premium reserve system financed by payroll fees. Presently, the fee is 6.3 per cent on average for the old age, disability and partial pension but varies depending on the composition of the work force. In most cases it is between 5 and 20 per cent. For those under the age of 28 the fee is 1.05 per cent of the salary (for the compensation at disability).

There is also a special supplement to the social security partial pension scheme. For income parts between 7.5 and 20 base amount reduced by decreasing the working hours up to 10 hours, the compensation is 55 per cent and for income parts between 20 and 30 base amount the compensation is 27.5 per cent.

Around 2000 employers having a total of 240 000 white-collar workers follow the ITP-plan but with pensions funded at the firms instead of at the insurance company SPP. The pensions are secured against insolvency by insurance policies taken at the FPG-insurance company (the scheme is called the FPG–PRI scheme). The fee varies with the number of insolvencies – in 1995 the fee was 0.3 per cent of the pension liability.

---

[15] The rest of the surplus is used to give a rebate on the fee the employer has paid.

Blue-collar workers in the private sector

During the latter half of the 1960s, LO became concerned with the issue of lowering retirement age, which was seen as one way of reducing inequities between blue-collar and white-collar workers. White-collar workers in the private sector and also those employed in the public sector could retire at age 65, while the general retirement age was 67. A decision was reached between LO and SAF in 1971, and the pension scheme, STP, went into effect on 1 July 1973. According to this scheme, STP 1 was paid between the ages of 65 and 67, followed by STP 2 at age 67 as a complement to the national basic and national supplementary pension (ATP). When the pension age in the national pension scheme was lowered from 67 to 65 years of age in 1976, the STP was changed to become a supplement to the national old age and supplementary pensions. In 1995 LO and SAF reached a new agreement regarding occupational pensions. The new pension system has been in force since 1996. Both the old system, STP (1973–95), and the new system (1996–) will be presented here.

The STP-pension depends on the number of qualifying years which must have been worked between the ages of 28 and 64 years. The right to receive an STP-pension requires a minimum of three STP years. Further, at least three STP years must have been earned between the ages of 55 and 64, or at least 0.25 STP years between age 63 and 64. In general, 30 STP years are required for full STP.

The size of the pension depends on the number of years worked and on the income earned between the ages of 55 and 60. The average of the three best years of this five-year period is calculated and called the 'pension wage'. Only earnings up to a ceiling of 7.5 base amount, the same ceiling as in the ATP-scheme, are included in the calculation of the pension. Full STP constitutes 10 per cent of the pension wage.

STP was financed by a payroll levy. The fee was set each year so that the receipts of it equal the expected costs of the life-long pensions of the persons who are pensioned that year. The method means that every year the employers pay a premium which corresponds to the sum which is necessary to allow those retiring during that year to receive life-long pensions.

The new pension system for blue-collar workers is also financed by a payroll fee. The system is a premium reserve system and the fee is 2 per cent of the salary. There will be no ceiling in the system, which is a change from the former system. On the other hand there will not be a higher compensation rate for earnings over the ceiling in the social security system as in the other three schemes. The fee may be placed either in AMF Pension, the insurance company of SAF and LO, or from 1 January 1997 also in other insurance companies.

The compensation will either be paid out as an annuity from the age of 65 for the rest of the lifetime or during a shorter time period.

In the new system workers aged 28 start to accumulate pension rights from 1 January 1996. Only those who were born in 1968 or later may have the maximum number of years with pension credits. Special arrangements have been made to guarantee the pension rights for those who were between the ages of 28 and 65 years by 31 December 1995. Those who reach the age of 65 in 1996 (born in 1931) get a full STP pension according to the former system. Those who were born in 1932 or later get a pension as if they had paid to the insurance system from the age of 28 for all years they have been employed. The compensation for the pension rights for years before 1996 will be financed by a special payroll fee (set to 1.5 per cent in the period 1996–99) and by the transfer of large surpluses (5000 million kronor) from another occupational insurance, the sickness and disability insurance scheme AGS.

Central government employees

The central government established a pension scheme long before the other sectors. This was an incentive for taking employment with the government for decades. When the ATP scheme was introduced in 1960 the central government pension scheme was constructed in a way so that this system guaranteed the total level, and the amount paid out from that system was determined by the difference between the pension that was guaranteed and the pension from the national social security pension schemes. In 1992, after an agreement between the government and the trade unions (PA-91), the pension system was changed so the compensation was determined without regard to the compensation from the social security schemes, i.e. the same type of system as that of the ITP pension.

The central government pension depends on the number of qualifying years and the size of the salary (overtime compensation excluded) received in the five years before retirement. Thirty years are required for full pension (either in the central government scheme or any of the other schemes). Years with employment from the age of 28 are included. Only years with at least 40 per cent of full-time full-year employment are counted. If the number of years is less than 30 the pension is reduced proportionally.

Full pension constitutes 10 per cent of the pension wage for the part of the salary which is below 7.5 base amount, 65 per cent for the salary between 7.5 and 20 base amount, and 32.5 per cent for the salary between 20 and 30 base amount. There is also a complementing defined contribution premium reserve part. The employer fee for that insurance (KÅPAN) is 1.9 per cent of the salary.

The retirement age is now 65 for almost all jobs in the central government, but large groups of employees still have the possibility of following earlier rules. Of those employed by the central government sector at present 35 per cent have a lower pension age than the general retirement age of 65, most of them having the option to retire sometime between the ages of 63 and 65. Their pensions are paid in total up to the age of 65 by the central government pension system.

There is also a special supplement to the social security partial pension scheme. For income parts between 7.5 and 20 base amount which are reduced by decreasing the working hours by up to 10 hours, the compensation is 55 per cent and for income parts between 20 and 30 base amount the compensation is 27.5 per cent.

The pension scheme for those employed in the governmental sector is a pay-as-you-go system.[16] The pensions are paid out by a special central authority and for most pensioners are financed by a payroll levy, at present 9.6 per cent (changed from 11 per cent from 1 July 1994). (The financial system is different for teachers and for those employed in some state authorities.)

Local government employees[17]

The pension scheme for those who work in local government has been modelled on the system for the pension scheme of the central government, but changes have been made in the central government pension scheme (see above) so that now there are some important differences.

---

[16] A governmental investigation proposed in 1995 that the pension scheme should be changed so that the fees should be set according to actuarial principles. See SOU 1995:9. No changes have yet been decided.
[17] See Ds 1995:46 and Björnstad and Kruse (1994) for more details regarding the scheme.

The local government pension depends on the number of qualifying years and the average salary during the best five of the last seven years before retirement (pension wage). In general, 30 years are required for full pension. Years with employment from the age of 28 are included. Only years with at least 40 per cent of full-time full-year employment are counted. If the number of years is less than 30 the pension is reduced proportionally.

Full pension including compensation from the two national schemes constitutes 96 per cent of the pension wage for the part of the salary which is below 1 base amount, 78.5 per cent of the salary between 1 and 2.5 base amount, 60 per cent of the salary between 2.5 and 3.5 base amount, 64 per cent of the salary between 3.5 and 7.5 base amount. On average it means an addition to the national pension schemes of 7 to 18 per cent of the salary at retirement for those with earnings of 7.5 base amount or lower. The compensation is 65 per cent of the salary between 7.5 and 20 base amount, and 32.5 per cent for the salary between 20 and 30 base amount. The pension is indexed to the base amount. The pension to be paid out from the local government pension scheme is the difference between the pension calculated that way and the pension according to the basic national pension and the national supplementary pension.

Of those employed by the local government sector, 65 per cent have a lower pension age than the general retirement age of 65, generally a flexible retirement age from 63 to 65. Most of those with a retirement age lower than 65 work in occupations where the majority are women. Many of those with a retirement age of 63 to 65 continue to work up to the age of 65. The pension for those retiring before 65 is paid in total by the local government until the age of 65.

There is also a special supplement to the social security partial pension scheme. The compensation for income parts between 7.5 and 20 base amount that are reduced by decreasing the working hours up to 10 hours is 55 per cent and for income parts between 20 and 30 base amount reduced by decreased working hours, the compensation is 27.5 per cent.

The pension scheme for those employed in the local governmental sector is a pay-as-you-go system. With the exception of the Stockholm municipality, the pensions are administered by an insurance company, KPA, which is owned by the local governments. However, each local government pays the pensions which are due to their respective former employees into KPA every year for further dispersion.

A comparison of the four schemes

The total compensation from each of the four systems is coordinated with other contractual pension systems. This means that someone who changes jobs, for example, from private to a municipal job or vice versa, gets credit for the total amount worked.

Common to all the four schemes is that you have to work up to the age of retirement to be entitled to a pension determined by the rules described above and summarized in Table 8.1. If a person leaves the labour force earlier he/she loses his/her pension rights in the occupational pension scheme but is instead granted an annuity to be paid out from the age of 65 when leaving. This annuity is not automatically indexed from the time the person leaves the job up to the age of 65 but only from the age of 65.[18] At an inflation rate like that of the 1970s and the 1980s, leaving the labour market early generally means a low occupational pension. This has been of special importance for women who more often than men leave the labour force for reasons other than retirement.

It is also important to note that there is a lower limit for the minimum number of working hours which qualify as a basis for entitlement to an occupational pension. The limit differs between the various schemes. In most cases the rules of the occupational pension schemes are more demanding than those of the national supplementary pension scheme (the ATP-scheme).

2.5   The private pensions – the third pillar[19]

There is also a third pillar in the pension system: private pensions. There are several forms of private pensions.

1)   One variety is private pension schemes that are connected to an occupational pension scheme. For example, those employed by the central government can, by paying an extra fee, get a higher pension from the occupational pension system (the premium reserve part).

---

[18] In the ITP-scheme, decisions to adjust for inflation have been made annually since 1985.
[19] See SOU 1990:77 for an overview of the private insurance pension schemes. The association of insurance companies, Svenska försäkringsföreningen, publishes a yearbook containing reports and statistics.

Table 8.1. – A comparison of the four occupational pension schemes

	White-collar workers (ITP)	Blue-collar workers Old (STP)	New	Central government	Local government
Principle for calculation of benefits	Defined benefit	Defined benefit	Defined contribution	Defined benefit	Defined benefit
Employment requirem. for full pension	30 years (after age 28)	30 years (after age 28)	37 years (after age 28)	30 years (after age 28)	30 years (after age 28)
Base for calculation	Salary year before retirement (plus defined contribution part)	Average of 3 of the 5 years between 55 and 59	Total earnings from age 28	Average of the 5 years before retirement (plus defined contribution part)	Average of the best five of the last seven years before retirement
Rate of compensation	10% –7.5 ba; 65% 7.5–20 ba; 32.5% 20–30 ba	10 % up to 7.5 base amount	c. 10 % (no ceiling)	10% –7.5 ba; 65% 7.5–20 ba; 32.5% 20–30 ba	96% –1 ba; 78.5% 1–2.5 ba; 60% 2.5–3.5 ba; 64% 3.5–7.5 ba; 65% 7.5–20 ba; 32.5% 20–30 ba
Financing principle	Premium reserve	Funds for those pensioned	Premium reserve	Pay-as-you-go	Pay-as-you-go
Financing rules	Payroll fee – on average 6.3%; 1.05% for those under 28	Payroll fee	Payroll fee 3.5% (2 % for the new system, 1.5 % for the old system)	Payroll fee 9.6 %	Pension costs paid from the municipality and the county to KPA for their own pensioners
Partial pension supplement	yes	no	no	yes	yes

Note: ba = base amount.

2) Many trade unions have agreements with an insurance company regarding a group private pension scheme which is optional to join for the members of the union. The pension is in most cases either as an annuity for all years after retiring or for a specified period (five, ten years) after retirement.

3) For some employees, generally high level employees, the firm buys or guarantees an extra pension as a part of the employment contract.

4) Quite common, especially in the crisis of the 1990s, is that a firm buys pension insurances to be able to lay off employees in an order other than that according to reversed seniority and by that be able to keep younger employees.

5) There are also private pensions which people buy directly from insurance companies.

The fee for a private pension insurance is tax deductible up to a ceiling (at present 1/2 to 1 base amount). Instead the pensions are taxed. Especially in the decades with high marginal taxes (1970s and 1980s) this gave strong incentives to buy a private pension. In recent years the difference in outgoing pensions between men and women from the other pension schemes has been debated and one result has been that the number of women who have bought private pensions has increased.

The number of new private pensions increased from 29 600 in 1978 to 386 800 in 1989. The total amount of fees that were paid increased from 194 to 6087 million SEK in the same period (after adjusting for inflation 13.7 times higher in 1989 than in 1978). Of the total funds of 130 billion in 1989, c. 80 billion was probably for pensions. The number of new pensions (the inflow) has decreased since 1989. One factor behind that development is probably that the lower marginal tax rates have made the tax deduction less favourable.

Table 8.2 shows the extent of savings in private pensions according to age group. Of the total number of people with a taxable income, 17.9 per cent made a tax deduction for a private pension insurance in 1994; in the age group 45–64 29.3 per cent did so. This means that in the next decades close to 1/3 of new retirees will have a private pension in addition to pensions from the national and occupational pension schemes.

Table 8.2 – The share of people in 1994 with taxable income, who receive tax deductions for private pension payments

Group	Percentage with tax deductions
All	17.9
–15 years	0.1
16–24 years	4.7
25–44 years	24.9
45–64 years	29.3
65–74 years	1.8
75– years	0.3
20–64 years	24.7

Source: Statistiska meddelanden, *Inkomst- och skattestatistik* 1994, Be 20 SM 9601.

3. The total system

The total income at old age is determined not only by the pension schemes but also by other sources of income. Table 8.3 shows the composition of earnings of households headed by people over the ordinary retirement age of 65 and by households headed by people aged 20–64. Pensions are the dominating source of income for people aged 65 and over. Pensions constitute less than 10 per cent of the total income before taxes for people under 65. The table also shows that the average disposable income per consumption unit is only about 14 per cent lower in households headed by people 65 or over than in households headed by people aged 20–64.

A study covering the development of the economic situation of pensioners between 1975 and 1993 (Ds 1993:93) shows that the standard of living rose for people aged 65 or over compared to those aged 18–64 in the period 1975 to 1990 – the main part of the increase occurring in the recession of the early 1980s when real wages, and thus the incomes of those of active age, fell. Also in the recession of the 1990s the relative position improved for those aged 65 or over mainly as a result of the maturing of the ATP-scheme (those reaching the age of 65 in 1990–93 have ATP-pensions to a higher extent and higher ATP-pensions than the generation of pensioners preceeding them.)

In Table 8.4 the pensions paid out to those aged 65 or over are compared with the average earnings of people aged 25–60 (pensions for men are compared with earnings for men, and pensions for women are

294

Table 8.3 – Income sources for households headed by people aged 20–64 and 65 or older in 1993 (thousand SEK)

	20–64	*65–*
Wages	179.6	8.6
Capital	8.4	13.3
Other earnings	8.1	4.0
Pensions and annuities	17.4	133.0
Other income transfers	45.3	8.7
– Taxes	70.0	40.4
Disposable income	189.2	127.7
Disposable income per consumption unit	101.8	87.8

Source: Statistiska meddelanden, *Inkomstfördelningsundersökningen 1993,* Be 21 SM 9501.

Table 8.4 – Average old age pensions paid out in 1994 for men and women aged 65 and over compared to average earnings for men and women aged 25–60 (excluding those without earnings)

	Men	*Women*
Basic pension	0.28	0.38
Basic pension + ATP	0.59	0.52
Basic pension + ATP + ITP/STP	0.81	0.77
Basic pension + ATP + central gov. pension	0.86	0.90
Basic pension + ATP + local gov. pension	0.84	0.78

Source: Statistiska meddelanden, *Inkomster och bidrag 1994,* Be 20 SM 9602.

compared with earnings for women). It shows that the total pension for those who only have pensions from the national pension schemes corresponds to 59 per cent of the average earnings for men, and 52 per cent for women. For those with occupational pensions the figures are much higher, 77 to 90 per cent. The reasons for the higher rate of total compensation are both the compensation from the occupational pension as such but also that those with occupational pensions have had higher earnings and therefore get a higher ATP-pension than those without an occupational pension.

Table 8.5 shows the percentage of people who have a pension and the average pension according to age. It shows that 4–5 per cent of those

Table 8.5 – The percentage of people with a pension in 1994 (all forms) and average size of the pension according to age

Age	Percentage with a pension		Average pension	
	Men	Women	Men	Women
16–19	4.5	4.4	27.8	26.0
20–24	1.8	1.7	42.3	38.4
25–34	2.4	2.8	49.5	45.7
35–44	4.8	6.7	65.5	60.0
45–54	9.1	14.4	80.2	71.0
55–59	24.4	30.5	99.6	77.1
60–64	70.0	71.8	117.4	79.5
65–69	99.3	98.8	152.6	93.6
70–74	99.5	99.1	144.6	86.5
75–79	99.6	99.4	135.8	81.7
80–	99.6	99.5	106.0	70.0

Source: Statistiska meddelanden, *Inkomster och bidrag 1994,* Be 20 SM 9602.

aged 16–19 had a pension; most of them are children receiving a child pension after a deceased parent. This number with a pension among those aged 20–34 is lower than for those aged 16–19. This increases from under 2 per cent for those aged 20–24 to 24.4 per cent for men and 30.5 per cent for women in the age group 55–59. Most of the people aged 20–59 who have a pension have a disability pension.

The share who have a pension is much higher among those aged 60–64 than for those aged 55–59, 70.0 per cent for men and 71.8 per cent for women. The high incidence is mainly a result of many people receiving a disability pension and many having partial pensions. Nearly everyone 65 years of age and over has a pension. The few exceptions are explained by some people choosing the option of a delayed enhanced pension (possible up to the age of 70), and by a few immigrants having arrived in Sweden at an age too high to qualify for a pension.

The table also shows that the pension is highest for those aged 65–69 and lowers gradually for those aged 60–74, 75–79 and 80 and over. The main explanations are the maturing of the ATP-pension scheme and that the pensions of the younger retirees are based on higher earnings as a result of the long-term growth of the wage level.

No information is given in Table 8.4 and Table 8.5 about the relative importance of the three pillars in the pension system. In Table 8.6 the percentages of people with different forms of pensions are given. The

Table 8.6 – The percentage of people with different forms of pensions in 1991

	66–			66–69		
	Men	*Women*	*All*	*Men*	*Women*	*All*
ATP	95	60	75	98	77	86
Widow's pension	–	35	20	–	21	11
Occupational pension	69	47	57	78	63	70
Private pension	11	5	8	15	8	11

Source: Jansson (1994).

Table 8.7 – Average pensions in 1991 (in SEK)

	66–			66–69		
	Men	*Women*	*All*	*Men*	*Women*	*All*
Basic pension + suppl.	28 000	34 100	31 500	28 200	31 000	29 700
ATP	65 200	23 100	40 900	80 800	36 300	56 900
Occ. pens.	17 100	7 500	11 600	19 200	8 300	13 300
Priv. pens.	3 400	1 100	2 000	4 500	1 900	3 100
Total pens.	113 700	65 800	86 000	132 700	77 500	103 000

Source: Jansson (1994).

large majority have ATP-pensions; the percentage is higher among men than women and higher among young retirees than among all retirees. The share with an occupational pension is lower, but more than 50 per cent have such a pension. The general pattern is the same – occupational pensions are more frequent among men than among women and more frequent among younger than among older retired people.

Table 8.7 shows the average pensions and how they are divided between different pension forms – the national pension is divided into the basic and the supplementary parts. It shows the importance of the national pension schemes. For those aged 66–69 these pensions constitute 84 per cent of all pension incomes; the occupational pensions constitute 13 per cent and the private pensions 3 per cent.

The ATP-scheme is a pay-as-you-go system but with considerable funds. Some of the occupational pension schemes are funded (accord-

Table 8.8 – Assets of the two systems (in billion SEK and as a percentage of GDP)

	AP-funds	Occupational funds	GDP	Assets as percentage of GDP
1980	165	53	531	41.1
1981	184	64	582	42.6
1982	205	77	636	44.3
1983	226	93	712	44.8
1984	246	111	797	44.8
1985	268	128	866	45.7
1986	295	153	947	47.3
1987	315	164	1023	46.8
1988	350	201	1114	49.5
1989	384	225	1233	49.4
1990	432	230	1360	48.7
1991	481	254	1447	50.8
1992	499	265	1442	53.0
1993	531	336	1446	60.0
1994	541	338	1525	57.6

Sources: Edebalk and Wadensjö (1989), SOU 1990:77, Statistiska meddelanden, *Nationalräkenskaper 1980–1994*, N 10 SM 9501, National Insurance Board (1996) and Annual Report from the occupational insurance schemes.

ing to different principles), and some are pay-as-you-go systems without any funding. The general development is shown in Table 8.8 (the funds in the firms belonging to the FPG/PRI scheme are not included). Of the total assets in the pension funds, the share belonging to the occupational pension schemes has gradually increased from 25 to close to 40 per cent. The total assets in the pension funds have increased more than the growth of the total economy – from c. 40 per cent of GDP to c. 60 per cent of GDP from 1980 to 1994 (the increase in the 1990s is partially explained by the drop in GDP caused by the recession).

4. The interrelation between the social insurance schemes and the occupational pension schemes

The presentation of the development of the pension schemes in section 2 indicates a close relationship in many instances between the development of the two systems. The influence goes in both directions between the first and the second pillars of the pension system.

The influence in the first decades of the twentieth century is mainly from the occupational pension schemes to the social insurance schemes. At the beginning of the century some groups (public sector employees, many white-collar workers in the private sector, some small groups of blue-collar workers in the private sector) already had occupational pensions. The national pension scheme founded in 1913 was a method of also giving other groups a pension at old age (most blue-collar workers in the private sector, the agricultural population), although low and to a large extent means-tested.

The national pension (in the 1930s and from 1948) gradually became less of a means-tested income support and more of an equal support for everyone in old age. The level of compensation also increased. The national old age pension after 1948 replaced social welfare as income support in old age for many of those who lacked or only had a low occupational pension. One factor behind this development of the national pension scheme was the existence of occupational pension schemes indicating a way of guaranteeing income support in old age.

In the late 1950s the national supplementary pension scheme, the ATP-scheme, was decided on in the *Riksdag* and came into force in 1960. One factor behind the development, also in this case, was the existence of occupational pension schemes. The blue-collar workers in the private sector (and many white-collar workers in lower positions, for example in the services sector) did not have occupational pensions and the LO and the Social Democratic Party saw it as an issue of equality to introduce a national supplementary pension scheme. The national schemes secure about 65 per cent income replacement for most people with an income below a certain ceiling. The compensation level was chosen with the replacement rate for public sector employees as a target.

The introduction of the national supplementary pension scheme influenced the design of the occupational pension schemes. The existing ones for blue-collar workers in the private sector were abolished – the compensation in most schemes was low and in most cases the pensions were only an employer guarantee which was dependent on the introduction of the national supplementary pension scheme. The occupational pension schemes in the other three major groups, however, continued but they were adjusted. For employees in the central and local government sectors the occupational pension schemes continued to guarantee the total pension level, higher in most cases than that of the ATP-scheme (the principle was changed in 1992 for the central government employees who had not retired yet). The occupational pension for the white-collar workers in the private sector, the ITP-scheme, was designed as an addition to the pension from the national schemes. In the early 1970s the blue-collar workers in the public sector also got an occupational pension as an addition to the pension from the national pension schemes.

The occupational pensions were not only additions to the old age pensions but also to the disability pensions and, for three of the four major bargaining areas, to the partial pensions when they were introduced in 1976. The occupational partial pension schemes compensated for losses in earnings over the ceiling (7.5 base amount before the reduction of working time).The replacement rate has been changed three times (from 65 to 50 to 65 to 55) and the replacement rate in the occupational pension schemes has been changed in the same way. When the maximum number of hours that are compensated was reduced in 1994 to 10, the corresponding change was made in the three occupational partial pension schemes.

Another example of an influence of a change in the national pension schemes on the occupational pension schemes is that when the possibility of disability pensioning for labour market reasons was discontinued from October 1991, LO and SAF reached an agreement on the introduction of a similar occupational pension scheme, TUFS, in 1993 (this scheme was abolished at least temporarily from 1996).

The influence has mainly been from the national to the occupational pension schemes since the introduction of the ATP-scheme in 1960. However, there are also examples of an influence from the occupational to the national pension schemes also in recent decades. The most obvious example is that the reduction of the retirement age in 1974 from 67 to 65 in the STP-scheme, an agreement between LO and SAF, was followed by a corresponding change of the retirement age from 67 to 65 in the national schemes from 1976. A driving force behind this change of the national retirement age was the Centre party (earlier called the Farmers party) which is widely supported among farmers, the major group with a retirement age of 67 after the agreement on a reduced retirement age for the blue-collar workers in 1974.

5. Some effects of the pension mix

The contractual insurances are of a considerable size and it is important to study their effects. The insurances can influence recruitment to the trade unions and also affect the stabilization, income distribution and resource allocation of the economy. Some of those effects will be dicussed briefly here.

One problem for trade unions, as for other interest organizations, is that the benefits from their activities do not only go to members but also to non-members. Wage rises that the unions have achieved are paid to non-union members as well. However, only members pay dues. This creates a 'free rider' problem. See e.g. Olson (1982). Therefore in addition to the general demands for wage increases and better employment conditions, they also have an incentive to push for measures which are more directly aimed at the members. These can be social insurances designed as member insurances or support to members when differences arise with the employer, for example about dismissals or promotion.

In a study of the development of union density in Denmark during the inter-war period, Pedersen (1982) has shown that the proceeds and costs of belonging to the union-connected unemployment benefit societies are important in explaining the variations of union density during this period.

Neuman and Rissman (1984) have studied the development of union density in the US in the last decades. Their results indicate that the state's expenses for social policy and the introduction of laws which strengthen the rights of employees can be factors behind the decline of union density in the US.

In Sweden there was a corresponding unrest within the trade unions in the 1960s. More and more of the unions' member-directed measures had been replaced by social insurances and it was considered only a matter of time before the union unemployment benefit insurance would be replaced by an obligatory national one.

The contractual insurances were thus something which could entice new members. It must be remembered that it was a question of contractual insurances not member insurances, but the benefits could still be directly connected to the organizations. Many members wanted extended social insurances and the contractual insurances are favoured tax-wise.

Union density in Sweden has also continued to rise from its previous very high level. However, perhaps there are more significant factors behind this development. Unemployment insurance has not been nationalized yet; it is still connected to the unions and the subsidization rate has increased greatly. Another factor is labour market legislation. When employment security was regulated by law in the middle of the 1970s, the Employment Protection Act was designed so that it was the

301

union and not the employee who took part in legal proceedings with the employer. This increased the importance of being a member of a union, as opposed to the situation in the US where labour market legislation has diminished the role of the union in conflicts.

The national social pension schemes are constructed such that they are redistributing. See Ståhlberg (1986). This redistribution goes to those with low incomes, amongst whom are those who have never had permanent employment. The occupational pension schemes on the other hand are constructed in another way. A large portion of the pensions are paid out to those with earnings over the ceiling in the national pension schemes. It means that the occupational pension schemes redistribute in favour of those with higher earnings (the exception is the scheme for blue-collar workers in the private sector). An alternative interpretation is different levels of fringe benefits according to the level of earnings. The redistribution of the occupational pension schemes means that the total scheme is more or less non-redistributing in any direction.

There are also elements of redistribution caused by the occupational insurances. Partly, there was a general subsidization of contractual insurances, and to some extent there occurs an (anticipated) redistribution between the unions. The risks of layoffs, illness, early retirements caused by disability, and work injury vary between unions. Redistribution via three contractual insurances – AGB, AGS and TFA according to union – have been calculated by Edebalk and Wadensjö (1989) for the period after the emergence of AGS and TFA and for AGB since 1980. These sums have been weighed with the relative size of the employer fees for the three insurances for 1985. Union wage data for 1980–85 have been used to calculate fees paid in. Certain smaller unions without comparable wage statistics have not been included in these calculations. The members of these unions amount to c. 5 per cent of those in LO who are covered by contractual insurances. The redistribution accounts for 8 per cent of the amounts paid out from the three insurances.

The tax subsidy to the contractual insurances was larger than the redistribution between unions. This subsidy was about three times as great as the redistribution between unions. This means that almost all unions received a net subsidy via the contractual insurances. With the tax reform of the early 1990s the subsidization has sharply declined.

The evolution of the national supplementary pension scheme has been much debated both before and after its inception. The occupational pension schemes on the other hand have been absent from the public debate even though they also cover almost everyone.[20] One explanation for this may be that the financial situation up to now has been rather uncomplicated. There are indications, however, that costs may increase considerably in the next decades and that financial problems may arise. Two of the factors leading to higher costs are related to demographic developments, two to prospective changes and lack of changes in the national supplementary pension scheme.

6.   The future development of the occupational pensions

The situation of the occupational pension schemes will probably be relatively uncomplicated for the rest of this decade. There may even be an argument for a strengthening of their role in the economy relative to that of the social insurance schemes. However, it is easy to see that from the beginning of the new century the financial problems will gradually increase for the occupational pension schemes just as they would have done for the national supplementary pension schemes if this system had not been changed. The problem will most likely be most serious for the pension scheme of the municipalities and counties. The pension costs of local government will increase faster than before at the same time as the costs for health care and services for old people will increase.

The reasons for the increasing problems of the occupational pension schemes are:

1) Changes in the female labour market participation may lead to consequences for the occupational pension schemes. As mentioned earlier, short part-time work does not lead to a qualifying year in the pension schemes (30 years are needed to get a full pension). However, persons with short-time work pay the payroll levy in most schemes. (The exception is the ITP-scheme; in the local government scheme there is not any payroll fee but an implicit one could be calculated). Related to this is that an occupational pension is only granted if a person works up to retirement. The annuity granted if leaving before retirement is lower (not always fully indexed).

---

[20] Exceptions are SOU 1990:76, Chapter 4:4, and studies published by the two organizations of local government: see Svenska Kommunförbundet & Landstingsförbundet (1992) and Björnstad and Kruse (1994).

Earlier, many women left the labour force before reaching retirement age after working for shorter and longer periods. They contributed to the financing of the pension schemes but they did not receive corresponding compensation. The female labour force participation is now becoming more and more similar to that of men. Almost everyone of active age is in the labour force, both men and women, and few work short part-time. This means that the costs of the pension schemes will increase. This will influence all pension schemes, but mostly that for those employed by local government as the proportion of female workers is much higher in that sector.

2) Another demographic factor influencing the revenues and expenditures of the pension schemes is the age distribution of the population. Changes in it mean that changes have to be made in the payroll levies. The size of the age cohorts varies greatly. The largest cohort is the group who were born in the 1940s – the baby-boom years. Most of them will begin to receive their old age pension between 2005 and 2015 according to the present regulations. The total costs of the pensions to be paid will be much higher when those born in the 1940s have retired and the number of those of active age who will pay fees will be fewer. Also here there are differences between the sectors. The sector with the highest share from the baby-boom cohorts is the local government sector. This sector expanded rapidly in the 1960s and the 1970s when those cohorts entered the labour market.

3) For many, the occupational pension scheme only provides an addition of about 10 per cent of the earlier income level to the pension from the two national schemes. For some persons the addition is much more substantial. Firstly and most important, three of the occupational pension schemes also cover earnings higher than 7.5 base amount, and the replacement rate for those parts of the earnings are much higher. Secondly, the pension level in the occupational pension schemes is based on the years immediately before retirement – not the 15 best years as in the national supplementary pension scheme. For those people where this makes a difference, the occupational pension scheme covers the difference (also here the STP-scheme differs). This is of most importance for those with a steep wage profile. Increasing real wages mean that more and more people get higher earnings than 7.5 base amounts. This together with a tendency to steeper wage profiles means that the costs for the pension schemes increase.

Table 8.9 – Total costs for payments of old age pension (billion SEK)

Year	Central government	Local government	ITP	STP
1989	2.7	1.6	3.7	2.5
1990	2.6	1.7	3.8	2.6
2000	1.8	2.2	5.4	3.1
2010	2.2	3.1	8.4	4.5
2020	3.5	4.2	12.4	6.7
2030	5.2	4.9	15.4	8.5

Source: SOU 1990:86, p. 126.

However, one part of the costs for the occupational old age pensions will decline. In 1990 35 per cent of all employees in the central government sector and 65 per cent of all employees in the local government sector had such a pension age. There has been a tendency in collective agreements to increase the age of retirement so that everyone, regardless of employment sector, would retire at the age of 65. This means that the costs for the pensions for those who retire earlier than 65 years of age will diminish.

A governmental committee presented a calculation in 1990 showing how the pension costs will develop in the next decades. See Table 8.9. The figures show that the costs increase rapidly, especially for the ITP-scheme. The reason for that is that the earnings of many people in the years before retirement are going to exceed the 7.5 base amount limit. The calculations build on simplifying assumptions (no part-time work, constant wage relations, etc.), and the costs of the old age pensions paid before the age of 65 are not included. The increases in the costs are probably greatly underestimated. Later calculations made by the insurance company of the local governments show that the cost in 2020 will be 15–20 billion SEK, not 4.2 billion SEK as estimated by the governmental committee. Note that the pension scheme for the blue-collar workers, the STP-scheme, has been changed.

The higher increase of costs in the ITP-scheme compared to the other schemes does not necessarily mean more financial problems. The ITP-scheme is, as mentioned, a premium reserve system and levies have continuously been paid to cover future costs. The problems may be greater for the pay-as-you-go schemes which have no funding of their liabilities (there is only a small fund for minor groups in the local

Table 8.10 – The situation of the pension schemes in 1992

Scheme	Number of persons concerned (millions)	Paid pension per year (billions)	Funds (billions)	Calculated debt (billions)
ITP	0.6	6.6	150	120
STP	1.0	3.0	90	180
Central gov.	0.4	7.0	0	80
Local gov.	1.2	3.9	2	120

Source: Svenska kommunförbundet & Landstingsförbundet (1992), p. 13.

government scheme). In Table 8.10 the financial situation in the early 1990s is presented.

The problems most likely will be small for the central government pension scheme. The increase in pension costs is smaller and happens later than in the other schemes, the costs are pooled between the different authorities and there is a well established system for financing the pensions – a proportional payroll fee. The problems will most likely be more severe for the local government pension scheme. The cost increase is higher, every local government pays its own costs, and there is no special financial system – it is just an item among others in the budget. The present changes in the social insurance system will also lead to problems if the pension scheme for local government employees is not changed. The pension scheme guarantees the total level and if the compensation from the social insurance system decreases the local government system has to cover the reduction.

References

Annual reports from the occupational pension schemes.

Björnstad, Sverre and Kruse, Agneta (1994), *Den kommunala pensionsskulden. - Metoder, redovisning, effekter,* Stockholm: KPA.

Classon, Sigvard (1988), *Kampen för tryggheten,* Stockholm: LO.

Ds 1993:93, *De äldres ekonomiska standard 1993.*

Ds 1995:29, *Vissa frågor angående allmänna egenavgifter.*

Ds 1995:41, *Reformerat pensionssystem – lag om inkomstgraderad ålderspension, m m.*

Ds 1995:46, *Kommunala avtalspensioner.*

Edebalk, Per-Gunnar and Wadensjö, Eskil (1988), 'Contractually Determined

Insurance Schemes for Manual Workers', in Bo Gustafsson and Anders Klevmarken (eds.), *The Political Economy of Social Security,* Amsterdam: North Holland.

Edebalk, Per-Gunnar and Wadensjö, Eskil (1989), *Arbetsmarknadsförsäkringar,* Ds 1989:68.

Edebalk, Per-Gunnar; Ståhlberg, Ann-Charlotte and Wadensjö, Eskil (1996), 'Avtalsrelaterade trygghetssystem vid sjukdom, arbetsskada och förtidspension', in SOU 1996:113, *En allmän och aktiv försäkring vid sjukdom och rehabilitering.* Del 2 Bilagor.

Framtidens pensioner – ett samrådsmaterial (1996), Linköping: Socialdemokraterna.

ILO (1984), *Into the Twenty-first Century: The Development of Social Security,* Geneva: ILO.

Jansson, Kjell (1994),'Fler pensionssparar – med lägre belopp', *Välfärdsbulletinen,* No. 2, 4–6.

Kangas, Olli and Palme, Joakim (1989), 'Public and Private Pensions. The Scandinavian Countries in a Comparative Perspective', *Swedish Institute for Social Research,* Meddelande 3/1989.

Kangas, Olli and Palme, Joakim (1992), 'Class-Politics and Institutional Feedbacks: Development of Occupational Pensions in Finland and Sweden', *Swedish Institute for Social Research,* Meddelande 3/1992.

Kruse, Agneta (1990), 'Demographic Structure and Labor Supply in a Pay-as-you-go Pension System', in Hans Carlsson and Bo Larsson (eds.), *Problems of the Mixed Economy: Cooperation, Efficiency, and Stability,* Amsterdam: North-Holland.

Kruse, Agneta and Söderström, Lars (1989), 'Early Retirement in Sweden', in Winfried Schmähl (ed.), *Redefining the Process of Retirement. An International Perspective,* Berlin: Springer-Verlag.

Molin, Björn (1965), *Tjänstepensionsfrågan. En studie i svensk partipolitik,* Göteborg: Akademiförlaget.

National Social Insurance Board (1996), *Statistikinformation* Is-I 1996:11.

Neuman, George R. and Rissman, Ellen R. (1984), 'Where Have All the Union Members Gone?', *Journal of Labor Economics,* Vol. 2, April.

Olson, Mancur (1982), *The Rise and Decline of Nations,* New Haven: Yale University Press.

Olsson, Lars (1996), 'I takt med tiden – arbetet, åldrande och pensionering', in Gunnar Aronsson and Åsa Kilbom (eds.), *Arbete efter 45,* Stockholm: Arbetslivsinstitutet.

Pedersen, Peder (1982), 'Union Growth in Denmark 1911–1939', *Scandinavian Journal of Economics,* Vol. 84, No. 4.

Proposition 1994/95:41, *Om förändringar i finansieringen av det allmänna pensionssystemet.*

Proposition 1994/95:150, *Reviderad finansplan m m.*

Proposition 1994/95: 250, *Reformering av det allmänna pensionssystemet.*

SAF (1954), *Betänkande av Svenska Arbetsgivareföreningens pensionskommitté,* Stockholm: SAF.

Schmidt, Folke (1974), *Allmänna och privata pensioner,* Stockholm: P.A. Norstedt & Söners förlag.

Sjuk- och arbetsskadekommittén (1995), 'Det kompletterande skyddet genom kollektivavtal', PM nr 37.

SOU 1938:18, *Betänkande med förslag till lag om frivillig pensionering av i enskild tjänst anställda m m.*

SOU 1946:26, *Tjänstepensionsförsäkringens organisation.* Bilaga B. 'PM angående de kommunala pensionerna'.

SOU 1950:33, *Allmän pensionsförsäkring.* Undersökning och förslag av pensionsutredningen.

SOU 1975:84, *Ersättning vid arbetsskada.* Betänkande av yrkeskadeförsäkringskommittén.

SOU 1990:76, *Allmän pension.*

SOU 1990:77, *Allmän pension.* Bilagor.

SOU 1994:20, *Reformerat pensionssystem.*

SOU 1995:9, *Fullt ekonomiskt arbetsgivaransvar.*

SOU 1996:83, *Allmänt pensionssparande.* Delbetänkande från Premiereservutredningen.

SOU 1996:113, *En allmän och aktiv försäkring vid sjukdom och rehabilitering.* Del 1. Slutbetänkande.

Ståhlberg, Ann-Charlotte (1986), 'Social Welfare Policy – Nothing but Insurances?', Institutet för social forskning. Meddelande 5/1986.

Ståhlberg, Ann-Charlotte (1995), 'Pension Reform in Sweden', *Scandinavian Journal of Social Welfare*, Vol. 4, 267–73.

Statistiska Meddelanden, Finansräkenskaper 1994, K11.

Statistiska Meddelanden, Inkomster och bidrag 1993, Be20 SM9502.

Statistiska Meddelanden, Inkomster och bidrag 1994, Be20 SM9602.

Statistiska Meddelanden, Inkomster och skatter 1994, Be20 SM9601.

Statistiska Meddelanden, Inkomstfördelningsstudien 1993, Be21 SM9501.

Svenska kommunförbundet & Landstingsförbundet (1992), 'Arbetsmaterial om avtalspensioner i kommuner och landsting', Stockholm: Svenska kommunförbundet & Landstingsförbundet, June.

Wadensjö, Eskil (1984), 'Disability Policy in Sweden', in Robert Haveman, Victor Halberstadt and Richard Burkhauser, *Public Policy Towards Disabled Workers*, Ithaca: Cornell University Press.

Wadensjö, Eskil (1990), 'Ekonomiska aspekter på avtalspensionerna' in SOU 1990:77, *Allmän pension.* Bilagor.

Wadensjö, Eskil (1991), 'Sweden: Partial Exit', in Martin Kohli et al. (eds.), *Time for Retirement: Comparative Studies of Early Exit from the Labor Force*, Cambridge: Cambridge University Press.

Wadensjö, Eskil (1996), 'Gradual Retirement in Sweden', in Lei Delsen and Geneviève Reday-Mulvey (eds.), *Gradual Retirement in the OECD-countries*, Aldershot: Dartmouth.

9

The British Case

Tony Lynes

Old age insurance in Great Britain comprises a state pension scheme covering virtually the whole population, occupational pension schemes which usually cover the employees of a single employer, and so-called 'personal pension schemes' through which individual employees and self-employed people can accumulate funds to purchase an annuity at retirement age. The state scheme provides, in effect, two pensions, one flat-rate and the other earnings-related, both payable to men at the age of 65 and to women at 60. Nearly all social insurance contributors, employed or self-employed, qualify for the basic flat-rate pension, but entitlement to the state earnings-related pension is restricted in a number of ways. Since it is based on contributions paid by employees from 1978 onwards, both the self-employed and those ex-employees who had retired before the scheme commenced are excluded, while those who retired in the first few years after 1978 receive only small additions to the basic pension. Moreover, an employer or an individual employee may contract out of the earnings-related pension, contributing to an occupational or personal pension scheme instead. The proportion of employees contracted out has risen rapidly and by 1992–93 only about 6.5 million out of some 22 million eligible employees were actually covered by the state earnings-related pension scheme (generally known by its unappealing acronym 'SERPS') (Department of Social Security 1996, p. 12).[1]

Occupational and personal pension schemes in Britain, therefore, operate to a large extent as a substitute for, rather than an addition to, the state scheme. They may, however, and in the case of occupational schemes generally do, provide more than the amount of pension for-

---

[1] As explained more fully below, an employee who is contracted out retains a residual entitlement to the state earnings-related pension.

gone in the state scheme. Moreover, it is open to either an employer or an individual employee to make additional contributions to an occupational or personal pension scheme, whether contracted out or not. For self-employed people, who are not covered by SERPS or by occupational schemes, voluntary contributions to a personal pension scheme, encouraged by tax relief, are an important means of supplementing the flat-rate state pension. The likely effect of current government policies in this field is that employees, too, will become increasingly dependent on voluntary savings and investment schemes to supplement the pensions provided under the existing legislation.

Pensioners whose total income from pensions and other sources is below a minimum level are entitled to means-tested benefits from central and local government departments. The first national minimum income for the elderly was introduced in 1940. It has been renamed several times and is now known as 'income support', providing minimum incomes not only for pensioners but for people under pension age who are not in full-time work. By 1970, nearly one in five recipients of the state pension were receiving income support (known at that time as 'supplementary pensions'). By 1993, following the introduction of a separate means-tested housing benefit, the proportion of retirement pensioners receiving income support, housing benefit or both was nearly one in four (House of Commons 1995a, columns *201–4*). For more than half a century, therefore, a substantial proportion of pensioners have been dependent on means-tested payments to provide them with a minimally adequate income. Many others survived on incomes below the minimum to which they were entitled: it is estimated that, in 1992, between 480 000 and 860 000 people aged 60 and over failed to claim income support, leaving unclaimed up to 30 per cent of the money available to them from this source (House of Commons 1995b, columns *105–6*).

1. The flat-rate basic pension

The post-war social insurance arrangements were enacted in 1946 and commenced in 1948. They were based broadly on the recommendations of the 1942 Beveridge Report for a system of flat-rate benefits, adequate for subsistence, covering a wide range of contingencies including widowhood, sickness and unemployment as well as old age, and financed by flat-rate contributions (Beveridge 1942). The importance attached by the post-war Labour government to raising the living standards of pensioners led to the rejection of Beveridge's recommendation that pension rates should be raised gradually over a period of 20 years. The increase in the pre-war 'old age pension' from £0.50 per person per week to £1.30 for a single person and £2.10 for a man with a dependent wife took place in 1946, preceding by nearly two years the comprehensive insurance scheme.

Despite these increases, the flat-rate pension remained inadequate for pensioners with no other income, leading to the long-term dependence on means-tested supplements noted above. Moreover, the 1946 National Insurance Act made no provision for further increases in benefit rates, other than a requirement to review them every five years. The pension rates introduced in October 1946 were to remain unchanged until September 1951, by which time prices had risen by about 28 per cent.

By the mid 1950s, concern was growing about the financial stability of the national insurance scheme. The number of elderly people was rising and the number receiving pensions was due to increase by about 8 per cent on a single day in July 1958, when people not insured prior to 1948 became entitled. Flat-rate contributions, necessarily limited to what the lowest-paid workers could afford, no longer seemed an adequate basis for financing social insurance. Both the Labour Party, then in opposition, and the Conservative government published proposals to increase contribution income by levying earnings-related contributions, either in addition to or in substitution for the existing flat-rate contributions. There were, however, fundamental differences between the two sets of proposals. The choice between them was one of the issues in the general election of 1959, which was to keep the Conservatives in power for another five years. The fundamental disagreement between the parties concerned the role of the state in pension provision. The Labour party believed that for large sections of the population only the state could provide adequate pensions, and was ideologically disposed to act on that belief. The Conservative party believed, on the contrary, that the provision of pensions above a flat-rate minimum was essentially a task for the private sector and, in particular, for occupational pension schemes established voluntarily by employers.

2. Earnings-related state pensions

2.1 Labour's national superannuation plan

The Labour Party's proposals for a 'national superannuation' scheme were published in 1957 (Labour Party 1957). Their main emphasis was on the need to make pensions more adequate, beginning with a substantial increase in the flat-rate pension. For the longer term, an additional earnings-related pension was proposed, providing the average male employee with a total pension of about half his pre-retirement earnings. The scheme was presented as a means of reducing inequalities between the 'privileged minority' of members of occupational pension schemes (commonly known as superannuation schemes; hence the proposal to call the new state scheme 'national superannuation') and the 'unprivileged majority' dependent wholly or mainly on state pensions.

A British occupational pension scheme usually covers defined categories of employees of a single employer. The number of separate schemes is therefore very large: the estimated number in the private employment sector in 1956 was between 35 000 and 40 000 schemes, with wide variations in the categories of employees covered and in the size and shape of the benefits provided. With about one-third of all employees covered by occupational schemes, there could be no question of compulsorily replacing them with a single national superannuation scheme. The Labour Party's proposal was that members of approved occupational schemes should be excluded from the earnings-related state pension unless they chose on an individual basis to 'contract in'. Thus was born the concept of *contracting out*, which was to play a crucial part in the developing relationship between state and occupational pensions.

The suggested conditions for approval of an occupational scheme included the requirement that both benefits and contributions 'should not compare unfavourably with those in the National Scheme'. The authors of the national scheme, however, drew their inspiration not from existing occupational schemes in Britain but from state pension schemes in other countries of Western Europe (Ellis 1989, p. 8). Radical changes would have been needed in most occupational schemes, especially in the private sector, to enable them to satisfy the condition of comparability. In particular, while nearly three out of four of the 3.8 million public sector employees covered by occupational schemes in 1956 were in schemes in which the pension was a proportion of earnings and, with some modifications, might have satisfied the contracting out conditions, in the private sector less than one in four scheme members were in schemes with pension formulas of this kind (Government Actuary 1958). Moreover, few private sector schemes offered any guarantee of pension increases to take account of inflation after retirement, an important element in the Labour party's proposals. The practical implications of contracting out were, therefore, highly problematic and any attempt to introduce the national superannuation scheme at that time would have encountered serious problems (Lynes 1963, pp. 28–9). The subsequent history of contracting out was to reflect the conflicting aims of, on the one hand, encouraging the growth or, at least, minimizing the disruption of occupational schemes and, on the other hand, protecting the interests of employees who either chose or were obliged to depend on those schemes as an alternative to the state scheme. The conflict has still not been fully resolved.

2.2 The 1961–75 graduated pension scheme

In the following year, 1958, the rival Conservative scheme was published (Ministry of Pensions and National Insurance 1958). Its stated aims were:

1) To place the National Insurance scheme on a sound financial basis.

2) To institute provision for employed persons who cannot be covered by an appropriate occupational scheme to obtain some measure of pension related to their earnings.

3) To preserve and encourage the best development of occupational pension schemes.

In contrast to the Labour proposals, the main emphasis was on restoring the financial equilibrium of the state scheme. The additional graduated (earnings-related) pension was, therefore, to be extremely modest, ensuring that most employers who wished to contract out (the decision was to be made by the employer, not by the individual employee) would be able to do so. Far from encouraging the best development of occupational pension schemes, both the graduated pension scheme itself and the contracting out conditions were designed to enable existing occupational schemes, often of extremely poor quality and wholly unprotected from inflation, to remain in existence. A man paying the maximum contribution to the state scheme throughout his working life was to receive an additional pension of £2.05 per week (the flat-rate basic pension was then £4 per week), while a woman drawing her pension at 60 would get at most an addition of £1.55; but these amounts were fixed in advance, in cash terms, with no provision for adjusting them in line with the cost of living or average earnings, either during working life or after retirement. Graduated pension rights earned by employees in their twenties or thirties, therefore, were likely to be almost valueless at retirement age. Contracted out schemes, similarly, were to be allowed to offer pensions entirely unrelated to the levels of prices or earnings on retirement.

As a result of the Conservatives' 1959 election victory, the graduated pension scheme commenced in 1961, remaining in force until 1975 when it was discontinued by the 1974 Labour government. At that point it was decided that preserved graduated pension rights should be inflation-proofed from then on. Employees who had been contracted out did not benefit from this change, but the sums involved were so small that the injustice aroused little concern. The contribution made by the 1961–75 scheme to pensioners' incomes, now or in the future, is negligible: more than half the 7.5 million graduated pensions in payment in September 1993 were of less than £2 a week (Department of Social Security 1994, p. 136) (the basic pension was then £56.10).

2.3   The 1975 Pensions Act: SERPS

Despite the obvious inadequacies of the graduated pension scheme and unsuccessful attempts by both Labour and Conservative governments to replace it (Ellis 1989, pp. 23–45), a major reform of state pensions did not take place until the introduction of the state earnings-related pension scheme (SERPS) in 1978. The Labour government had inherited the previous Conservative government's Social Security Act of 1973, which had not yet been implemented and whose purpose was to confirm occupational schemes as the main providers of earnings-related pensions, the role of the state being confined as far as possible to providing the flat-rate basic pension. As in the 1961 graduated scheme, the aim was not to raise the standards of occupational schemes (except in one respect, referred to below in section 4.3) but to enable as many employers as possible to contract out. The Labour party, on the other hand, still favoured a system of state pensions which, while not overtly discouraging occupational pension schemes, would avoid many of their defects and would itself be adequate for those with no other source of retirement income. The government decided, therefore, not to implement the pension provisions of the 1973 Act, which were replaced by SERPS under the Social Security Pensions Act 1975 (Ellis 1989, pp. 46–7). The 1975 Act embodied a new approach (explained below) to the problem of allowing contracting out without compromising the standards of the state scheme. To avoid any suggestion that the government was hostile to occupational schemes, the reduction in state scheme contributions for contracted out employees was deliberately set slightly above the estimated cost of the benefits which the occupational schemes were required to provide.

The SERPS pension was to be a proportion of the individual's earnings between the lower and upper limits of, in 1975 terms, £10 and £70 per week, the lower limit being the amount of the basic pension while the upper limit was about 1.5 times average male earnings. The intention was that these limits, as well as the flat-rate pension, would rise annually in line with average earnings. At pension age, each year's earnings were to be revalued in line with the rise in average earnings, and the pension was to be based on the individual's best 20 years of revalued earnings, at the rate of 1.25 per cent of each year's relevant earnings. Thus, after paying into the scheme for 20 years or more, a person would receive an annual pension of roughly 25 per cent (20x1.25 per cent) of his or her earnings, in addition to the basic pension. This formula did not quite measure up to the Labour Party's 1957 slogan of 'half pay in retirement' but, for single people in the middle range of earnings, it offered a combined pension of between a third and a half of pre-retirement earnings. Widows were to inherit the whole of their husbands' earnings-related pension as an addition to their own, subject to a maximum, and the scheme also provided invalidity pensions.

The effect of the complex contracting out provisions of the 1975 Act was that all employees with earnings above the lower limit were to benefit from SERPS to a greater or lesser extent, the state retaining an important residual responsibility for the earnings-related pensions of contracted out employees. This made it possible to introduce the new scheme without requiring occupational schemes to match its benefits in all respects.

To contract out, a scheme had to satisfy two main conditions. The first amounted to a broad definition of a 'good' occupational pension scheme: it must provide an earnings-related pension, accruing at an annual rate of at least 1.25 per cent of pensionable earnings – the 'requisite benefits' condition. The earnings used as a basis for calculating the pension could be either those of the period preceding pension age or the person's average earnings over the whole period of membership of the occupational scheme; but in the latter case, each year's earnings were to be revalued, as in the state scheme, to take account of increases in average earnings (the significance of the choice of methods is explained below).

The second condition was designed to limit the demands placed on occupational schemes to what they could realistically be expected to provide. Each member of a contracted out scheme was to receive from it a 'guaranteed minimum pension' (GMP), similar but not identical to the full SERPS pension, the main differences being, first, that the GMP was to be calculated year by year and would not take into account the 'best 20 years' rule and, secondly, that the GMP calculated at pension age would not be indexed thereafter but would remain payable at the same rate, regardless of subsequent increases in prices or average earnings. In other respects, too, contracted out schemes were not obliged fully to match the state scheme's benefits. For widows, they had to provide a pension of only half the pension based on the husband's contributions, leaving the other half to be provided by the state scheme; and they were not required to provide invalidity pensions, which would also remain the responsibility of the state.

To protect the rights of contracted out employees, the state pension was to be calculated in two stages. First, the pension (including any post-retirement increases) was to be calculated as if the person had never been contracted out. Then, the GMP to be provided by the occupational scheme was deducted. Thus, the pensioner and/or his widow would receive from the two schemes, as a minimum, approximately the same amount of pension as the state scheme alone would have provided. In most cases, the occupational pension would be more than the GMP, and the total pension would therefore be more than the pensioner would have obtained from the state scheme alone.

3. Cutting back state pensions

It was at first generally believed that SERPS, with its contracting out provisions designed to enable the continuation and growth of good occupational schemes, had provided the basis for a lasting 'pensions consensus'. Even when the Conservatives again returned to power in 1979, it seemed that the established pattern of incoming administrations overturning the pension plans of their predecessors was not to be repeated. This, however, was the point at which concern about demographic trends became a dominant factor in social security planning. Moreover, the Thatcher government was even more strongly committed than previous Conservative administrations to the transfer of functions from the public to the private sector, to containing or reducing public expenditure and to making British industry more competitive by reducing employers' costs. As a result, between 1980 and 1995, a series of steps were taken aimed at reducing the level of pensions promised by the state, while widening the coverage but reducing the average cost of occupational and personal pensions by encouraging the growth of defined-contribution schemes.

The main change affecting the basic pension was enacted in 1980. Over the whole post-war period, its value had risen broadly in line with average earnings, at first on an ad hoc basis but, since 1974, as a legal requirement (under severe pressure to restrain public expenditure, the Labour government had circumvented the requirement in one year, 1977). In 1980 the link with average earnings was repealed and, since then, the basic pension has been tied to the index of retail prices. As a result, between 1979 and 1994, the basic pension for a single person, as a proportion of average earnings, fell from 23.2 per cent to 17.5 per cent (Bradshaw and Lynes 1995, p. 10). By the year 2050, if average earnings rise in real terms by 1.5 per cent per annum and the basic pension continues to rise in line with prices, it will be about 7 per cent of average men's earnings and 9 per cent of average women's earnings (Government Actuary 1995, p. 7). The idea of a basic pension sufficient to meet the minimum needs of elderly people has been abandoned. While a change of government might prevent the process from being taken further, the cost of restoring the 1979 relationship between the basic pension and average earnings would be far too great to contemplate in the foreseeable future. Present indications (in June 1996) are that a new Labour government would not even reintroduce the automatic link with average earnings for future pension increases.

The main cuts in SERPS were made by the Social Security Act 1986. A 'green paper' published by the government in 1985 (*Reform of Social Security* 1985, Vol. 1) had proposed that SERPS should be abolished. From the end of the century, contributions of at least 4 per cent of earnings would have to be made to an occupational or 'personal' pension scheme in respect of each employee, at least half being paid by the employer. The most striking innovation, compared with the existing contracting out provisions, was that the compulsory second tier would consist to a large extent of 'money purchase' (defined-contribution) schemes. It was envisaged that all personal pension schemes and most new occupational schemes would be of this type. The availability of personal pension schemes for those not covered by occupational schemes would, it was believed, remove the need for the state to provide earnings-related pensions.

There was little support for this proposal, even from the insurance companies which stood to gain from selling occupational and personal pension schemes to a captive market. The prospect of organizing pension schemes for millions of low-paid and mobile workers was not attractive. From the point of view of the Treasury, abolishing SERPS would greatly reduce expenditure but only in the long term. Meanwhile, to cover the cost of pensions already in payment, contributions to the state scheme would have to be redistributed, with those previously contracted out losing their contribution rebate and gaining nothing in return.

When the government's firm proposals (*Reform of Social Security: Programme for Action* 1985) were published at the end of 1985, therefore, they included the continuation of SERPS, but with drastic cuts for those reaching pension age after the end of the century. The cuts included the reduction of the earnings-related pension from 25 to 20 per cent of earnings and the abolition of the 'best 20 years' rule, so that the pension would be based on earnings over a person's whole working life (non-earning years due to child-rearing or sickness were to be excluded). Widows were to suffer the biggest cuts, since, in addition to the reduction in the pension earned by their own contributions, they would in future inherit only half their husbands' SERPS pension instead of the whole of it.

A report (Government Actuary 1986), accompanying the government's proposals, showed the very substantial effect on the cost of retirement pensions and other contributory benefits, taking into account not only the changes then proposed but also the policy already adopted of tying the basic pension to an index of prices rather than earnings. The separate and combined effects over the period from 1986–87 to 2053–54, for retirement pensions only (the effects on survivors' and invalidity benefits were roughly similar), are shown in Table 9.1. The table does not show the savings that had already resulted from the price-indexation of the basic pension between 1980 and 1986. What it does

Table 9.1 – 1986 estimates of cost of retirement pensions (£ billion at November 1985 prices)

Year	Basic pension		SERPS		Total	
	(a) With earnings uprating	*(b)* With prices uprating	*(c)* Existing	*(d)* Proposed	*(a)+(c)*	*(b)+(d)*
1993–94	19.4	17.4	1.1	1.1	20.5	18.5
2003–04	22.5	17.4	4.3	4.2	26.8	21.6
2013–14	28.8	19.2	10.1	7.5	38.9	26.7
2023–24	37.0	21.2	16.9	10.3	53.9	31.5
2033–34	47.2	23.4	25.5	13.2	72.7	36.6
2043–44	50.9	21.7	29.0	13.6	79.9	35.3
2053–54	55.9	20.5	32.3	14.6	88.2	35.1

Notes:
1. Earnings are assumed to rise 1.5 per cent p.a. more than prices.
2. Half a million additional persons are assumed to be contracted out of SERPS (an increase from 9.75 million to 10.25 million).

Source: Government Actuary 1986, pp. 10–11.

show is that future price-indexation and the 1986 cuts in SERPS were expected to halve the total cost of retirement pensions by about 2035, compared with what it would otherwise have been (only a small part of the expected saving was a result of the assumed increase in the numbers contracted out).

Despite the cuts, the figures show the total cost of state pensions nearly doubling between 1993–94 and 2033–34, a period over which the number of contributors per pensioner was expected to fall substantially. Taking into account the assumed increase in average earnings, however, the burden on contributors would have been much smaller than these figures suggest. A table in the same report showed the national insurance contribution rates for employed persons (including the employer's contribution) corresponding to the benefit costs in Table 9.1. The figures, reproduced in Table 9.2, represent the contributions required to cover the cost of all social insurance benefits, not just retirement pensions. The corresponding contribution rate for 1986–87, based on similar assumptions as to unemployment etc., would have been 15.7 per cent. Tying the basic pension to prices rather than earnings

Table 9.2 – 1986 estimates of contribution rates for employees not contracted out (percentage of earnings)

Year	Existing scheme		Proposed scheme	
	With earnings uprating	With prices uprating	With earnings uprating	With prices uprating
1993–94	15.8	14.5	15.9	14.6
2003–04	17.0	14.3	17.0	14.1
2013–14	20.0	15.4	18.9	14.3
2023–24	23.4	16.8	20.9	14.4
2033–34	27.3	18.5	23.2	14.5
2043–44	25.3	16.5	21.0	12.2
2053–54	24.2	15.0	20.0	10.8

Source: Government Actuary 1986, p. 14.

would, alone, have resulted in the contribution rate peaking at 18.5 per cent in the 2030s and falling to 15 per cent by 2053–54. With the SERPS cuts added to the savings on the basic pension, contribution rates were expected to be lower at the height of the expected demographic crisis than in the 1980s and would then fall steeply.

The biggest change brought about by the 1986 Act was the addition of defined-contribution or 'money purchase' schemes to the types of schemes allowed to contract out and, in particular, the introduction of an option for individual employees to arrange their own 'personal' pension schemes on a money purchase basis through insurance companies and other financial institutions. Since the amount of pension produced by such schemes is unpredictable, they could not be required to guarantee a minimum pension: instead, they were to receive a minimum contribution, equivalent to the 'contracted out rebate' (the reduction in social security contributions for contracted out employees). As an initial boost, they received from the National Insurance Fund an additional 'incentive payment' of 2 per cent of the employee's relevant earnings. This was originally intended to continue for five years, but the government decided to allow personal pension schemes to be backdated to April 1987, thus extending the incentive payments to six years. A similar incentive was given for newly contracted out occupational schemes, whether of the money purchase type or not. The unexpectedly dramatic results are described below.

Another package of economy measures was enacted in 1995. The most important of these were the raising of the age at which women qualify for a state pension from 60 to 65, thus equalizing pension ages for men and women, and the termination of the arrangements described above by which the state scheme was to retain part of the liability for the pensions of contracted out employees. The change in women's pension age will take place over a ten-year period, between 2010 and 2020.

In the light of the figures in Tables 9.1 and 9.2, it may seem surprising that further reductions in the cost of state pensions were considered necessary. The Conservative government, however, remained strongly committed to reducing both public expenditure and taxation (social insurance contributions, unlike contributions to occupational and personal pension schemes, are regarded as a form of taxation). There had, moreover, been major changes in the demographic forecasts since 1986. The 1986 report from which the figures in Tables 9.1 and 9.2 are taken showed the number of recipients of the basic state pension in Great Britain rising from 9.8 million in 1993–94 to 13.4 million in 2033–34, then falling to 11.9 million in 2053–54 (Government Actuary 1986, p. 22). Only four years later, a report from the same source (Government Actuary 1990, p. 27) estimated the number of pensioners in 2030–31 as 15.2 million, falling to 14.2 million by 2050–51; and yet another report, in January 1995, showed an even bigger increase in the number of pensioners, reaching 16.9 million in 2030–31, with a further rise to 17.4 million in 2040–41, falling to 16.8 million by 2050–51 (Government Actuary 1995, p. 11). In short, assuming no change in pension ages, the expected increase in the number of pensioners, over the period up to 2030–31, was now twice as great as had been anticipated in 1986; and the subsequent fall was not expected to occur until after 2040–41, leaving nearly as many pensions in payment in 2050–51 as in 2030–31.

A number of factors contributed to these startling changes in the demographic prospect. Among them were changes in the assumptions regarding migration, mortality and ages of retirement. Their combined effect is reflected in the contribution rates required to finance pensions and other social insurance benefits. Instead of remaining roughly constant up to 2033–34, as shown in the last column of Table 9.2, the latest estimates show that, without the 1995 economy measures, contribution rates would have risen between 2010–11 and 2030–31 from 17.6 per cent to 20.0 per cent, falling to 16.8 per cent over the two following decades (the increase in the number of pensioners between 2030 and 2040 being more than compensated by the assumption that the basic pension would remain price-indexed while contributions rose in line with earnings). The changes enacted in 1995 are expected to restore the 1986 forecast of roughly constant contribution rates up to 2030–31 (Government Actuary 1995, pp. 14, 21).

A major uncertainty in these projections is the band of earnings on which contributions will be payable. This is of crucial importance for the future role of SERPS, since the earnings-related pension will be based on those earnings. The intention when SERPS was introduced, on which the logic of the pension formula depended, was that the lower and upper earnings limits would rise annually, roughly in line with average earnings. These limits, however, are linked to the basic pension (the lower limit is approximately equal to the basic pension, while the upper limit is between 6.5 and 7.5 times as high) which, since 1980, has risen in line with prices instead of earnings. This has already resulted in a fall in the lower and upper limits relative to average earnings, to about 16 per cent and 119 per cent of male average earnings in April 1994. If the process continues and the annual increase in earnings is 1.5 per cent above the increase in prices, the upper earnings limit will be about the same as male average earnings in 2005 and about two-thirds of male average earnings in 2030, by which date the lower earnings limit will also have fallen to about half its present level in relation to earnings. Eventually, most contributors will have earnings above the upper limit and their contributions and pensions will, in effect, cease to be earnings-related. It seems most improbable that this will actually be allowed to happen. More likely outcomes are that either SERPS will, after all, be abolished or the legislation will be amended to allow the earnings limits to rise with average earnings.

4. Occupational pension schemes

A series of surveys of occupational pension schemes in the United Kingdom, carried out by the Government Actuary's Department in 1956 and at four-yearly intervals since 1963, provides a valuable record of their development, from which most of the information in this section is derived. The membership figures from successive surveys are shown in Table 9.3. Changes in the total membership since the late 1930s are summarized in the report on the latest of these surveys:

> Just before the Second World War there were only about 2.5 million members of occupational pension schemes, or about 15 per

Table 9.3 – Employees in occupational pension schemes 1953–91, United Kingdom (millions)

Year	Private sector		Public sector		Total members	Total employed	Percentage employed who are members		
	Men	Women	Men	Women			Men	Women	Total
1953	2.5	0.6	2.4	0.7	6.2	21.9	34	18	28
1956	3.5	0.8	2.9	0.8	8.0	22.7	43	21	35
1963	6.4	0.8	3.0	0.9	11.1	22.9	63	21	48
1967	6.8	1.3	3.1	1.0	12.2	23.2	66	28	53
1971	5.5	1.3	3.2	1.1	11.1	22.5	62	28	49
1975	4.9	1.1	3.7	1.7	11.4	23.1	63	30	49
1979	4.6	1.5	3.7	1.8	11.6	23.4	62	35	50
1983	4.4	1.4	3.4	1.9	11.1	21.1	64	37	52
1987	4.4	1.4	2.8	2.0	10.6	21.6	60	35	49
1991	4.5	2.0	2.3	1.9	10.7	22.5	57	37	48

Source: Government Actuary 1994, p. 4.

cent of the workforce, but during the 1950s and most of the 1960s the number of people in schemes grew rapidly to reach about half the number of employees in employment, at which level it has remained. In the private sector, coverage peaked at the end of the 1960s and then fell to about 40 per cent as a result of fewer male manual workers' being covered. It has remained at about this level ever since... In the public sector the percentage coverage has always been higher than in the private sector, although there has been a continued decline from the high point reached in 1983. (Government Actuary 1994, p. 3)

Public sector schemes, like public sector employers, are typically large, while private sector schemes often cover only a small number of employees, either because the employer is small or because the scheme has been set up for a small number of highly paid executives. According to the Government Actuary's broad estimates, the number of private sector schemes rose from 35 000–40 000 in 1956 to around 128 000 by 1991. The increase is accounted for mainly by small schemes administered by insurance companies. The estimated number of schemes in the private sector with 1000 or more members rose only from about 600 in 1956 to about 800 in 1991 (Government Actuary 1958, pp. 2, 4; 1994, p. 30). The larger schemes are generally 'self-administered', managing their own investments; but insurance companies also play a part in self-administered schemes, managing the investments of the smaller schemes and insuring the benefits payable on a member's death.

In contrast to the pay-as-you-go financing of state pensions, all occupational schemes in the private sector and many of those in the public sector are funded, their investments being held by trustees or financial institutions legally separate from the employer (although, as the Maxwell affair demonstrated (Social Security Committee 1992), this has not always prevented manipulation or misappropriation by an unscrupulous employer). This is seen as an inevitable consequence of the British system of single-employer schemes, whose financial security can be assured only by advance funding of their liabilities and by separating their assets from those of the employer. The value of pension scheme assets in the United Kingdom in 1993 was estimated at £600 billion, compared with the 1992 figures of £160 billion in Germany and £140 billion in the Netherlands – the two other European countries with the largest volume of pension funds (House of Commons 1996b, columns 474–5). The fact that these assets do nothing to enhance the well-being of the current generation of pensioners goes some way towards explaining why most British pensioners' incomes remain relatively low compared, for example, with the incomes of French pensioners.

An equally important characteristic of most single-employer occupational pension schemes, particularly in the private sector, is that their creation and subsequent development is strongly influenced by the perceived interests of the employer. This is seen most clearly in relation to the preservation of the pension rights of 'early leavers' – employees who change their employment before pension age – discussed more fully below. Given that one motive for the provision of occupational pensions is to retain valued employees who might otherwise be tempted to move, employers are not inclined to confer generous benefits on those who leave before pension age and offer their services to a competing employer. Similarly, from the employer's point of view, it is more important to provide attractive benefits at the point of retirement than to maintain or increase the value of pensions in payment. Employers' attitudes to occupational pensions depend crucially on the state of the labour market. As a recent survey of the British economy (Hutton 1995, p. 203) puts it:

> Firms competed to offer them when labour market conditions were tight in the post-war period. With high and permanent unemployment there is increasingly less need to offer pension funds to attract staff and new companies tend to regard them as an unnecessary and expensive luxury.

4.1 The growth of final salary schemes

The most obvious change in the characteristics of occupational schemes, up to the end of the 1970s, was the steady growth of 'final salary' schemes, in which the pension was calculated as a proportion of the employee's earnings in the period preceding retirement. The oldest occupational scheme, the civil service superannuation scheme, provided a model which other schemes increasingly emulated. Under the civil service scheme, a pension of 1/80 of 'final salary' is paid for each year of service. In addition, a lump sum of 3/80 of final salary per year of service is paid on retirement (i.e., 1.5 years' salary after 40 years' service). The combined value of the pension and the lump sum is roughly equivalent to a pension of 1/60 of final salary per year of service, and the formula adopted in other schemes based on this model was generally a

Table 9.4 – Manner of calculation of pension, private sector, 1963

	Percentage of members
Dependent on salary range from time to time	29
Fraction of salary for each year of service	23
Fixed amount	1
Fixed amount per year of service	26
As secured by contributions	4
Other bases	15
No pension provided	2
	100

Source: Government Actuary 1966, p. 32, Table 35.

pension of 1/60 per year of service with an option to commute a quarter of it for a lump sum on retirement, thus reducing the pension to 1/80 per year of service.

The adoption of this model was encouraged by the rules regarding tax exemptions for pension scheme contributions and investment income. The Finance Act 1947 gave legal force to the standards previously applied by the Inland Revenue department, requiring that, as a condition of approval for tax purposes, both the aggregate value of the benefits and the proportion payable as a pension rather than as a lump sum were to be 'reasonably comparable' to those 'usually afforded by statutory superannuation schemes'. The significance of the rule that not more than a quarter of the total benefits could be paid as a lump sum was that lump-sum payments were generally not taxable. The civil servants' lump-sum payment on retirement had its origins in a campaign by civil servants for similar payments on death before retirement. The spread of lump-sum retirement benefits to other schemes, however, was almost entirely due to the fact that they were tax-free.

Before the 1939–45 war, final salary pension schemes were almost entirely confined to non-manual workers (hence the use of the term 'salary' rather than 'wage'). The Government Actuary's survey for 1963 showed that only 23 per cent of members of private sector schemes were in schemes which calculated the pension as 'a fraction of salary for each year of service' (Government Actuary 1966, p. 32). Table 9.4, taken from the 1963 survey report, shows the proportions in schemes of different types. Schemes in which the pension was 'dependent on salary range from time to time' were sometimes known as 'average salary schemes', the pension accruing in each year being roughly proportional to that year's earnings, with no provision for revaluation to take account of subsequent changes in the general level of earnings or prices. 'Fraction of salary for each year of service', on the other hand, meant in most cases that the pension was based on salary for a period of not more than five years preceding retirement – most commonly three years.

The proportion of private sector scheme members in schemes of this kind (which can conveniently, if not altogether accurately, be described as final salary schemes) rose rapidly in the 1960s and 1970s: from 23 per cent in 1963 to 55 per cent in 1967 (Government Actuary 1968, p. 19), 62 per cent in 1971 (Government Actuary 1972, p. 26), 79 per cent in 1975 (Government Actuary 1978, p. 49), and over 90 per cent in 1979 (Government Actuary 1981, p. 40). Over the same period there was a marked shortening of the periods of earnings used as a basis for calculating the pension in these schemes, thus bringing the earnings base closer to actual final salary. By 1979, over half the members of private sector final salary schemes could expect their pensions to be based on only one year's earnings (usually a year ending within the 12 months preceding retirement); in very few cases were earnings averaged over more than three years (Government Actuary 1981, p. 45). For public sector schemes, the normal averaging period was reduced from three years to one year in 1971.

Both the growing popularity of final salary schemes and the shortening of the period of earnings used for calculating pensions owed much to the inflationary conditions of the post-war period and the consequent erosion of the value of pensions based on average career earnings. Final salary schemes were now seen as a means of raising the standards of provision for manual workers. By the 1970s, trade unions representing manual workers in the private sector, which had not in the past taken much interest in occupational pensions, regarded final salary schemes as a desirable objective, even though basing the pension on a person's earnings at the end of his or her working life was not necessarily the best formula for their members.

There was an equally significant shift in the attitude of the insurance companies. An actuarial textbook published in the 1950s described the provision by insurance companies of 'pensions bearing a definite relation to salaries at date of retirement' as impracticable, because the risks involved were 'not susceptible of reasonable actuarial assessment' (Crabbe and Poyser 1953, p. 4). Faced with the growing demand for final salary schemes and the risk of losing their share of the pensions market, the insurance companies adapted their actuarial techniques. The results were noted by the Government Actuary in the report on his 1975 survey:

> Whereas, in the past, schemes insured with life offices have tended not to offer benefits depending on salaries of employees at or near retirement, this is now not the case and of the 20 350 schemes where all the contributions are paid to the life offices about 15 150 (74 per cent) offer final-salary benefits. (Government Actuary 1978, p. 35)

As noted above, the proportion of private sector scheme members in final salary schemes was even higher: 79 per cent in 1975. Most of the other 21 per cent were manual workers in flat-rate schemes; the once popular average salary and 'salary range' schemes had practically disappeared. In the public sector, nearly all schemes, including those established in the 1940s and 1950s for workers in the newly nationalized industries, were on a final salary basis (Government Actuary 1978, p. 49).

The growth of final salary schemes up to 1975 was not materially influenced by developments in the state scheme, but it was to be an important factor in determining the form that contracting out took under Labour's 1975 Pensions Act (SERPS). And, in turn, the SERPS contracting out conditions were to give a further boost to the spread of final salary schemes from 1975 on.

4.2 Exclusion of women

The membership of occupational schemes has always consisted mainly of men in full-time employment. Since 1978, under the Social Security Pensions Act 1975, occupational schemes have been required by law to give men and women equal access to membership, and a more general requirement of equal treatment, in respect of pensionable service from 17 May 1990, is imposed by article 119 of the Treaty of Rome. Yet a large proportion of women continue to be excluded. According to the Government Actuary, the lower level of membership among women in 1991, shown in Table 9.3, was mainly due to the fact that in Britain a much higher proportion of women than of men work part-time (Government Actuary 1994, p. 4) (although part-time work is now

Table 9.5 – Part-time employees' pension scheme coverage, 1991 (thousands)

	Men		*Women*		*Total*	
	Employees	*Members*	*Employees*	*Members*	*Employees*	*Members*
Private sector	450	30	3250	450	3700	480
Public sector	200	50	1400	320	1600	370

Source: Government Actuary 1994, p. 11, Table 2.9.

becoming increasingly common among men). Table 9.5 shows that coverage of part-time workers of both sexes and in both private and public sectors was low.

Final salary schemes are particularly unsuitable for part-time workers. Hours of part-time work often fluctuate, making it unsatisfactory to relate pension entitlement to the number of hours worked during a relatively short period preceding retirement. Part-time work is also often intermittent, resulting in loss of pension rights when employment is interrupted. The increasing prevalence of final salary schemes, therefore, has played a part in keeping the coverage of women employees much lower than that of men. Recent events may, however, be expected to result in more part-time women being covered. The growth in the number of money purchase schemes, stimulated by the fact that since 1988 they have been allowed to contract out of SERPS, should encourage the inclusion of part-time workers. It has also become clear, as a result of recent judgments by the European Court of Justice, that where part-time workers are predominantly women their exclusion from an occupational scheme may be illegal on grounds of sex discrimination.

4.3 Early leavers

Occupational pensions have traditionally been regarded as private arrangements between employers and employees in which the state should not interfere. The main departures from this principle are the conditions which schemes must satisfy in order to qualify for tax reliefs and, since 1961, the conditions for contracting out of the graduated pension scheme and SERPS. There is, however, one other aspect of occupational pensions which, by the mid 1960s, was causing sufficient concern for the government to consider the need for legislation: the treatment of 'early leavers'. As we have already noted, employers did not see it as being in their interests to reward those who chose to leave their employment before pension age. In most cases, early leavers either lost their accrued pension rights entirely, possibly receiving a refund of contributions, or were awarded a deferred pension based on their salary at the time of leaving, no allowance being made for increases in earnings, or even in prices, between leaving and reaching pension age. The loss of pension resulting from a change of employment some years before pension age could be very substantial.

The first attempt at a partial solution to this problem was made in 1973. The Social Security Act 1973 provided for the preservation of the pension rights of early leavers, but normally only on the basis of their salary and length of service at the time of leaving. Even this plainly inadequate obligation, which came into force in April 1975, applied only to employees over the age of 25 who had completed at least five years' pensionable service, but it was extended to those under 25 in 1986 and the minimum period of service was reduced to two years in 1988.

The situation was improved by the introduction of SERPS in 1978. The guaranteed minimum pension (GMP) provided by a contracted out occupational scheme had to be not only preserved but increased in line with average earnings up to pension age (the liability for preservation and revaluation could either be retained by the scheme or transferred wholly or in part to the state scheme, on terms laid down in the legislation). This applied only to pension rights accruing from 1978 on and did not apply to pension rights in excess of the GMP or to occupational schemes which were not contracted out. Nevertheless, the requirements had a wider impact on occupational schemes in the private sector (in the public sector, preserved pensions were already generally subject to revaluation in line with prices). The Government Actuary's 1979 survey showed that only about 8 per cent of employees in the private sector were in schemes whose rules provided for preserved pensions to be increased, but by 1983 just over 40 per cent of private sector scheme members were entitled to such increases, generally of a fixed percentage (most commonly 3 per cent) (Government Actuary 1991, p. 61). Thus, while employers were increasingly recognizing the injustice of freezing pension rights at the point of leaving, the action taken to correct it, in most cases, fell far short of enabling employees to change jobs without loss of pension rights.

Further legislation followed, requiring the revaluation of preserved pensions of employees leaving on or after 1 January 1986 in line with the increase in prices, or by 5 per cent per annum compound if this was less. At first, the revaluation requirement applied only to the pension accrued since January 1985, but from January 1991 leavers are entitled to revaluation of the whole of their preserved pension.

A minority of members of the Pension Law Review Committee (the Goode Committee) which reported in 1993 considered that preserved pension rights ought to be revalued in line with average earnings rather than prices, subject to a maximum annual rate of increase. The majority, however, disagreed, arguing that there was 'no reason why the employer should be expected to pay the cost of relating pensions for leavers to projected final earnings, since this was never part of the bargain, and the cost could be substantial' (Pension Law Review Committee 1993, p. 298). No further improvement in the statutory revaluation requirements can, therefore, be expected in the near future. The Government Actuary's 1991 survey showed that a significant minority of private sector employees were then entitled to full price-indexation of preserved pensions without a 5 per cent limit (Government Actuary 1994, p. 78). The schemes providing this degreee of protection may, however, have been those transferred in recent years from the public sector, where full price-indexation is the norm. For most members of final salary schemes in the private sector, loss of pension rights will remain a significant deterrent to leaving before pension age.

4.4 Indexation of pensions in payment

While the effects of freezing preserved pensions of early leavers do not become fully evident until they reach pension age, the effects of rising prices on pensions already in payment are felt from week to week and are much more clearly understood. Until recent times, however, it was not considered practicable for private sector schemes to guarantee pension increases in line with prices, although it was the normal practice in public sector schemes from 1971 on. The possibility of tying pensions in payment to an index of average earnings was not even considered. In a report published in 1972, a director of a leading firm of pension consultants, commenting on the government's recent commitment to annual reviews of state pensions, wrote:

> ...the introduction of a regular review related specifically to a price index is bound to increase pressure on occupational

schemes to follow suit. The risk, however, is an uninsurable one –
no insurance company will guarantee to match increases in the
cost-of-living index – and it is unlikely that many employers will
feel able to underwrite an unconditional guarantee of this sort.
(Michael Pilch, foreword to Kingston 1972).

This view was borne out by the Government Actuary's 1971 survey.
Although 70 per cent of private sector scheme members (excluding
schemes with less than 25 members) were eligible for 'some form of aug-
mentation after retirement', in about three out of four schemes the
increases were given ad hoc from year to year, and even where they were
automatic the average increase was well below the rate of inflation
(Government Actuary 1972, pp. 37–8).

The high rates of inflation in the 1970s concentrated attention on
the problem and by 1987 nearly half of all private sector occupational
pensioners were receiving increases promised by the rules of the
scheme, though these varied from 2 per cent to 5 per cent and the
increases actually granted remained to a large extent discretionary
(Government Actuary 1991, p. 47). By 1991, 80 per cent of private sector pensioners were entitled to limited increases under the scheme rules
(Government Actuary 1994, p. 63). The assumption made in 1975 that
occupational schemes could not be required to provide such increases
was plainly no longer valid, and the SERPS contracting out rules were
amended, requiring contracted out schemes to provide inflation-proofing up to a maximum of 3 per cent in any year for GMPs accrued since
April 1988; the state scheme would remain responsible for the excess
over 3 per cent. The Social Security Act 1990 gave the government
power to require increases in line with prices up to 5 per cent per year
(known as 'limited price indexation' or LPI) in pensions in excess of the
GMP. This requirement will come into force in April 1997. From then
on, the state scheme's responsibility for inflation-proofing GMPs will
cease and private sector occupational pensioners can expect the purchasing power of their pensions to be maintained fully only during periods of low or moderate inflation.

5.   Contracting out

Some of the ways in which state and occupational pension schemes have
influenced each other in Britain have already been mentioned. The

early growth of occupational schemes for non-manual workers was clearly related to the inadequacy of state pensions and their failure to take into account differences in earnings. The coverage of occupational schemes, however, was extremely uneven. The growing inequalities between occupational pensioners and those wholly dependent on the state pension provided the main justification for the Labour Party's attempts, from 1957 on, to introduce a substantial earnings-related addition to the state pension, culminating in the 1975 Pensions Act. More recently, concern about the rising cost of state pensions, for which the 1975 Act was partially responsible, has resulted in legislation aimed at promoting private pension schemes, both occupational and personal, to reduce the burden on the state. The most direct interaction between state and occupational or personal pension schemes, however, has resulted from the arrangements for contracting out of part of the state scheme. Successive stages of this interaction are described below.

5.1 The 1961–75 graduated pension scheme

One of the explicit aims of the graduated pension scheme – the Conservative answer to Labour's national superannuation plan – was to encourage the best development of occupational schemes. Employers could contract out if their occupational schemes provided pensions at or above the maximum level of the state's graduated pension. Most schemes giving pensions based on length of service, whether calculated as a percentage of earnings or not, satisfied this condition. In addition, taking into account the reduction in national insurance contributions resulting from contracting out, insurance companies were able to offer employers the option of setting up new occupational schemes, mainly for male manual workers, at the minimum level required for contracting out and at a lower cost than that of paying full contributions to the state scheme.

The popularity of schemes of this kind, known as 'Q schemes', was reflected in the Government Actuary's 1963 survey, showing an increase since the previous survey in 1956 in the number of schemes offering pensions of a small fixed amount per year of service. Over the same period, 1956–63, the proportion of private sector scheme members in schemes limited to manual workers had grown dramatically, from 10 per cent to 40 per cent, and the proportion of private sector male manual workers covered by occupational schemes had risen from 38 per cent to

55 per cent (the proportion of female manual workers covered had fallen, probably because the lower average earnings of women made contracting out less attractive). So far as manual workers were concerned, therefore, far from encouraging the best development of occupational schemes, the contracting out conditions had produced a new generation of schemes which, while cutting employers' costs and increasing the insurance companies' profits, did little to improve their members' pensions and were to vanish almost without trace within less than twenty years. The role played by the insurance companies is indicated by the increase in the proportion of private sector scheme members in wholly or partly insured schemes from 53 per cent to 60 per cent between 1956 and 1963 (Government Actuary 1966, pp. 9–10, 12, 32).

For non-manual workers, the graduated scheme was almost irrelevant. Although contracting out involved little or no change in their existing occupational schemes, the general standard of those schemes continued to improve, with a rapid growth both in the number of employees in final salary schemes and in the proportion accruing pension at the rate of 1/60 of salary per year of service (the maximum allowed under the tax rules). If the graduated scheme played any part in encouraging these trends, it was probably through its sheer inadequacy: if this was the best that the state could do, the only hope of obtaining adequate retirement incomes was through improved occupational schemes. Indeed, one of the most striking improvements in occupational schemes in the decade following the introduction of the graduated scheme was in the provision of widows' pensions, despite the fact that the contracting out conditions did not require any provision at all for widows (Government Actuary 1968, p. 26; 1972, p. 40).

5.2   The 1969 national superannuation plan and the public sector

In general, the abortive attempts of both Labour and Conservative governments to introduce new pension arrangements in the late 1960s and early 1970s had little impact on the development of occupational schemes. There is, however, one important exception to this statement. The Labour government's 1969 plan for a national superannuation scheme included proposals for contracting out which differed radically from both the party's 1957 plan and the contracting out arrangements of the graduated pension scheme. It was now recognized that occupational schemes could not realistically be required to match the benefits of the new state scheme. In particular, it was argued, they could not guarantee the revaluation of pension rights either during a person's working life or after retirement. The proposal, therefore, was that a contracted out scheme should be required to provide, for each year of contracted out employment, a pension of a fixed percentage of the member's earnings in that year, which would remain unchanged regardless of any subsequent changes in earnings or prices. The amount of pension calculated in this way would be deducted from the state pension. A contracted out employee would therefore receive part of the pension for each year of employment from the occupational scheme and part from the state scheme. The perceived advantage of this arrangement was that improvements in the state scheme need not be inhibited by the inability of occupational schemes to guarantee matching benefits. But there was a corresponding disadvantage: if the new earnings-related state pension was added to the occupational pension from a final salary scheme, and the combined pension was reduced only by the much smaller amount which the occupational scheme was required to pay under the contracting out rules, the amount remaining could well be higher than would be considered either necessary or desirable. In the long run, therefore, if not immediately, the government's proposals seemed likely to result in final salary schemes being cut back to make room for the new state pension.

The problem was acute for public sector employees, who enjoyed the highest standard of occupational provision and felt most at risk of having it reduced. The local government officers' trade union, NALGO, was particularly vociferous in protesting against the proposals. The civil service unions, representing national government employees, pursued their negotiations with less publicity, through a joint negotiating committee. By the time the committee reported in February 1972 (Civil Service Joint Superannuation Review Committee 1972), there had been a change of government and the new Conservative government had published its own pension proposals, which could have been implemented without any major change in the civil service scheme, apart from improvements in the preservation of pension rights of early leavers. Nevertheless, the government felt obliged to implement the recommendations of the joint committee. The civil service and other public service employees to whose schemes similar improvements were made were, therefore, the main beneficiaries of the proposals which the Labour government had failed to enact before its defeat in the 1970 general election. Paradoxically, a plan intended to raise the standard of state pensions for those without occupational provision had the effect, instead, of posthumously bringing about major improvements in what were already among the most generous occupational schemes. The pensions paid by these schemes were in future to be increased regularly in line with prices, with a special increase to restore the original value of those already in payment; they were to be based on pensionable pay in the best of the last three years of service (normally the last year), instead of on the average of the last three years; widows' pensions were to be raised from one-third to one-half of the husband's pension; and there were to be improvements in ill-health pensions, widows' pensions where the husband died in service, and the preserved pension rights of employees leaving before retirement age.

5.3   SERPS

The improvements that had taken place in occupational pension schemes, in both public and private sectors, were reflected in the conditions laid down in the Social Security Pensions Act 1975 for contracting out of the state earnings-related pension scheme (SERPS). The Government Actuary's 1975 survey showed not only that about 80 per cent of private sector occupational scheme members and nearly all those in the public sector were in final salary schemes (most of the remainder were in flat-rate schemes for manual workers, of the kind used for contracting out of the 1961 graduated pension scheme – not the type of scheme that the Labour government was anxious to protect) but also that far more schemes were now providing widows' pensions: in the private sector, the proportion of male members in schemes providing a widow's pension on death in service had risen from 39 per cent in 1971 to 54 per cent in 1975, and far more schemes were now paying widows' pensions on death after retirement as an additional benefit rather than through allocation of part of the husband's pension rights (Government Actuary 1978, pp. 33–4, 64, 68). The effect of the new contracting out rules was to consolidate these advances by building them into the conditions for contracting out.

Although the effect of the 1975 Act was to confirm the predominance of final salary schemes, it actually provided for two types of occupational schemes to contract out: first, the conventional final salary type, with a minimum accrual rate of 1/80 of salary per year of membership and, secondly, schemes providing pensions based on each year's earnings revalued in line with average earnings up to pension age. The latter alternative was offered in recognition of the disadvantages of final salary schemes for manual workers whose earnings peaked some time before retirement. Schemes of the revalued salary type, however, hardly existed and, if the government hoped in this way to encourage their creation, that hope was to be disappointed. The occupational pensions 'industry' was not interested in developing new products for the benefit of manual workers so long as it was able to sell the old ones, and the trade unions, which might have been expected to show more interest, did not, perhaps because of a feeling that manual workers were likely to do better in partnership with their higher-status non-manual colleagues than by demanding schemes of their own. Even where, as was commonly the case, an employer had separate schemes for manual and non-manual employees, the manual workers' scheme was generally of the final salary type: the Government Actuary's 1979 survey (SERPS had commenced in 1978) showed that out of 4.8 million contracted out employees only about 10 000 were in 'revalued current salary' schemes (Government Actuary 1981, p. 42).

For final salary schemes, contracting out of SERPS proved extremely popular. Indeed, for most, it was a condition of their continued existence. This had not been the case under the 1961 graduated scheme: in 1967, about 30 per cent of occupational scheme members in the private sector and 70 per cent in the public sector, a total of about 5.3 million, were contracted out (Government Actuary 1968, pp. 12–13). By 1979, over 10 million employees were contracted out of SERPS, including virtually the whole of the public sector and 80 per cent of private sector scheme members (85 per cent of those in private sector final salary schemes) (Government Actuary 1981, pp. 23, 42). There has been little change since then in the proportions contracted out, apart from the effects, discussed below, of the growth of money purchase schemes.

It should be stressed, however, that members of contracted out schemes were originally intended to derive considerable benefit from SERPS. As in the abortive 1969 scheme discussed in section 5.2 above, it was assumed that occupational schemes could not be required fully to match the benefits of the state scheme, and that contracting out must involve a partnership in which occupational schemes did what they could, leaving the state scheme to do the rest. Although the occupational scheme was responsible for providing a guaranteed minimum earnings-related pension (GMP) at retirement age, inflation-proofing of the GMP after retirement was to be provided by the state scheme, which was also to play a major part in preserving the rights of early leavers. Earn-

337

ings-related invalidity pensions were to be provided by the state regardless of whether the recipient was contracted out; and responsibility for earnings-related widows' pensions was to be shared between the occupational scheme and SERPS. Subsequent legislation has changed all this. The Social Security Act 1986 halved the entitlement of widows to inherit their husbands' SERPS pensions; earnings-related invalidity benefits were first reduced and then abolished with effect from April 1995 (those in payment at that date will continue but their cash value will be frozen); and from April 1997 the state scheme will no longer play any part in inflation-proofing occupational pensions accruing from then on. In short, the partnership between SERPS and contracted out occupational schemes will cease and members of contracted out schemes will be wholly dependent on them for their earnings-related pension.

5.4 Money purchase (defined contribution) schemes

In April 1988, money purchase or 'defined contribution' schemes were added to the types of occupational schemes allowed to contract out. Individual employees were also given the option of contracting out through savings schemes, known as 'personal pension schemes', operating on a money purchase basis. Since employers were no longer permitted to make membership of occupational schemes compulsory, actual or potential members could decide, instead, to invest in a personal pension scheme, although, by doing so, they would normally lose the advantage of any contribution by the employer above the legal minimum.

The advantage of an occupational scheme based on money purchase, from the employer's point of view, is that the cost is established at the outset. Provided that he has made the required contributions to the scheme, he has no responsibility for the size of the pension, which depends on investment yields and on the state of the annuity market when a member reaches pension age. A significant growth of money purchase schemes was noted by the Government Actuary in his 1983 survey of occupational schemes, before they became eligible for contracting out. Money purchase, he commented, 'is a convenient arrangement among highly mobile staff, since the pension liability in respect of a particular period of service is defined in terms of the contributions paid into the scheme, thus avoiding the uncertainties associated with the costs of providing benefits related to final salary' (Government Actuary 1986, p. 44). The effect, however, is to shift the uncertainty from the cost incurred by the employer to the benefits received by the employee: pure money purchase schemes cannot determine in advance the value of the pension in relation to pre-retirement earnings. But money purchase does also have advantages for employees. In particular, the treatment of early leavers is greatly simplified: the member's share of the fund can easily be either preserved or transferred to another scheme and, in either case, will continue to appreciate until the pension becomes payable.

By 1991, the number of private sector employees covered by money purchase occupational schemes had risen from 240 000 in 1983 to 900 000, about 14 per cent of all private sector scheme members. They were heavily concentrated in small schemes with less than 100 members, most of whom were not contracted out (including a very large number of schemes with less than 12 members, averaging about 3 members each – a large proportion of them probably senior staff). Most of those in schemes with 100 or more members were contracted out, but in all less than 8 per cent of contracted out occupational scheme members were in money purchase schemes. The Government Actuary's enquiries showed no large-scale shift from final salary to money purchase benefits among the larger schemes (Government Actuary 1994, p. 31). It appears, therefore, that the growth of money purchase schemes has occurred mainly among employers setting up a scheme for the first time. The trend away from defined benefits and towards defined contributions can, however, be expected to continue, resulting in a long-term diminution of the average level of occupational pensions.

6.   Personal pensions

6.1   Annuities for the self-employed

Before 1988, while it was possible for any individual to make provision for his or her own retirement by saving and investing money in a variety of ways, it was mainly self-employed people who did so by using part of their earnings to purchase deferred annuities. The self-employed were excluded from state pensions insurance until 1948. Those contributing to the national insurance scheme from then on became eligible for pensions, subject to the normal age conditions, ten years later. Both the 1961 graduated pension scheme and the 1978 SERPS, however, excluded them. The most that a person who is self-employed for the whole of his/her working life can expect to receive from the state, apart from means-tested benefits, is the flat-rate basic pension. Private provision by self-employed people for their retirement is encouraged by income tax reliefs, broadly comparable to those enjoyed by employees, provided that the contributions paid to an insurance company or other financial institution do not exceed a certain proportion of their net earnings. That proportion has varied over the years and depends on the person's age, but the current limits are between 17.5 per cent and 40 per cent of earnings. In 1992–93, out of about 3 million self-employed people, about 0.6 million were contributing to a personal pension scheme and 1.1 million to a retirement annuity contract (House of Commons 1996a, columns *219–20*). Many others were undoubtedly saving for their retirement in other ways, but it is likely that a substantial proportion were not.

6.2 'Appropriate' personal pensions

Since July 1988, so-called appropriate personal pension (APP) schemes, provided by insurance companies, banks, etc., have been available to employees as a means of contracting out of SERPS. As a minimum, the contracting out rebate – the reduction in national insurance contributions payable by contracted out employees and their employers – must be invested in the personal pension policy. For the first six years, an additional 2 per cent of the relevant band of earnings was transferred to the scheme from the National Insurance Fund – a direct subsidy to the employees concerned from the general body of contributors. Because the contracting out rebate did not vary with the age of the employee, the option of having it paid into a personal pension scheme was far more attractive to younger employees (whose contributions would accumulate interest for a longer period) than to those nearer retirement; hence the vast majority of employees taking up the option were under 40.

The government's expectation was that about 500 000 employees would contract out through an APP scheme (Government Actuary 1986, p. 9), but a combination of government and commercial advertising (the latter accompanied by an assortment of gift offers, including free cinema tickets), together with the activities of an army of ill-trained and commission-hungry salesmen posing as 'financial advisers', resulted in the sale of far more schemes than had been expected. Nearly 2 million people took advantage of the opportunity to backdate their schemes to the earliest permitted starting date, April 1987. Over 5.3 million, including about 2 million women, contributed to APP schemes in 1991–92, though many had ceased to do so by the end of the year, when the number of APP holders was 4.7 million (according to the Department of Social Security, 'Terminations could have been for many reasons, e.g. retirement, transfer to another type of scheme or death', but, given the small numbers in the higher age groups, neither retirement nor death is likely to have accounted for many of the drop-outs) (Department of Social Security 1993). The cost to the National Insurance Fund of the 2 per cent incentive for APP schemes was about £3.7 billion at 1995–96 prices. Taking into account the normal contracting out rebate, APPs had cost the Fund over £14 billion over the six-year period 1987–93 – a massive loss which had to be made good by a variety of expedients, including relieving the fund of the cost of certain benefits and filling the remaining gap with a subsidy from tax revenues (House of Commons 1995d, columns *1019–20*).

The minimum contributions to an APP scheme, consisting of the contracting out rebate and the 2 per cent incentive, could be supplemented by either the employee or the employer. Employers with their own occupational schemes, however, were not keen on supplementing the contributions of employees who opted out of those schemes, while those without occupational schemes generally had no reason to do so. More than half the APP schemes in force in 1993–94 were based on minimum contributions (House of Commons 1995b, column *113*).

By the end of 1993 it had become apparent that very large numbers of APP schemes had been sold to employees for whom they were clearly not appropriate. Many had been persuaded to opt out of, or not to join, occupational schemes which would have been much more advantageous to them. An investigation was carried out by the Securities and Investments Board (SIB – a body set up by the government to regulate the financial services 'industry') and in October 1994 the providers of APPs were instructed to review over a two-year period all cases in categories where mis-selling was thought likely to have occurred and, where necessary, to restore those concerned to the position they were in before signing the APP contract. This has involved a vast amount of work. By the end of 1995, about 5 million questionnaires had been sent to people in the groups most likely to have been affected. Numerous problems were encountered, including legal actions challenging SIB's right to issue such instructions. Reinstating the rights of those concerned was far from simple, since occupational pension schemes could not be compelled to re-admit past members, and still less to restore the pension rights lost during their period of non-membership. In May 1996, the chief executive of SIB admitted, 'progress so far in actually delivering redress to investors who have been harmed has been much slower than we had anticipated' (Securities and Investments Board 1996, p. 3).

The fact that the contracted out rebate was not related to the age of the employee meant not only that APPs were more attractive to younger employees but also that, at some point, an employee contributing to an APP scheme would find that SERPS was better value. A leading firm of actuaries calculated in 1993 that the 'pivotal ages' at which people should be advised to transfer back to SERPS were 47 for men and 39 for women, although the pivotal ages quoted by insurance companies varied between 40 and 52 for men and 30 and 47 for women. Whatever the correct figures may have been, the implication was that, contrary to the government's policy of reducing reliance on SERPS, most people would discontinue their APP contributions and return to SERPS long before reaching retirement age.

To forestall these developments and make APPs more attractive to older workers, the government decided to introduce a system of age-related contracting out rebates. As a temporary measure, an additional 1 per cent rebate was introduced in 1993 for APP holders aged 30 and over. A more general system of age-related rebates will commence in April 1997. It will apply to contracted out money purchase occupational schemes as well as to personal pension schemes. In spite of this, however, the Department of Social Security estimates that the number of APP contributors will fall from 4.2 million in 2010 to 2.8 million in 2030. The reason given for this is that, while the age-related rebates will enable most APP holders to maintain their plans until retirement, they will reduce the incentive for younger people to contribute to an APP (House of Commons 1995c, columns *1099–1100*).

The government is also taking action to mitigate one of the major hazards of personal pensions, arising from their money purchase basis: the fact that the capital sum accrued in the scheme must be used at pension age to purchase an annuity, the size of which depends on the annuity rates currently offered in the financial market. The scale of the risk is illustrated by Table 9.6, showing the average of the four best annuity rates offered by insurance companies in March of each year from 1990 to 1994, taken from surveys published in the monthly journal *Pensions World*. The implication of these figures is that, for example, while a man reaching pension age in March 1990 with a personal pension policy worth £10 000 could buy an annuity of £1460, a man four years younger,

Table 9.6 – Insurance companies' annuity rates: average of best four, 1990–94

	Annuity per £1000 purchase money	
	Man aged 65	Woman aged 60
	£	£
1990	146.05	127.57
1991	137.39	118.22
1992	127.52	107.58
1993	114.50	94.07
1994	107.40	87.67

Source: Pensions World, 1990–94.

reaching pension age in March 1994, would have received an annuity of only £1074. The difference, in percentage terms, was even greater for a woman. The solution promised by the government is to allow the purchase of the annuity to be deferred up to the age of 75, meanwhile allowing part of the capital sum or the interest from it to be spent. While this may reduce the risk, however, it will not eliminate it, since it will still be necessary to guess the right moment at which to convert the capital into an annuity. As the above figures show, guessing wrong by even one year could make a significant difference to the size of the annuity.

7. The changing composition of pensioners' incomes

The effects of the changes in pension provision and other factors on the incomes of pensioners over the period from 1979 to 1993 are illustrated by Table 9.7, showing the average gross incomes of single pensioners (men aged 65 and over, women aged 60 and over) and pensioner couples (husband aged 65 or over or female head of household aged 60 or over) living in private households in 1979, 1989 and 1993, at July 1993 prices. The table shows a real increase in gross income of 51 per cent for single pensioners and 43 per cent for pensioner couples, with big increases in occupational pensions and investment income accompanied by a smaller increase in state benefits and a substantial decline in earnings.

Table 9.7 – Average gross incomes of pensioner units, by source, 1979, 1989 and 1993, at July 1993 prices, and percentage change 1979–93

	1979 £	1989 £	1993 £	% change 1979–93
Single pensioners				
Benefit income	58.80	67.30	77.30	+ 32
Occupational pension	10.30	21.30	26.00	+ 152
Investment income	9.40	20.80	19.30	+ 105
Earnings	6.00	5.00	5.40	− 10
Other income	0.60	0.50	0.40	− 30
Total gross income	85.00	114.90	128.40	+ 51
Pensioner couples				
Benefit income	88.90	98.70	112.30	+ 26
Occupational pension	33.10	55.90	69.30	+ 109
Investment income	17.70	41.20	40.70	+ 130
Earnings	26.50	23.10	16.30	− 38
Other income	0.90	0.60	0.70	− 18
Total gross income	167.00	219.50	239.40	+ 43

Source: Department of Social Security 1995, p. 6.

Earlier retirement and rising rates of incapacity account for the fall in earnings and for part of the increase in income from benefits and occupational pensions. Most of the weekly benefit income consisted of the state retirement pension; the basic pension alone, for a single pensioner with full entitlement, was £54.15 per week from January to March 1993 and £56.10 from April. The policy of tying the basic pension to an index of prices, however, implies that little, if any, of the real increase in benefit income can be ascribed to increases in the basic pension. Part of it resulted from the growth of SERPS pensions, which hardly existed in 1979 but accounted for about 5.7 per cent of the cost of retirement pensions in 1993–94, and part from the increased value and take-up of means-tested benefits (particularly housing benefit) and disability benefits. There was also an increase in the pensions paid under the 1961–75 graduated pension scheme as the oldest pensioners were replaced by those young enough to have contributed to it.

The proportion of pensioner units (single and couples) receiving some investment income rose from 62 per cent in 1979 to 73 per cent in 1993. The importance of this source of income, however, is considerably less than the figures in Table 9.7 would suggest. Although the average amount received by those with some investment income in 1993 was £37.40 per week, the median was only £8.70, indicating that most of it went to a small proportion of wealthy pensioners (Department of Social Security 1995, p. 10). The median for all pensioner units, including those with no investment income, would have been considerably less than £8.70. For most pensioners, investments were not a significant source of income.

Occupational pensions were a much more important component of pensioners' incomes. Here, too, the distribution was markedly unequal. The proportion of pensioner units with occupational pensions rose from 43 per cent in 1979 to 54 per cent in 1989 and 62 per cent in 1993 as members of schemes set up in the past two or three decades reached retirement age and the effects of improved arrangements for preservation of pension rights on changes of employment became apparent. But this still left more than one in three pensioner units without occupational pensions, and the proportion was nearly as high among those recently retired (up to five years over state pension age). For those actually receiving an occupational pension, the average weekly amount in 1993 was £54.10 for single pensioners and £94.70 for couples (these figures are not directly comparable with those in Table 9.7, being based in part on data from the Government Actuary's surveys of occupational schemes). The corresponding median values, however, were little more than half these amounts: £27.30 for single pensioners and £53.70 for couples (Department of Social Security 1995, p. 11). As an indication of the relative importance of occupational pensions, these figures may be compared with the flat-rate basic state pension rates for the year 1993–94: £56.10 for a single person and £33.70 for a wife dependent on her husband's insurance (making a total of £89.80 for a couple, and more than this if the wife's personal entitlement exceeded £33.70).

In comparing the incomes received from state benefits and occupational pensions, it should be noted that, where an employee has been contracted out of SERPS, at least part of the occupational pension is substituted for, rather than additional to, the state pension. In September 1993, out of 10.1 million state retirement pensions in payment, 2.2 million (21.8 per cent) were reduced by an average of £11.55 per week because, for part of the period since 1978, their recipients had been contracted out. For men aged 65–69, the proportion was 53.5 per cent and the average deduction £23.47; both the proportions and the average amounts were lower for older pensioners and for women (Department of Social Security 1994, p. 128). These amounts can be regarded as

Table 9.8 – State pension payable to a man on average male earnings reaching age 65 in selected years from 1996 to 2040, at 1996 prices and as a percentage of average male earnings

	Basic pension £	Earnings-related pension £	Total pension £	Percentage of average male earnings
1996	61.15	77.30	138.45	34.9
2000	61.15	84.80	145.95	34.7
2010	61.15	85.50	146.65	30.0
2020	61.15	94.80	155.95	27.5
2030	61.15	102.10	163.25	24.8
2040	61.15	105.40	166.55	21.8

Source: House of Commons 1996c, columns 229–32.

part of the SERPS pension, paid by occupational schemes acting as agents for the Department of Social Security.

For most pensioners, therefore, the state retirement pension remains by far the most important source of income, but it is clearly the intention of the present Conservative government that this situation should change. Table 9.8 shows the value of the state pension (basic and SERPS – the small amounts payable under the 1961–75 graduated pension scheme are excluded) for a man with average male earnings which rise by 1.5 per cent yearly throughout his working life, reaching pension age in selected years between 1996 and 2040. The freezing of the real value of the basic pension inevitably reduces its value relative to average earnings. The SERPS pension increases but by a smaller per-centage than average earnings, as the reduction in the rate of accrual under the 1986 Social Security Act takes effect. The overall effect is to reduce the combined pension from around 35 per cent of earnings in 1996 to 22 per cent in 2040.

It is important to note, however, that these estimates relate only to employees who pay full social security contributions throughout their working lives from 1978 on and are never contracted out. Already only a small minority of those reaching pension age are in this situation, and the proportion is likely to fall still further. If present policies continue, occupational and personal pensions will constitute an increasing pro-portion of pensioners' incomes in the twenty-first century. The ability of these schemes to provide adequate retirement incomes remains extremely doubtful. The risks inherent in money purchase schemes, to which all personal pensions and an increasing proportion of occupational pensions will be subject, make the future level of pensions unpredictable. The relatively low level of contributions to these schemes makes it almost inevitable that their benefits will be lower than those offered (but, because of the treatment of early leavers, often not delivered) by occupational schemes of the final salary type. Whatever the eventual outcome may be, money purchase schemes remain a gamble; and, as with all forms of gambling, there will be losers as well as winners.

8.   Conclusion

The history of pension provision in Great Britain over the past half century can be seen largely as a series of inter-reactions between social insurance and employer-based occupational pension schemes, with individually negotiated personal pension schemes acquiring a significant role in the past decade. Until the 1950s the two sectors – social and occupational – had developed independently: for most people, there was only the inadequate flat-rate state pension, supplemented by means-tested assistance, while a privileged minority could expect to retire with an additional pension from an occupational scheme. The degree of privilege conferred by membership of an occupational pension scheme, however, varied widely, both because of differences between the schemes set up by different employers and because the value of the pension to an individual employee depended crucially on continuity of membership of the scheme up to retirement age.

By the late 1950s, it was clear that the role of the state as pension provider must be extended. The system of flat-rate state pensions financed by flat-rate contributions could no longer be sustained without either placing an unacceptable burden on low-paid contributors or meeting a large part of the cost from general taxation. At the same time, it was recognized that the flat-rate pension was too low to meet the needs of the majority of pensioners who did not have occupational pensions. The introduction of an additional earnings-related contribution offered both a solution to the immediate financial problem and a means of funding a more adequate level of pensions. The plans put forward by the two main political parties in 1957–58 had two features in common: contributions would in future be based, in part at least, on individual earnings, and the new earnings-related contributions would earn the right to an earnings-related pension, to be added to the existing flat-rate pension.

Behind these common features lay radical differences of approach, which were to be reflected in a series of competing plans over the next twenty years. The Labour Party, while accepting that occupational schemes must have a continuing role, wanted a state pension scheme of high quality, which could bear comparison with the best that Britain's European neighbours could offer. For an occupational scheme to be allowed to serve as a substitute for the earnings-related element of the state scheme, it would have to be shown that its members would receive at least as good a pension. If occupational schemes of inferior quality were discontinued as a result, this would hardly be a matter for regret, since their members would fare better in the state scheme. In later versions of the Labour plan, however – including the SERPS scheme enacted in 1975, which remains in operation today – it was recognized that even those occupational schemes generally regarded as of good quality would have great difficulty in matching fully the benefits of the state scheme. The system of 'contracting out', therefore, developed into a partnership between the state and the better occupational schemes, in which the state provided or guaranteed those elements of the pension which were judged to be beyond the competence of the occupational schemes.

The Conservative Party favoured a much more modest role for the state scheme. While it might be necessary to provide a small earnings-related supplement to the pensions of those outside the reach of occupational schemes – mainly low-paid, casual or mobile workers, including a large proportion of female employees – the state's main responsibility would remain the provision of the basic flat-rate pension. Supplementary pensions, whether based on individual earnings or not, would be provided mainly by employers, acting either independently or through the insurance companies. As it became increasingly clear that membership of occupational pension schemes of the traditional 'defined benefit' type was unlikely to extend to much more than half the employed population, leaving the rest dependent on the state, the Thatcher government in the 1980s sought other ways of stimulating private pension provision. The principal method adopted was to modify the contracting out conditions so as to allow defined contribution or 'money purchase' schemes – including the new generation of 'personal' pension schemes – to be used as an alternative to SERPS.

Since 1980, the role of the state has been reduced still further, both by the freezing of the real value of the basic pension and by cuts in the future value of SERPS pensions. At the same time, the principle that employees contracted out of SERPS should be guaranteed a pension of at least equivalent value has been abandoned. For those contracted out through money purchase schemes, such a guarantee is no longer feasible, since the value of their pensions depends on future investment yields and annuity rates. In addition, the effect of the 1995 Pensions Act will be to dissolve the partnership between the state scheme and occupational defined benefit schemes – a partnership which, until now, has ensured that members of the latter would not suffer any loss of pension through being contracted out.

The retirement prospects of the minority of employees who remain full members of the state scheme are decidedly bleak, compared with what they were led to expect when SERPS commenced in 1978. Neither the flat-rate basic pension nor the earnings-related SERPS addition will have anything like the value intended by the Labour government twenty years ago. Indeed, those due to retire in the mid twenty-first century have had their pension expectations halved. The figures in Table 9.8 show only part of the picture, since the basic pension is already some 25 per cent lower than it would have been if the link with average earnings had been maintained. Moreover, Table 9.8 does not show the effect of the abolition of the 'best twenty years' rule, which would only have affected those retiring in the next century and after.

For those, by now a large majority, who are contracted out of SERPS, the outlook is hardly better and the reality could turn out to be a great deal worse. If present policies continue, they too will face a steady diminution in the relative value of the basic pension as average earnings rise. If they rely on an occupational scheme of the defined benefit type for an additional earnings-related pension, they will no longer be able to look to the state scheme either to protect their 'guaranteed minimum' pension rights if they change jobs before pension age or to ensure that the value of the guaranteed minimum pension is not eroded by inflation after they retire. And if, instead, they opt for a money purchase scheme at the minimum level required by the contracting out rules, the resulting pension is likely to be small as well as unpredictable.

In this situation, the commercial purveyors of a variety of savings and investment schemes, some more reputable and less risky than others, will be able to argue with increasing conviction that the only way of avoiding abject poverty in the years of retirement is by investing in their wares. The brief history of the selling of personal pension schemes to a gullible public since 1988 should provide a warning of the likely consequences. The idea of restoring to the individual worker the responsibility of providing for his or her own retirement may be ideologically attractive, and criticism of such a policy may be condemned as paternalist; but there is little reason to assume that unrestrained market forces will result in most people buying during their working lives the means of obtaining the income they will need during twenty, thirty or more years of retirement. If the price to be paid for the freedom to organize one's own pension turns out to be a growing level of poverty, inequality and insecurity in old age, it may not take many years for the policy-makers to rediscover the virtues of social insurance.

References

Beveridge, Sir William (1942), *Social Insurance and Allied Services*, London: HMSO.

Bradshaw, Jonathan and Lynes, Tony (1995), *Benefit Uprating Policy and Living Standards*, York: Social Policy Research Unit.

Civil Service Joint Superannuation Review Committee (1972), *Civil Service Superannuation*, London.

Crabbe, R.J.W. and Poyser, C.A. (1953), *Pension and Widows' and Orphans' Funds*, Cambridge: Cambridge University Press.

Department of Social Security (1993), *Personal Pension Statistics 1991/92*, London: HMSO.

Department of Social Security (1994), *Social Security Statistics 1994*, London: Government Statistical Service.

Department of Social Security (1995), *The Pensioners' Income Series 1993*, London: Government Statistical Service.

Department of Social Security (1996), *Pension Scheme Contributors 1986/87 to 1992/93*, London: Government Statistical Service.

Ellis, Bryan (1989), *Pensions in Britain 1955–1975*, London: HMSO.

Government Actuary (1958), *Occupational Pension Schemes*, London: HMSO.

Government Actuary (1966), *Occupational Pension Schemes: A New Survey by the Government Actuary*, London: HMSO.

Government Actuary (1968), *Occupational Pension Schemes: Third Survey by the Government Actuary*, London: HMSO.

Government Actuary (1972), *Occupational Pension Schemes 1971: Fourth Survey by the Government Actuary*, London: HMSO.

Government Actuary (1978), *Occupational Pension Schemes 1975: Fifth Survey by the Government Actuary*, London: HMSO.

Government Actuary (1981), *Occupational Pension Schemes 1979: Sixth Survey by the Government Actuary*, London: HMSO.

Government Actuary (1986), *Social Security Bill 1986: Report on the Financial Effects of the Bill on the National Insurance Fund,* London: HMSO.

Government Actuary (1990), *National Insurance Fund Long Term Financial Estimates: Report by the Government Actuary on the Second Quinquennial Review under Section 137 of the Social Security Act 1975,* London: HMSO.

Government Actuary (1991), *Occupational Pension Schemes 1987: Eighth Survey by the Government Actuary,* London: HMSO.

Government Actuary (1994), *Occupational Pension Schemes 1991: Ninth Survey by the Government Actuary,* London: HMSO.

Government Actuary (1995), *National Insurance Fund Long Term Financial Estimates: Report by the Government Actuary on the Third Quinquennial Review under Section 137 of the Social Security Act 1975,* London: HMSO.

House of Commons (1995a), *Parliamentary Debates 7 February 1995,* London: HMSO.

House of Commons (1995b), *Parliamentary Debates 1 May 1995,* London: HMSO.

House of Commons (1995c), *Parliamentary Debates 18 July 1995,* London: HMSO.

House of Commons (1995d), *Parliamentary Debates 8 November 1995,* London: HMSO.

House of Commons (1996a), *Parliamentary Debates 23 January 1996,* London: HMSO.

House of Commons (1996b), *Parliamentary Debates 12 February 1996,* London: HMSO.

House of Commons (1996c), *Parliamentary Debates 20 March 1996,* London: HMSO.

Hutton, Will (1995), *The State We're In,* London: Jonathan Cape.

Kingston, N. (1972), *Pensions Today,* London: British Institute of Management.

Labour Party (1957), *National Superannuation: Labour's Policy for Security in Old Age,* London: Labour Party.

Lynes, Tony (1963), *Pension Rights and Wrongs,* London: Fabian Society.

Ministry of Pensions and National Insurance (1958), *Provision for Old Age: The Future Development of the National Insurance Scheme,* London: HMSO.

Pension Law Review Committee (1993), *Pension Law Reform, Vol. I: Report,* London: HMSO.

Reform of Social Security (1985), London: HMSO.

Reform of Social Security: Programme for Action (1985), London: HMSO.

Securities and Investments Board (1996), Speech by Andrew Winkler, Glasgow, 3 May 1996 (text released to press), London: SIB.

Social Security Committee (1992), *Second Report: The Operation of Pension Funds,* London: HMSO.

10

Enterprise and the State: Interactions in the Provision of Employees' Retirement Income in the United States

Lucy apRoberts and John Turner[1]

1. Introduction

Compared to continental Western Europe, the United States has an underdeveloped welfare state. In France, for example, the state provides many employee welfare benefits directly to employees. When the state does not provide a specific benefit directly, it often does so indirectly through legislation requiring employers to provide it.

In the United States, public programmes simply do not exist for some welfare benefits, and when they do exist they provide relatively low benefits. The state does not provide benefits indirectly either – legislation requiring US employers to provide benefits is practically nonexistent. Benefits that are mandatory for most European employers to provide – vacations, maternity leave, sick leave – are left up to American employers to provide, or not, to employees.

Retirement pensions, as well as disability pensions, in the United States have been provided primarily by the nationwide social security system since the 1950s. Provision of additional retirement income is left to private initiative – to workers and their employers. There is a widespread belief that private initiative can provide employees with adequate supplementary social welfare. This laissez-faire approach has strongly marked the American social welfare system and persistently colours policy debates. Its proponents often contend that private initiative can

---

[1] The material in this chapter is the responsibility of the authors and does not represent the position of any organization with which they are affiliated.

provide adequate supplementary social welfare for employees and can substitute for state action.

American commentators generally do not distinguish between decisions taken by employees as individuals and decisions taken by employers concerning employee welfare. Both are called 'private'. When used this way, the adjective 'private' glosses over the contrasting institutional arrangements through which 'private' welfare systems can be set up and run. In the United States, most 'private' welfare benefits for private sector employees are provided through 'welfare enterprise' – through plans created by companies.

The adjective 'private' also diverts attention from the many ways the state intervenes in 'private' systems. The state may make 'private' protection mandatory, and that has been discussed in the United States. Short of actually mandating coverage, the state has set up incentives for participating in private systems, particularly through the tax system. Finally, the state regulates the financing of private systems and the rules that govern how benefits are allocated to employees. Thus, American 'private' retirement systems are very much the result of public as well as private initiatives.

This chapter analyses interactions between enterprises and the state by examining the history of US occupational retirement pensions. The chapter addresses the question, why have state-enterprise interactions changed over time? The state and enterprises are seen to have reacted to each other and to external economic and demographic developments as they have pursued their goals.

The analytical framework is as follows. Both the state and enterprises have goals to pursue concerning the provision of pensions by enterprises. The state wishes to encourage the development of occupational pensions in order to increase employees' retirement income without increasing social security payments. Enterprises wish to use occupational pensions as a tool for personnel management. Their goals include discouraging employee turnover among certain categories of employees and encouraging retirement at certain ages. These goals lead the state and enterprises to act. The state provides tax incentives for occupational pensions, and enterprises require long periods of work for vesting. In turn, these actions lead to reactions by the other party. The reactions may reinforce the original action or may limit the ability of the original party to pursue its goals. For example, enterprises respond to the tax incentives by providing pension plans, supporting the original action. The government reacts to plans that require lengthy vesting by mandating minimum vesting rules, restricting the original action. The anticipation of reactions affects the actions taken. For example, because occupational pensions are provided voluntarily, governmental regulations may take into account the reaction that instead of strengthening the occupational pension system, a regulation may cause enterprises to end their pension plans.

A subtheme is the unintended consequences of state action. Some governmental actions that are taken for reasons unrelated to occupational pensions, such as changes in tax rates, have important effects on pensions, and often actions taken to influence pensions have unintended effects.

2.   A note on terminology

Although not normally used by Americans, but rather by the British, we use the term 'occupational' to refer to American employee welfare plans. That term stresses the idea that employees' affiliation to such plans occurs due to the jobs they hold, and hence distinguishes between individual decisions and decisions concerning groups of employees, which are not necessarily supported by particular individual workers concerned themselves.

The term 'occupational' also has the advantage of encompassing employee benefit plans in both the private and public sectors. Occupational benefit plans are more widespread in the public sector than in the private sector, but otherwise public and private sector plans are quite similar. It is useful to have a term that applies to both and distinguishes them from national social security.

Americans sometimes refer to occupational retirement plans in both the private and public sectors as 'employers' pension plans'. While, like 'occupational' this term has the advantage of applying to both the public and private sectors, it masks the role that unions often play in occupational plans. At least in the private sector, unions negotiate every aspect of the rules of retirement plans covering union members and the rules of such plans are part of the union contract. Some industries have what Americans call 'multiemployer' plans, which are negotiated by a union with an employers' association representing a number of companies. The union participates in running these plans and in deciding on financing policies and pension fund investments. It seems inappropriate to refer to collectively bargained company or multiemployer plans as 'employers' plans'.[2]

Another comment on terminology concerns the distinction between defined contribution and defined benefit plans. Standard American usage is misleading for many Americans and even more so for foreigners. A defined contribution plan is a benefit plan under which the employer does not promise a certain level of benefits to employees. Benefits depend on contributions paid into the plan during the employee's career and on the returns on the investments of the plan fund. A defined benefit plan is a plan through which the employer promises a certain level of benefits, which depend on the employee's length of service and earnings. The employer's commitment to employees does not involve contributions to the plan fund but the benefits actually paid out.

The differences between the two types of plans as they operate in the United States are far more wide-reaching than these definitions indicate. A major difference is that defined benefit pension plans generally pay lifetime annuities commencing at retirement, whereas defined contribution plans generally provide lump sums upon the employee's ending employment with the employer providing the plan.

A recent draft of a framework produced by Eurostat's European System of Integration Social Protection Statistics (ESSPROS) provides a definition of social welfare that is to be applied to European Union statistics. The term used for 'social welfare' is the newer European term 'social protection'. This definition can be applied to American occupational defined benefit and defined contribution plans to see how they fit into the framework. Most American occupational savings plans would not be considered an element of social protection under the European Union definition.

One aspect of this definition is that social protection must constitute a form of protection against certain risks, one of which is old age. Eurostat specifically states that 'payments made by employers to their employees under saving schemes' are considered part of gross wages and salaries and not part of social protection (Eurostat 1995, section 2.15). Unlike wages, employees generally do not dispose of contributions to a savings plan until they leave their employer. However, when employees do leave their employer, whatever their age, the decision to save or

---

[2] Further discussion of pension terms and their application to international comparison of retirement systems may be found in apRoberts (1993).

spend the money, and the choice of what it is spent on, are entirely individual. Plans that pay lump sums and that offer neither retirement annuities nor survivors' annuities do not afford employees protection against certain risks.

American employees who withdraw capital from an occupational savings plan are free to use it to purchase annuities from an insurance company. However, the Eurostat definition of social protection encompasses individual insurance contracts on condition that the insurer charge premiums that are 'not proportional to individual exposure to risk' (Eurostat 1995, section 2.13). An insurance policy offered to a group of employees working in the same company or in the same sector that enables all members of the group, regardless of sex or physical health, to purchase annuities at the same price would correspond to this definition. But annuities sold to employees individually by an insurance company that charges premiums on the basis of individual life expectancy would not correspond to this definition.

In this chapter, we consider pension plans to be plans that pay annuity benefits at retirement. Because defined contribution plans generally do not pay annuity benefits, and the lump-sum benefits they pay are frequently paid before retirement, we do not include them in our discussion of pension plans. Defined contribution plans might more appropriately be classified as savings plans, or possibly in some instances retirement savings plans. It is noteworthy that often when employees covered by a defined contribution plan are asked on a survey if they are covered by a pension plan their response is 'No'. See Doescher (1994).

Private sector plans will be discussed at more length than public sector plans. One reason is that more information is readily available on private sector plans. This is due partly to the fact that the American public sector is small relative to the public sector in continental Western Europe. There are few public sector enterprises in the United States. More fundamentally, it is because public sector plans are subject to few federal regulations.

3.   A history of interactions between enterprises and the state

The interactions between enterprises and the state have changed over time, in part as a reaction to external economic and demographic circumstances such as population aging, conditions in the labour market, and the federal budget deficit. The following analysis breaks the historical development of occupational pensions in the United States into various subperiods, some of them overlapping, that have been characterized by a particular form of enterprise-state interaction.

3.1 Occupational pensions before social security: a relatively passive role of the state, 1900–35

As in other industrialized Western countries, modern American retirement plans originated in initiatives of certain employers, with little impetus from the state. The first employers to systematically pay pensions to older employees were, as in other countries, public administrations and some large private companies, notably railroads, telegraph and telephone, and large manufacturers (Williamson 1992). Some of these employers had previously developed the practice of keeping long-term, old employees on their payrolls but assigning them to jobs that were not taxing, often at lower wages than they had received when younger. That policy provided for their welfare without having them retire.

Some employers subsequently resorted to paying a retirement pension as a more efficient way of coping with older workers without appearing inhumane. Retirement with a pension also helped motivate younger employees to stay with the same employer throughout their careers, since departure before retirement age meant losing all pension rights.

As of 1921, federal tax law allowed companies to write off as a business expense contributions to a fund destined to pay deferred payments to employees.[3] This regulation applied not only to occupational pension plans but also to profit-sharing plans. Returns on investments made by such a fund were also tax exempt.

This law marked the beginning of federal involvement in the provisions of occupational pensions. Because of the tax system, the state necessarily is involved in pension plans. The involvement, however, can be neutral, where pensions are treated equivalently to other types of expenditures, or the involvement can favour or disfavour pensions. Treating pensions as a business deduction is neutral involvement in that it treats current wages and future pension benefit payments equivalently, both being treated as deductible business expenses. Allowing investment

---

[3] For the history of tax regulations concerning pensions, see McGill (1979, - Chapter 2).

earnings to accrue tax free, however, favours pension savings over other forms of savings that are taxed.

Many of the oldest occupational pension plans in the United States were set up by public administrations for civil servants. Timing of plan establishment and practices varied greatly from one jurisdiction to another, given the decentralization of American government. The federal government, states, townships, and counties had autonomous jurisdiction over the salaries and working conditions of the civil servants they each employed. Furthermore, pension plans for different categories of employees – teachers, firemen, policemen, hospital personnel, office workers – were created at different times with different rules. The federal government did not set up its own civil service pension plan until 1920, later than many state or local governments, one sign of the relative weakness of the central state. Many state and local governments set up plans in the nineteenth century.

In the private sector, a number of large companies started pension plans in the 1910s and 1920s. At their height in the 1920s, these plans covered about 14 per cent of workers in the private sector. These plans were part of a broader movement called 'welfare capitalism', which ended with the Great Depression (Brandes 1976). Its leaders were corporate heads who advocated employer paternalism with the idea that employers should provide for the welfare of employees and their families.

Advocates of this movement were also interested in proving that large corporations, which the public viewed with increasing suspicion, had a sense of social responsibility to the community at large and to their own employees. Company initiatives in this direction included not only pension plans, but provision of many other services and benefits: schools, housing, churches, shops, recreation facilities, medical care, sick pay, and vacations. The most extreme form was the 'company town', isolated from other communities, where the company owned every business and provided every service.

As in other industrializing countries, American unions sometimes provided welfare benefits for their members. Provision of retirement pensions, however, quickly proved to be beyond the financial resources of most unions, especially when membership began to decline after 1920 (Quadagno 1988, pp. 56–60). By 1930, around 20 per cent of union members had a union pension plan (Ghilarducci 1992, p. 30). The onset of the Depression, however, caused the failure of many union and company plans.

3.2 The advent of social security: the impact of a more active state on occupational pensions

In 1935, the federal government passed the Social Security Act, which created a national retirement pension plan for employees aged 65 and over, financed through payroll taxes split evenly between employers and employees. This legislation was in part a response to the failure of occupational pension plans and private savings. It was also motivated by widespread misery among older Americans at a time when unemployment affected up to a quarter of the working population. The state wanted to alleviate poverty among the elderly and to encourage them to leave the work force so that jobs would go to the young.

The same legislation made unemployment insurance nationwide and started a programme of means-tested assistance for people aged 65 and over. Of these programmes only the retirement plan was purely national, financed and administrated on a national basis with the federal government deciding on contribution and benefit levels. The national nature of the plan was a major innovation in a country where social welfare had previously been the province of the separate states.

The system began to pay benefits in 1940, marking a major change in the interaction between the state and enterprises in the provision of retirement income. Social security changed the shape of pre-existing retirement plans, as it grew to become the main source of retirement income for the majority of Americans. Much of the expansion of coverage by occupational plans occurred in the 1950s when social security was firmly in place.

Social security originally covered only employees of commerce and industry, but in the 1950s and 1960s, the social insurance system gradually extended coverage. Over the 1950s, coverage became mandatory for the self-employed, who today are required to pay both the employer's and the employee's share of contributions. It also became mandatory for domestic workers, farmers and farm labourers.

When social security was created, public sector employees were not allowed to affiliate. In 1951, administrations were allowed to affiliate employees who had no occupational plan. The decision was up to the employer, not the employee. In 1955, affiliation was authorized for those who had an occupational plan and many proceeded to join. In 1984, the federal government affiliated all newly hired civil servants.[4] In 1990,

---

[4] The federal government had affiliated the armed forces in 1956.

Congress voted to make affiliation to social security obligatory for public sector employees with no occupational plan and now more than three-quarters of state and local government employees are covered. The expansion of social security coverage occurred in part to improve social security financing by bringing in new taxpaying workers.

While social security may have had a negative impact on the generosity of some existing pension plans, on net its effect on the development of occupational pensions may have been positive. Social security benefits are set at such a low level that most retired workers come nowhere near maintaining their standard of living if they rely solely on social security. Thus, social security does not eliminate the need for supplementary pensions.

The structure of social security benefits affects the characteristics of the work force covered by occupational pensions. The social security benefit formula is heavily weighted in favour of workers with low career average wages. The replacement rate is high for these workers, and few of them are covered by occupational pension plans.

An employee who has earned the average annual wage throughout a full career and begins to get a pension at the earliest possible age of 62 will get a pension equivalent to 35 per cent of his or her career-end wage. In contrast, someone who has always earned the equivalent of 75 per cent of the average wage will have a replacement rate of 48 per cent, while someone who has always earned the equivalent of 150 per cent of the average wage will have a replacement rate of 29 per cent.

For workers earning above a ceiling amount, further increases in earnings do not raise social security benefits. The ceiling is high compared to wages: it is equal to 2.4 times the average annual wage, and only 6 per cent of employees earn more. The replacement rate for someone who has always earned the ceiling is 19 per cent. Because of the weighting of the benefit formula in favour of low wage workers, and because of the ceiling on social security benefits, higher paid workers with full careers are 'disadvantaged' under social security.

While social security has been designed to favour low wage earners and those with intermittent careers, occupational plans on the whole favour high wage earners and employees who do not interrupt their careers. This complementary pattern did not develop by accident but developed through the interactions of the state and enterprises. Social security is designed to provide relatively generous benefits to low wage workers who are not likely to be covered by an occupational pension. For higher wage workers, social security benefits are relatively small (in comparison to earnings), leaving room for occupational pensions.

Occupational plans that adjust benefits in such a way as to take social security pensions into account are said to be 'integrated' with social security. Because social security is heavily weighted in favour of employees with low career average wages, integration offsets this tendency by guaranteeing higher benefits proportional to wages for employees with higher career wage levels. Two techniques of integration have developed. One, called 'step rate', consists of defining two accrual rates for benefits: a lower one for earnings below the social security ceiling and a higher one for earnings above the ceiling. The other, called 'offset', consists of promising a certain total benefit, adding up social security and the occupational pension. The occupational plan then pays the difference between the social security pension and the total pension. The changes that have evolved over time in integrated schemes are discussed in detail later in the section on state regulation.

Unions demanded integration as a strategy for campaigning for both improvements in social security and the creation of occupational pension plans at the end of the 1940s. At that time, social security pensions were very low for all workers. Unions pushed for occupational plans having a 100 per cent offset of social security benefits. Thus, the plans negotiated at this time provided for a total benefit that included the social security pension and the occupational pension, the latter being financed completely by the employer. Union leaders, particularly Walter Reuther of the United Auto Workers, calculated that this arrangement would give the employers who signed such agreements a direct financial interest in increases in social security benefits. Shortly after the three major automobile manufacturers signed such agreements, in 1950, Congress enacted the first increase in social security since the beginning of the programme – an increase of 77 per cent. The result was an immediate and large saving for companies that were financing offset integrated plans (Quadagno 1988, pp. 162–8).

Subsequently, Congress established a pattern of enacting regular increases in social security pensions, and unions dropped this tactic and opposed integration between occupational plans and social security. Negotiated plans in the private sector are now usually not integrated.

3.3 State interventions on taxes, wages and industrial relations in the 1940s: their impact on the development of occupational pensions

The growth of pension coverage in the private sector was encouraged by the high income tax rates during World War II and the Korean War. At the same time, however, the growth of pension coverage, among both unionized and nonunionized workers, was also encouraged by rules concerning wage and price controls during World War II and during the Korean War in the early 1950s. Workers could not receive wage increases, but they were allowed increases in pension benefits. Furthermore, high tax rates on corporate profits in these periods gave employers a new financial incentive for setting up pension plans or increasing pension promises under existing plans.

The court system also encouraged the growth of occupational pension coverage. A major court decision of 1949 gave unions the right to bargain not only on wages but also on occupational pension plans, as well as many other 'fringe' benefits. Under the Taft-Hartley Act of 1947, employers were obliged to bargain with unions on behalf of unionized employees concerning wages, hours of work, or other conditions of employment. Shortly after the law was passed, the management of the Inland Steel Company decided to unilaterally fix a mandatory retirement age as a feature of the company pension plan. The steel workers' union contested the decision and a federal court ruled that the company had to negotiate decisions concerning its pension plan. Pension plans thus became a mandatory subject of bargaining. Following this decision, many unions negotiated pension plans. Previously pension plans had often been regarded as a management tool by unions.

3.4 The monopoly of enterprises in providing retirement income

An aspect of retirement income provision in the United States that has been present in all periods is that enterprises have been given a near monopoly on the provision of tax-favoured retirement income.

Only employer contributions to an occupational pension plan are tax deductible. Employee contributions to an occupational pension plan in the 1920s, that is, to a defined benefit plan were, and still are, included in the employee's taxable income. This tax rule is a state action that discourages employee contributions. It is to the employee's financial advantage to have the employer alone finance a pension plan rather than receiving an equivalent salary raise and then using it to contribute after-tax dollars to a pension plan. By contrast, tax regulations in many other countries allow tax-free employee contributions as well as employer contributions, or at least accord similar tax treatment to both (Dilnot 1992).

The near monopoly of employers is also seen in the tax treatment of personal retirement savings. Individual Retirement Accounts have a low maximum annual contribution of $2000 per worker plus $250 for a nonworking spouse, while the maximum for occupational plans is many times higher ($30 000 for most defined contribution plans).

The Taft-Hartley Act of 1947 also had another major impact on occupational pension plans for union members. The legislation expressly forbade unions from being sole managers of pension funds, which had sometimes been the case in multiemployer plans. Funds of collectively bargained plans can be unilaterally managed by employers or jointly managed by employers and a union. Funds of multiemployer plans are generally jointly run, the trustees being half union and half representatives of the negotiating employers' organization.

3.5 Direct state regulation of occupational pensions since 1974: an expanding role in determining the structure of occupational plans

Two major changes in government regulations concerning older workers have occurred since 1974. First, there have been major reforms in occupational retirement plan regulations. Second, legislation regarding the rights of older workers has been modified, mostly to prevent discrimination against them based on age.

Up until 1974, public policy towards private sector occupational plans mainly concerned the tax exemptions on employer contributions designed to encourage creation and operation of occupational pension plans. Employees' rights were poorly protected. Those laid off just before reaching retirement age could lose all occupational pension rights, no matter how many years they had been affiliated to a plan. Employees had no legal protection for their occupational pensions in the event of employer bankruptcy.

In 1974, Congress passed a major reform in pension law, the Employee Retirement Income Security Act, commonly known as ERISA. This legislation was motivated by highly publicized cases where long-tenure employees had been denied benefits. This legislation broke with the past – the federal government intervened in private sector pension policy in many areas where it had not done so previously. Among other changes, the 1974 law required vesting of occupational pension rights for the first time. Up until then, even long-term employees could lose all rights to an occupational pension if they left an employer. Since 1974, there have been almost yearly additions or modifications to the original legislation, which has gradually become more restrictive.[5]

The general rationale behind these regulations is that occupational retirement plans that benefit from tax exemptions are a matter of public concern. Since taxpayers bear part of the cost of such plans, the federal government is perceived as having a duty to see that the plans are run in such a way as to further the national interest. This has been interpreted as necessitating intervention in two areas: (1) the state should see that benefits are distributed fairly, and (2) the state should ensure that employees' pensions are adequately secured.

The state has always stopped short of mandating coverage for all employees. It has also stopped short of requiring coverage for all employees within an establishment or enterprise once a plan has been set up. Part-time employees and seasonal employees may specifically be excluded. An enterprise may define a subgroup of employees to be covered by a plan, subject to approval of the Internal Revenue Service that must ascertain that the definition is 'nondiscriminatory' (McGill and Grubbs 1989, p. 86). This regulation allows unions to negotiate a plan covering a particular bargaining unit within an enterprise. It also allows an employer to set up separate plans for different categories of personnel or plans for some categories and not for others.

Concern with equity in distribution of benefits has resulted in a number of regulations regarding criteria that plans may use to determine who among the employees who belong to a covered category of personnel may or may not be excluded from an occupational pension plan. These regulations are designed to prevent exclusion on the grounds of age and exclusion of mobile employees. In particular, the 1974 law also required plans to affiliate newly hired older employees if they were more than five years from reaching the plan's retirement age. The Omnibus Budget Reconciliation Act of 1986, which generally took effect in 1988,

---

[5] Hoopes and Maroney (1992) provide a useful chronology of major changes since 1974.

required that older employees of any age be affiliated to a plan under the same conditions as younger ones.

State actions sometimes do not achieve their desired goals because of reactions of employers. Aspects of occupational pension reform designed to protect the rights of older workers have increased the costs of employing them, and thus may have a negative effect on the hiring of the older workers they are designed to protect.

Regulations have gradually set up limits on integration of occupational plans with social security. Integration is more widespread in the private sector than in the public sector. In the private sector, integration was considered to be justified for two reasons. First, it was sometimes argued that employees with different wage levels should get about the same replacement rate in retirement. Each employee's total pension, counting social security and an occupational pension, should be proportional to wages. The basic principle behind this idea is that inequalities in wages should be extended into retirement. Secondly, employers contended that since they pay social security contributions, they should be able to recoup what they have spent on social security in the form of reductions in occupational pensions.

Regulations concerning integration protect the rights of the employees who have relatively low wages. Offset integration of private sector occupational plans with social security was limited in 1974 in that an occupational plan was forbidden to cut pensions in payment following increases in social security pensions. Prior to this change, cost-of-living increases in pensions being paid out by social security could result in equal cutbacks in pensions in payment from occupational plans. In other words, increases in social security could result in immediate and full equal decreases in payments from occupational plans, a feature that gave employers who finance occupational benefits, but not retired employees, an interest in social security increases. The Tax Reform Act of 1986, which generally took effect in 1989, defined new limits on disparities between occupational pension benefits between high and low wage earners working in the same enterprise, including even workers who are not covered by a plan. Furthermore, plans may no longer take into account social security benefits due for years of work with other employers.

Concern over nonpayment of occupational pension promises by inadequately funded plans prompted another series of regulations. In 1974, ERISA made funding of occupational pension plans obligatory and the law defined a limited number of actuarial funding methods for

Table 10.1 – Coverage rate of the work force by occupational plans in the private sector, 1975, 1987 and 1992: defined benefit plans and defined contribution plans (percentage of the private sector work force)

Type of Plan	1975	1987	1992
Defined benefit only	30	13	9
Defined contribution only	6	15	20
Defined benefit or defined contribution + secondary defined contribution plan	9	18	17
Total with an occupational pension or savings plan	45	46	46

Sources: Beller and Lawrence (1992, Table 4.12); US Department of Labor, Pension and Welfare Benefits Administration (1996).

determination of tax exemptions. In order to further protect employees, a form of state-run reinsurance was instituted. The Pension Benefit Guaranty Corporation guarantees occupational pensions up to a fairly generous limit for employees whose employers have gone bankrupt leaving an inadequate fund.

A major trend in federal intervention in the provision of occupational pensions has thus been to reduce the risks to workers participating in occupational pension plans. Defined contribution plans are less expensive to provide and entail more risk for the worker and less for the employer than do traditional defined benefit pension plans. To some extent the efforts of the state to reduce pension risks have been offset by actions taken by enterprises that have increased pension risks. This occurred through the trend towards defined contribution plans and away from defined benefit plans.

Between 1975 and 1992, defined contribution plans became increasingly common, rising from 15 per cent to 37 per cent. Increasingly employees who have a defined benefit plan have acquired a defined contribution plan in addition. At the same time, an increasing proportion of the private sector work force has only a defined contribution plan, without a defined benefit plan (Table 10.1).

State interventions have tended to become more restrictive over the past 20 years as the state has gained experience in regulating occupational pensions. The interventions have also become more sharply focused. While the state has the goal that occupational pensions be adequately funded, it now much more restrictively regulates both overfunding and underfunding than it did a few years ago.

An important trend in American public policy towards occupational pensions is to encourage work at later ages. This public policy trend seems to run counter to the desires of employers. Sheppard (1991, p. 278) describes this situation in his contribution on the United States to a comparative study of retirement age trends in the United States and Europe:

> The history of retirement in the United States involves a scenario of seemingly opposite or conflicting policy directions resulting from the government's efforts to raise age at exit or to restrain the drift toward early exit and the employer world's efforts to expand on and accelerate the rate of early exit.

In comparison, in continental Europe there was a certain coordination, or at least coincidence, of state and employer policies towards older workers whereby public policy reinforced employers' tendencies to encourage older workers to leave their work forces. See other chapters in this book, especially those on France, Germany and the Netherlands.

So long as the decision to provide an occupational pension plan is voluntary for employers, the state is limited in the actions it can take to regulate pension plans by the threat of employers to not provide them. If the state regulates occupational pensions in such a way as to make them too costly, or to overly reduce their positive features for employers, then employers will react by not providing them.

3.6 The impact of federal budgetary policy in the 1980s and 1990s: reducing the tax subsidy to occupational pensions

A major trend in federal intervention in the provision of occupational pensions has been to reduce the tax subsidy provided them, starting noticeably with the Tax Reform Act of 1982. This trend has been motivated by two factors. First, the tax subsidy to occupational pensions has grown with the growth in total assets in the occupational pension system, which itself has been caused by the aging of the population and the maturing of the occupational pension system. Second, the large deficit in the federal budget has forced Congress to look for ways to reduce tax subsidies. Thus, the state has two conflicting goals – the goal of increasing occupational pension coverage and the goal of reducing the budget deficit. The second goal, while not directly relating to occupational pensions, has important implications for them since it results in a reduction in the generosity of the tax treatment of occupational pensions.

4. The present US retirement system

4.1 A major transformation in occupational plans

The US occupational pension system has changed greatly in the past decade due to the decline of defined benefit pension plans. Following years of growth, the number of participants in defined benefit plans peaked in 1984 at 41.0 million, and has stagnated despite continued growth of the labour force. In 1992, there were 39.5 million participants in defined benefit plans.

The true magnitude of the decline in the occupational pension system, however, is hidden in the statistics on number of participants because those numbers include retirees whose benefits are based on their earlier work. The decline in defined benefit plans is seen more starkly in the statistics on active participants – workers currently accruing benefits. The number of active participants in defined benefit plans peaked in 1984 at 30.2 million, and by 1992 had fallen to 25.4 million. The number of active workers in defined benefit plans in 1992 was less than in 1975, the first year for which a consistent series of statistics is available.

The decline in defined benefit plans has occurred at least in part due to government regulations that have made them more expensive to provide, that have reduced the extent to which they can be funded, and that have reduced their usefulness to employers as a tool to manage personnel tenure.

By comparison, in 1975, there were 11.2 million active participants in defined contribution plans, and by 1992 that number had tripled to 38.9 million. Since 1984, there have been more active participants in defined contribution plans than in defined benefit plans (US Department of Labor 1996).

US occupational pension coverage statistics, while appearing straightforward to interpret, are in fact complex. While it is clear that defined benefit plans have declined, the numerical dominance of defined contribution plan participants is partially because of the growth of defined contribution plans as secondary plans for workers having a primary defined benefit plan (Table 10.1).

A major aspect of the growth in defined contribution plans has been the growth of 401(k) plans. These plans were first available when section 401(k) was added to the Internal Revenue Code (the tax code) in 1979. They have two important features. First, employee contributions are tax deductible, while employee contributions to defined benefit plans and most other defined contribution plans are not. Second, employee participation is voluntary, while employee participation in most other plans is automatic because the contributions are made entirely by the employer.

The growth of 401(k) plans was made possible by government policy that made these plans available to workers. Their growth, however, followed clarifying regulations implemented in 1981. By 1984, these plans had 7.5 million active participants. That number has continued to grow rapidly, and in 1992 reached 22.4 million. Three million more active participants were added in 1992 alone (US Department of Labor 1996).

A related trend is the change in coverage rate over time. Occupational pension coverage measured in terms of the responses of individuals to the question 'are you covered by a pension plan?' has declined. While occupational pension coverage defined to include defined contribution plans has changed little over time, pension coverage defined by workers' responses to the above question has declined because many workers do not consider their defined contribution plans to be pension plans.

This decline is troubling because at the same time the generosity of social security is diminishing. Starting in the year 2000, the age at which full retirement benefits can be received is being pushed back. The projected deficit in social security makes further declines in social security generosity likely. Thus, there appears to be a double decline in the two major sources of retirement income, causing many policy analysts to worry that the baby-boom generation is saving inadequately for its future retirement. To better understand the base from which these changes are occurring, section 4.3 analyses the sources of retirement income for current retirees.

Table 10.2 – Total cash payments from the three pillars for those age 55 or older, 1992 (billions of 1992 dollars)

Source		
Total	605.1	
First pillar	307.0	
Social security: retirement and survivors'		254.9
Retired workers, 62–64		16.7
Retired workers, 65+		185.0
Disabled workers, 60–64		6.9
Disabled workers, 55–59		5.0
Spouses, 62–64		2.0
Spouses, 65+		10.8
Widows & widowers, 60–64		3.8
Widows, 65+		37.8
Public assistance		7.4
Veterans' benefits, workers' injuries or illnesses, unemployment insurance		13.8
Federal civil service retirement, 1990		33.2
Railroad retirement		7.7
Second pillar	259.2	
Private sector occupational plans, including disability		182.0
State and local government occupational plans, including disability		77.2
Third pillar	38.9	
Life insurance payments to annuitants, 1990		35.4
Individual Retirement Accounts, Keogh plans		3.5
GDP	5950.7	

Sources: Social Security Administration (1995); Yakoboski and Silverman (1994); US Department of Commerce (1995); authors' calculations.

4.2 The relative size of the three pillars

The relative importance of the government, employers and individuals as sources of retirement income for older Americans can be seen by examining payments made to beneficiaries age 55 or older. Table 10.2 shows figures for 1992 and Table 10.3 gives the figures in less detail for 1980.

Retirement income sources can be divided into three categories or pillars. The first pillar is the government, the second is employers, and the third is individuals. The third pillar is small compared to the other

Table 10.3 – Total cash payments from the three pillars for those age 55 or older, 1980 (billions of 1980 dollars)

Source		
Total	202.3	
First pillar	140.6	
Social security: retirement and survivors'		105.1
Public assistance		2.7
Federal civil service retirement		15.5
Veterans retirement		12.5
Railroad retirement		4.8
Second pillar	51.5	
Private sector occupational plans, including disability		36.4
State and local government occupational plans, including disability		15.1
Third pillar	10.2	
Life insurance payments to annuitants		10.2
GDP	2708.0	

Sources: US Department of Commerce (1992); Social Security Administration (1982).

two as a source of retirement income. It is composed of payments specifically destined to provide income to individuals after a certain age, which are set up by the individuals themselves. It has two components in the 1992 table: annuities paid out by individual life insurance policies, and payments (usually as lump sums) from individual accounts. The individual accounts are of two types: Individual Retirement Accounts (IRA), which may be opened by any worker, and Keogh plans, which may be opened by the self-employed for themselves and their employees.

Table 10.4 sums up the information, presenting total payments for each pillar as a percentage of Gross Domestic Product (GDP) for the two years. These tables take into account money income from all types of benefit programmes that go to people age 55 or over.

A few comments are in order concerning the tables. While nearly all the figures in Table 10.2 are for 1992, a few of the figures are for 1990, but have been expressed in 1992 dollars, adjusting for changes in the Consumer Price Index. Table 10.2 shows payments from social security's disability insurance programme (DI) made to beneficiaries age 55 or

Table 10.4 – Cash payments from the three pillars for those age 55 or older as a percentage of GDP, 1980 and 1992

Pillar	1980	1992
First pillar	5.2	5.1
Second pillar	1.9	4.4
Third pillar	0.4	0.7
Total	7.5	10.2

Sources: Tables 10.2 and 10.3.

over, but in the 1980 data it was not possible to isolate payments from disability insurance to people over 55 from payments to younger beneficiaries. Hence, social security disability insurance is not included in the total for social security in Table 10.3.

In these tables, occupational pensions paid by the federal government to its employees, a form of occupational pensions, are counted as part of the first pillar, which is made up of public, legally obligatory pensions. Pensions paid by other levels of government – states, municipalities, counties – are counted as part of the second pillar, which is made up of contractual, occupational pensions. This distinction is somewhat arbitrary in that pensions paid by any level of government can be considered public and obligatory, or could be considered as provided by the government as an employer. In Table 10.3, Individual Retirement Accounts are not included. These accounts were only authorized by legislation in 1974, so that by 1980 total retirement income from them was negligible.

Table 10.4 gives a rough idea of the relative importance of the three pillars in 1980 and 1992, based on the figures in Tables 10.2 and 10.3. Total cash payments relative to GDP to people age 55 and over were considerably higher in 1992 than in 1980: 10.2 per cent of GDP in 1992 versus 7.5 per cent in 1980. Payments from the first pillar, which are mostly from social security, have remained stable relative to GDP at about 5.2 per cent, which represented over two-thirds (69 per cent) of the total in 1980 and half (50 per cent) in 1992. While payments from the third pillar increased relative to GDP between 1980 and 1992, they still comprised only 0.7 per cent of the total in 1992, hardly much of a 'pillar' as a source of retirement income for Americans.

There has, however, been a marked increase in the relative impor-

Table 10.5 – Percentage of units aged 65 and older with money income from specified sources, 1962–92

Source	1962	1971	1976	1980	1988	1992
Social security: retirement, survivors' and disability	69	87	89	90	92	92
Public sector occ. plans	5	6	9	12	14	15
Private sector occ. plans	9	17	20	22	29	32
Earnings	36	31	25	23	22	20
Income from assets	54	49	56	66	68	67
Public assistance	13	10	11	10	7	7

Source: Susan Grad (various years).

tance of payments from the second-pillar payments from occupational retirement plans. Much of this increase comes from private sector occupational savings plans. In 1980, savings plans (defined contribution plans) paid out a third of all cash paid by private sector occupational plans, whereas in 1992 they paid out about half (US Department of Labor 1996). Most of the payments from savings plans are in the form of lump sums upon an employee's departure from a job, whatever the employee's age.

4.3 Older Americans' income sources

The US Bureau of the Census regularly conducts a survey called the Current Population Survey, in which participants are asked about their sources of income. Tables 10.5, 10.6, and 10.7 present data on the sources of income of aged households from this source. The age of a household, or 'unit,' is defined as the age of the individual, if the person is single, and the age of the older of the two individuals in a couple. Hence, among units aged 65 and older are many individuals who are younger but who are married to someone who is at least 65.

Table 10.5 gives the frequency of income from various sources for units age 65 or over for years when the survey on benefits was conducted between 1962 and 1992. The category 'income from assets' includes income from investments made with capital distributed by occupational savings plans. The assets of occupational savings plans represent a large

Table 10.6 – Percentage shares of aggregate income of units aged 55 and older, 1984 and 1992

Year	1984			1992		
Age	55–61	62–64	65+	55–61	62–64	65+
Social security	2	12	38	2	14	40
Public sector occ. plans	3	5	7	4	7	9
Private sector occ. plans	2	6	6	4	8	10
Earnings	78	57	16	79	56	17
Income from assets	11	16	28	9	11	21
Public assistance	1	1	1	1	1	1
Total	100	100	100	100	100	100

Source: Susan Grad (various years).

and increasing proportion of total household assets in the United States. Hence the amount of income derived from lump sums paid by such plans is growing, but a breakdown is not available on how much of the income from assets comes from this type of capital.

The figures in Table 10.5 reflect the broadening of social security coverage over the period. This is reflected with some time lag, since new beneficiaries must have contributed for a minimum period to qualify for a retirement pension.

The frequency of income from occupational retirement plans – both public and private – rose significantly over the period, reflecting the expansion of affiliation. Altogether, only 14 per cent of aged units received income from an occupational plan in 1962, while in 1992 the proportion was 32 per cent. Many occupational pension plans, when set up, quickly pay benefits on the basis of past service, which is work for the employer before the creation of the plan.

The frequency of labour earnings for the older population dropped significantly between 1962 and 1992, reflecting the trend towards withdrawal from the work force at earlier ages. Nonetheless, many older Americans work for pay beyond age 65, far more than in continental Europe. The earnings from work among older households are also due to younger spouses who work after their partner has retired.

Since 1980, about two-thirds of older Americans have received income from assets. Some of this income is derived from capital paid out by occupational retirement and savings plans.

Table 10.7 – Distribution of income from each source by quintile, units aged 65 and older, 1990 (percentages)

Source of income	1st	2nd	Quintile 3rd	4th	5th
Social Security	10	18	22	25	26
Occupational plans	1	4	12	27	57
Earnings	0	1	5	15	79
Asset income	1	3	8	18	70
Other	17	15	16	20	32
Total	4	9	13	22	52

Source: Reno (1993).

Public assistance for the elderly is mostly comprised of income from a means-tested programme for handicapped people and people aged 65 or over called Supplementary Security Income (SSI). As older households have received more income from other sources, the frequency of public assistance receipt dropped from 1962 to 1988. It did not drop, however, from 1988 to 1992.

Table 10.6 gives a picture of the composition of older households' income in two years, 1984 and 1992. This table presents the percentages of aggregate income of the aged that come from different sources. As pointed out by Rein and Stapf (1996), the statistics in this table differ from statistics that take the average across individuals of the percentage of income derived from different sources. The statistics based on the percentages of aggregate income are disproportionately affected by the income receipt patterns of wealthy aged units.

In the age group 65 or over, income from social security has risen slightly as a percentage of total income, from 38 per cent in 1984 to 40 per cent in 1992. In both years, it is by far the largest single source of income for this age group. Occupational pensions represented only 13 per cent in 1984 and 19 per cent in 1992.

Table 10.7 shows the share of income from each source that goes to each income quintile. Distribution of income from a source is equal if the percentage is 20 per cent for each quintile. Social security pensions are the most equally distributed of the different categories of income. The poorest quintile receives 10 per cent of social security pension payments and the richest quintile receives 26 per cent. Asset income and earnings are the most unequally distributed of income types, with the highest quintile receiving 70 per cent of asset income and 79 per cent of earnings. The latter figure arises because the wealthier older population more often work for pay than the middle quintiles and their earnings are higher.

Occupational pensions are less concentrated among the most wealthy than asset income or earnings. However, the bottom two quintiles – the poorest 40 per cent of the elderly population – receive only 5 per cent of the income from occupational pension plans.

5.   Summary and conclusion

The state has various goals concerning the provision of occupational pensions by enterprises. These goals include reducing risk to workers, assuring an equitable distribution of benefits, encouraging pension coverage, and limiting the tax loss to the Treasury. In recent years, encouraging older workers to continue working in their early and mid sixties may have become a goal. The state pursues these goals through tax subsidies, laws and regulations, and court decisions. In addition, it pursues these goals through the structure of social security, which provides benefits at moderate levels in order to leave room for occupational pensions. Enterprises' goals include attracting workers, reducing worker turnover, and influencing retirement age.

Providing equality of treatment for all forms of retirement income has not been a goal of government policy. An outcome of occupational pension policy is that in the United States enterprises have a monopoly on the provision of tax-favoured retirement savings. The limits on contributions to Individual Retirement Accounts, which individual employees may use to provide retirement income, are much lower than the limits for occupational pension or savings plans.

Enterprises have reacted in various ways to the actions taken by the government in pursuit of its goals. The provision of tax incentives to encourage occupational pension coverage has increased the provision of pensions. The reduction of tax benefits to occupational pensions to reduce the federal deficit has probably had the unintended consequence of reducing coverage. The enactment of regulations to reduce the risks workers face in defined benefit plans has had the intended effect for some plans, but has had the unintended effect of reducing occupational pension coverage. It is as yet unclear whether governmental action encouraging delayed retirement will be supported by changes in occupational pensions that also encourage delayed retirement or whether enterprises will attempt to offset governmental action by changes in pension plans that are more favourable to early retirement.

The use of occupational pensions by enterprises to reduce employee turnover has caused a reaction from the government in the form of laws that limit the ability of enterprises to use pensions in this way. Some enterprises have reacted to these laws by terminating their occupational pension plans. Because employers voluntarily provide occupational pension plans, the threat that they will terminate their plans limits the government's ability to impose costly regulations.

At the same time, regulations have allowed, and in some ways actually encouraged, expansion of the occupational savings plans that seem to have replaced occupational pension plans to some extent in the private sector.

Occupational pension plans can be considered a component of social welfare, while occupational savings plans do not constitute a form of social welfare according to the European Union definition outlined at the beginning of this chapter. Recent developments in American company policies can be interpreted as a decline in the 'welfare enterprise,' that is, a decline in social welfare provided through plans set up by companies for their own employees.

In traditional American laissez-faire ideology, 'welfare enterprise' is sometimes considered an alternative to the welfare state. Proponents of this ideology tend to view occupational retirement plans not merely as supplements to social security but as substitutes for social security. Given the present decline of occupational pension plans and the growth of savings plans, it is essential for this argument that savings plans be perceived as a substitute for pension plans, both occupational plans and social security. This may be one of the reasons why savings plans are so often called pension plans.

In the area of retirement, the American 'welfare enterprise' has long supplemented social security pensions for a minority of retired employees. If present trends continue, the 'welfare enterprise' will fade as pension plans are replaced by occupational savings plans.

References

apRoberts, Lucy (1993), 'Complementary Retirement Pensions: Towards a Definition of Terms', *International Social Security Review*, Vol. 46, 51–66.

Beller, Daniel J. and Lawrence, Helen H. (1992), 'Trends in Private Pension Plan Coverage', in John A. Turner and Daniel. J. Beller (eds.), *Trends in Pensions 1992*, Washington, DC: US Government Printing Office.

Brandes, Stuart D. (1976), *American Welfare Capitalism 1880–1940*, Chicago: The University of Chicago Press.

Dilnot, Andrew (1992), 'Taxation and Private Pensions: Costs and Consequences', in *Private Pensions and Public Policy*, Paris: OECD.

Doescher, Tabitha A. (1994), 'Are Pension Coverage Rates Declining?', in Richard P. Hinz, John A. Turner and Phyllis P. Fernandez (eds.), *Pension Coverage Issues for the '90s*, Washington, DC: US Government Printing Office.

Eurostat (1995), *ESSPROS Manual 1995*. Volume 1: 'General Principles and the Core System', Brussels: Eurostat.

Ghilarducci, Teresa (1992), *Labor's Capital: The Economics and Politics of Private Pensions*, Cambridge, Mass.: The MIT Press.

Grad, Susan (1994), *Income of the Population Aged 60 and Older*, and various other years, Washington, DC: US Social Security Administration.

Hoopes, Terence J. and Maroney, Kevin (1992), 'Appendix II: Summary of Federal Legislation Affecting Private Employee Pension Benefits', in John A. Turner and Daniel J. Beller (eds.), *Trends in Pensions 1992*, Washington, DC: US Government Printing Office.

Kohli, Martin, Rein, Martin, Guillemard, Anne-Marie and Gunsteren, Herman van (eds.) (1991), *Time for Retirement: Comparative Studies of Early Exit from the Labor Force*, Cambridge: Cambridge University Press.

McGill, Dan M. (1979), *Fundamentals of Private Pensions*, 4th edition, Homewood, Illinois: R.D. Irwin.

McGill, Dan M. and Grubbs, Donald S. Jr. (1989), *Fundamentals of Private Pensions*, 6th edition, Homewood, Illinois: Irwin.

Quadagno, Jill (1988), *The Transformation of Old Age Security: Class and Politics in the American Welfare State*, Chicago: The University of Chicago Press.

Rein, Martin and Stapf, Heinz (1996), 'Income Packaging and Economic Wellbeing at the Last Stage of the Working Life', LIS Working Paper.

Reno, Virginia P. (1993), 'The Role of Pensions in Retirement Income: Trends and Questions', *Social Security Bulletin*, Vol. 56 (Spring), 29–43.

Sheppard, Harold L. (1991), 'The United States: The Privatization of Exit', in Martin Kohli et al. (eds.), op. cit.

Social Security Administration (1982, 1995), *Annual Statistical Supplement to the Social Security Bulletin*, Washington, DC: US Government Printing Office.

Tilove, Robert (1976), *Public Employee Pension Funds*, New York: Columbia University Press.

US Department of Labor, Pension and Welfare Benefits Administration (1996), 'Abstract of 1992 Form 5500 Annual Reports', *Private Pension Plan Bulletin* (Winter).

US Department of Commerce (1992), *Survey of Current Business, the National Income and Product Accounts of the United States: Statistical Supplement, 1959-1988,* Vol. 2, Washington, DC: US Government Printing Office.

US Department of Commerce (1995), *Survey of Current Business, the National Income and Product Accounts of the United States,* Washington, DC: US Government Printing Office.

Williamson, Samuel H. (1992), 'US and Canadian Pensions before 1930: A Historical Perspective', in John A. Turner and Daniel J. Beller (eds.), *Trends in Pensions 1992,* Washington, DC: US Government Printing Office.

Yakoboski, Paul and Silverman, Celia (1994), 'Baby Boomers in Retirement: What Are Their Prospects?', in Dallas L. Salisbury and Nora Super Jones (eds.), *Retirement in the 21st Century: Ready or Not,* Washington, DC: Employee Benefit Research Institute.

Index

AAW-1976   *225-7*
Abel-Smith, Brian   *7*
ABP Law   *222*
actuarial pensions   *277*
Adenstedt, Erik   *51*
AGB   *283, 302*
AGIRC   *67-80, 82, 84-92, 94, 96, 98*
AGS   *283, 284, 288, 302*
Ahrend, Peter   *19, 111, 118, 120, 144*
AKW   *254*
Allmendinger, Julia   *8*
AOW (Old Age Act)   *222-4, 234-8, 251-2, 254-5, 260, 263-4*
AP-funds   *298*
APP schemes   *340-41*
ARRCO   *67-8, 71-82, 84-92, 94-5*
ASF   *88-90*
ATP   *27, 270, 278-81, 283, 285, 287-8, 291, 294-7, 299-300*
Auerbach, Alan   *8, 9*
Ausgleichszulage (means tested supplement to pension)   *37-8, 41, 45-6*
Austria   *7, 23, 29, 33-64*
Austrian Association of Pension Funds   *57-8*
AWBZ   *254*
AWW Act   *223*

Barber case   *138*
base amount   *27, 268, 270, 275-6, 278, 281, 286-7, 289-90, 292-3, 300, 304-5*

Bauer, Uwe   *127*
Beamten or Civil Service Pensions
Becker, Gary   *53*
BetrAVG   *110, 118, 132-4, 141*
Beveridge, William   *310-11,*
Beyer, Jürgen   *133, 139*
Biffl, Gudrun   *48*
Bismarck   *109*
Blomsma, Martin   *234*
Boltanski, Luc   *68*
book reserves   *58, 77, 92-3, 110, 117-9, 137, 139, 183, 186*
Boychuk, Terry   *19*
BPF   *222, 242*
Bradshaw, Jonathan   *317*
Brandes, Stuart   *358*
bridging jobs   *9*
Broeder, Arie den   *226*

CAO   *224, 232, 263-4*
Castellino, Onarato   *152, 166*
Caussat, Laurent   *82*
CNPF   *70–71, 87*
company pensions funds   *151, 206-7, 211*
compulsory supplementary schemes   *73-4, 77*
contracting out   *26, 195-6, 206-7, 312, 332-9, 348-50*
contributory pensions   *65*
Cornilleau, Gérard   *92*
Cozzolino, Maria   *175, 184*
Crabbe, R.J.W.   *137*
Cutler, David   *7*

defined benefit   17, 19, 75, 90, 144, 218, 286, 292, 348-9
defined benefit plans   19, 144, 355, 366, 368-9, 376
defined contribution, defined contribution plans   276, 366
Denmark   23-4, 119, 301, 307
Di Biase, Rita   172
disability pensions   13, 17-18, 49, 157-8, 170, 178-9, 267-8, 270-72, 274-5, 285, 300, 352
Dobbin, Frank   19
Doescher, Tabitha   356
Dyer, John   196, 209

early exit   14, 17, 31-2, 246, 265, 273, 284, 308, 367, 378
early retirement   5, 7, 9, 14, 17-18, 38, 61, 63, 77, 88-9, 134, 136, 171, 178-9, 192, 254, 302, 307, 377
Edebalk, Per Gunnar   302
efficiency wages   52, 56, 61
Ellis, Bryan   312, 315
employees' pensions funds   196, 199-201, 206-7, 209-13, 216, 218
Employment Protection Act   301
ERISA   363, 365
Esping-Andersen, Gösta   5
European Union   9, 31, 62, 87, 193, 355, 377
Eurostat   14, 21, 22-3, 174-5, 194, 253, 355-6, 378

farmers' old age provision   114
Fase, Wil   258
Ferrera, Maurizio   151
Finance Act 1947   326

FNS (National Solidarity Fund)   65
Förster, Wolfgang   107, 144
FPG-PRI scheme   281, 286, 289
France   4, 21-4, 29, 65-98, 206, 352, 367
Franco, Daniele   180
Friot, Bernard   69
Fujii, Tokozu   200
functional income distribution   41-2
FVP-fund   240

Gales, B.P.A.   222
Gassner-Möstl, E.   57
George, Rainer   109, 113
Germany   5, 7-8, 12, 18, 21, 23, 29-30, 56-7, 99-148, 324, 367
Ghillarducci, Teresa   358
Gini coefficient   26
GMP   316, 330, 332, 337
Gokhale, Jagadeesh   8, 9
Goode report   26
graduated pension scheme   313-14, 329, 333-4, 336, 339, 344, 346
Grubbs, Donald   364

Hannah, Leslie   18
Heppt, Ehrenfried   102, 122
Herd, Richard   7, 13, 21
Hofer, Helmut   55
Holzmann, Robert   61
Hutton, Will   325

IBM   185
INAIL   153, 158
income packaging   28, 65, 80, 378

Individual Retirement Accounts (IRA) *363, 370-72, 376*
INPDAP *155, 157, 159*
INPS *153-9, 178*
integrated pensions schemes *119-20*
integrative pension funds *182*
IRCANTEC *67, 79*
Italy *12, 21, 23-4, 29, 149-94*
ITP *281, 285-6, 288, 291-2, 295, 300, 303, 305-6*
ITPK *286*

Jansweiler, Roel *238, 260*
Japan *11-12, 16, 23, 29-31, 195-219*

Kam, Flip de *241*
Kammern (pension scheme for professionals) *34*
Kohli, Martin *5*
Kotlikoff, Laurence *8, 9*
Keogh (plans) *370-71*
Kroon, J. *229*
Kuné, Jan *222*

Lackner, Karin *39*
Lacroix, Jacqueline *80*
Lindbeck, Assar *2, 53*
LPI (limited price indexation) *332*
lump-sum benefits *188, 200, 356*
Lutjens, Erik *241*
Lutz, Hedwig *43*
Lynes, Tony *95, 313, 317*

mandatory retirement *164, 267, 198, 216*
Matschke, Manfred Jürgen *120*

Maxwell (affair) *324*
McGill, Dan *364*
Meijnen, J. *229*
Montedison *185*
Mooslechner, Peter *53, 56, 58*
Moynihan (Senator) *13*
Murakami, Kioyshi *200*

1946 National Insurance Act *311*
Netherlands *13, 16-18, 22-4, 26, 28-9, 31-2, 118, 220-65, 324, 367*
Netter, Francis *69*
Neuman, George *301*
Niermann, Udo *140*
Nypels, Frans *241*

Offe, Claus *4*
Olivetti *185*
Olson, Mancur *301*
Olsson, Lars *282*
Omnibus Budget Reconciliation Act 1986 *364*
OPF *222, 244*
Oswald, Christiane *109, 113*
Oversloot, Johannes *224*

Pace, Daniele *183*
part-time employees' pension scheme *329*
pay-as-you-go system *6, 31, 34, 96, 201, 205, 213, 218, 223, 233-4, 242-3, 250, 255-6, 260-61*
PAYE system *207*
Pedersen, Peder *301*
pension credits *91, 274-6, 278, 288*
1992 Pension Reform Act *135, 141*

Pensionskassen *117, 145*
Pensionsversicherungsanstalt
(PV-Anstalt) *34, 47*
personal pensions *3, 5-6, 13-15,*
19-20, 22, 29, 198, 207, 211,
317, 339-43, 346-7
PGGM *240, 243-4, 262*
PLE *284*
poverty *15, 25-7, 37, 41, 113,*
142, 180, 223, 259, 349-50, 359
Poyser, C.A. *327*
premium reserve system *276,*
286-7, 305
private pension *8, 15, 18-19, 24,*
28, 30, 32, 96, 100, 131, 135,
148, 168, 174, 182, 187-8, 191,
194, 214, 218-19, 224-5, 241,
259, 291-3, 296-7, 307, 333,
348, 378
401k programs *14, 20, 22, 469*
Proto, Gaetano *175, 184*
PSW *224, 241, 243, 259*

Q schemes *333*
Quadagno, Jill *358, 361*
quasi-funded scheme *13*

Rainwater, Lee *26*
redistributive effects *41-2, 82,*
166-7, 174, 193
Rein, Martin *1, 375*
Renault *4, 70*
replacement rate *14, 17, 29, 50,*
60, 66-7, 72, 80, 82-3, 91-2,
106, 127-8, 134, 161-4, 168,
187, 190-91, 360, 365
Reuther, Walter *361*
Reynaud *68, 74, 75*
Rhein-Kress, Gabi von *48*
Rissman, Ellen *301*

Rosanvallon, Pierre *78, 94*
Rössler, Norbert *144*

salary reduction plans *20*
Schmähl, Winfried *100, 101,*
109, 113, 124, 136, 140, 141
Schnapper, Dominique *94*
Schneider, Hans-Peter *126*
self-employment pension *163*
seniority pension *160, 163-4,*
169, 178
SERPS *309-10, 314-20, 322, 328-*
30, 332, 336-40, 342, 344-6,
348-9
severance pay, severance payments, *52, 150-51, 168, 174-7,*
181, 186-9, 191-2
Shapiro, Carl *53*
Sheppard, Harold *367*
Silburn, Roland *3*
SKP *280*
Smeeding, Tim *26*
Snower, Dennis *53*
social contributions *153*
social pensions *154*
social plans (SOP) *17, 232*
social protection *1-3, 10, 12, 17-*
18, 23, 25, 220-22, 247-51, 253,
256, 355
solidaristic wage policy *284*
Sonderunterstützung *38-9, 61*
SPP *280-81, 286*
Ståhlberg, Ann-Charlotte *302*
Stapf, Heintz *375*
statutory pension insurance
101-2, 104, 106, 107, 109, 110-
11, 113-14, 118-21, 124, 127-9,
132-7, 139-41, 144
Stefanis, Hans *39*
step rate *361*

Sterdyniak, Henri   92
Stiglitz, Joseph   53
STP   283-5, 287-8, 292, 295, 300, 304-6
Supplementary Security Income (SSI)   375
survivor benefits   8, 22
survivors' pension   37, 39, 170, 178
Sweden   8, 11-13, 15-17, 22-3, 25-7, 29, 32, 206, 266-308

Taft-Hartley (Act)   362-3
Tálos, Emmeric   38, 43
TAV-Act   228
tax qualified plans   195
Tax Reform Act 1986   365, 367
TBA-Act   228
teinen (age of retirement from 'life-long' jobs)   11, 195, 198
TFA   283, 302
TGL   283
Thatcher, Margaret   317
Timmermans, J.M.   251
Titmuss, Richard   4
Torrey, Barbara   26
Trommer, Willem   232
TUFS   18, 284, 300
Turner, John   7, 16, 19, 28, 30
TZ-Act   228

United Kingdom (Great Britain, Britain, UK)   2, 13, 15-17, 23-4, 26-7, 29, 95, 119, 142, 195, 309-51
United States (US)   8-9, 11-13,

18-20, 22-4, 28-31, 136, 206, 301, 302, 352-79
UNIRS   71
Unterstützungskassen   117, 148
Urbitch, Christian   139
Url, Thomas   53, 56, 58

VAM-1980   235
Van den Noord, Paul   7, 13, 21
VBL (Versorgungsanstalt des Bundes und der Ländes)   126-8
Veldkamp, G.   222, 223
Verbon, Harry   223, 224
veterans' schemes   114
Vollman, Kurt   58
Vroom, Bert de   232
VUT, VUT-schemes   17, 221, 231, 233-4, 255, 262

Wadensjö, Eskil   302
WAO-1967   225-6
Watanabe, Noriyusu   7, 16, 19, 28, 30
widows' pensions   135, 334, 336, 338
Williamson, Samuel   357
Winters, W.   223, 224
WKA-1991   235
Wolf, Walter   58, 59
Wörister, Karl   38, 43
WW-1949   225
WWV-1964   225, 229

ZFW   254
ZW-1967   226

This is a very timely book given the worldwide discussion these days of pension reform and privatization. It should prove extremely useful to academics and policy makers concerned with the future of the welfare state in general and the reform of social security programs in particular.'
– Lee Rainwater, Harvard University, USA

The economic demands of an ageing population, coupled with the crisis of public spending pose one of the greatest challenges to social policy, in both the East and West. This book focuses on the political economy of pensions, particularly on the interaction between private and state provision.

Enterprise and the Welfare State argues that there is more to welfare than simply provision by the state and so the focus of this book is on the welfare society rather than the welfare state. This requires a new system of statistical accounting and a different focus for case studies. A multidisciplinary approach is used to examine the design of the pensions system in nine countries with different institutional welfare mixes. Using a common conceptual framework, it compares and contrasts the goals and realities of the welfare systems in France, Germany, The Netherlands and Sweden, where strong occupational pensions are in operation, with the more modest welfare states in Japan, the United Kingdom and the United States. Each country case study provides a grounded analysis of the evolution of pension design and traces the impact of the policies on the economic well-being of the aged and the performance of the economy. It offers new data on the level of spending of enterprise based occupational pensions and examines the implications for redistribution resulting from changes in the design of state and occupational pensions.

This book will be essential reading for academics, students and public policy makers interested in the economics of welfare, social policy and the future of pension provision.

Martin Rein is Professor of Social Policy in the Department of Urban Studies and Planning at the Massachusetts Institute of Technology, USA and **Eskil Wadensjö** is Professor of Labour Economics in the Swedish Institute for Social Research at Stockholm University, Sweden.

EDWARD ELGAR PUBLISHING

8 Lansdown Place, Cheltenham, Glos, GL50 2HU, UK
Tel: +44 (0)1242 226934 Fax: +44 (0)1242 262111
Email: Info@e-elgar.co.uk

6 Market Street, Northampton, MA 01060, USA
Tel: +1 413 584 5551 Fax: +1 413 584 9933
Email: rhenning@e-elgar.com

http://www.e-elgar.co.uk

ISBN 1-85898-664-8

9 781858 986647

DATE DUE

THE LIBRARY STORE   #47-0103 Pre-Gummed